Our Moral Life in Christ

SEMESTER EDITION

The Didache

[DID-uh-kay]

The *Didache* is the first known Christian catechesis. Written in the first century, the *Didache* is the earliest known Christian writing outside of Scripture. The name of the work, "*Didache*," is indeed appropriate for such a catechesis because it comes from the Greek word for "teaching," and indicates that this writing contains the teaching of the Apostles.

The *Didache* is a catechetical summary of Christian sacraments, practices, and morality. Though written in the first century, its teaching is timeless. The *Didache* was probably written by the disciples of the Twelve Apostles, and it presents the Apostolic Faith as taught by those closest to Jesus Christ. This series of books takes the name of this early catechesis because it shares in the Church's mission of passing on that same Faith, in its rich entirety, to new generations.

Below is an excerpt from the *Didache* in which we see a clear example of its lasting message, a message that speaks to Christians of today as much as it did to the first generations of the Church. The world is different, but the struggle for holiness is the same. In the *Didache*, we are instructed to embrace virtue, to avoid sin, and to live the Beatitudes of our Lord.

My child, flee from everything that is evil and everything that is like it. Do not be wrathful, for wrath leads to murder, nor jealous nor contentious nor quarrelsome, for from all these murder ensues.

My child, do not be lustful, for lust leads to fornication, nor a filthy-talker nor a lewd-looker, for from all these adulteries ensue.

My child, do not be an interpreter of omens, since it leads to idolatry, nor an enchanter nor an astrologer nor a magical purifier, nor wish to see them, for from all these idolatry arises.

My child, do not be a liar, for lying leads to theft, nor avaricious nor conceited, for from all these thefts are produced.

My child, do not be a complainer, since it leads to blasphemy, nor self-willed nor evil-minded, for from all these blasphemies are produced.

Be meek, for the meek will inherit the earth.

Be long-suffering and merciful and guileless and peaceable and good, and revere always the words you have heard.[1]

The *Didache* is the teaching of the Apostles and, as such, it is the teaching of the Church. Accordingly, this book series makes extensive use of the most recent comprehensive catechesis provided to us, the *Catechism of the Catholic Church*. The *Didache* series also relies heavily on Sacred Scripture, the lives of the saints, the Fathers of the Church, and the teaching of Vatican II as witnessed by the pontificates of John Paul II and Benedict XVI.

1. Swett, Ben H. "The Didache (The Teaching)." © January 30, 1998. http://bswett.com/1998-01Didache.html

Our Moral Life in Christ

⊰— SEMESTER EDITION —⊱

Author: Rev. Peter V. Armenio
General Editor: Rev. James Socias

MIDWEST THEOLOGICAL FORUM
Woodridge, Illinois

Published in the United States of America by

Midwest Theological Forum
1420 Davey Road
Woodridge, IL 60517

Tel: 630-739-9750 Fax: 630-739-9758
mail@mwtf.org www.theologicalforum.org

Copyright ©2009, 2012 Rev. James Socias
All Rights Reserved
First Edition
ISBN 978-1-890177-69-0

Nihil Obstat
The Reverend Louis J. Cameli, S.T.D.
Censor Deputatus
July 19, 2008

Imprimatur
The Very Reverend John F. Canary, S.T.L., D. Min
Vicar General, Archdiocese of Chicago
August 8, 2008

The *nihil obstat* and *imprimatur* are official declarations of ecclesiastical authority that a book is free from doctrinal and moral error. No implication is contained therein that those who have granted the *nihil obstat* or the *imprimatur* agree with the content, opinions, or statements expressed in the work. Nor do they assume any legal responsibility associated with the publication.

Author: Rev. Peter V. Armenio
General Editor: Rev. James Socias
Editor in Chief: Jeffrey Cole
Editorial Board: Rev. James Socias, Rev. Peter V. Armenio, Dr. Scott Hahn, Jeffrey Cole
Other Contributors: Gerry Korson
Design and Production: Marlene Burrell, Jane Heineman of April Graphics, Highland Park, Illinois

Acknowledgements

Excerpts from the English translation of the *Catechism of the Catholic Church* for the United States of America, copyright ©1994, United States Catholic Conference, Inc.—Libreria Editrice Vaticana. Used with permission.

Excerpts from the English translation of the *Catechism of the Catholic Church: Modifications from the Editio Typica*, copyright ©1997, United States Catholic Conference, Inc.—Libreria Editrice Vaticana. Used with permission.

Scripture quotations are adapted from the *Revised Standard Version of the Bible*, copyright ©1946, 1952, 1971, and the *New Revised Standard Version of the Bible*, copyright ©1989, by the Division of Christian Education of the National Council of the Churches of Christ in the United States of America, and are used by permission. All rights reserved.

Excerpts from the *Code of Canon Law, Latin/English Edition*, are used with permission, copyright ©1983 Canon Law Society of America, Washington, DC.

Citations of official Church documents from Neuner, Josef, SJ and Dupuis, Jacques, SJ, eds., *The Christian Faith: Doctrinal Documents of the Catholic Church*, 5th ed. (New York: Alba House, 1992). Used with permission.

Excerpts from *Vatican II: The Conciliar and Post Conciliar Documents, New Revised Edition* edited by Austin Flannery, OP, copyright ©1992, Costello Publishing Company, Inc., Northport, NY, are used with permission of the publisher, all rights reserved. No part of these excerpts may be reproduced, stored in a retrieval system, or transmitted in any form or by any means—electronic, mechanical, photocopying, recording or otherwise, without express written permission of Costello Publishing Company.

Disclaimer: The editor of this book has attempted to give proper credit to all sources used in the text and illustrations. Any miscredit or lack of credit is unintended and will be corrected in the next edition.

Library of Congress Cataloging-in-Publication Data
Armenio, Peter V.
    Our moral life in Christ : semester edition / author, Peter V. Armenio ; general editor, James Socias. – 1st ed.
        p. cm. – (The Didache series)
    Includes bibliographical references and index.
    ISBN 978-1-890177-69-0 (hc : alk. paper)
    1. Christian ethics – Catholic authors. I. Socias, James. II. Title.
BJ1249.A75 2009b
241'.042 – dc22

                                            2009017361

The Midwest Theological Forum *Our Moral Life in Christ, Semester Edition* student text, copyright © 2009, has been judged to be in conformity with the *Catechism of the Catholic Church* by the Subcommittee on the Catechism, United States Conference of Catholic Bishops.

Printed in Canada

TABLE OF CONTENTS

TABLE OF CONTENTS

TABLE OF CONTENTS

The Marriage of the Virgin (detail) by Besozzo.

ABBREVIATIONS USED FOR THE BOOKS OF THE BIBLE

OLD TESTAMENT

Genesis	Gn	Tobit	Tb	Ezekiel	Ez
Exodus	Ex	Judith	Jdt	Daniel	Dn
Leviticus	Lv	Esther	Est	Hosea	Hos
Numbers	Nm	1 Maccabees	1 Mc	Joel	Jl
Deuteronomy	Dt	2 Maccabees	2 Mc	Amos	Am
Joshua	Jos	Job	Jb	Obadiah	Ob
Judges	Jgs	Psalms	Ps	Jonah	Jon
Ruth	Ru	Proverbs	Prv	Micah	Mi
1 Samuel	1 Sm	Ecclesiastes	Eccl	Nahum	Na
2 Samuel	2 Sm	Song of Songs	Sg	Habakkuk	Hb
1 Kings	1 Kgs	Wisdom	Wis	Zephaniah	Zep
2 Kings	2 Kgs	Sirach	Sir	Haggai	Hg
1 Chronicles	1 Chr	Isaiah	Is	Zechariah	Zec
2 Chronicles	2 Chr	Jeremiah	Jer	Malachi	Mal
Ezra	Ezr	Lamentations	Lam		
Nehemiah	Neh	Baruch	Bar		

NEW TESTAMENT

Matthew	Mt	Ephesians	Eph	Hebrews	Heb
Mark	Mk	Philippians	Phil	James	Jas
Luke	Lk	Colossians	Col	1 Peter	1 Pt
John	Jn	1 Thessalonians	1 Thes	2 Peter	2 Pt
Acts of the Apostles	Acts	2 Thessalonians	2 Thes	1 John	1 Jn
Romans	Rom	1 Timothy	1 Tm	2 John	2 Jn
1 Corinthians	1 Cor	2 Timothy	2 Tm	3 John	3 Jn
2 Corinthians	2 Cor	Titus	Ti	Jude	Jude
Galatians	Gal	Philemon	Phlm	Revelation	Rev

GENERAL ABBREVIATIONS

AG	*Ad Gentes Divinitus* (Decree on the Church's Missionary Activity)
CA	*Centesimus Annus* (On the Hundredth Anniversary)
CCC	*Catechism of the Catholic Church*
CDF	Congregation for the Doctrine of the Faith
CIC	*Code of Canon Law* (*Codex Iuris Canonici*)
CPG	*Solemn Profession of Faith*: Credo of the People of God
CT	*Catechesi Tradendæ* (On Catechesis in our Time)
DCE	*Deus Caritas Est* (God is Love)
DD	*Dies Domini* (The Lord's Day)
DH	*Dignitatis Humanæ* (Declaration on Religious Freedom)
DoV	*Donum Vitæ* (Respect for Human Life)
DV	*Dei Verbum* (Dogmatic Constitution on Divine Revelation)
DS	Denzinger-Schonmetzer, *Enchiridion Symbolorum, definitionum et declarationum de rebus fidei et morum* (1985)
EV	*Evangelium Vitæ* (The Gospel of Life)
FC	*Familiaris Consortio* (On the Family)
GS	*Gaudium et Spes* (Pastoral Constitution on the Church in the Modern World)
HV	*Humanæ Vitæ* (On Human Life)
IOE	*Iura et Bona* (Declaration on Euthanasia)
LE	*Laborem Exercens* (On Human Work)
LG	*Lumen Gentium* (Dogmatic Constitution on the Church)
MF	*Mysterium Fidei* (The Mystery of Faith)
PH	*Persona Humana* (Declaration on Sexual Ethics)
PL	J.P. Migne, ed., *Patrologia Latina* (Paris: 1841-1855)
PT	*Pacem in Terris* (On Establishing Universal Peace)
QA	*Quadragesimo Anno* (The Fortieth Year)
RP	*Reconciliatio et Pænitentia* (On Reconciliation and Penance)
RH	*Redemptor Hominis* (The Redeemer of Man)
SC	*Sacrosanctum Concilium* (The Constitution on the Sacred Liturgy)
SRS	*Solicitudo Rei Socialis* (On Social Concerns)
SS	*Spe Salvi* (In Hope We Are Saved)
USCCB	United States Conference of Catholic Bishops
VS	*Veritatis Splendor* (Splendor of the Truth)

Foreword

The Lord Jesus, divine teacher and model of all perfection, preached holiness of life (of which he is the author and maker) to each and every one of his disciples without distinction: "You, therefore, must be perfect, as your heavenly Father is perfect" (Mt 5:48). For he sent the Holy Spirit to all to move them interiorly to love God with their whole heart, with their whole soul, with their whole understanding, and with their whole strength (cf. Mk 12:30), and to love one another as Christ loved them (cf. Jn 13:34; 15:12). (Dogmatic Constitution on the Church)

The common shared vocation for all Christian believers is holiness. The heroes and heroines of our Faith are celebrated for their faithfulness to Christ and his Church. We call them saints. We should all be saints in the making. But saints in the making need the example and knowledge of those entrusted with passing on the understanding of our faith.

One needs only to look at our present culture. Moral bankruptcy surrounds us. Attacks on the dignity of human life from conception to natural death continue. Greed and irresponsibility have injured our national economy. Even our ability to practice our faith is challenged.

Our Moral Life in Christ focuses the intellectual, moral, and formational development in living a life joined to the Mystery of our Lord. This foundation affords the Christian with the only true alternative to a world which often rejects the spiritual and substitutes its own brand of convenience for that which is "right" and "true." The foundation of course is Christ and his Church.

The "culture of life" needs champions in today's society. Our Moral Life in Christ offers to the student those reasons which direct us to live for the good of all our brothers and sisters. Grounded in the Ten Commandments, these corner stones tie our humanity together in actions that call us to understand our human nature. The mystery of Christ illumines those right actions so that we might live fully the life gifted to us.

I have had the privilege of using Our Moral Life in Christ in class and found it to be thoughtful, concise and timely. Students enjoyed the examples, and the moral content always reflected a fidelity to the Magisterium of the Church. All hope to have material that speaks to and challenges the student to go beyond—to take the next step. In the moral life, this commitment is necessary to be a living reflection of Christ in the world. The authors of Our Moral Life in Christ have given an instrument to the teacher to fulfill that task—to call us to holiness through our Lord Jesus Christ.

Most Rev. Jerome E. Listecki
Bishop of LaCrosse

"He will be great, and will be called the Son of the Most High;
and the Lord God will give to him the throne of his father David."

—Luke 1:32

The Basis for Morality and Moral Theology

CHAPTER 1

The Basis for Morality and Moral Theology

*I*magine an athlete who participates regularly in sporting events—a football player, for example. He and his teammates want to win every game, and their ultimate goal is to win a championship. To reach that goal requires that he and every other player on his team perform to the very best of their ability.

In order to perform at the highest level, each player must prepare himself well and do what is expected of him. He studies the team's playbook in great detail, so that he knows every formation and what he is supposed to do on every single play. He goes out with his team and practices these plays many times until executing them becomes almost second nature. He works out regularly to build his strength and improve his endurance, so he will not tire as easily. He knows the rules of the game and strives to remain disciplined enough to avoid being penalized for breaking those rules. He and his teammates work at how to use time well, so that the clock does not run out at the end of the game while they are still behind in the score. He keeps his eyes always focused on the prize.

The Bible of Ripoll opened to Genesis. We need to study our "playbooks," the Bible and the teachings of the Church, to learn what Jesus expects of us.

The life of a Christian is a lot like that—at least it ought to be. To live in this world the way Christ taught us takes preparation. We need to study our "playbooks"—the Bible and the teachings of the Church—to learn what Jesus expects of us. If we want to become stronger, with the indispensable help of God's grace, we must "work out" our faith regularly through prayer, the sacraments, growth in virtue, and service to others. To avoid being penalized, we need to learn the rules Christ asks us to live by, and we must discipline ourselves accordingly with self-control. God's laws are the means required by human nature to fulfill our innate desire for happiness. We must use our time well and keep our eyes focused always on the ultimate prize—eternal life and happiness in Heaven.

Christ became man, suffered, died, and rose again from the dead so that we might enjoy eternal life with God. His sacrifice on our behalf saves us from the power of sin and death that is reflected in the perils that arise from using our God-given free will in making wrong moral choices and thereby acting sinfully. Rather than abandon us to our sinful tendencies, Christ invites us—every one of us—to share in his life, both in this world and the next.

To accept his invitation requires not only that we have faith, but also that we live according to that faith by using our free will to make good moral decisions. We must, in other words, live our moral life in Christ.

> The *preparation of man* for the reception of grace is already a work of grace...
>
> Indeed we also work, but we are only collaborating with God who works, for his mercy has gone before us. It has gone before us so that we may be healed, and follows us so that once healed, we may be given life; it goes before us so that we may be called, and follows us so that we may be glorified; it goes before us so that we may live devoutly, and follows us so that we may always live with God: for without him we can do nothing.[1] (CCC 2001)

Moses Receives the Tables of Law on Mount Sinai. Although the *Catechism* links all of its moral teachings to the Ten Commandments—including those very "thou shalt nots"—the Commandments themselves are rooted in an even more fundamental principle, as the Gospels tell us.

FOR DISCUSSION

✠ What would happen if you played a game in which everyone could make up his or her own rules?

✠ What does it mean to "share in the life of Christ"?

✠ Did Jesus indicate how his followers should live?

✠ Who is harmed if we do not always do our best and "follow the rules"? Ourselves? Others?

✠ What is the connection between freedom and living a moral life in Christ?

✠ The creation story[2] teaches us about human dignity and the sacredness of life. What other lessons does it give us about moral theology?

✠ What does it mean when we say that God created us in his image and likeness?

INTRODUCTION

Morality refers to the standards by which we judge actions to be good or evil. *Moral law* refers to the standards of human behavior that were established by God and are taught by the Catholic Church.

In recent decades, there has been heated controversy over how to define certain standards of behavior for society as they relate to a number of disputed issues. Those who support a "woman's right to abortion," for example, have clashed frequently with those who believe the unborn child has a "right to life." The strong tensions and lively discussions that result are indications that while most people agree in the existence of some kind of moral standards, there is broad disagreement as to what exactly those moral standards should be.

Those who form their consciences according to the teachings of Christ believe in an *objective morality*, one that is rooted in the fundamental dignity of the human person and the sacredness of human life. Those who have not received the same moral education and formation might hold to a *subjective morality*, one that can vary from situation to situation and from one personal opinion to another. This line of thinking is called *moral relativism*.

The Samaritan Woman at the Well by Carracci. Love of God and neighbor—Jesus himself fulfills the precepts of the Law: "You shall love your neighbor as yourself."

Moral theology is the study of the principles and actions revealed to us by Jesus Christ and taught by the Catholic Church that will guide us to a life of holiness and eternal salvation. It also includes the study of principles and actions that can be known by reason through the natural law, with the help of grace.

Besides exploring Catholic moral teaching, this textbook aims to show not only how human reason leads us to affirm an objective moral law, but also how respecting this law can help bring us true happiness and make us better human beings—how we become, as St. Paul tells us, a new creation in Christ.[3]

This first chapter presents an overview of the basic principles of Christian morality and clarifies some common misconceptions. Understanding these principles is vitally important if we are to appreciate more completely the richness and depth of Catholic moral teaching.

WHAT THE MORAL LAW IS NOT

Moral law is not just about human sexuality. Mention the word "morality," particularly in the context of Catholic moral teaching, and many people are likely to think first of issues pertaining to sexuality and marriage. More to the point, they are reminded of the "thou shalt nots" of human relationships, as though moral law represents a severe restriction on human freedom.

The fact of the matter is that although moral law does govern issues such as premarital sex, adultery, abortion, contraception, and homosexual behavior, in its totality, it is far broader than that. Catholic moral teaching also has much to say about topics such as war, health care, economics, poverty, discrimination, calumny, and criminal justice.

The third section of the *Catechism of the Catholic Church*, the official presentation of Catholic beliefs and teachings, explains the Church's position on a wide variety of modern moral concerns. It is important to bear in mind that Divine Revelation of the moral law and the teachings of the Church reflect the natural law, which is innate to human nature and established by reason.

Temptation on the Mount by Duccio. Jesus' morality is not a morality of rules, but rather a morality that includes laws and precepts. Moral laws help us differentiate between good and evil.

Natural Law is the participation of man in the plan of God. It is the objective order established by God that determines the requirements for people to thrive and reach fulfillment, enabling man "to discern by reason the good and the evil, the truth and the lie."[4]

Moral law is not just about rules, but about happiness. When morality is seen only as a series of cold and rigid "thou shalt nots," it is easy to think of it in negative terms as a list of somewhat arbitrary restrictions on human freedom. That view misses the point entirely. The moral law essentially puts the human person in a position to achieve happiness.

> Man is made to live in communion with God in whom he finds happiness: "When I am completely united to you, there will be no more sorrow or trials; entirely full of you, my life will be complete."[5] (CCC 45)

Although the third section of the *Catechism* links all of its moral teachings to the Ten Commandments—including those very "thou shalt nots"—the commandments themselves are rooted in an even more fundamental principle, as the Gospels tells us.

When Jesus was asked which commandment was the greatest, he replied: "You shall love the Lord your God with all your heart, and with all your soul, and with all your mind. This is the greatest and first commandment. And a second is like it, You shall love your neighbor as yourself. On these two commandments depend all the law and the prophets."[6] It is precisely in living these commandments that a person becomes fulfilled and truly happy, for the commandments ultimately lead us to God.

> Endowed with a spiritual soul, with intellect and with free will, the human person is from his very conception ordered to God and destined for eternal beatitude. He pursues his perfection in "seeking and loving what is true and good."[7] (CCC 1711)

Love of God and neighbor, then, is the basic principle on which moral law is based. Catholic moral teaching provides the answer to this critical question: How can we best reflect our love for God and other people in our thoughts, words, and deeds?

Baptism of Christ by Cima.
Jesus himself fulfills the precepts of the law: "Let it be so now; for thus it is fitting for us to fulfil all righteousness." (Mt 3: 15)

Moral law is not just about precepts. Christianity is more a message of salvation and holiness than a set of moral teachings. Nevertheless, to reach perfection or holiness, commandments and counsels are vital. In Jesus' preaching, there are concrete prohibitions, such as adultery, avarice, rash judgments, divorce, blasphemy against the Holy Spirit, and scandal to the innocent.[8]

Jesus himself fulfills the precepts of the Law. He observes the Sabbath, he fasts, he obeys the purification laws, and he goes to Jerusalem to celebrate the Jewish feasts.[9]

Jesus' morality is not a morality of rules, but rather a morality that includes laws and precepts. These laws and precepts exist in order to guide people to a good life. Moral laws help us differentiate between good and evil; they show us the path that we need to follow if we want to please God, achieve true perfection, and obtain salvation.[10]

Morality does not mean being "moralistic." Unfortunately, people who embrace Christian morality sometimes make poor ambassadors for the Christian Faith. They, too, sometimes tend to reduce the moral law to a mere set of rules, a checklist of behavior that they see as the primary indicator of a moral life in Christ. Mix that with a degree of *triumphalism*—an excess of pride that leads them to think themselves superior to others, sometimes called a "holier than thou" attitude—and they can quickly be seen not as witnesses to the Faith, but as cold and judgmental moralizers.

It is important to live according to Church teaching, but it is even more important that we do so with the love described in the Great Commandment.

It is as easy for us today to slip into a moralistic mentality as it was for the Pharisees in Jesus' time. In fact, the Old Testament, which includes an extensive set of moral guidelines given by God to the Jewish people, often was reduced to a narrow, legalistic, and sometimes hypocritical model of morality. This explains Jesus' critical attitude toward many of the ideas preached by the religious leaders of his time.[11]

CHARACTERISTICS OF THE MORAL LAW

Moral law comprises the objective standards authored by God and taught by Church authority.

Moral law is a demand of our Faith. Although Christianity involves much more than the observance of moral law, to live according to the moral law is a requirement of the Christian life.

When the rich young man asked Jesus how he could attain eternal life, Jesus made it abundantly clear that adherence to the commandments was a vital first step.[12] The Great Commandment of love does not at all weaken the force of the Ten Commandments; rather, it brings context to the commandments and describes the interior spirit with which we are to embrace the moral law. A full commitment to the moral law is essential if we are to live out our vocation to holiness and abide by Christ's new commandment of love.

Moral law is guided by the cardinal virtues. At Baptism, we receive from the grace of God the four *cardinal virtues* of prudence, justice, fortitude, and temperance, along with the *theological virtues* of faith, hope, and love. These virtues assist the Christian in living the commandments because they are the foundation for all moral virtues. The exercise of these virtues can help us achieve the proper disposition to draw closer to God and to know him and love him more completely:

✤ *Prudence* enables us to choose the right course of action inspired by the moral law.

✤ *Justice* enables us to render what is due to God and neighbor.

✤ *Fortitude* enables us to perform good actions amid obstacles and difficulties.

✤ *Temperance* enables us to control our passions in order to maintain a clear mind and a strong will.[13]

The cardinal virtues enable us to live the Christian life, and counteract the effects of Original Sin and the resultant vices of ignorance, malice, infirmity, and sensuality (concupiscence).

The infused virtues received at Baptism are certainly not fully developed virtues, but must be strengthened through human effort expressed in a repetition of virtuous actions.

> The moral virtues grow through education, deliberate acts, and perseverance in struggle. Divine grace purifies and elevates them. (CCC 1839)

As always, holiness is an interplay between God's grace and the struggle to practice virtue.

✤ *Faith* enables us to believe the truths revealed by Christ and transmitted by his Church.

✤ *Hope* assists us in trusting that God will give us the means to salvation and holiness.

✤ *Charity* enables us to love God and others with the very love of Christ.

From a Christian point of view, loving God and loving others allows a person to reach a joy that the world cannot offer.

Moral law provides the way to true happiness. Because the moral law is rooted in love, living by its ideals prepares us for an ever-deepening relationship with God. It is a pathway toward a liberating happiness that results from drawing ever closer to Christ. The promise is that if we totally immerse ourselves in Christ's life and teachings, we will find it a most rewarding, peaceful, and spiritually gratifying experience.

From a Christian point of view, loving God and loving others allows a person to reach a joy that the world cannot offer. Therefore, by living by the commandments, a Christian not only grows in virtue, he or she is also empowered to give himself or herself more completely and more joyfully to the service of God and neighbor.

The moral life leads us to knowledge of the inner life of God and his plans for us. By living a moral life, which is the fruit of God's assistance, an individual becomes more receptive to God's grace. This increase of sanctifying grace and faith leads to a deeper knowledge of the mystery of God.

Faith is a supernatural gift from God. In order to believe, man needs the interior helps of the Holy Spirit. (CCC 179)

Only with the light of Faith and God's grace are we able to have greater knowledge and understanding of God's inner life. At the same time, a well-grounded moral life is crucial.

> The mystery of the Most Holy Trinity is the central mystery of the Christian faith and of Christian life. God alone can make it known to us by revealing himself as Father, Son, and Holy Spirit. (CCC 261)

Moral law is based on the Divine Wisdom of God. Just as the physical laws governing physics, chemistry, and biology were discovered rather than invented by man, the moral law is also not man's own creation. The different laws governing the universe reflect the influence of an all-knowing Supreme Being; the same is true of the moral law.

The Holy Trinity by Pereda. The moral person acquires the wisdom to appreciate and penetrate the mysteries of God as a Trinity of divine persons. Moral standards are inscribed on the heart of every human person by God himself.

Moral standards are inscribed on the heart of every human person by God himself. This universal *natural law* recognizes the dignity of every person and his or her right to freedom. Derived from this dignity is an equality among all·persons and, consequently, unalienable rights corresponding to the person's exalted value.

> The natural law, present in the heart of each man and established by reason, is universal in its precepts and its authority extends to all men. It expresses the dignity of the person and determines the basis for his fundamental rights and duties. (CCC 1956)

At the same time, the human condition affected by Original Sin requires that natural law be revealed as well. It is through a deepening knowledge of the objective norms of morality that the conscience becomes well formed and, thereby, trustworthy. The natural moral law finds its ultimate source in God's eternal wisdom. In the Book of Exodus, God explicitly revealed the law of the Ten Commandments to Moses, which is a privileged expression of the natural law. In Jesus' teaching ministry, God's law was fulfilled and brought to perfection to be taught by the Church and lived by all the faithful.

Abiding by moral law draws us closer to Christ. We have pointed out that the standards of Christian morality are objective rather than subjective because they are determined neither by general consensus nor by individual preference, but by God's plan for us. The commandments given by God to the Jewish people were perfected and explained by Christ, who emphasized love of God and neighbor as the basis for all moral law. This perfected law taught by Christ serves as a pathway toward our ultimate happiness and growth in holiness.

Pope John Paul II, in his encyclical *Veritatis Splendor* ("The Splendor of Truth"), reiterates how the Ten Commandments are a vital preliminary step for the full experience of a moral life in Christ.

MORAL LAW AND FREE WILL

At the time of creation as described in the Book of Genesis, God blessed Adam and Eve with complete self-control over their minds, wills, and passions. This complete self-mastery enjoyed by our first parents ended when they disrupted their harmony with God by violating his command.

This sin, because it was the first sin and the forerunner of all subsequent sins, is called *Original Sin*. Original Sin caused a deep wound in the soul of every human being. As a consequence, the human person suffers from a clouded mind, a weakened will, and disordered passions—in other words, a tendency to sin. Together with this severe debilitation to the soul, our first parents lost their original holiness and justice.

> Adam and Eve transmitted to their descendants human nature wounded by their own first sin and hence deprived of original holiness and justice; this deprivation is called "original sin." (CCC 417)

Although God's natural law is inscribed in our very soul, our sinful nature makes it difficult for us to make the right moral decisions on our own. Because of these inherited limitations, we need God's help to distinguish good choices from evil choices.

Scripture teaches that Adam and Eve were made in God's own image; and through the merits of Jesus Christ received in the Sacrament of Baptism, we are restored in his image. This belief is an important incentive for us to conduct ourselves according to the requirements of our God-given dignity. God reveals not only the fact that we are made in his image, but also the moral principles we must embrace and the evil actions we must avoid.

God the Father, in his infinite love for us, draws us into the light and life of Jesus through the moral law he has revealed. In this sense, fidelity to the commandments of God serves as a preparatory step for a deeper friendship with Christ.

MORAL LAW AND GRACE

Grace, the divine life of God in the soul, is a supernatural gift bestowed on us through the sacrifice of Jesus Christ for our salvation. It is a gratuitous gift which we can never deserve or earn through our own action.[14] This grace enables us to share the life of Jesus Christ and assists us in conforming our lives to his teachings.[15] Grace is the indispensable help that God gives us, allowing us to respond to his call to holiness in our lives and to become his adopted sons and daughters.

> Grace is the help God gives us to respond to our vocation of becoming his adopted sons. It introduces us into the intimacy of the Trinitarian life. (CCC 2021)

Expulsion of Adam and Eve by Milani. As a consequence of Original Sin, the human person suffers from a clouded mind, a weakened will, and disordered passions.

There are two kinds of grace:

Sanctifying grace is the grace that confers a new life on our souls—that is, a sharing in the life of God himself. It is a gift through which the Triune God—Father, Son, and Holy Spirit—dwells in the soul. We first receive this grace in the Sacrament of Baptism, and it is nourished by the Eucharist. If we lose it through mortal sin, sanctifying grace can be restored to us by the Sacrament of Reconciliation.

Sanctifying grace unites us to God and makes us "pleasing to God" (cf. CCC 2024), but in an incomplete way. In Heaven, we will be united to God completely and will see him face-to-face. That is why we call sanctifying grace "the seed of eternal life."

The Disciples of Jesus Baptizing by Procaccini. We first receive sanctifying grace in the Sacrament of Baptism, and it is nourished by the Eucharist. We call sanctifying grace "the seed of eternal life."

Actual grace is a temporary grace given by God. Through actual grace, God helps us to obtain, preserve, and grow in sanctifying grace by giving us the knowledge and strength to do what is good and right. When we pray for God's grace to guide us in making a difficult decision or to give us strength to resist a temptation, it is actual grace that we receive.

Actual grace is necessary for all who have attained the use of reason. Without its help, we would not be able to remain faithful to the commandments because we would not have the strength to resist the power of temptation.[16]

> What is the ultimate source of this inner division of man? His history of sin begins when he no longer acknowledges the Lord as his Creator and himself wishes to be the one who determines, with complete independence, what is good and what is evil. "You will be like God, knowing good and evil"[17]: this was the first temptation, and it is echoed in all the other temptations to which man is more easily inclined to yield as a result of the original Fall.

> But temptations can be overcome, sins can be avoided, because together with the commandments, the Lord gives us the possibility of keeping them: "His eyes are on those who fear him, and he knows every deed of man. He has not commanded anyone to be ungodly, and he has not given anyone permission to sin."[18] Keeping God's law in particular situations can be difficult, extremely difficult, but it is never impossible. (*Veritatis Splendor*, 102)

We might ask: If sanctifying grace is present to those who are baptized, then why do so many baptized individuals lead such poor moral lives?

God, who is rich in mercy and love, takes the initiative in helping us to live the commandments and pursue a life of holiness. In other words, God makes the first move in assisting us to embrace his will. At the same time, our freedom is indispensable in responding to God's promptings and inspirations.

> The divine initiative in the work of grace precedes, prepares, and elicits the free response of man. Grace responds to the deepest yearnings of human freedom, calls freedom to cooperate with it, and perfects freedom. (CCC 2022)

Nevertheless, grace cannot operate in a vacuum. It is a gift that will assist a person who sincerely commits himself or herself to keeping the moral law and makes every effort to do so. As human beings we do not have the capacity of perfectly discerning good from evil; and even after Baptism, we still have the temptation to sin. However, the teachings of Jesus Christ, and the grace which he gives us, assist us in living the Christian vocation.

Those who lack that commitment and effort or who rationalize their own behavior as exempt from the moral law will not be aided by the grace they have received. In the case of the baptized person who truly tries to live the commandments, however, God's grace will always be present.

Think of faith and grace as gifts, like those we might receive at Christmas or at our birthday celebration: If we receive a gift but decide not to unwrap it, we cannot put that gift to good use. We must respond to the gifts of faith and grace with our own free will.

MORAL LAW AND THE CHRISTIAN VOCATION

The moral law is not just for Catholics or for Christians. It is not even meant solely for theists, those who at the very least believe in God. To commit and conform to the moral law is to pursue a life of holiness—and, as the Second Vatican Council taught based on the Gospels, every human person is called by God to a life of holiness, to a life that requires a degree of self-control in order to overcome our inherent tendency to sin.

The history of peoples scattered in every corner of the world, gives tangible evidence that man by nature is a religious being. Virtually every group of people and civilization from the dawn of human history practiced forms of religious worship, and acknowledged a being or beings greater than themselves. The fact that man is a religious being by nature, leads him to grasp, at least in part, the moral law.

> **Man is by nature and vocation a religious being. Coming from God, going toward God, man lives a fully human life only if he freely lives by his bond with God. (CCC 44)**

Everyone is called to a life of holiness. Jesus calls every baptized individual to fully embrace his teachings. By virtue of the Sacrament of Baptism, every Christian has a vocation—a call from God—to become completely centered on Christ. All Christians are called to the holiness proclaimed by the Gospels and found throughout the New Testament.[19]

Jesus Preaching on the Mount by Doré. Everyone is called to a life of holiness. The only appropriate response to our call to holiness is to follow the example of the life of Jesus Christ.

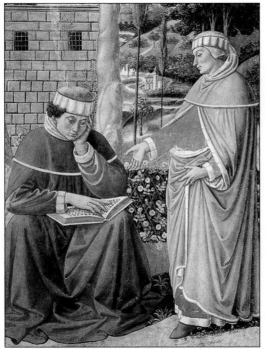

St. Augustine Reading the Epistle of St. Paul
by Gozzoli. Through intense prayer and study of the
Gospels, St. Augustine was able to amend his sinful life
and embrace his call to holiness.

Because God gave us free will, it is entirely our own choice whether we accept or reject this call to holiness. Since our vocation is a call from God, it requires our response. If we fail to respond, our relationship with God will be incomplete, and, as a consequence, we will deprive ourselves of the complete joy and fulfillment that he wants to bestow on us.[20]

The only appropriate response to our call to holiness is to follow the example of the life of Jesus Christ—his dispositions, actions, and teachings. The moral law gives us the necessary tools and directions to guide us in following in Christ's footsteps. That is the fundamental vocation of every person.

Living our vocation requires free will and self-control. The Gospel tells us of two aspects of freedom that are vital in following Christ's teachings. First, an individual must want to follow Christ and live by his teachings.[21] Secondly, he or she must have sufficient self-control and self-mastery to live the high standards of love and sacrifice exemplified by Christ. These standards are expressed in the Ten Commandments, the Beatitudes, and the Sermon on the Mount.

St. Augustine, one of the greatest figures in Catholic history, is a case in point. For many years, although he had an interior desire to live a life of holiness, he lacked the self-control and self-mastery to do so and instead led an unchaste life. Only after Augustine made the decision to pray intently for chastity did he find the strength, obtained through grace, to amend his life and live by the moral law—in other words, to live a moral life in Christ.

VOCATION AND DISCIPLESHIP

The call of Jesus is a call to discipleship with Jesus as the divine teacher (cf. Mt 23:7-8). The relationship between teacher and disciple describes the relationship between Christ and those who believe in him. The word *disciple* ("follower") indicates an individual who has adopted another person's way of life and taken on his or her particular type of discipline.[22]

To be a disciple of Christ is to imitate Christ. A disciple must learn from his or her master or teacher. The Christian disciple strives to imitate Christ and apply his instructions to his or her own particular circumstances. Every gesture, action, and word in the life of Christ serves as an inexhaustible source of instruction for a full moral life.

> "The whole of Christ's life was a continual teaching: his silences, his miracles, his gestures, his prayer, his love for people, his special affection for the little and the poor, his acceptance of the total sacrifice on the Cross for the redemption of the world, and his Resurrection are the actualization of his word and the fulfillment of Revelation."[23] (CCC 561)

Christ's life and teachings are meant to be expressed in our daily lives. But how do we actually go about imitating Jesus Christ and practicing his teachings?

Jesus' life and Death exemplify the virtues to which he calls us. Christ's suffering and Death reveal an example of Christian virtues in practice *par excellence*. The pain and anguish Christ endured in his Passion are a moving lesson in forgiveness, patience, humility, and his love for us. Jesus himself invites us to conform our lives to his. "I have given you an example, that you should do as I have done to you."[24]

As Pope John Paul II points out in *Veritatis Splendor*:

> Following Christ is not an outward imitation, since it touches man at the very depths of his being. Being a follower of Christ means becoming conformed to him who became a servant even to giving himself on the Cross.[25] Christ dwells by faith in the heart of the believer[26] and thus the disciple is conformed to the Lord. This is the effect of grace, of the active presence of the Holy Spirit in us. (*Veritatis Splendor*, 21)

As disciples, we can be incorporated into the life of Christ. If we freely choose to live the moral law and to seek holiness as disciples of Christ, we can gradually become incorporated into the life of Christ through the Holy Spirit, transforming our hearts and minds into those of Christ. In practical terms, that means that through this transformation we would increasingly love, think, and act according to Christ's example and teachings. Sanctifying grace initiates this transformation; actual grace assists us in our commitment as disciples of Christ and identifies us with him.

Apostles Peter and Paul by El Greco.
"I have been crucified with Christ; it is no longer I who live, but Christ who lives in me; and the life I now live in the flesh I live by faith in the Son of God, who loved me and gave himself for me." — St. Paul (Gal 2:20)

A person who is identified with Christ and consequently lives his life in this manner sees the world in a whole new way. This growth in union with Jesus Christ enables the person to see the infinite wisdom and love with which God has created the world. The person filled with Christ sees the exalted dignity of every human being and thereby sees the need to love and serve everyone. Being united to Christ, by its very nature, involves the embracing of suffering as a way of sharing in Christ's Cross. Thus, the work of grace, together with the will to live by God's commandments, empowers the person to think with the mind of Christ and to love with the heart of Christ.[27]

St. Paul spells out the goal of the Christian life in his letter to the Galatians: "It is no longer I who live, but Christ who lives in me."[28] These interior sentiments of St. Paul express the goal of every Christian.

He who believes in Christ has new life in the Holy Spirit. The moral life, increased and brought to maturity in grace, is to reach its fulfillment in the glory of heaven. (CCC 1715)

CHRISTIAN MORALITY IN ACTION

We have already begun to see how our moral choices are interconnected with virtually every aspect of our lives. In this section, we will examine how morality, free will, our actions, and our interior dispositions are all inextricably interrelated.

Our actions express our moral dispositions. Actions undertaken through our own free will express our values, our moral dispositions. A person who values virtue will strive to tell the truth, act justly, and treat others kindly. If our free will, assisted by grace, inclines us to live by the moral law as disciples of Christ, that interior disposition will be reflected in our actions.[29]

Transfiguration of Christ by Bellini.
In order to follow Christ, we must accept the moral law as expressed in the commandments and the teachings of Christ.

In the Gospel of St. Luke, Jesus speaks of the connection between our exterior acts and interior dispositions:

> For no good tree bears bad fruit, nor again does a bad tree bear good fruit; for each tree is known by its own fruit. For figs are not gathered from thorns, nor are grapes picked from a bramble bush. The good man out of the good treasure of his heart produces good, and the evil man out of his evil treasure produces evil; for out of the abundance of the heart his mouth speaks. (Lk 6: 43-45)

The Beatitudes, which express the heart of Christian morality, also speak to the interior attitude of the person. If we first accept and pursue the ideals of mercy, purity of heart, and peace, we will act more fully as merciful, pure, and peaceful people.[30]

Our actions express our free will. Good actions result from good choices, which are exercises of our free will to choose good over evil. If we truly commit to living the commandments according to Christ's message, our free will, assisted by grace, will increasingly conform to the will of God.

That is not to say that an individual who is committed to Christ cannot be tempted or even fall from grace by sinning. Tendency toward sin is a consequence of our wounded human nature, so we can never presume ourselves to be completely invulnerable to temptation and sin. What it does mean is that our commitment to living a moral life in Christ, assisted by our good will and God's grace, will help us grow in strength and self-control so that we will be able to avoid transgressing the moral law.

> Do you not see that whatever goes into the mouth passes into the stomach, and so passes on? But what comes out of the mouth proceeds from the heart, and this defiles a man. For out of the heart come evil thoughts, murder, adultery, fornication, theft, false witness, slander. These are what defile a man; but to eat with unwashed hands does not defile a man. (Mt 15:17-20)

Just as concrete acts express our dispositions to pursue the moral law, our passions, appetites, thoughts, and words will begin little by little to reflect our free choice in striving to live a moral life in Christ.

> Jesus brings God's commandments to fulfillment, particularly the commandments of love of neighbor, by interiorizing their demands and by bringing out their fullest meaning. Love of neighbor springs from a loving heart which precisely because it loves, is ready to live out the loftiest challenges. (*Veritatis Splendor*, 15)

Our decisions and actions must be informed by the moral law. In order to follow Christ, we must accept the moral law as expressed in the commandments and the teachings of Christ. Acceptance inevitably must lead to our choosing to conform our interior dispositions and free will to that moral law. In turn, our decisions, because we have committed to orient them to the moral law, must be expressed in moral actions.

Grace, as we have seen, plays a critical role, even an indispensable one, in our ability to live the moral law. We can call upon this grace, particularly in the Sacraments of Reconciliation and the Holy Eucharist, to strengthen our resolve and our discernment to choose what is right and to grow in virtue. Earlier in this chapter, we noted that grace cannot operate in a vacuum; put positively, we might say that "grace builds upon nature," as the adage goes, meaning that our dispositions and will must be engaged in order to make use of the grace received from God and through the sacraments.[31]

EFFECTS OF THE MORAL LIFE IN CHRIST

Christian morality is a *positive morality* that prescribes what a person, motivated by the love of God, ought to do in order to imitate the life of Christ. As we have seen, the moral law cannot be reduced to a merely *negative morality* motivated solely by fear of punishment, one that involves exclusively a series of "thou shalt nots." Also, Pope John Paul II taught that, with regard to the Decalogue, the commandments are phrased in the negative to indicate a minimum threshold of behavior.[32]

It is true that the moral law includes many prohibitions such as those found in the Ten Commandments themselves. All that goes against the love of God and neighbor, of course, is forbidden. Nevertheless, Jesus' moral teachings on the whole stress the good that we must do much more than the evil that we must avoid. Rather than stopping at a list of "do's" and "don'ts," the Lord reveals what type of persons we *should be* in order to live justly, be happy, and find fulfillment.

In pursuing the moral life, it is best to be motivated by love of God and neighbor rather than by fear of punishment. As St. John points out: "There is not fear in love, but perfect love casts out fear. For fear has to do with punishment, and he who fears is not perfected in love."[33]

Christian morality serves and safeguards human dignity. When we act morally, we act in accordance with our own human dignity and the dignity of others as well. The Great Commandment to love God with our whole heart, soul, and mind calls us to recognize that we must serve God, who made us in his own

Last Judgment and the Wise and Foolish Virgins by Unknown Flemish Master. In Jesus' parable, it is not just that the foolish virgins acted wrongly, but that they did not act wisely.

image and calls us to communion with him; the second part of the Great Commandment, that we must love our neighbor as ourselves, reminds us that we must treat other persons with great respect, for they, too, were made in God's image and are likewise called to communion with him. The entire moral law is based on the love expressed in this Great Commandment, a love that respects the dignity of every person.

The choice to serve Jesus is the choice to respond to love with love. Jesus tells us the parable of two sons who were commanded by their father to do work.[34] The answer to the question of "Who is the son who loved his father?" is the son who did his father's bidding. A person demonstrates his love of the Father by doing as Jesus asks.

The twenty-fifth chapter of St. Matthew's Gospel summarizes the judgment that Christ will impose on each person based on what they did or did not do on earth. Jesus' condemnations are leveled against those who have been negligent or deficient in loving others and not solely on those who have done evil deeds. In Jesus' parable, it is not just that the foolish virgins acted wrongly, but that they did not act wisely.[35] In the parable of the talents, the men who received five and ten

Parable of the Good Samaritan by Conti. We can use our freedom to do what is morally good, which helps strengthen us against sin; or, we can abuse it by making immoral choices. Christian morality is at the service of love.

talents are rewarded because they increased them, while the one who received only one talent is condemned because he refused to make use of the talent that he was given.[36] These parables place heavy emphasis on God's pleasure with those who do good and his displeasure with those who fail to do good.

St. Matthew goes on to describe how, at the time of judgment, Jesus will demand each of us to account for the good we have done and the good we have failed to do. Did we feed the hungry? Did we give shelter to the homeless? Did we visit the sick?[37] In the Last Judgment of Matthew's scenario, those who did good for others are saved, and those who did evil or failed to do good are condemned.

Christian morality is at the service of freedom. The magnificent gift that God bestows on every human being that sets us apart from the rest of creation is our intellect and our will, grounded in the soul. Precisely through these spiritual faculties, we are endowed with the gift of freedom.

> Endowed with a spiritual soul, with intellect and with free will, the human person is from his very conception ordered to God and destined for eternal beatitude. He pursues his perfection in "seeking and loving what is true and good."[38] (CCC 1711)

We can use our freedom to do what is morally good, which helps strengthen us against sin; or, we can abuse it by making immoral choices, which further diminish and cloud our discernment and resolve to choose and act wisely. This diminished capacity for discernment represents a restriction on our freedom.

God wants us to freely choose his divine life. In this sense, he took a risk when he created the human person with a free will. Given the very nature of freedom, God allows us to make choices freely, regardless of whether those choices have good or bad effects on us and those affected by our decisions. When we practice the message preached by Christ, we acquire the highest degree of freedom.

The basic message preached by Christ is a call to freedom: "For you were called to freedom, brethren."[39] When some early Christians misunderstood the freedom for which "Christ has set us free," St. Paul warned them not to use their freedom as an "opportunity for the flesh," but for the good.[40] When we practice the message preached by Christ, we acquire the highest degree of freedom.

This freedom is what St. Paul was talking about: "For freedom Christ has set us free; stand fast therefore, and do not submit again to a yoke of slavery."[41] And again: "You who were once slaves of sin have become obedient from the heart to the standard of teaching to which you were committed and having been set free from sin, have become slaves of righteousness."[42]

Christian morality is at the service of love. For the Christian, every aspect of morality begins and ends in love. The Christian moral message begins with God

St. Paul Writing His Epistles by Tournier. The command to love is proclaimed not only by Jesus, who calls it "my commandment" and "new," but also by the apostles in addressing the first Christians.

offering his love to us and culminates with the new commandment of love.[43] Christ calls his followers to love as he has loved. To take on the heart of Christ should be the goal of every Christian.

The command to love is proclaimed not only by Jesus, who calls it "my commandment" and "new," but also by the Apostles in addressing the first Christians. St. Paul praises love in his "hymn of love" that concludes: "So faith, hope, and love abide, these three; but the greatest of these is love."[44]

St. John, who relates the love of God with the love of neighbor, teaches:

> Beloved, let us love one another; for love is of God, and he who loves is born of God and knows God. He who does not love does not know God; for God is love. In this the love of God was made manifest among us, that God sent his only Son into the world, so that we might live through him. In this is love, not that we loved God but that he loved us and sent his Son to be the expiation for our sins. Beloved, if God so loved us, we also ought to love one another. (1 Jn 4: 7-11)

Love for God authenticates our love for our neighbor, and our love for our neighbor is indispensable evidence of our genuine love for God.

PERSONAL FRUITS OF THE MORAL LIFE IN CHRIST

In the New Testament, Jesus teaches that Christians must live up to high standards of morality. Christian morality requires not just a decent or honorable existence, but a saintly life modeled on Christ. It is through following Christ and seeking to abide by these moral standards that we can respond to his call to holiness and find true happiness.

Keeping the moral law leads to holiness. As we have seen earlier in this chapter, every baptized person is called to a life of holiness, as taught by the Second Vatican Council document *Lumen Gentium*. This life of holiness, as we have also seen, is made possible through the power of grace especially when derived from the sacraments. Our pursuit of holiness assists our efforts to make morally good choices, and the converse is also true. Our commitment to keeping the moral law leads us to growth in holiness as well.

> In particular, the *life of holiness* which is resplendent in so many members of the People of God, humble and often unseen, constitutes the simplest and most attractive way to perceive at once the beauty of truth, the liberating force of God's love, and the value of unconditional fidelity to all the demands of the Lord's law, even in the most difficult situations. (*Veritatis Splendor*, 107)

To emphasize the message of the Beatitudes, Jesus places his moral teaching side-by-side with the "Old Law" of the Old Testament, which, in God's plan, was a preparation for the "New Law."[45] In fact, he repeats

Moses and the Tablets of Law by Ribera (left); *Sermon on the Mount* by Bloch (right). To emphasize the message of the Beatitudes, Jesus places his moral teaching side-by-side with the "Old Law" of the Old Testament, which, in God's plan, was a preparation for the "New Law." In so doing, Jesus fulfills the commandments.

these juxtapositions six times: "You have heard that...but I say to you...."[46] In so doing, Jesus fulfills the commandments, enriches their moral content, and urges that they be put into practice with the help of the Holy Spirit.

> Thus it is evident to everyone that all the faithful of Christ of whatever rank and status, are called to the fullness of the Christian life and to the perfection of charity; by this holiness as such, a more human manner of living is promoted in this earthly society....They must follow in his footsteps and conform themselves to his image seeking the will of the Father in all things. (*Veritatis Splendor*, 16)

"You, therefore, must be perfect, as your heavenly Father is perfect."[47] Reflecting this call of Jesus, Vatican II declares that every baptized person is called to seek holiness.[48]

Keeping the moral law leads to happiness. It is basic Christian belief that God created us to know, love, and serve him in this world so that we can be eternally happy with him in the next life. A first step in knowing, loving, and serving God is our effort to keep the moral law as taught by Jesus Christ.

The *Catechism of the Catholic Church* reminds us that Jesus teaches that there is an intimate link between happiness and good moral behavior: "The moral life, increased and brought to maturity in grace, is to reach its fulfillment in the glory of heaven."[49] Obedience and conformity to God's will thus result in a foretaste here on earth of the perfect happiness that awaits us in Heaven.[50]

Keeping the moral law calls us to justice. Christian morality includes the achievement of a more just world and everlasting life. In understanding Christian morality, however, it is important to avoid two extremes.

One extreme is to limit the consideration of moral behavior exclusively to terms of social justice and what benefits the common good at the present moment. The other extreme is to limit the scope of morality to individual actions that only have a spiritual benefit to that individual, and which exclude the seeking of justice and well-being for other people in the present life.

Because Christians are citizens of both this world and the next, the moral law calls us to try to establish a more just and peaceful society on earth while at the same time ensuring our personal behavior is in accord with the moral law.

Vatican II summarizes this idea in the following statement:

> This Council exhorts Christians, as citizens of both cities, to perform their duties faithfully and in the spirit of the Gospel. It is a mistake to think that, because we have here no lasting city, but seek the city which is to come, we are entitled to shirk our earthly responsibilities; this is to forget that by our faith we are bound all the more to fulfill these responsibilities according to the vocation of each one. (*Gaudium et Spes*, 43)

WHAT IS MORAL THEOLOGY?

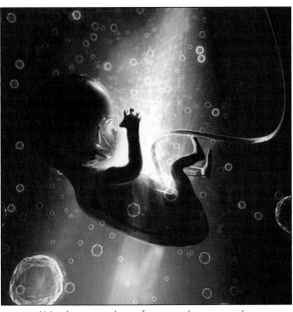

Using human embryos for research are examples of the inadequacy of human reason when separated from the moral truths of the Church.

Moral theology is the study of both the principles and actions revealed to us by Jesus Christ and taught by the Catholic Church that will lead us to a life of holiness and to eternal salvation. It is concerned with the good and the evil of human actions and of the individual person who performs these actions.

Moral theology is based on Divine Revelation. The foundation for moral theology, as is true with all branches of theology, is Divine Revelation, which is transmitted to us through Sacred Scripture and Divine Tradition and communicated to us by the Magisterium, the teaching authority of the Catholic Church. It acknowledges that the origin and purpose of all moral actions are found in God.

Moral theology is beyond human reason, but not contrary to human reason. Moral theology responds to the inquiries of human reason. When human reason is separated from the wisdom of God as found in the teachings of the Church, false conclusions are often reached that can have disastrous effects for the individual and society at large. Opinions that advocate abortion, same-sex partnerships, and stem-cell research using human embryos are examples of the inadequacy of human reason when separated from the moral truths of the Church. Moral theology also includes the study of both moral principles and actions that comprise the natural law, which is inscribed in the mind and heart of every individual and can be known by reason, with the help of grace.

Moral theology is compatible with natural sciences. The natural sciences have a role to play in corroborating theology. The moral teachings of the Church, for example, may use modern scientific findings in the area of psychology or medicine to support what Christ has ultimately revealed.

Moral theology recognizes and understands the dignity of the human person. The moral law taught by Christ, and interpreted and transmitted by the Catholic Church, derive from the Great Commandment of love, which itself comprises the call to respect the dignity of all human persons.

The Adoration of the Trinity by Dürer. What makes the human person unique is that through the soul, every man and woman is made in the image of God.

THE CHRISTIAN CONCEPT OF MANKIND

Moral theology and the moral law serve to guide the moral choices we face and to evaluate the free-will decisions we make. How we exercise our free will in making moral decisions will have a profound impact not only on our happiness on earth, but also on the eternal destination of our immortal souls. By extension, therefore, moral theology and the moral law are necessary for the good of our immortal souls.

Understanding a few truths about the human soul and its inherent dignity will help enlighten our study of moral theology.

Our immortal souls are what make us human. The existence of an immortal soul in each person is what distinguishes us from animals. Unlike the animals, we are made in God's own image, and our soul is the spiritual mark that sets us apart. Our capacity to know and love God and neighbor finds its origin in our immortal soul.

Recognition of the soul is essential for human dignity. Many people today do not believe in the existence of the soul. They accept the false claim that if something cannot be directly experienced, measured, or observed by our senses, then it cannot be known with certainty. They dismiss human conscience as nothing more than the product of neurological processes or psychological influences.

That erroneous and artificial separation of our conscience from God's wisdom leads to belief in a subjective morality rather than an objective morality. The disregard for the human soul leads to a materialistic view of the human person and, consequently, to serious offenses against human dignity.

Our desire to search for truth is evidence of the existence of the soul. The universal human desire for knowledge, truth, personal fulfillment, and a meaningful life points to man's spiritual nature. The progress derived from the human mind in its search for truth and the love expressed by the human heart is ongoing testimony that each person has an immortal soul.

The human soul is created by God. The Church teaches that each human soul is created directly by God at the moment of conception. Together, the physical and spiritual components comprise a new human life.

What makes the human person unique is that through the soul, every man and woman is made in the image of God. Like God, although in a lesser manner, we have the capacity for intellect, free will, and immortality.

The human person comprises a body and a soul. We are both physical beings and spiritual beings. Although every human being is composed of a body and a soul, the human person is not merely a soul residing or imprisoned within the body, as some ancient philosophers taught. Nor is the person merely a sophisticated or high-tech machine. Rather, the entire body is enlivened by the soul, and the soul is created to take up the form of the body, giving it the capacity for spiritual operations such as knowledge, acts of faith and love, and supernatural life.[51]

> The unity of soul and body is so profound that one has to consider the soul to be the "form" of the body: i.e., it is because of its spiritual soul that the body made of matter becomes a living, human body; spirit and matter, in man, are not two natures united, but rather their union forms a single nature. (CCC 365)

Death temporarily separates the soul from the body. At death, the soul, which is essential for human life on earth, is separated from the body. While the soul continues to exist, the mortal body is rendered lifeless and decomposes. At the end of time, according to Catholic teaching, the soul will be reunited with the body in its glorified state.

The Baptism by Longhi. Upon receiving Baptism, the soul is purified of Original Sin. The person, through the infusion of sanctifying grace, is raised to the status of a child of God.

Moral theology involves both the physical and spiritual realities of the human person. Since the human person is both a physical and spiritual reality, morality is concerned with both the body and the spirit, for "in fact, body and soul are inseparable: in the person, and the willing agent, and in the deliberate act, they stand or fall together."[52]

Our own experiences illustrate how the physical and spiritual are interrelated. People who stay in shape through exercise, for example, say it helps them relieve stress and lifts their spirits. Likewise, when we feel depressed, sad, or humiliated, it is often expressed through our physical bodies—a tight throat, abdominal pain, or general malaise.

While man is a religious being by his nature, the need for enlightenment, purification, and strength make the sacramental life necessary. The sacraments, which were instituted by Christ, also point to the unity of body and soul. In each sacrament, spiritual graces are received through a physical sign—the water of Baptism, for example, or Sacred Chrism.

In Baptism, the soul is united to Christ. Upon receiving Baptism, the soul is purified of Original Sin, receives the Holy Spirit, and is incorporated into the life of Christ. Through this Sacrament, the soul shares in the divine life of God in a new and elevated way. By the grace of Baptism, the person, through the infusion of sanctifying grace, is raised to the status of a child of God. A permanent and indelible mark is imprinted on the soul whereby the person becomes a member of Christ's Mystical Body, the Church, and the baptized person is united to the Death, burial, and Resurrection of Christ and becomes a new creation in Christ Jesus.

The Blessing by Simonet. In the Sermon on the Mount, as told by Matthew, Jesus set a higher standard for his followers: "You have heard that it was said, 'You shall love your neighbor and hate your enemy.' But I say to you, Love your enemies and pray for those who persecute you, . . ." (Mt 5:43-44)

These graces received in the Sacrament of Baptism are strengthened and completed in the Sacrament of Confirmation, which more perfectly binds a person to Christ's Mystical Body, the Church.[53] The soul is nourished further by the Body of Christ in the Sacrament of the Eucharist, which further transforms a person in Christ.[54]

Through the Sacraments of Baptism and Confirmation, the laity have a share in the priestly, prophetic, and kingly mission of Jesus Christ. Precisely by their presence in the midst of the world, the laity respond to the call to holiness by bringing Christ into all areas of human society: families, friends, and associates, etc. In this manner, the command of Christ to "make disciples of all nations"[55] is brought to fruition.

MORAL EXPECTATIONS OF CHRISTIANS

It is reasonable to expect that the elevation of the human soul at Baptism places higher moral expectations on all baptized Christians.

> Christian, recognize your dignity. For now, you partake of divine nature; do not degenerate by turning back to your past state. Remember what Head you belong to and to what body you are a member of. Remember that you have been snatched away from the power of darkness to be transported to the light of the kingdom of God. (St. Leo the Great, *The Sermon on the Nativity*, 21, 2-3)

The moral responsibility of Christians. Do Christians have an obligation to behave differently from the unbaptized? Is there a Christian morality that is distinct from non-Christian religious moral standards? Are there specific moral precepts that are expected of a Christian?

The answer is "yes" to all three questions. The moral responsibility for a follower of Christ is far greater than for those who do not follow Christ. These high standards required of a Christian find their origin and principle in the elevation of the soul to a new life in Christ through sanctifying grace.

This new life in Christ also implies a calling to achieve the kind of spiritual and moral ideals expressed in the Beatitudes. The high vision mapped out by the Beatitudes—to be poor in spirit, merciful, meek, humble, and pure of heart—can be achieved only through the exercise of the theological virtues of faith, hope, and charity, which are gratuitously given at Baptism. Christ's New Law, summarized in the Beatitudes and elaborated in the Sermon on the Mount, presupposes the help of sacramental grace.

Jesus sets higher standards for his followers. "A new commandment I give to you, that you love one another; even as I have loved you, that you also love one another," Jesus said.[56] This statement not only envelops the commandments, and indeed the entire moral law, as expressions of love, it also demands that we love others just as Christ loves us—with a supernatural love rather than a merely human love.

In the Parable of the Good Samaritan, the Christian is called to love even those whom the world considers unlovable.[57] Jesus condemned the Old Law of retaliation—"an eye for an eye, a tooth for a tooth"[58]—by calling for a response of unconditional love. The Lord wants us not just to forgive our enemies, but to love them as well.

In the Sermon on the Mount,[59] Jesus perfects the Old Law into a New Law of love. In return, Jesus promises an unimagined happiness to those who follow his commandments: "If you keep my commandments, you will abide in my love, just as I have kept my Father's commandments and abide in his love. These things I have spoken to you, so that my joy may be in you, and that your joy may be full."[60]

MORAL REQUIREMENTS FOR MAN AS A SOCIAL BEING

Since the time of Aristotle, it has been said that the human being is by his very nature a social being. Relating to other persons is very much a part of the human condition.

This is reflected in the sacraments, especially in the Sacraments of Baptism and the Eucharist, which have both individual and communal characteristics. In Baptism, the person being baptized is united both to Christ and to the members of his Mystical Body, the Church. In Holy Communion, the gathered community, united to all of the faithful throughout the world, is strengthened and renewed in its union with Christ. While an individual relationship with Christ is essential, the Christian is never alone. Instead, he or she is an integral part of God's family.

> The human person needs to live in society. Society is not for him an extraneous addition, but a requirement of his nature. Through the exchange with others, mutual service and dialogue with his brethren, man develops his potential; he thus responds to his vocation.[61] (CCC 1879)

Because personal interests can sometimes overshadow social duties, it is necessary to stress social morality. Vatican II states the "need to transcend an individualistic morality."[62]

A large portion of the *Catechism of the Catholic Church* is dedicated to the social teaching of the Church, which deals with those actions that impact on the "human community."[63] The teaching of the Church clearly states that Christian morality cannot be limited to the individual at the expense of his or her social duties. The Vatican II document *Gaudium et Spes* explains this well.

> The pace of change is so far-reaching and rapid nowadays that no one can allow

In Holy Communion, the gathered community, united to all of the faithful throughout the world, is strengthened and renewed in its union with Christ.

himself to close his eyes to the course of events or indifferently ignore them and wallow in the luxury of a merely individualistic morality. The best way to fulfill one's obligations of justice and love is to contribute to the common good according to one's means and the needs of others, even to the point of fostering and helping public and private organizations devoted to bettering the conditions of life. (*Gaudium et Spes*, 30)

OUR SOURCES OF MORAL THEOLOGY

Every branch of study must accept certain self-evident truths as a starting point in order to do any meaningful research. The study of history, for instance, begins with the recognition that actual events took place. Only after investigating specific episodes can the historian pick up certain trends and develop explanations as to the causes and effects of these trends.

Sciences are also interrelated, as various disciplines make use of the facts and findings of other disciplines. This is especially true of chemistry, physics, and engineering, which rely heavily on advanced mathematical calculations.

Similarly, moral theology uses its own particular sources along with other disciplines to reinforce its teachings. As in all of theology, as we said earlier, moral theology draws its principles from Divine Revelation found in Sacred Scripture and Sacred Tradition, which together form one sacred Deposit of Faith entrusted to the Church. The Magisterium of the Church then interprets and teaches from this sacred Deposit of Faith revealed by God himself.

The Inspiration of St. Matthew by Caravaggio. The Apostles and early Christians were inspired to record Christ's life and teachings. In doing so, they were led by the Holy Spirit, who safeguarded these divine truths from error.

The marvel of Divine Revelation is that God reveals his inner life to men and women, by inviting them into a loving relationship. This invitation to friendship includes a rich array of truths connected with God's love for us, and instruction on how to respond to his love.

The God of our faith has revealed himself as He who is; and he has made himself known as "abounding in steadfast love and faithfulness."[64] God's very being is Truth and Love. (CCC 231)

This Divine Revelation reaches its climax with the Incarnation and in Jesus' public life and teachings and ultimately in his Paschal Mystery.

Moral theology represents the development and growth in understanding of these moral truths. Throughout history, the Church has applied the moral truths revealed by God to specific situations that have called for moral evaluation or clarification. Theologians, through the light of human reason and in full respect for existing Church teachings, can draw new understanding of the truths contained in this sacred Deposit of Faith transmitted by the Church.

Sacred Scripture. Divine Revelation, as transmitted to us through Sacred Scripture, involves a divine illumination in the minds and wills of certain individuals chosen to record that which was inspired by God. These divinely inspired truths that embrace both the Old and New Testaments are ultimately designed to assist every person in finding salvation through the discovery and acceptance of God's will. This divine

Transfiguration by Previtali. The life of Jesus is used as the primary example of how a believer learns to live a Christian life.

inspiration and Revelation reaches its climax with the Incarnation and in Jesus' public life and teaching, together with his Death and Resurrection.

The Apostles and early Christians were inspired to record Christ's life and teachings. In doing so, they were led by the Holy Spirit, who safeguarded these divine truths from error.

Christian morality is especially drawn from the New Testament, which contains the teachings of Christ. In the Gospels, we find two main sources of moral theology:

✤ The life of Jesus, which is used as the primary example of how a believer learns to live a Christian life;

✤ The teachings and preaching of Jesus—his words, deeds, and precepts—which constitute the "moral rule of Christian life."[65]

The rest of the New Testament is also used as a source for moral theology. The Apostles, besides recounting the moral teachings of Christ, explained other precepts derived from these teachings and applied them to the different circumstances of the early Church communities.[66]

However, not all biblical teachings were meant to be binding forever. The Old Testament contained many circumstantial precepts that were superseded by Jesus' preaching. For instance, the practice of divorce, which was permitted under certain conditions by Moses, was later prohibited by Jesus who restored the original dignity of the marital covenant established by God in creation.[67]

Sacred Tradition. The word "tradition" comes from the Latin *tradere*, which means "to pass on." Sacred Tradition refers to the living transmission of the Gospel of Jesus Christ. This message of salvation, whether oral or written, is conserved and handed on as a Deposit of Faith through apostolic succession under the guidance of the Holy Spirit.

Tradition is the very life of the Church. Through Tradition, the Church, in her doctrine, life, and worship, transmits to every generation what she believes.[68] The writings of the early Church Fathers give "witness to the life-giving presence of this Tradition, showing how its riches are poured out in the practice and life of the Church, in her belief and her prayer."[69]

The Magisterium. The Church's teaching office, known as the Magisterium, is a word that is derived from the Latin *magister*, which means "teacher." It refers to the authority of the pope and the bishops united with him in matters of faith and morals.

The realm of faith and morals embrace every theme that is connected to the contents of Divine Revelation. The Church, through the guidance of the Holy Spirit, has the authority to define and interpret the truths and directives derived from Sacred Scripture and Tradition, including "moral questions that fall within the natural law and reason."[70]

> But the task of giving an authentic interpretation of the Word of God, whether in its written form or in the form of Tradition, has been entrusted to the living teaching office of the Church alone. Its authority in this matter is exercised in the name of Jesus Christ. Yet this magisterium is not superior to the Word of God, but is its servant. It teaches only what has been handed on to it. At the divine command and with the help of the Holy Spirit, it listens to this devotedly, guards it with dedication and expounds it faithfully. All that it proposes for belief as being divinely revealed is drawn from the single deposit of faith. (*Dei Verbum*, 10)

The teachings of the hierarchy—the popes, the councils, and the bishops in their dioceses—began with the Apostles. The head of the Church, the pope, by divine institution, enjoys complete, immediate, and universal power over the care of souls. Christ promised that the pope would be guided by the Holy Spirit to authentically interpret the Christian doctrinal and moral message as the head of the college of bishops.[71]

The Magisterium defines both the truths of the Faith and the Church's moral teachings, and transmits them to every generation.[72] Under certain conditions, the pope, or the whole hierarchy in union with the Holy Father, can make infallible pronouncements regarding faith and morals. This phrase "faith and morals" can be found in many documents of Catholic Tradition, indicating that these teachings are preserved from error and therefore must be accepted as ultimately coming from Christ himself.

Pope Benedict XVI.
Christ promised that the pope would be guided by the Holy Spirit to authentically interpret the Christian doctrinal and moral message.

> The Church's magisterium intervenes not only in the sphere of faith, but also, and inseparably so, in the sphere of morals. It has the task of "discerning...those acts which in themselves conform to the demands of faith and foster their expression in life and those which, on the contrary, because intrinsically evil, are incompatible with such demands."[73] In proclaiming the commandments of God and the charity of Christ, the Church's magisterium also teaches the faithful specific particular precepts and requires that they consider them in conscience as

Triumph of St. Thomas Aquinas by Gozzoli. St. Thomas' great work *Summa Theologiæ* is a document of the Church's Magisterium. One of 33 Doctors of the Church, St. Thomas, a Dominican priest, is considered by many to be the Catholic Church's greatest theologian and philosopher. He was the foremost classical proponent of natural theology and the father of the Thomistic school of philosophy and theology.

morally binding. In addition, the magisterium carries out an important work of vigilance, warning the faithful of the presence of possible errors, even merely implicit ones, when their consciences fail to acknowledge the correctness and the truth of the moral norms, which the magisterium teaches. (*Veritatis Splendor*, 110)

Natural law. Natural law and the moral principles intimately linked to the requirements of human dignity are another source of moral theology. This notion of right and wrong is derived from the very wisdom of God. As man deliberates and chooses actions to achieve personal perfection and happiness, he continues to discover the objective moral guide given by God.

The natural law is written and engraved in the soul of each and every man, because it is human reason ordaining him to do good and forbidding him to sin. But this command of human reason would not have the force of law if it were not the voice and interpreter of a higher reason to which our spirit and our freedom must be submitted.[74] (CCC 1954)

Natural sciences and moral theology. The natural sciences, which are based on reason alone, are especially useful in elaborating upon and corroborating the moral doctrine of the Church. However, as Revelation goes beyond human reason alone, natural sciences are only supplementary; that is, they neither substitute for nor diminish the authority of Scripture and Tradition, including the Magisterium, which constitute the true sources of moral theology.

CONCLUSION

Terms such as "morality," "the moral law," and even "sin" often make people uncomfortable because they associate these terms with a spirit of judgmentalism and narrow-mindedness. The prevailing mind of many Western societies today is a secularizing trend that increasingly views matters of morals and truth as subjective in nature, so much so that if one dares to publicly state a Christian or Catholic position on a given

Crucifixion by Mantegna. Although every person enjoys the dignity of being made in the image of God, every person has moral weaknesses and is inclined to sin.

issue affecting public policy, that person is accused of imposing his or her personal moral views—or the moral views of his or her particular church—on others. While there is often a call to respect diverse points of view, it sometimes becomes clear that this tolerance for opinions stops short of respecting anything that smacks of traditional Christian or Catholic morality.

Catholics, too, can sometimes become shy about expressing their faith, either out of ignorance or out of fear of not being accepted by others. Sometimes a Catholic will be sheepish and almost embarrassed about aspects of the moral law that do not fit the currents of popular opinion. Sometimes, sadly, a Catholic will not accept certain teachings of the Church.

Christ was sent by the Father to bring his message of love, hope, and reconciliation to all people. Christ fulfilled this mission perfectly through his life of self-sacrifice and obedience, through his teachings, and through his Passion, Death, and Resurrection. In faithful obedience to the command that Christ gave his Apostles, the Church continues his mission and will continue to do so until Christ comes again. In this mission, the Church is aided by the Holy Spirit, who is the "principal agent of the whole of the Church's mission."[75]

Because the Holy Spirit perpetually guides the Catholic Church in developing and safeguarding her teachings, we as believers enjoy a certainty that we possess objective moral truth without the possibility of error. Moral theology is a reflection upon revealed truth as expressed in Sacred Scripture, Tradition, and natural law. The process of interpreting, explaining, and applying Divine Revelation falls to the Magisterium under the loving direction of the Holy Spirit.

Divine Revelation teaches us that the human person has an inherent dignity. Although every person enjoys the dignity of being made in the image of God, every person has moral weaknesses and is inclined to sin. The reality of Original Sin points out the precarious state in which each person finds himself:

> When man looks into his own heart, he finds that he is drawn toward what is wrong and sunk in many evils...Man therefore is divided in himself. As a result, the life of men, both individual and social, shows itself to be a struggle, and a dramatic one, between good and evil, between light and darkness. (*Gaudium et Spes*, 13)

Through the Sacrament of Baptism a person is formed in the image of Christ and can again enjoy the divine life offered by his Redemption. This realistic view of the human condition helps us to aspire to a life of

Cupola of Genesis, Basilica of St. Mark, Venice. This mosaic depicts episodes of the Book of Genesis, from the Creation of the Heavens and Earth to the Expulsion from Eden. "The Lord God took the man to put him in the Garden of Eden to till it and keep it. And the Lord God commanded the man, saying, 'You may freely eat of every tree of the garden; but of the tree of the knowledge of good and evil you shall not eat, for in the day that you eat of it you shall die.'" (Gn 2:15-17)

morality. In seeking that life of morality, we must remain aware of our continuous need of God's grace, for only with grace are we able to live a faithful life of prayer and sacrifice, making good moral decisions based upon the rich teachings of the Catholic Church.

To understand the true source and purpose of the moral law, it is critical to appreciate how the Ten Commandments, the Gospels, and the teachings of the Church call us to a life that leads to our eternal salvation. If we believe that God loves us and desires our happiness, both on earth and in Heaven forever, then it follows that our discipleship in Christ, the moral law, and the life of holiness to which he calls us are indeed the paths of greatest love, the road he has set before us that leads us to Heaven.

We will explore the implications of that call further in the chapters ahead.

SUPPLEMENTARY READING

On the love of God and neighbor, serving others, and human dignity:

1. Love of God and love of neighbor are thus inseparable, they form a single commandment. But both live from the love of God who has loved us first. No longer is it a question, then, of a "commandment" imposed from without and calling for the impossible, but rather of a freely-bestowed experience of love from within, a love which by its very nature must then be shared with others. Love grows through love. Love is "divine" because it comes from God and unites us to God; through this unifying process it makes us a "we" which transcends our divisions and makes us one, until in the end God is "all in all" (1 Cor 15:28).

— Pope Benedict XVI, *Deus Caritas Est*, 18

2. There are some also who, either from zeal in attending to their own business or through some sort of aversion to their fellowmen, claim that they are occupied solely with their own affairs, without seeming to themselves to be doing anyone any injury. But while they steer clear of the one kind of injustice, they fall into the other: they are traitors to social life, for they contribute to it none of their interest, none of their effort, none of their means.

— Cicero, *De Officiis*, Bk. I, 9

3. It is in accordance with their dignity that all men, because they are persons, that is, beings endowed with reason and free will and therefore bearing personal moral responsibility, are both impelled by their nature and bound by a moral obligation to seek the truth, especially religious truth. They are also bound to adhere to the truth once they have come to know it and direct their lives in accordance with the demands of truth.... In availing of any freedom man must respect the moral principle of personal and social responsibility; in exercising their rights individual men and social groups are bound by the moral law to have regard for the rights of others, their own duties to others and the common good of all. All men must be treated with justice and humanity.

— *Dignitatis Humanæ*, 2 and 7

Pope Benedict XVI celebrates the Eucharist in São Paulo, Brazil. "Love of God and love of neighbor are thus inseparable, they form a single commandment."

VOCABULARY

ACTUAL GRACE
This supernatural, free, and undeserved help from God that is given for specific circumstances to do good and avoid evil.

AMORALITY
Outside the sphere of moral sense; an attitude that lacks any moral orientation, dispensing from all moral norms; attitudes or orientations not characterized as either good or evil.

BEATITUDE
Happiness or blessedness, especially the eternal happiness of Heaven, which is the vision of God and a participation in the divine nature. This is the greatest human desire.

CHRISTIAN MORALITY
Moral norms to be followed because a Christian is incorporated into Christ through Baptism.

CHRISTIAN VOCATION
God's call to each person by which he is incorporated into Christ through grace and becomes a member of the Mystical Body of Christ. As one of God's people, he partakes in the life of the Church.

CHRISTIANITY
A name derived from Christ, the Anointed One. The set of beliefs, practices, and morals in imitation of and commanded by Jesus Christ.

DISCIPLE
From the Latin verb *discere*, "to learn." One who accepted Jesus' message to follow him, especially one of the Twelve; this term can also refer to a Christian of any age because he is a follower of Christ.

ENCYCLICAL
A letter written by the pope to all the world's bishops and occasionally to all the faithful. It usually expounds on some aspect of Church teaching.

FREEDOM
The power rooted in reason and the will, to act or not to act, and so to perform deliberate actions on one's own responsibility.

FREE WILL
This gift from God includes the power of directing one's own actions without constraint. This makes possible the choice to love God.

GRACE
The free and unmerited favor of God given first of all through the sacraments. Grace is a share in the divine life infused into the soul by the Holy Spirit to heal from sin and to sanctify.

HOLINESS
Spiritual perfection or purity because of likeness unto God who is perfectly Holy. The free dedication of a Christian to the will of God and the participation in the life of grace. Holiness is the perfection of charity. It is also referred to as sanctity, saintliness, and sacredness.

IMMORALITY
A quality, character, or conduct in violation of moral law.

INFALLIBILITY
Immunity from error and any possibility of error. The pope enjoys this charism by virtue of his office when, "as supreme pastor and teacher of the faithful...he proclaims by a definitive act a doctrine pertaining to faith or morals."[76] The college or body of bishops is also infallible, when, in union with the pope, they definitively proclaim doctrines pertaining to faith and morals to be held by the universal Church, above all in an Ecumenical Council.

LAW OF CHRIST
An interior law that stems from grace—in connection with life in Jesus—and becomes a norm or impulse for imitating Christ and acting like him.

LOVE (CHARITY)
The theological virtue by which a Christian loves God above all things for His own sake, and loves his neighbor as himself for the love of God.

LUMEN GENTIUM
Latin name for the "Dogmatic Constitution on the Church," a key document from the Second Vatican Council.

VOCABULARY Continued

MAGISTERIUM
The name given to the teaching authority of the Church, entrusted to the pope and the bishops in communion with him.

MATERIALISM
An unhealthy attachment to material goods and wealth, particularly when it diminishes virtue and distracts from attention to the spiritual life.

MORALITY
The doctrine or system by which actions are judged to be good or evil. Morality looks to those human acts that impact the human person and affect his or her eternal destiny.

MORAL LAW
The ethical norms, authored and revealed by God and safeguarded by the Church, imposing obligations on the conscience of each person.

MORAL RELATIVISM
The view that there is no absolute or universal moral law or truth, resulting in a morality determined by cultural factors or personal preference.

MORAL THEOLOGY
The subset of theology that makes use of reason to offer practical judgments, under the guidance of divine revelation, in order to direct human acts towards their supernatural end: God.

NATURAL LAW
The participation of man in the plan of God in relation to human life and action, insofar as the mind can understand it. The objective order established by God that determines the requirements for people to thrive and reach fulfillment. Natural law "enables man to discern by reason the good and the evil, the truth and the lie" (CCC 1954).

NATURE
The essence of a being considered as the principle of its activity and defining its particular characteristics.

NEW BEING IN CHRIST
The supernatural condition of the baptized, by which one participates in the life of Jesus.

OBJECTIVE MORALITY
Standards of conduct that are universal rather than conditioned by culture or personal preference.

ORIGINAL SIN
Adam and Eve's abuse of their human freedom in disobeying God's command. As a consequence they lost the grace of original holiness and justice and became subject to the law of death; sin became universally present in the world; and every person is born into this condition. This sin separated mankind from God, darkened the human intellect, weakened the human will, and introduced into human nature an inclination toward sin. With Original Sin, man lost the inner harmony between his mind, his will, and his passions. Also, after this "First Sin," every person would be destined to die.

PLURALISM
The existence of a variety of opinions, ideas, or beliefs within human society, some of which contradict others. A plurality in the application of moral principles and social customs is valid insofar as it does not contradict God's Revelation, Church teaching, and sound reason.

POSITIVE MORALITY
A moral code that prescribes what ought to be done.

REASON
The intellectual power or faculty which is ordinarily employed by man in adapting thought or action to some end; the guiding principle of the human mind in the process of thinking.

SACRED TRADITION
From the Latin for "handed down," this refers to a teaching, whether written or oral, entrusted by Christ to the Apostles and their successors, and which has been transmitted by teaching to each generation of Christians through Apostolic Succession.

VOCABULARY Continued

SANCTIFYING GRACE
The free and unmerited favor of God given through the sacraments. Sanctifying grace heals and sanctifies human nature wounded by sin by giving man a share in the divine life infused into the soul by the Holy Spirit.

SECULARISM (or SECULAR HUMANISM)
The doctrine that morality should be based solely on well-being in the present life, paying no heed to life after death.

SERMON ON THE MOUNT
One of Jesus' first and most famous proclamations of the Gospel. The Beatitudes and the Lord's Prayer are among some of the teachings given in the Sermon on the Mount.

THEOLOGICAL VIRTUES
Faith, hope, and charity. Infused in the soul at Baptism, these enable a Christian to partake of the divine nature; they are called "theological" because they originate with God and have him as their object.

VATICAN II
Shorthand for the Second Vatican Council (1962-65), the most recent of the Ecumenical Councils of the Catholic Church.

VERITATIS SPLENDOR
Latin title for "The Splendor of Truth," a 1993 encyclical of Pope John Paul II that explored the fundamental questions of the Church's moral teachings.

VIRTUE
A habitual and firm disposition to do good.

Communion of the Apostles by Signorelli. The Christian disciple strives to imitate Christ and apply his instructions to his or her own particular circumstances.

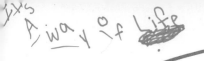

STUDY QUESTIONS

1. What is morality?

2. Why is it important to be a "moral person"?

3. Explain the difference between an objective morality and moral relativism.

4. Name several social and political issues today that pertain to the moral law.

5. Why is the view that Christianity is "a mere set of rules" incorrect?

6. Explain how the Ten Commandments can be summed up in the Great Commandments of love of God and love of neighbor.

7. Why do moral laws and precepts exist?

8. Name three ways in which Jesus fulfilled the requirements of civil law.

9. Name one moral action. What are its positive consequences? Name one immoral action. What are its negative consequences? Explain how immoral actions indicate a lack of love.

10. How do Christian ethics differ from secular ethics?

11. Read the story of the rich young man (Mt 19:16-23). According to the story, why is the "moral life" necessary?

12. Explain each of the four cardinal virtues. How are these virtues necessary to live a truly human life?

13. What are the origins and goals of Christian morality?

14. What does the word *concupiscence* mean? Use a dictionary if necessary. What does it mean for the Christian life?

15. How was the "Divine Law" revealed to mankind?

16. Why can human reason never be the last word in regards to morality?

17. Explain the difference between sanctifying grace and actual grace.

18. What is the "vocation" shared by all the baptized?

19. God calls everyone, but each individual must respond. What is the proper response to God's call?

20. Sanctifying grace enables a person to share in the actual life of Christ. Explain what this means in the life of a Christian.

21. Explain the following terms: "Put on Christ," "born again," and "formed in Christ."

22. Someone might say that as long as you love God, your actions are not relevant. Using the image of the tree and its fruit, explain why this idea is not correct. Using the same image, explain what must come before good moral actions.

23. The Sacraments of Reconciliation and the Holy Eucharist fortify a person in living a virtuous life. Explain.

24. Read the Parable of the Sheep and the Goats (Mt 25:31-46). How does one show love of God? What happens to those who fail to show love of neighbor?

25. If human beings have caused so much harm throughout history, then why would God have created humans with free will?

26. Explain how sin diminishes freedom, and how moral actions increase freedom.

27. "Love for God guarantees the authenticity of the love for neighbor, and the love for neighbor is an indispensable evidence of a genuine love for God." Explain.

28. What is the link between happiness and moral behavior? How can moral behavior result in a foretaste of Heaven in the here and now?

29. Explain how God is the origin and end of all good moral actions.

30. What is the purpose of moral theology?

STUDY QUESTIONS Continued

31. What often happens to societies that reject the moral law revealed by God?

32. Define secular humanism. Can human reason on its own determine moral truths without error? Explain.

33. What is a "materialistic view" of the world?

34. Explain why "scientism" will always fail to answer the basic problems of mankind.

35. What is the error of a "purely spiritual" viewpoint?

36. What is a soul?

37. What comprises a human body?

38. Explain how Christ recognized the reality of body and soul in instituting the sacraments.

39. What is the effect of Baptism on a person?

40. Why is a Christian held to a higher standard of conduct?

41. Where can these higher standards mapped out by Christ be found?

42. Read Matthew 5: 38-48. List the ways in which Jesus perfected the Commandments.

43. Explain why the "Social Teaching" of the Church is important.

44. From what sources does moral theology draw its principles?

45. How can one be sure that the Bible is without error?

46. Why cannot Catholics just read the Bible and figure out doctrines for themselves? Your answer should refer to the intentions of Christ in founding the Church. How can Catholics have assurance that the moral teachings of the Church are correct?

47. Why is it a responsibility of Catholics to have a good understanding of the Catholic Faith?

Matthew and the Angel by Rembrandt.
Divine Revelation, transmitted to us through Sacred Scripture, involves a divine illumination in the minds and wills of certain individuals chosen to record that which was inspired by God.

PRACTICAL EXERCISES

1. Apply the story of the rich young man to your own life. Are there things in your life that take precedence over God? Make a list of things that you might change in your life so that God takes center stage.

2. The unChristian lifestyle of some Christians harms the spread of the Gospel message. What great responsibility does each Christian have in this regard? What changes might you make in your life to better reflect the message of Christ to others?

3. What "talents" has God given you? Make a list. What are ways in which you might multiply these talents for God?

4. Reflect on the Parable of the Sheep and the Goats in Matthew 25. Think of concrete ways in which you could show love of God by serving those in need.

5. Vatican II states that "a man is more precious for what he is than for what he has" (*GS* 35). Explain how this sentence defines the Christian vocation and moral life in Christ.

6. Read and comment on Chapter 25 of St. Matthew's Gospel. What importance do sins of omission have in relation to the understanding that Christian moral life is a "following of Christ"?

7. Explain the ramifications of Christ's words in Matthew 15:10-20.

8. Reflect for a moment: What are the things that make you truly happy in life? Friendship, relationships, family, love, God...? Are these material realities? How would adopting a materialistic viewpoint fail to make you happy?

9. Read the Sermon on the Mount (Mt 5:1–7:29). Make a list of some of these "high standards" to which a Christian is held. Reflect on these standards in prayer.

10. By doing good works a person merits an increase of grace in the soul. Grace is the divine life of God. This means effectively that the presence of God grows within the soul when we model our lives on Christ. Think of some concrete things that you could do for others that would increase God's presence in your soul.

11. What are some of the moral principles expressed in the New Testament? Name some of the principles proposed by Christ himself in the following passages:

- Mt 5:21-48
- Mk 9:42-48; 10:1-12
- Lk 17:1-4
- Jn 13:34-35

12. Compare and contrast the moral precepts of the Old and New Testaments. Begin with the Ten Commandments in Exodus 20, and the Beatitudes in Matthew 5:1-12. What is the relationship between the Law of God as expressed by Moses on Mount Sinai and Jesus in the Sermon on the Mount? Discuss their similarities and reconcile their differences.

13. Read Chapter 5 of *Lumen Gentium* about the "universal call to holiness." What are the practical consequences that might arise from the principles laid out in this document?

14. According to the *Catechism of the Catholic Church* (1033-1037), what does the existence of Hell reveal about humanity's destiny and proper end?

15. Is it possible to accept the challenge to be holy in your life today? Explain your answer in two paragraphs.

FROM THE CATECHISM

135 "The Sacred Scriptures contain the Word of God and, because they are inspired, they are truly the Word of God."[77]

382 "Man, though made of body and soul, is a unity."[78] The doctrine of the faith affirms that the spiritual and immortal soul is created immediately by God.

418 As a result of Original Sin, human nature is weakened in its powers; subject to ignorance, suffering, and the domination of death; and inclined to sin. This inclination is called "concupiscence."

520 In all of his life Jesus presents himself as *our model*. He is "the perfect man,"[79] who invites us to become his disciples and follow him. In humbling himself, he has given us an example to imitate, through his prayer he draws us to pray, and by his poverty he calls us to accept freely the privation and persecutions that may come our way.[80]

742 "Because you are sons, God has sent the Spirit of his Son into our hearts, crying, 'Abba! Father!'"[81]

1280 Baptism imprints on the soul an indelible spiritual sign, the character, which consecrates the baptized person for Christian worship. Because of the character Baptism cannot be repeated.[82]

1823 Jesus makes charity the *new commandment*.[83] By loving his own "to the end,"[84] he makes manifest the Father's love which he receives. By loving one another, the disciples imitate the love of Jesus which they themselves receive. Whence Jesus says: "As the Father has loved me, so have I loved you; abide in my love." And again: "This is my commandment, that you love one another as I have loved you."[85]

1833 Virtue is a habitual and firm disposition to do good.

1840 The theological virtues dispose Christians to live in a relationship with the Holy Trinity. They have God for their origin, their motive, and their object—God known by faith, God hoped in and loved for his own sake.

1975 According to Scripture the Law is a fatherly instruction by God which prescribes for man the ways that lead to the promised beatitude, and proscribes the ways of evil.

Statue of Pope John Paul II in Madrid, Spain. Pope John Paul II's encyclical, *Veritatis Splendor* (The Splendor of Truth) is a document of the Church's Magisterium. This encyclical is one of the most comprehensive, philosophical teachings of moral theology in the Catholic tradition.

Calling of the Apostles by Ghirlandaio. Our discipleship in Christ, the moral law, and the life of holiness to which he calls us are indeed the paths of greatest love, the road he has set before us that leads us to Heaven.

ENDNOTES – CHAPTER ONE

1. St. Augustine, *De Natura et Gratia*, 31: PL 44, 264.
2. Cf. Gn 1: 26-31; 2: 15-25
3. Cf. 2 Cor 5: 17.
4. CCC 1954.
5. St. Augustine, *Conf.* 10, 28, 39: PL 32, 795.
6. Mt 22: 37-40; cf. Lk 10: 25-28, Mk 12: 28-34.
7. *GS* 15 § 2.
8. Cf. Mt 5: 27; Mt 5: 19-24; Mt 7: 1-6; Mk 10: 2-9; Mk 3: 28-30; Mt 12: 31-37; Mt 18: 1-5.
9. Cf. Mk 1: 21; 6: 2; Lk 4: 16; Mk 11: 1-11; Mt 4: 1-2; Lk 2: 21-39; 2: 40-52; 3: 21-22; Lk 2: 41; Jn 5: 1; 7: 10; 11: 5.
10. Cf. *VS* 12-13; 95-97.
11. Cf. Mt 12: 1-14, 22-30; 23: 1-33.
12. Cf. Mt 19: 17.
13. Cf. CCC 1834.
14. Cf. Rom 11: 6.
15. Cf. CCC 2021.
16. Cf. *VS* 102.
17. Gn 3: 5.
18. Sir 15: 19-20.
19. Cf. Mk 8: 34; Mt 19: 16.
20. Cf. *VS* 10; cf. Lk 18: 18-27.
21. Cf. *VS* 11, 19; cf. Lk 9: 23.
22. Cf. *VS* 19-21.
23. John Paul II, CT 9.
24. Cf. *VS* 19-21; Jn 13: 15.
25. Cf. Phil 2: 5-8.

26. Cf. Eph 3: 17.
27. Cf. *VS* 19-21.
28. Gal 2: 20.
29. Cf. Lk 6: 43-45.
30. Cf. *VS* 19-21.
31. Cf. *VS* 16.
32. Apostolic Letter, *Dilecti Amici*, March 31, 1985.
33. 1 Jn 4: 18.
34. Cf. Mt 21: 28-32.
35. Cf. Mt 25: 1-13.
36. Cf. Mt 25: 14-30.
37. Cf. Mt 25: 31-46.
38. *GS* 15 § 2.
39. Gal 5: 13.
40. Gal 5: 1; Gal 5: 13; cf. Gal 6: 18.
41. Gal 5: 1.
42. Rom 6: 17-18.
43. Cf. *VS* 13-14.
44. Jn 15: 12; Jn 13: 34; 1 Cor 13: 13.
45. Mt 5: 1-12; Lk 6: 20-26.
46. Mt 5: 21-48.
47. Mt 5: 48.
48. Cf. *LG* 39-41.
49. CCC 1715.
50. Cf. *VS* 12.
51. Cf. Council of Vienne (1312): DS 902.
52. *VS* 49.
53. Cf. *LG* 11.
54. Cf. CCC 1275, 1694.
55. Mt 28: 19.

56. Jn 13: 34.
57. Cf. Lk 10: 29-37.
58. Cf. Mt 5: 38-40.
59. Mt 5.
60. Jn 15: 10-11.
61. Cf. *GS* 25 § 1.
62. *GS* 30.
63. Cf. CCC 1877-1948.
64. Ex 34: 6.
65. *VS* 20.
66. Cf. *VS* 26.
67. Cf. Mk 10: 2-12; Mt 5: 27-32; 19: 3-12.
68. Cf. CCC 78.
69. CCC 78.
70. CCC 2050.
71. Cf. *VS* 27, 30.
72. Cf. *VS* 110.
73. *DV* 16.
74. Leo XIII, *Libertas præstantissimum*, 597.
75. John Paul II, *RMiss* 21.
76. CCC 891.
77. *DV* 24.
78. *GS* 14 § 1.
79. *GS* 38; cf. Rom 15: 5; Phil 2: 5.
80. Cf. Jn 13: 15; Lk 11: 1; Mt 5: 11-12.
81. Gal 4: 6.
82. Cf. DS 1609 and DS 1624.
83. Cf. Jn 13: 34.
84. Jn 13: 1.
85. Jn 15: 9, 12.

Freedom and Conscience

CHAPTER 2

Freedom and Conscience

The freedom to make choices—free will—is at the very heart of the human person's exalted place in creation. It is part of what distinguishes us from the animals and is related to our capacity for reason, our capability to understand and discern good from evil, and the existence of our immortal soul with which we were created.

The concept of free will, however, can be misunderstood. Too often, freedom or free will is thought of as "the freedom to do whatever one wants." The most radical form of this misconception presupposes that the options we face have no objective value or moral implications, but only subjective values. In this view, our choices are not really a matter of choosing good versus evil, or of greater good versus lesser good, or of lesser evil versus greater evil. Every choice is seen as an exercise of personal preference, so much so that deciding whether or not to cheat on income taxes, shoplift, or commit adultery is erroneously perceived as having approximately the same moral gravity as choosing a flavor of ice cream.

But that is not what free will is truly meant to be. From a moral perspective, as Pope John Paul II pointed out, free will means "freedom to do what one ought."[1]

God has endowed us with this freedom so that we can willingly choose to return his love, and to love others as he has loved us. Love, by its very nature, is a free gift of self, and therefore it is intimately linked to the exercise of freedom.

In his book, *The Source of Christian Ethics*, Servais Pinckaers discusses two ideas of freedom. He speaks of a *freedom of indifference* and a *freedom of excellence* discussed in the writings of the Church Fathers and St. Thomas Aquinas. In a nutshell, he states that freedom of indifference is the power to choose between contraries, usually between good and evil. Freedom of excellence can be defined as the power to act freely in the pursuit of human perfection and everlasting joy.

It is important not to limit the role of freedom to the ability to choose between a virtuous act and a sinful one (freedom of indifference). The beauty of this gift consists in the capacity to choose to love God and others (freedom for excellence), and with the grace of God, becoming holy.

FOR DISCUSSION

✠ Why is it necessary to follow the will of God if we wish to be free?

✠ Are we responsible for disciplining ourselves and ordering our lives in such a way that we can objectively seek the truth which will set us free?

✠ Which moral acts make us truly free?

✠ What do we mean when we say that sin enslaves a person?

✠ What is conscience?

✠ How does the conscience aid a person who seeks to live a truly Christlike life?

✠ How does a person develop the conscience so that he or she can be confident of right judgments?

"If you continue in my word, you are truly my disciples, and you will know the truth, and the truth will make you free," Jesus says.[2] Later in the chapter, he also says plainly that "everyone who commits sin is a slave to sin."[3]

Truth liberates us to know and choose what is ultimately best for us, while sin makes us slaves. Knowing and keeping the moral law that is rooted in Divine Revelation grants us true freedom. Ignoring or denying the truth and going against the moral law actually restricts our freedom. The truest exercise of freedom is choosing to "do what one ought," and that will always be the will of God.

An essential theme in moral theology involves how to apply the moral law to concrete actions and situations. To evaluate the moral value or relative goodness of an action requires us to use our consciences correctly.

INTRODUCTION

What is the relationship between freedom and morality? When must a person take full responsibility for a particular act that he or she has committed?

Love of God and love of neighbor are the perfect motivations for a Christian to live a moral life in Christ, while fear of the consequences of immoral actions is an imperfect motivation. However, both incentives are grounded in a belief in the moral truths revealed by Christ and taught by the Church.

Even for the most devout believer, the moral life is always a struggle, and the greatest saints of history have had to deal with the temptation to sin. As Catholics, we find strength for that struggle through prayer and the grace of the sacraments, particularly the Sacraments of Reconciliation and the Eucharist. Although our free will and commitment to the moral law empower us to make good moral choices, temptation remains a formidable adversary that can weaken us and cause us to sin through poor moral choices.

Denying Satan by Bloch.
Truth liberates us to know and choose what is ultimately best for us, while sin makes us slaves. As Christians, we believe that God, through his Son Jesus Christ, revealed to us the fullness of truth that can lead us to everlasting life.

As we read at the beginning of this chapter, Jesus taught his disciples that choosing to do the will of the Father would lead them to the truth that would set them free: "If you remain in my word, you will be my disciples, and you will know the truth, and the truth will set you free."[4] Being a faithful disciple of Christ does not make us less free; rather, it gives us greater freedom because it liberates us from the sinfulness that would otherwise enslave us, thereby allowing us to fulfill the purpose for which we were created and to achieve true happiness.

As Christians, we believe that God, through his Son Jesus Christ, revealed to us the fullness of truth that can lead us to everlasting life. The teachings of Christ as mediated through the Church teach us what we must do, or avoid doing, in order to live in that truth.

We have seen how Christians who have received the truth of Divine Revelation and the grace of Jesus Christ are called to live by high moral standards. The principles behind the moral law, however, apply to all people. These principles include the truths that:

✤ The moral law increases freedom, rather than limiting it;

✤ Freedom requires every person to be responsible for his or her actions;

✤ Through a well-formed conscience, and making the necessary effort to know the truth, each person has the capacity to discover God's will within his or her own heart.

The rest of this chapter will explore different facets of freely chosen moral acts as they lead the person into a greater union with Christ.

THE MORAL LIFE

Before discussing moral acts, it would be helpful to revisit some basic principles regarding the moral life in the context of the universal experiences of the human condition.

Plato and Aristotle, detail from *School of Athens* by Raphael. Plato was a classical Greek philosopher, who, together with his mentor, Socrates, and his student, Aristotle, helped to lay the foundations of Western philosophy. Plato was a mathematician, writer of philosophical dialogues, and founder of the Academy in Athens, the first institution of higher learning in the western world.

Every human person must face moral decisions. The choice between good and evil will accompany all of us for the duration of our lives on earth. There are obvious exceptions, of course, such as children below the "age of reason" and individuals with mental disabilities or other impairments who do not possess a true faculty for the use of reason. These exceptions are to be understood whenever we speak of moral acts or moral choices in general.

The human preoccupation with the struggle of good versus evil has been the great drama of mankind throughout history. Great literature, profound philosophical thought, and the development of law all concern notions of good and evil. Because this universal struggle is at the very core of human experience, the study of ethics and moral theology is of vital importance to us all.

Socrates (470-399 BC) put it well when he said that "the science of good and evil" is the most important of all the forms of knowledge because it places us on the road to true happiness. Plato (424-348 BC) wrote similarly: "Still, I should like to examine further, for no light matter here is at stake, nothing less than the rule of human life."[5]

Every human person has the necessary free will to make moral decisions. Every person who is faced with a moral decision has the possibility and the power to choose from among the options presented. The power to choose what is good and right is always accompanied by the power to choose what is evil and wrong. Even those who are unbaptized or do not practice Christianity and are not explicitly aware of the moral law can make moral decisions to the extent of their ability in accordance with the natural law written on the human heart.

Every human person is morally responsible for his or her own moral acts. We have the ability and the opportunity to reason and evaluate the various choices set before us, along with their corresponding consequences. Then, we must make a choice and will to carry out the chosen act. This interplay between the mind and the will makes a person responsible for his or her actions and determines whether the act is virtuous or sinful.

THE MORAL ACT

Not every act performed by a human is a moral act. As used in philosophy and theology, the term "moral act" refers to any action that results from a deliberate choice between good and evil, or between different degrees of goodness.

a. A moral act involves both deliberation and choice. For an act to be a moral act, it must be preceded by deliberation, i.e. premeditated, and chosen freely. The acts of breathing, walking, and yawning have no moral value because they are not the fruit of deliberation and choice. They are simply physical actions that are performed unconsciously. Therefore, they are never considered moral actions.

b. A moral act has a moral content. A moral act proceeds from a moral decision, a choice between good and evil, or between a greater good and a lesser good. Some actions, while involving deliberation and choice, are not moral acts because the choices are morally indifferent. This would be the case, for example, when deciding whether to have a dish of vanilla ice cream or chocolate ice cream. Neither option would be considered wrong, nor is one choice better than the other.

Additional considerations, however, could turn even the choice of ice cream into a moral decision. Examples would include a teenager taking ice cream from the kitchen freezer when his parents

Christ and the Adulteress by Turchi. The term "moral act," as used in philosophy and theology, refers to any action that results from a deliberate choice between possible good and evil actions. "And Jesus said, 'Neither do I condemn you; go, and do not sin again.'" (Jn 8: 11)

specifically forbade it, or scooping the last of the vanilla ice cream in order to spite a sibling who is allergic to chocolate. Such factors transform the decision to a choice between acting in a way that expresses love of neighbor or acting in a way that is selfish or hurtful to others.

c. A moral act is a personal act. The criteria of deliberation and choice involve the intellect and the will, which are faculties of the soul. Moral acts involve the complete person, body and soul. As Pope John Paul II wrote, "Human acts are moral acts because they express and determine the goodness or evil of the individual who performs them."[6]

For better or for worse, moral acts contribute toward forming our character and our virtue. This truth is related to what we stated in the first chapter: Moral acts express and influence our dispositions and our will because our actions, dispositions, and will are interrelated. Every moral act we commit leaves us either better off or worse, more virtuous or less virtuous, closer to God or further away from God. It never leaves us exactly the same.

These ideas are well expressed by the philosopher Aristotle (384-322 BC):

> For man, when perfected, is the best of animals, but, when separated from law and justice, he is the worst of all; since armed injustice is the more dangerous, and he is equipped at birth with arms, meant to be used by intelligence and virtue, which he may use for the worst ends. Wherefore, if he has not virtue, he is the most unholy and the most savage of animals, and the most full of lust and gluttony. But justice is the bond of men in states, for the administration of justice, which is the determination of what is just, is the principle of order and political civil society.[7]

KNOWLEDGE AND MORAL RESPONSIBILITY

If Christ connects knowledge of the truth to keeping his commandments and to freedom, then what is the relationship between knowledge and moral responsibility?

A key factor in our moral responsibility for our actions rests in the knowledge of moral truth—that is, the ability to distinguish between right and wrong. Because every individual has an innate grasp of at least some standard of correct behavior, every person is accountable for his or her actions.

The knowledge which enters into each and every moral act determines the corresponding level of moral responsibility. An adult is more culpable for lying than a seven-year-old child, since the adult is expected to have a fuller grasp of the obligation to speak truthfully. The greater the knowledge of certain rules of good moral conduct, the greater the responsibility. That is why we as Christians are held to a higher standard of moral behavior: we are presumed to be more fully aware of what the moral law entails.

We cannot perform an evil act unless, at some level, we know it is evil. A person who acts through an ignorance that cannot be overcome (i.e., invincible ignorance) is not morally culpable. However, if we have at least some suspicion that an action might be wrong, then we have a moral obligation to resolve that doubt by gathering the necessary knowledge before acting. If we deliberately carry out a wrong action when we had prior doubt as to whether it was right or wrong, then we have committed a sinful act.

A good analogy is that of a deer hunter in the woods: if he hears a rustling in the brush but does not see what is causing it, he cannot simply fire his rifle at the source of the noise. He must first determine whether the rustling is caused by a deer or by another hunter.

Because there are different levels of knowledge, it is common in moral theology to classify actions that have been prompted by either full knowledge or partial knowledge of the appropriate moral principles. A corollary of the preceding discussion is that knowledge is thus a consideration in evaluating the relative virtue or sin of a given moral act.

Satan tempts Jesus on the pinnacle of the temple. Detail from *Three Temptations of Christ* by Botticelli.

The virtue in a moral act is determined in part by knowledge. A virtue is something that enables a person to act according to right reason enlightened by faith. Every action that is virtuous—an action that reflects the moral law and corresponds to the requirements of human dignity—presupposes knowledge of what is morally good.

For example, the virtuous act of giving a monetary contribution to a charitable organization involves knowing about how just and important it is to give to those in need. Familiarity with the standards of honesty and justice enables a person to act virtuously in putting in a full day's work, paying bills, and giving an accurate report on job performance. Every virtuous act, therefore, is preceded by a general knowledge of objective moral criteria and a specific application of that knowledge to a concrete act.

The sinfulness of an act is determined in part by knowledge. Just as knowledge enters into every virtuous action, it also serves as a condition for sinful actions. For an action to be considered sinful, the subject must be aware that the act violates the moral law.

For a person to be morally culpable for missing Mass on Sunday, he or she must first realize that it is a serious obligation to attend Sunday Mass. Complete, invincible ignorance of a moral teaching exonerates the individual of moral responsibility for that act; partial, invincible ignorance will partially exonerate the individual. The degree of moral responsibility for a given moral act, considering that the appropriate means were applied to inform the conscience, is proportionate to the level of awareness that the action was sinful.

Even when the moral responsibility for a moral act is mitigated by lack of knowledge about its sinfulness, the damage resulting from that act is still done. For example, even though an individual, who is somehow oblivious to the moral obligations to refrain from suggestive movies or magazines, may be partially inculpable for his ignorance, the act nevertheless causes negative moral effects on his or her mind, heart, passions, and will.

A lack of knowledge, nevertheless, is not the only attenuating factor mitigating the culpability for violations of the moral law. Fear and overwhelming duress, as well as other psychological or social factors, can lessen or even remove personal responsibility for a moral action.

The Temptation of Adam (detail) by Tintoretto. The virtue in a moral act is determined in part by knowledge. A virtue is something that enables a person to act according to right reason enlightened by faith.

> The imputability or responsibility for an action can be diminished or nullified by ignorance, duress, fear, and other psychological or social factors. (CCC 1746)

THE GIFT OF HUMAN FREEDOM

Freedom is a gift that makes the human person unique. Every man and woman is endowed with the power to love, which expresses a person's highest calling. Love is intimately connected to freedom, since it involves freely glorifying God and helping one's neighbors.

To truly love as Christ loves involves the gift of oneself to another. In order to give ourselves, we must exercise our freedom in choosing what is good. This is equally true for any virtuous act. To be just, merciful, chaste, or honest, we must have the freedom to choose these actions as well as the freedom to convert these choices into actions.

To enjoy the freedom that comes from self-mastery, we must actually choose to live according to the moral law. It is precisely in choosing to follow the moral law that we become the true master of ourselves and are transformed into a new creation. This self-mastery has the power to liberate us from inordinate passions and make us truly free. Wrong choices make us slaves to sin and to our own passions.

If in our freedom we enjoy a high degree of self-control, we can seriously pray, joyfully bear suffering for the sake of Christ, and find fulfillment in serving the needs of others. If we use this marvelous gift well, we can be transformed in such a way that the image of Christ clearly emerges in us. With the aid of grace, we can become empowered to love with the love of Christ himself.

> By free will one shapes one's own life. Human freedom is a force for growth and maturity in truth and goodness; it attains its perfection when directed toward God, our beatitude. (CCC 1731)

The improper use of freedom leads to immorality and self-destruction. The person ends up being a slave to his or her passions in such a manner that freedom is reduced and can be virtually lost. Freedom is one of the central themes of moral theology because it is innately involved with the pursuit or rejection of the moral law given by God.

SEVERAL ASPECTS OF HUMAN FREEDOM

a. Human freedom is not absolute—rather, it is limited. Human freedom, although quite real, is finite and limited by what is good and our individual circumstances. Every person needs to nurture his or her freedom by freely choosing those actions that contribute to his or her virtues as a person and as a follower of Christ:

> Rational reflection and daily experience demonstrate the weakness which marks man's freedom. The freedom is real but limited....Human freedom belongs to us as creatures; it is a freedom which is given as a gift, one to be received like a seed and to be cultivated responsibly. It is an essential part of that creaturely image, which is the basis of the dignity of the person. (*Veritatis Splendor*, 86)

Free will is a powerful gift. By using our freedom to do good, it can serve as a transforming force for the development of our skills and virtues, for growth in our ability to love as Christ loves and to experience true happiness. By the same token, misuse of our freedom in order to make poor moral choices robs us of dignity, distances us from God, and causes us to fall short of the happiness that God intends for us. Human freedom, then, is not an absolute in the sense that we can do anything we want without consequences.

The very purpose of freedom is to choose and perform good actions which will lead us to God.

God has chosen each of us for himself to share his eternal life. The freedom we have is the freedom to establish a loving relationship with Jesus Christ through the action of the Holy Spirit. The subordination of the world to the teachings of Christ is the greater use of freedom.

b. Freedom and knowledge are intimately related. Earlier we discussed how freedom, the moral law, and truth are related according to the words of Jesus himself: Christ and his teachings are the source of truth, and this truth makes us free.[8]

According to the Christian faith and the Church's teaching, "only the freedom which submits to the Truth leads the human person to his true good. The good of the person is to be in the Truth and to do the Truth."[9] (*Veritatis Splendor*, 84)

The intimate relationship between freedom and truth can be easily impeded or severed when a person tries to determine truth subjectively without regard to the moral law. Remember that the moral law is objective, and is therefore not a matter of mere personal preference or opinion. The relative good or evil of an act cannot be reduced simply to what "feels right" or is done with good intentions:

> In this way, the inescapable claims of truth disappear, yielding their place to a criterion of sincerity, authenticity, and "being at peace with oneself," so much so that some have come to adopt a radically subjectivistic conception of moral judgment. (*Veritatis Splendor*, 32)

c. Human freedom is ordered toward good. The very purpose of freedom is to choose and perform those good actions which will lead us to God, the ultimate source of all true and lasting happiness. It is better to view freedom as the capacity ultimately to find life in Christ. We enjoy the greatest true freedom when we choose to avoid sin and do the will of the Father.

> Man gains such dignity when, ridding himself of all slavery to the passions, he presses forward towards his goal by freely choosing what is good, and, by his diligence and skill, effectively secures for himself the means suited toward this end. (*Gaudium et Spes*, 17)

Sin enslaves us to evil. This is the meaning of St. Paul's words: "do you not know that if you yield yourselves to anyone as obedient slaves, you are the slaves of the one whom you obey, either of sin, which leads to death, or of obedience, which leads to righteousness?"[10]

The intimate relationship between freedom and truth is reiterated by the *Catechism of the Catholic Church.*

> **The more one does what is good, the freer one becomes. There is no true freedom except in the service of what is good and just. The choice to disobey and do evil is an abuse of freedom and leads to "the slavery of sin."[11] (CCC 1733)**

d. With freedom comes responsibility. There is no such thing as freedom that is independent of responsibility. Even on a strictly human level, we acquire and grow in freedom when we exercise responsibility and accountability. A child who responsibly exercises the freedom given by his or her parents is given more freedom. Consider Jesus' parable of the talents. The "good and faithful" servants who handled the master's money responsibly were given greater freedom and responsibility, while the servant who acted irresponsibly was "thrown into the outer darkness."[12]

> **Freedom makes man *responsible* for his acts to the extent that they are voluntary. Progress in virtue, knowledge of the good, and ascesis [rigorous self-discipline] enhance the mastery of the will over its acts. (CCC 1734)**

e. God respects our freedom. The reality of free will answers questions that at first glance seem difficult to answer. How can a God who is all-good and all-powerful allow such horrid evils as famine, genocide, the AIDS virus, and war to prevail in this world? How could God, if he truly loves every human person, allow for the possibility of an eternal Hell?

The answers to these seeming contradictions rest on human freedom. God has taken a certain risk in creating us and endowing us with free will.

God creates us in his image and likeness, gives us freedom, and invites us to cooperate willfully in his plan of creation. However, we suffer from the consequences of Original Sin and it is only through the merits of Christ that we can have the freedom to love God, to seek God, and to abide by his moral law. The freedom to choose correctly necessarily entails the option to reject God or to be indifferent to him and his will for us.

Out of respect for the freedom he grants us, God neither forces us to make the right choices nor prevents us from making wrong choices. Otherwise, we would not be free. Evil in the world, even that which reaches monumental proportions, is the bitter fruit of our evil choices. We cannot blame God for the evils that find their origins in our abuse of freedom.

f. God's grace is not imposed on us, but must be freely received. Jesus Christ died for our sins so that every person might enjoy the fullness of freedom and reach everlasting life. Through his Death and Resurrection, there is a superabundance

Christ in the Wilderness by Kramskoy.
"Then Jesus was led up by the Spirit into the wilderness to be tempted by the devil. And he fasted forty days and forty nights, and afterward he was hungry." (Mt 4: 1-2)

of grace for the forgiveness of sins, healing, and the salvation of every person. These graces have multiple effects. Received through the sacraments, they enlighten us to know what is right and strengthen our will to do what is right in order to fulfill God's will. God's graces overcome all by supplementing the flaws in our human ability and by enabling us to follow him.

The grace of God, however, does not diminish our freedom. Rather, it helps us to see the truth more clearly, and it gives us the required strength to conquer our passions. The proper use of freedom, with the help of grace, enables us to gradually align our will with God's will, as the *Catechism* reminds us:

> The grace of Christ is not in the slightest way a rival of our freedom when this freedom accords with a sense of the true and the good that God has put in the human heart. On the contrary, as Christian experience attests especially in prayer, the more docile we are to the promptings of grace, the more we grow in inner freedom and confidence during trials, such as those we face in the pressures and constraints of the outer world. By the working of grace the Holy Spirit educates us in spiritual freedom in order to make us free collaborators in his work in the Church and in the world. (CCC 1742)

g. The moral law enhances freedom. The moral law does not suppress freedom, but rather enhances it. Freedom is not license to make choices that are contradictions to the moral law. If we respect the inalienable rights of others and subject our passions to the demands of the Gospel, then we abide by God's law and therefore are truly free. The perfection of freedom presupposes and requires fidelity to the law of God. As Pope John Paul II taught:

> God's law does not reduce, much less do away with human freedom; rather, it protects and promotes that freedom. In contrast, however, some present-day cultural tendencies have given rise to several currents of thought in ethics which center upon an alleged conflict between freedom and law. These doctrines would grant to individuals or social groups the right to determine what is good or evil. Human freedom would thus be able to "create values" and would enjoy a primacy over truth, to the point that truth itself would be considered a creation of freedom. Freedom would thus lay claim to a moral autonomy which would actually amount to an absolute sovereignty. (*Veritatis Splendor*, 35)

Perfect freedom is expressed in the exercise of the virtue of prudence, which is the ability to make and carry out correct moral choices. Only a free person can make correct choices and carry them through to completion.

The Fathers of the Church called conscience "the spark of the Holy Spirit," "the sacredness of man," and "the sanctuary of God."

Title *Topic*

WHAT IS A CONSCIENCE?

The word *conscience* itself is derived from the Latin *cum scientia*, which means "with knowledge."

Like the terms "freedom" and "free will," the concept of conscience can often be misunderstood today. Popular wisdom often equates conscience with "feeling okay" about a decision or, more precisely, "not feeling guilty" about an action. People appeal to the role of their personal conscience in statements such as, "I ask that my conscience be respected," "Your conscience may say this is wrong, but my conscience sees things differently," or, "My conscience allows me to do this."

St. Paul by Di Bartolo. In the New Testament, the term "conscience" is mentioned more than thirty times in reference to the need for good moral behavior.

Properly understood, conscience is a practical judgment of right reason made by the intellect regarding the good or evil of a particular act in light of objective moral standards—the moral law. Conscience is not a feeling, nor an emotion, nor a hunch; nor is it the mere absence of guilt or regret. It is not a theoretical judgment on whether something is good or evil, but rather a practical judgment regarding a moral act.[13] Since conscience is a function of reason and intellect that evaluates the moral content of a given action, the person who acts according to conscience, or in opposition to it, is responsible for his or her actions.[14]

The gifts of the Holy Spirit received at Baptism help to enhance the effectiveness of conscience in making sound moral judgments, keeping in mind the natural law, the teachings of Christ, and the Magisterium. It is intimately involved in every effort of discernment, whether that discernment involves a moral decision, a vocation, or a self-examination of personal sins and virtues. "When he listens to his conscience," says the *Catechism of the Catholic Church*, "the prudent man can hear God speaking."[15]

His conscience is man's most secret core, and his sanctuary. There he is alone with God, whose voice echoes in his depths. By conscience, in a wonderful way, that law is made known which is fulfilled in the love of God and of one's neighbor. (*Gaudium et Spes*, 16)

SOURCES OF THE CONSCIENCE

Conscience is a vitally important faculty for the Christian who is trying to lead a moral life in Christ. How are we to consult our conscience, and how can we be sure that our conscience is telling us the truth? First, we should be aware of a few basic principles regarding conscience:

Conscience is addressed in Divine Revelation. The Old Testament indicates that God interacts with our human consciences: "He searches out the abyss, and the hearts of men."[16] It teaches that the wicked person, "distressed by conscience…has always exaggerated the difficulties."[17] Moreover, in the Eastern tradition, the Old Testament stresses the intimacy of conscience to the point of identifying it with the heart. The Scripture counsels: "Let not loyalty and faithfulness forsake you; bind them about your neck, write them on the tablet of your heart."[18]

In the New Testament, the term "conscience" is mentioned more than thirty times in reference to the need for good moral behavior. St. Paul clearly states that the pagans are at fault for all their corruption, as "their conscience also bears witness."[19] He also encourages the Christians to carry out proper conduct, "not only to avoid God's wrath, but also for the sake of conscience," for they will have to give an account to God for their conscience.[20]

Conscience is known through our own human experiences. The natural law is inscribed in the heart of every person. In the intimacy of our hearts, we can make free choices, and conscience will assist us in those choices. This assistance is always available to us, even though the standards it sets cannot always be articulated immediately. Nevertheless, it serves as a guidepost for choices regarding concrete actions.

When a mother asks her son a question about his conduct at school, for example, the son is presented with an interior law that urges him to tell the truth. If he actually chooses to lie, his heart or conscience indicates to him the wrongness of the lie, even though he may proceed with untruthful statements.

Within our human intellect there exists a practical moral deliberation. We constantly ask ourselves, "Is this the right thing to do?" or, "Does this act reflect what is morally correct?" We may ignore or barely notice the ethical question at the moment due to our blinding passions, weak will, or apathy, but the question is raised in the depths of our souls.

It is not an exaggeration to state that conscience is absolutely vital, both in indicating what is right and in reacting to what is wrong. There exist innumerable examples where a person suffers a lifetime of sorrow due to a grievously sinful action that went against conscience.

Personal experience demonstrates that the power of conscience is very real. The advice columns are filled with people who are dealing with regrets over choices they have made without consulting or abiding by their consciences. The conscience is indeed a moral voice that does not keep silent, but rather appraises and reprimands, exhorts and corrects.

The human conscience must be habitually enlightened by moral truth according to the guiding light of the Ten Commandments and Christ's teachings on charity in order to function properly.

NATURE OF THE CONSCIENCE

According to St. Paul, conscience in a certain sense confronts each of us with God's law, and thus becomes a "witness" for us—a witness of our own faithfulness or unfaithfulness to our moral beliefs. Only God has full access to that witness.[21]

The exercise of moral conscience is more than an obligation; it is also a right. It is through our consciences that we see and recognize the demands of the Divine Law. We are bound to follow this conscience faithfully in all our activities so that we may draw closer to God, who is our ultimate goal. Therefore, we must not be forced to act against conscience, nor may we be prevented from acting according to conscience, especially in religious matters.[22]

A good conscience applies moral truth. One of the biggest misconceptions regarding conscience is that it can create and apply its own moral standards. This belief is steeped in the error of subjective morality, the perspective that has given rise to everything from telling a "white lie" to "pro-choice" positions.

Conscience, if it is to be reliable, must make its judgments consistent with objective moral truth, which is the moral law. If it does not, then that conscience is in error and is not to be trusted. In the spiritual world, as well as in the physical, the truth is objective, and it must be obeyed and applied accordingly. A "conscience" that acts against truth is no conscience at all. It is outside the power of individual conscience to be the source of its own moral truth.[23]

Conscience fails when the natural law is ignored or misunderstood. Failures of conscience in recognizing fundamental human rights have led to untold numbers of grave injustices in the course of human history. The human conscience must be habitually enlightened by moral truth according to the guiding light of the commandments and Christ's teachings on charity in order to function properly. Therefore, if it is to be of any help to us at all in discerning right from wrong, our conscience must be properly formed according to the objective moral law.

Conscience is not an infallible guide. There is always the possibility of error in one's judgments. Therefore, to act "in good conscience," one must first seek to know what is truly and morally good. The person who has become blind to the truth through habitual sin or who simply refuses to see or acknowledge moral truth will have significantly suppressed the effective function and purpose of the conscience.

FORMATION OF CONSCIENCE

Homer and His Guide by Bouguereau. "Our inviolable rule ought to be never to do anything that wounds our conscience or that makes us ashamed of ourselves."

Since it is through conscience that we judge our actions, such judgments should always be made with a correctly formed conscience. Therefore, we have the obligation to form our consciences in such a manner that its judgments habitually reflect the teachings of Jesus and his Church.

Although the natural law is inscribed on the human heart, we must be taught and directed in how to evaluate moral situations so as to live the moral life in Christ. This training begins with learning the basics such as the Ten Commandments and the Beatitudes, but it cannot end there.

The most critical area of moral training is the *formation of conscience*. A conscience that is properly formed knows not only *what* the moral teachings of Christ and his Church are, but also how to apply them to concrete, real-life situations.

The better our consciences are formed, the more effective and trustworthy they will be in guiding us to good moral choices. Because situations we encounter can be so varied and complex, formation of conscience is necessarily an ongoing duty.

As is immediately evident, the *crisis of truth* is not unconnected with this development. Once the idea of a universal truth about the good, knowable by human reason, is lost, inevitably the notion of conscience also changes. Conscience is no longer considered in its primordial reality as an act of a person's intelligence, the function of which is to apply the universal knowledge of the good in a specific situation and thus to express a judgment about the right conduct to be chosen here and now. Instead, there is a tendency to grant to the individual conscience the prerogative of independently determining the criteria of good and evil and then acting accordingly. Such an outlook is quite congenial to an individualistic ethic, wherein each individual is faced with his own truth, different from the truth of others. Taken to its extreme consequences, this individualism leads to a denial of the very idea of human nature. (*Veritatis Splendor*, 32)

HOW TO DEVELOP A WELL-FORMED CONSCIENCE

Since everyone has the duty to follow the dictates of a properly formed conscience, it follows that everyone is required to form the conscience according to the moral law taught by Jesus Christ and transmitted by the Church. An individual can enjoy the absolute assurance that if one sincerely tries to know and understand the teachings of the Catholic Church on moral matters, and attempts to apply that knowledge to his or her actual situations and circumstances, then he or she will be acting in good conscience.

There are several specific means that have proven particularly effective in the formation of conscience.[24]

a. Learn the moral teachings of the Catholic Church. In consulting our consciences, it may not be sufficient to simply have good will and a sincere desire to do what is right. For example, well-meaning people may feel under certain circumstances that divorce and remarriage without a declaration of nullity is morally acceptable, or that the direct killing of innocent people in a wartime situation would not violate the moral law. The presence of emotion, compassion, or strong loyalties can cloud the conscience and influence its discernment.

The faithful of the Catholic Church are blessed with a Magisterium that over the centuries has preserved and developed objective teachings on faith and morals that are faithful to Scripture and Sacred Tradition and can never change. We can study the *Catechism of the Catholic Church* and be assured that these teachings represent the mind of Jesus Christ, who established the Church's teaching authority that has been handed down to us today.

b. Approach matters of faith and morals with an attitude of humility. A proper disposition in favor of Church teaching is essential for developing and consulting the conscience. An attitude of faith and obedience is required to accept these teachings, even if they seem beyond human understanding or opposed to the conventional wisdom of today's culture. This obedience with respect to the teachings of the Church in many instances leads to a clearer and more profound understanding of the moral law.

St. Augustine by Foppa. The faithful of the Catholic Church are blessed with a Magisterium that over the centuries has preserved and developed objective teachings on faith and morals that are faithful to Scripture and Sacred Tradition and can never change.

> The highest norm of human life is the divine law-eternal, objective and universal-whereby God orders, directs and governs the entire universe and all the ways of the human community by a plan conceived in wisdom and love. Man has been made by God to participate in this law, with the result that, under the gentle disposition of divine Providence, he can come to perceive ever more fully the truth that is unchanging. Wherefore every man has the duty, and therefore the right, to seek the truth in matters religious in order that he may with prudence form for himself right and true judgments of conscience, under use of all suitable means. (*Dignitatis Humanæ*, 3)

The Church possesses the fullness of truth, and we would be extremely negligent if we ignore her teachings or refuse to be guided by her wisdom. Decisions made due to this negligence run a high risk of error and will often lead us into a sinful course of action.

c. **Engage in sincere prayer and meditation.** Prayer is conversation with God. It is through prayer that God communicates his will. Fundamentally, the role of conscience is to discern God's will in a particular moral situation. Prayer, therefore, must accompany the development as well as the deliberations of the well-formed conscience.

Knowledge of Church teachings alone would give conscience the right information and criteria for proper moral behavior, but that knowledge would not lead the person into a deeper sharing in Christ's life. It is

St. Dominic in Prayer by El Greco. Prayer is conversation with God. It is through prayer that God communicates his will.

through personal and frequent prayer that we can grow closer to God and develop a relationship with him—what we commonly call the "interior life." Through our interior life, in concert with spiritual direction, we can be assured that our consciences will remain well-formed and in conformity with the teachings of Christ and his Church.[25]

Contemplation of the Word of God as found in Scripture, especially the Gospels, should be a vital component of Christian prayer. This prayerful meditation on Christ's words, which are "spirit and life,"[26] and the frequent reception of the Holy Eucharist, are sure means to enhance knowledge and truth in our lives and provide a sound basis for both moral judgments and moral behavior.

d. **Develop and maintain a well-formed conscience through frequent and honest self-examination.** The careful and prayerful interior evaluation of our thoughts, words, and deeds is called an *examination of conscience*. Examination of conscience is analogous to the review of game films by a sports team. The players and coaches review the film to identify mistakes and make the necessary changes and adjustments, thereby improving their game. Likewise, examination of conscience reviews our own lives with an eye toward avoiding sin and growing in virtue.

The entire Sermon on the Mount in the Gospel of Matthew serves as a marvelous reference for self-examination. Jesus' teachings on mercy, judgment, humility, purity, and prayer, as well as the Ten Commandments and the teachings of the Church, ought to be a model for evaluating our own behaviors and attitudes. The Beatitudes, too, are helpful in looking at our spiritual practices of poverty, humility, obedience, mercy, peacefulness, and faithfulness. Many prayer books include a rather solid and detailed examination of conscience, often following the structure of the Ten Commandments, that can help us in our self-examination.

An examination of conscience, however, must go beyond a dry analysis of our conduct. It must also lead to sincere repentance, which includes contrition for our sins and purpose of amendment (i.e., the intention to avoid sin in the future). Our examination—ideally performed daily, particularly at day's end before retiring for the night—must end with a firm resolution to avoid the sins and near occasions of sin that have confronted us. It does little good to acknowledge sins if we fail to commit to eliminating them from our lives. An act of contrition, whether formally recited or improvised from the heart, is a good way to conclude the day's examination.

e. Participate frequently in the Sacrament of Reconciliation. The ultimate goal of the examination of conscience is a conversion of heart leading to the Sacrament of Reconciliation, which results in a cleansing of the soul and a strengthening of the will. Frequent Confession with due sorrow and repentance is a commendable practice that is invaluable for the formation of conscience. The Parable of the Prodigal Son[27]—in which a wayward son repents of his sins and returns home to a loving, welcoming, and forgiving father—illustrates the same moving episode that occurs every time we return to the Sacrament of Reconciliation.

Frequent Confession with due sorrow and repentance is a commendable practice that is invaluable for the formation of conscience.

f. If possible, seek spiritual direction. Many people like to consult a spiritual director with whom they can discuss their interior lives and find help in matters of conscience. Prudence is required here to ensure finding a director who is himself or herself well-versed in the teachings of the Catholic Church and their applications to the moral life. Often a priest, although he may not always be able to offer extended spiritual direction in the Sacrament of Reconciliation, will be happy to meet privately for spiritual direction.

Although many errors of conscience stem from bad formation early in life, a correctly formed conscience can also suffer harm at any age and by many causes if true vigilance is not maintained through regular examination of conscience, prayer, and continued formation. Conscience and judgment can be corrupted and distorted for many reasons. Some of the most common causes are those set forth in the *Catechism*.

> Ignorance of Christ and his Gospel, bad example given by others, enslavement to one's passions, assertion of a mistaken notion of autonomy of conscience, rejection of the Church's authority and her teaching, lack of conversion and of charity: these can be at the source of errors of judgment in moral conduct. (CCC 1792)

CONSCIENCE AND THE NEW COMMANDMENT

It is fair to say that the pitfalls to forming a good conscience are many. We know that we, as Christians and especially as Catholics, must form and nurture our conscience with prayerful attention to the moral law. In order to handle and overcome the contradictory moral messages permeating society and popular culture and the effects of spiritual apathy among others, we must understand Church teaching ourselves and be prepared to explain and defend it when necessary. This is part of the call of the baptized to both live the Faith we have received and to evangelize the world.

Moral issues are often the topic of discussion in the classroom, at the dinner table, in the media, and around the workplace. The lay faithful present in these contexts may represent the only voice capable of guiding others to the truth, beginning with a more profound understanding of the natural law. Since every person is endowed with the capacity to reason and thus is capable of understanding truth, it would be insufficient for us to simply exhibit the moral law as a set of rules to be obeyed. Invoking a rule simply because it is a rule, even if it comes from God, is not nearly as effective as communicating a moral principle in a gentle but convincing manner.

The moral teachings of the Church are not unreasonable rules, but rather directives that make eminent sense. Given the moral controversies in modern society, the followers of Christ must be especially prepared to articulate the Church's teachings in a kind yet persuasive way.

Christ Carrying the Cross by Titian.
The "law of the gift" signifies that every person has a vocation to love as Christ loves.

Though it is true that a good conscience finds its inspiration in the moral law and its many applications taught by the Church, it must also be motivated by the universal call to holiness and the desire to imitate Christ. The Christian conscience must not only judge or determine a course of action according to its compatibility with the Ten Commandments, but also in light of the example of Christ as seen in the Gospels.

The modern follower of Christ must invoke his conscience with the perennial question: "What action will be best?" or "What action would Christ want me to choose?" The question behind the popular "WWJD?" wristbands that still circulate today is actually an extremely valid one that should be part of any deliberation of conscience: "What would Jesus do?" Conscience, formed according to the heart of Christ, will make charity with others a priority and the constant companion for every deliberate action.

CONCLUSION

The spiritual faculty of free will elicits choices and prompts actions that can transform or degrade the person. Only the human person can forge his or her destiny for good or for evil. The rest of living creation fulfills its functions according to a predetermined dynamism. Put there by God, plant life enjoys a life principle and acts according to its nature and purpose in creation. Likewise, animals and other living creatures that inhabit the land and sea all live, eat, interact, and reproduce according to a standard code dictated by nature.

It is man alone who has freedom. Created in the image and likeness of God, it is man who dominates the material world, and can thus choose to cooperate with God in his act of creation. With this powerful gift of freedom and the help of God's grace, man can transform the world into a haven of justice, charity, and peace, or he can destroy himself.

Every free act leaves a change in the person, whether for better or worse. The human person is not a static being, but someone who morally grows or diminishes. Aided by grace, man by his very nature is intended to be another Christ, provided that the mind and will are directed to follow in Christ's footsteps:

> The kingdom of Christ is the kingdom of freedom. In it the only slaves are those who freely bind themselves, out of love of God. What a blessed slavery of love, that sets us free! Without freedom, we cannot respond to grace. Without freedom, we cannot give ourselves freely to our Lord, for the most supernatural of reasons, because we want to.[28]

Conscience is the practical judgment on the morality of a given action. It leads a person either to perform an action or to refrain from carrying it out. As a faculty of reason, conscience must humbly seek the truth guided by the teachings of the Church. Every person has the obligation to form his or her conscience according to the objective standards of God's law and Christ's teachings. Fidelity to a right and true conscience is a concrete way of being faithful to God himself.

A properly formed conscience perfects and cultivates a person's dignity and chooses actions that lead to true happiness. The Magisterium of the Church is the most certain guide to the will of God and therefore must play a vital role in forming one's conscience.

As a way of life, the words of St. Paul are worth noting: "Brethren, I have lived before God in all good conscience up to this day."[29] The greatest happiness, according to classical thought, is to have a well-formed and clear conscience.

St. Paul Preaching in Athens by Raphael.
The Magisterium of the Church is the most certain guide to the will of God and therefore must play a vital role in forming one's conscience.

SUPPLEMENTARY READING

1. Condemned To Freedom?

Most people love freedom when it means being able to do whatever they feel like doing. But they don't love freedom when it means the responsibility of making moral choices and living with the results. Freedom is not easy. But today we want everything to be easy. That's why our political freedom is currently in great danger. Freedom is not in danger in places like Poland today, because it is not easy there. Poles know the value of freedom. They had to struggle for it, and pay for it. But whether or not we have political freedom, everyone has moral freedom. Every human being has the free will to choose between good and evil, and the responsibility to do so. That's essential to human nature. That's why we are all "condemned to freedom."

— Peter Kreeft, *Making Choices: Practical Wisdom for Everyday Moral Decisions*, pp. 13-14

2. On True Freedom

A certain type of man feels, on every conceivable occasion, that his rights are threatened, or trespassed upon. He always keeps on his guard lest some impairment of his rights should escape his attention. Dominated by his fear of such an injury or encroachment, he seldom stops to consider whether a thing is valuable in itself or not, whether it glorifies God or offends him. Hence, his vision of various situations is obscured; his capacity of adequate judgment is blunted. He is incapable of a free, unwarped response to values. In his mind, the theme of his rights overshadows the question of the objective value involved; thus, instead of a disinterested love of truth and of right he is likely to develop a bitter and cantankerous attitude. Indeed, his inordinate insistence on his rights may sometimes tempt him to ride roughshod over those of others. Such people, in their cramped egoism, are as far remote from true freedom as it is possible to be.

— Dietrich von Hildebrand, *Transformation in Christ*, p. 207.

3. The Conscience Must Be Informed

Conscience must be informed and moral judgment enlightened. A well-formed conscience is upright and truthful. It formulates its judgments according to reason, in conformity with the true good willed by the wisdom of the Creator. The education of conscience is indispensable for human beings who are subjected to negative influences and tempted by sin to prefer their own judgment and to reject authoritative teachings.

— CCC 1783

4. The Conscience is a Precious But Delicate Guide

Conscience is a precious but delicate guide. Its voice is easily distorted or obscured. To dictate to conscience is to silence and, eventually, to destroy it. Conscience must be listened to and listened to sensitively. It needs to be interrogated, even to be cross-examined.

And only those who habitually interrogate their conscience and are ready to pay heed even to its awkward answers, will not cheat their conscience or be cheated by it.

— Cormac Burke, *Conscience and Freedom*, 25.

5. Having a Plan of Life

Try to commit yourself to a plan of life and to keep to it: a few minutes of mental prayer, Holy Mass—daily, if you can manage it—and frequent Communion; regular recourse to the Holy Sacrament of Forgiveness—even though your conscience does not accuse you of mortal sin; visiting Jesus in the Tabernacle; praying and contemplating the mysteries of the Holy Rosary, and so many other marvelous devotions you know or can learn.

You should not let them become rigid rules, or watertight compartments. They should be flexible, to help you on your journey you who live in the middle of the world, with a life of hard professional work and social ties and obligations which you should not neglect, because in them your conversation with God still continues. Your plan of life ought to be like a rubber glove which fits the hand perfectly

— St. Josemaria Escriva, *Friends of God*, 149.

ADVANCED CONCEPTS

HOW IGNORANT ARE YOU?

We have stated that an individual who commits a moral act without the knowledge that it is sinful might not have moral responsibility for that act. In other words, a sinful act committed in total ignorance of the moral law is not a sin.

Here we must introduce the distinctions between two types of ignorance—*vincible ignorance* and *invincible ignorance*.

Vincible ignorance occurs when we lack knowledge regarding some aspect of the moral law because of a failure of due diligence on our part. In such a situation, we are responsible, at least to some degree, for any sin that is committed because of that lack of knowledge.

For example, if we realize that the cashier at the supermarket has overpaid us in change from our purchase, but we remain silent instead and do not seek to confirm this suspicion, we are responsible for a sin because our ignorance was surmountable—we could have simply gone over the receipt with the cashier or manager to redress the mistake.

Invincible ignorance occurs when knowledge of certain moral laws is impossible. Those who have never had the opportunity to hear the message of Christ and who act in a way considered acceptable in their own society may not be held morally accountable for actions that transgress the moral law. The presumption here is that the individual in question—who, as we have discussed previously, has the Divine Law written on his heart—is one who seeks the truth and follows that truth as best he understands it.

Invincible ignorance can also result from psychological limitations or mental illness. A person with mental illness who commits suicide is not held morally responsible because of his or her diminished capacity to make good moral decisions. This diminished capacity is recognized as a legal defense in many countries for those accused of crimes. Diminished capacity may also be temporary, as in the case of extreme fear, duress, or shock, and may be influenced by many factors such as habit or culture.

While none of these reasons should be used as an excuse to "do whatever one wishes," we must remember that God in his omniscient wisdom knows all and judges each person mercifully and justly according to his or her works.[30]

Pope Paul VI opened the second session of the Second Vatican Council on September 29, 1963.
Gaudium et Spes (*Joy and Hope*), the Pastoral Constitution on the Church in the Modern World, was one of the important accomplishments of the Second Vatican Council and is a document of the Magisterium.
"Conscience is man's most secret core, and his sanctuary" (*Gaudium et Spes*, 16).

VOCABULARY

BLESSED
As used in the Beatitudes, it means "bliss"—
a reference to the ultimate happiness of Heaven.

CONCUPISCENCE
Human appetites or desires remain disordered due to the temporal consequences of Original Sin. This remains even after Baptism and constitute an inclination to sin. This term is often used to refer to desires resulting from strong sensual urges or other things of the world.

CONSCIENTIOUS OBJECTION
A personal appeal that to carry out a particular action that has been ordered by legitimate authority would be against one's own conscience.

CULPABLE
The quality of being guilty or deserving punishment for participation in sin.

DELIBERATION
The premeditation or forethought that weighs one's options before making a moral act.

DOUBTFUL CONSCIENCE
Judgment of conscience that occurs when there is doubt about the good or evil of an act done or omitted. Unless one is required to act immediately, the person is required to determine the moral rectitude of an act before acting on a doubtful conscience (cf. CCC 1787-1789).

EVIL
That which is opposed to the moral law and thus entails sin.

EXAMINATION OF CONSCIENCE
Prayerful self-reflection on one's words and deeds in light of the gospel to determine how one has sinned against God. This is necessary to prepare for the Sacrament of Penance.

FREEDOM OF EXCELLENCE
The power to act freely in the pursuit of human perfection.

FULL KNOWLEDGE
The clear and deliberate knowledge of the merit or sinfulness of an action. It is required as a condition before a person can be guilty of sin.

HUMAN ACT
An act that is performed with both knowledge and free will. Human acts, depending upon the degree of knowledge and freedom involved in their commission, are either morally good or morally evil.

IGNORANCE
The lack of knowledge.

INDIRECT RESPONSIBILITY
The attribution of a secondary effect that follows as a natural result from the primary effect.

INVINCIBLE IGNORANCE
Ignorance that cannot be overcome by ordinary diligence. The guilt of a sin committed under invincible ignorance is not imputed to the sinner. This ignorance can be a lack of knowledge, either of fact or of law, scarcity of evidence, insufficient time or talent in the person, or some other factor.

MORAL ACT
Any human act that has a moral content and involves deliberation and choice.

PARTIAL KNOWLEDGE
Knowledge that is incomplete due to the presence of some obstacle interfering with a moral judgment.

PRUDENCE
The ability to discern the most suitable and moral course of action.

RESPONSIBILITY
The demand for an account of one's acts; it includes accepting the consequences of those acts.

SUBJECTIVE MORALITY
Moral standards that are not universal but are decided upon by the individuals involved.

VINCIBLE IGNORANCE
Lack of knowledge for which a person is morally responsible due to lack of diligence.

VIOLENCE
Coercion or the application of an external force against a person's will.

STUDY QUESTIONS

1. What are reasons why Christians should try to live a moral life?

2. What gives freedom to a Christian?

3. How does God accomplish his reconciliation with man?

4. Explain how, in following God's moral law, we become free.

5. Explain why moral theology is of the utmost importance for all people.

6. If the incorrect use of free will degrades us and harms others, why would God have given us free will?

7. How is free will different from instinct as found among animals?

8. Explain why a person is responsible for his or her actions.

9. On what standards is moral theology based?

10. Explain what makes an action a moral act. Give examples.

11. "Every act which is elicited by both deliberation and free choice has an effect on both the individual and on others." Explain.

12. What is the relationship between knowledge and moral responsibility?

13. "Those who have had the benefit of God's Divine Revelation given through Jesus Christ are held to a higher moral standard." Explain.

14. Two people perform the same good action. One does so out of societal conformity and the other because he or she understands it is a virtuous act. What is the difference?

15. Is it unjust to hold one person morally responsible for a bad action while another is excused because of complete ignorance? Explain.

16. Explain how a person suffers the consequences of incorrect moral behavior even if he or she is ignorant of being wrong. List some examples.

17. What is the difference between vincible and invincible ignorance?

18. A person is not held morally accountable for an immoral action if he or she acted in ignorance. However, that person is held accountable if the ignorance was vincible. Reconcile these two statements.

19. Why must love, by its very nature, be freely given?

20. The capacity to give oneself requires self-mastery. Explain.

21. How can our "environment" have an effect on our freedom?

22. Explain how wrong choices diminish our freedom.

23. Explain why truth can never be a subjective opinion.

24. How does a person find happiness?

25. How does human society show its belief that we are responsible for our actions? List several examples.

26. Why would an all-loving God allow so much human suffering? Where does human evil and suffering come from?

27. Why do human beings sometimes choose incorrectly? How can human beings choose correctly?

28. What is the relationship between habit and moral choices?

29. What is the relationship between following the law and freedom?

30. Why is conscience considered sacred in Christian tradition?

STUDY QUESTIONS Continued

31. What is conscience, and how does it aid us in our choices?

32. What happens to the conscience at Baptism?

33. What is the purpose of the conscience as mentioned in the New Testament?

34. Explain how conscience acts as a witness for us.

35. The Ten Commandments and the Sermon on the Mount are sources of moral truth. Can a person simply read the Bible and reach his or her own conclusions about moral truth? Explain.

36. If Divine Law is inscribed on the human heart, then why must the conscience be formed?

37. What are some circumstances that might hinder a person's conscience from functioning properly or according to its created purpose?

38. If moral truths are not subjective, where can Catholics go to learn the objective truths regarding moral decisions?

39. What prerequisites are necessary to properly form one's conscience?

40. What more is needed to imitate the life of Christ than just possessing knowledge of his teachings?

41. What is "interior life"? How is it formed, and what is its purpose?

42. What is the purpose of an examination of conscience? What must it lead to in order to be useful?

43. Other than the forgiveness of sins, what is the role of a confessor in the Sacrament of Reconciliation?

44. Read the Parable of the Prodigal Son (Lk 15:11-32). Who do the Father and the two sons represent? What does it tell us about each of these persons?

45. Explain how an action can be sinful, even if a person does not know that it is sinful.

46. Man must not be forced to act contrary to his conscience, nor prevented from acting according to his conscience, yet a conscience which views immoral acts as moral (e.g., racism) cannot be obeyed. Explain this seeming contradiction.

47. One must always obey the conscience that is truly and correctly informed. How can a person know whether his or her conscience is truly and correctly informed?

48. What is the error of moral relativism? In addition to those listed in the chapter, give examples of incorrect moral judgments that are prevalent in modern society.

49. How would you answer someone who tells you that his or her conscience dictates that every woman should have a right to have an abortion?

50. In a debate over abortion, a Catholic says that it is wrong because the Church says so. While true, how might this answer be inadequate? Prepare a better response.

51. Explain how a correctly formed conscience can become distorted or degraded.

52. When a person does something that he or she knows is wrong, it is often difficult the first time, but afterwards becomes easier. Explain.

53. What must the faithful do to help others properly form their consciences?

54. What should be the center of the Christian life? Explain.

55. What is the Magisterium, and what is its role in the formation of the conscience?

PRACTICAL EXERCISES

1. Imagine that human beings act simply according to a programming or instinct and are therefore not responsible for their actions. How would society be different? How would this affect ideas of crime and punishment, love and sexual morality, the way that we treat others, etc.?

2. List two examples of actions which in and of themselves are good. Explain how the choice between these two could be a moral decision.

3. Think of an example of an action where there might be doubt as to its moral correctness. Why must one resolve this doubt before acting? What are ways in which this doubt could be resolved?

4. What would be the consequences if a person tried to substitute subjective opinion for objective mathematical or scientific truths? Give examples. Apply this reasoning to objective moral truths.

5. Explain St. Paul's understanding of human freedom as evidenced in the following passages of Scripture:

   - Rom 6: 11-23; 7: 2-12; 8: 1-5
   - Gal 4: 21-23

6. Improper use of the will can lead to licentiousness, an excessive enjoyment of sensual pleasures that respects no moral precepts or standards. Explain the significance of the following scriptural texts:

   - Rom 6: 15
   - 1 Cor 6: 12; 10: 23
   - Gal 5: 13

7. To what degree does God respect our freedom as human beings? Are there ever instances in which he will act directly to interfere with a person's freedom? Why or why not? Do you ever wish that God would act differently? What would be the positive and negative consequences of his doing so?

8. Think of some examples of when you were bothered by your conscience for something that you had done wrong. What are ways that you can unburden your conscience?

9. An improper environment, lack of moral education, or immoral customs and lifestyles, may easily hinder the conscience's power to judge correctly. Give examples of situations in modern society that might fit this definition. Explain how these influences affect everyone and might hinder the conscience from judging correctly.

10. *Veritatis Splendor* states that once the idea of objective moral truth is discarded in favor of subjective truth, a form of individualism takes over which can lead to the denial of our human nature. What are some instances in which basic human rights have been violated in society? Explain whether these violations fit the situation outlined by *Veritatis Splendor*.

11. A friend tells you that after receiving the Sacrament of Confirmation he or she does not need to study "religion" anymore. How would you answer?

12. Following the format of an "examination of conscience," write your own, making it applicable to your own life and personal situation.

13. The role of a spiritual director is to help a person in his or her journey toward a life of holiness. Spend a few minutes in quiet reflection, carefully examining those areas of your life which might be holding you back from a life lived more in union with Jesus Christ. How might a spiritual director help you? If you have a spiritual director, speak to him or her about these things. If not, ask a priest if you can speak to him about spiritual direction.

PRACTICAL EXERCISES Continued

14. The word "conscience" appears thirty times in the New Testament. Explain the exact meaning St. Paul intends when he speaks of conscience in three or four of the following instances:

- Rom 2:15; 13:5
- 1 Cor 8:12; 10:27-29
- 2 Cor 1:12; 5:11
- 1 Tm 1:19
- Heb 10:22

15. What are some situations that occur in daily life that might create problems for one's conscience?

16. Reflect on instances in your own life in which conscience played a role in determining your response to a particular situation or problem, and describe how you responded in each situation.

St. Peter Preaching in the Presence of St. Mark by Fra Angelico.
In the end, those who pretend to deny conscience or imply that it is only a cultural prejudice of religion expose their own hypocrisy and a true lack of sincerity.

FROM THE CATECHISM

1744 Freedom is the power to act or not to act, and so to perform deliberate acts of one's own. Freedom attains perfection in its acts when directed toward God, the sovereign Good.

1745 Freedom characterizes properly human acts. It makes the human being responsible for acts of which he is the voluntary agent. His deliberate acts properly belong to him.

1747 The right to the exercise of freedom, especially in religious and moral matters, is an inalienable requirement of the dignity of man. But the exercise of freedom does not entail the putative right to say or do anything.

1748 "For freedom Christ has set us free."[31]

1760 A morally good act requires the goodness of its object, of its end, and of its circumstances together.

1795 "Conscience is man's most secret core, and his sanctuary. There he is alone with God whose voice echoes in his depths."[32]

1796 Conscience is a judgment of reason by which the human person recognizes the moral quality of a concrete act.

1798 A well-formed conscience is upright and truthful. It formulates its judgments according to reason, in conformity with the true good willed by the wisdom of the Creator. Everyone must avail himself of the means to form his conscience.

1800 A human being must always obey the certain judgment of his conscience.

1802 The Word of God is a light for our path. We must assimilate it in faith and prayer and put it into practice. This is how moral conscience is formed.

2017 The grace of the Holy Spirit confers upon us the righteousness of God. Uniting us by faith and Baptism to the Passion and Resurrection of Christ, the Spirit makes us sharers in his life.

ENDNOTES – CHAPTER TWO

1. *Centesimus Annus*, 4-5.
2. Cf. Jn 8: 31-32.
3. Jn 8: 34.
4. Jn 8: 31-32.
5. Plato, *The Republic*, I, 352d.
6. *VS* 71.
7. Aristotle, *Politics*, 1, 2.
8. Cf. Jn 8: 32.
9. Pope Pius XII, *Address to the International Congress on Moral Theology*, 970.
10. Rom 6: 16.
11. Cf. Rom 6: 17.
12. Cf. Mt 25: 14-30.
13. Cf. CCC 1778.
14. Cf. *VS* 57.
15. CCC 1777.
16. Sir 42: 18.
17. Wis 17: 11.
18. Prv 3: 3.
19. Rom 2: 15.
20. Rom 13: 5; cf. 2 Cor 4: 2.
21. Cf. *VS* 58.
22. *DH* 3.
23. Cf. Pope John Paul II, *Discourse to Scientists*, May 8, 1993.
24. Cf. CCC 1783-1785.
25. Cf. CCC 1799.
26. Jn 6: 63.
27. Cf. Lk 15: 11-32.
28. St. Josemaria Escriva, *Christ Is Passing By*, 184.
29. Acts 23: 1.
30. Cf. CCC 1735.
31. Gal 5: 1.
32. *GS* 16

Morality in Law
and Action

CHAPTER 3

Morality in Law and Action

When in the course of human events, it becomes necessary for one people to dissolve the political bands which have connected them with another, and to assume among the powers of the earth, the separate and equal station to which the Laws of Nature and of Nature's God entitle them, a decent respect to the opinions of mankind requires that they should declare the causes which impel them to the separation.

We hold these truths to be self-evident, that all men are created equal, that they are endowed by their Creator with certain unalienable Rights, that among these are Life, Liberty, and the pursuit of Happiness;

That to secure these rights, Governments are instituted among Men, deriving their just powers from the consent of the governed;

That whenever any Form of Government becomes destructive of these ends, it is the Right of the People to alter or to abolish it, and to institute new Government, laying its foundation on such principles and organizing its powers in such form, as to them shall seem most likely to effect their Safety and Happiness.

—*The Declaration of Independence*

INTRODUCTION

Imagine living in a city that had no laws, one in which the citizens could behave however they wanted without restriction or consequences. Theft, murder, drunkenness, perversion—all of these would take place without the slightest legal sanction. Would that be a pleasant place to live?

Imagine driving on a highway with no traffic laws, where everyone could drive as fast and recklessly as he or she chose without regard for other drivers. Would that be a safe road to travel on a family vacation?

FOR DISCUSSION

✛ What is the definition of law?

✛ What is the relationship between human laws and the moral law as set forth by God?

✛ Do moral laws and civil laws make conflicting demands upon human behavior?

✛ How are conflicts between conscience and law to be resolved?

✛ Can laws legislate morality? Should they?

Imagine that professional basketball teams decided to dispense with the rules and regulations of the game and play without referees. There would be no fouls called, no game clock, no consistent system of scoring. The result would be chaotic and meaningless.

Life would be dangerous without rules and laws to govern behavior, even on the level of recreational sports or driving to work. Without a developed body of law to keep order, society would fall into a chaos that would threaten the dignity and perhaps even the very life of every human person. For civil harmony, the common good, the protection of rights, and the enjoyment of freedom in society, laws are absolutely necessary.

We have seen that for a human action to be considered a moral action, it must involve a decision and a choice. Furthermore, moral actions leave the subject morally changed—the individual either becomes a better person or a worse person, but never remains the same.

This chapter will discuss those actions peculiar to man that have profound moral ramifications both on him and those around him. Our human will, expressed through choices and actions, can either transform us with the aid of grace into a reflection of Christ or can enslave us to passion and sin.

WHAT IS LAW?

What is law? The general definition is that law is an ordinance of reason that exists for the common good and is affirmed by legitimate authority through an official process. Let us look at these requirements one at a time. All just law finds its origin in the mind of God, who communicates his divine plan to man.

The Thirteenth Amendment to the United States Constitution officially abolished slavery in every state. It was adopted as law on December 6, 1865. President Lincoln and others were concerned that Lincoln's Emancipation Proclamation would be considered a temporary war resolution. Because of this uncertainty, they supported the new Amendment as a means to guarantee the permanent abolition of slavery.

Law is an ordinance of reason. Laws are not the result of some capricious initiative by someone in authority. Rather, they are the fruit of reasoned deliberation to address the needs of the human person and society.

Laws exist for the common good. Society is organized and assisted through the enactment of appropriate laws. These laws protect its citizens, and their application is designed to aid society as a whole so that everyone's basic rights are respected. Taxes are imposed on citizens so that the fundamental needs of society are met—sanitation, safety, assistance in the case of injury, protection of property, and so on. Laws, therefore, are enacted to preserve and promote the common good by regulating in fairness how people interact with one another and with the greater environment.

Law is made by those in legitimate authority. Only those who have justly received the power to govern have the right as well as the obligation to make laws that will serve the just needs of the people. Natural law affirms that only those invested with legitimate authority can pass and enforce laws. Legitimate authority comes ultimately from God, as the Lord told Pontius Pilate.[1]

Laws must be legislated in an official manner. Laws cannot be passed in an arbitrary way. Rather, they must follow an established protocol to ensure that those laws are officially legislated and published. The citizens would be at the mercy of their rulers if the passage of laws were not the result of a generally accepted and recognized process.

TYPES OF LAW

A justice system that includes a court of law and the imposition of penalties to secure some sort of reparation for damages implies the existence of a standard of morality. All just law finds its origin in the mind of God, who communicates his divine plan to man. The multitude of Divine Laws embraces the entire universe. The clearest and greatest revelations of the will of God the Father, expressed in his laws for human actions, were communicated through his Son Jesus Christ.[2]

> There are different expressions of the moral law, all of them interrelated: eternal law—the source, in God, of all law; natural law; revealed law, comprising the Old Law and the New Law, or Law of the Gospel; finally, civil and ecclesiastical laws. (CCC 1952)

Eternal law, according to St. Thomas Aquinas, is "nothing other than the plan of divine wisdom as directing all acts and movements."[3]

St. Thomas' statement is a development of the ideas of ancient Greek thinkers such as Plato and Aristotle. Centuries before Christ, ancient philosophers observed the intricate harmony and order in the world they called the *cosmos*. They speculated that an unknown, all-powerful, and all-knowing being, both created and organized the world that perhaps at first was a jumble of matter they called *chaos*.

Over the course of centuries, human society has expressed fascination that the world is not only a harmonious and intricate unity, but also is continuously governed by laws intrinsic to creation itself. One does not have to be a professional philosopher to appreciate that a simple planet is governed, as it were, by biological or physical laws that are perpetually fixed.

Even on a superficial level, one can readily recognize an intelligent and loving hand governing the universe. The world is sustained in a finely tuned and profoundly logical unity. This vast and rich intelligence is evident in the vastness of the universe as well as in the minute details of subatomic particles. There is an "intelligent design" to all of creation that points not only to the Creator, but also to the observable and demonstrable laws of physics and other sciences by which creation exists.

Evidence of God's care and guidance is present in all of creation. Every law, whether physical, moral, or man-made, is derived from God's eternal law. God's plan and direction of the entire created world is the foundation and basis of all true law (cf. *VS* 43).

> The supreme rule of life is the divine law itself, the eternal objective and universal law by which God out of his wisdom and love, arranges, directs, and governs the whole world and the paths of the human community. God has enabled man to share in this divine law, and hence man is able under the gentle guidance of God's providence increasingly to recognize the unchanging truth. (*Veritatis Splendor*, 43)

Natural law "is nothing other than the rational creature's participation in the eternal law."[4] The natural law is simply the eternal law as it applies to human life. As we have seen in previous chapters, it is written in the heart of every human person—meaning that "deep down" in each person there is an innate sense of order, an awareness of right and wrong. The natural law shows us the inherent dignity of the human person and how to attain our proper end. It encompasses the essential precepts of the moral life, the principal precepts being expressed in the Ten Commandments.[5] The natural law is universal and its authority extends to all human beings.[6] It is something that sets mankind apart from all creation.

Whereas physical laws are mechanical, natural law is not. If we want to boil water, we need to raise the temperature of the water high enough and it will boil; if we want to throw a ball to another person, we must judge how hard and how far to throw it, make the proper motion with the arm, and let go of the ball at the proper moment. We cannot simply "will" that water boil or that a thrown ball reaches its target.

By contrast, to obey the natural law requires an exercise of the mind and the will. Unlike the physical laws, the natural law is never imposed upon us. One chooses to obey a moral principle or to reject it. To go against natural law knowingly and willingly is an offense against God. When a person rejects these moral obligations, as we have seen, it is detrimental to his or her freedom, dignity, and happiness.

St. Thomas Aquinas in Glory between St. Mark and St. Louis of Toulouse by Carpaccio.
The *Summa Theologiæ*, written 1265-1274, is the most famous work of St. Thomas Aquinas (ca. 1225-1274).
It was intended as a compilation of all of the main theological teachings of that time. It summarizes
the reasonings for almost all points of Christian theology in the West. The *Summa's* topics follow a cycle:
the existence of God, God's creation, Man, Man's purpose, Christ, the Sacraments, and back to God.
It is famous for its five arguments for the existence of God, the *Quinquæ viæ* (five ways).

Revealed law is the law as revealed by God. It is found in the Old Law of the Old Testament and finds its fulfillment in the New Law, which was ushered into our world with the coming of Jesus Christ. Also called the "Law of Grace" or "Law of the Gospel," this law makes it possible for us to model ourselves after the life of Jesus.[7]

The New Law is called a *law of love* because it makes us act out of love infused by the Holy Spirit, rather than from fear; a *law of grace*, because it confers the strength of grace to act, by means of faith and the sacraments; a *law of freedom*, because it sets us free from the ritual and juridical observances of the Old Law, inclines us to act spontaneously by the prompting of charity and, finally, lets us pass from the condition of a servant who "does not know what his master is doing" to that of a friend of Christ—"For all that I have heard from my Father I have made known to you"—or even to the status of son and heir.[8] (CCC 1972)

Cleansing the Temple by Bloch.
The New Law was ushered into our world with the coming of Jesus Christ. It fulfilled the Old Law revealed by God in the Old Testament.

Ecclesiastical law, called canon law, is the law that governs the Church in the organization of the hierarchy, in liturgical and penitential practices, and in other matters. These laws are both aids and directives for clergy and laity alike to enable the people of God to faithfully practice the Catholic Faith.

Civil law consists of laws enacted by civil governments for the common good of a particular sector of society or an entire country. These laws, in order to be true laws, must be derivations from and applications of the Ten Commandments. Laws on traffic, the environment, zoning, and crime are examples of this type of law.

JUST CIVIL LAW

St. Thomas Aquinas taught that for laws to be just or even valid, they must reflect some aspect of the natural law articulated by the Ten Commandments. In fact, a civil law that is in contradiction to the natural law is not even considered a valid law.

It is easy to see that all just laws have a foundation based on the truth. It is evil to kill an innocent person, not just because the law prohibits it, but because every person has the right to life. Similarly, it is evil to blaspheme against God, not just because it is prohibited by the Second Commandment, but because it offends his infinite goodness and dignity. It is also evil to slander, because a person's reputation belongs to him and is intimately linked to human dignity, and therefore laws against slander are not just an arbitrary prohibition.

The same ideas are connected to what is good for man. For example, to help rehabilitate a criminal is good, not only because society seeks to include marginalized people, but because it restores human dignity. To give alms to one who needs them is good, not merely because some organization requires it, but because it is a practice of charity. To demand the fulfillment of a penalty is good, not just because society seeks to punish criminals, but because it brings about justice.

All civil laws that meet the prerequisite of being derived from some facet of the Ten Commandments are binding and must be obeyed. St. Thomas outlines the following conditions necessary for a law to be valid and just:

A just civil law must promote the common good. According to the *Catechism*, "The common good consists of three essential elements: respect for and promotion of the fundamental rights of the person; prosperity, or the development of the spiritual and temporal goods of society; the peace and security of the group and of its members."[9]

A just law must seek the good of all members of society, not just of a select group. By contrast, a law that seeks only the good of a certain segment of society while neglecting the rest would be unjust. This would be the case of a law that required military service of only the poorer members of society while exempting the wealthy. A just law must also defend human rights and promote the social development of society as a whole.

A just civil law must reflect an "equality of proportion." The burden of the law's fulfillment must be shared by all members of society and not just by some. A law that taxes the citizens of a society for a common purpose is just, and all members of that society must pay their share of taxes. However, they should bear the burden of the tax in proportion to their ability to pay. To demand an amount of payment from someone whose income is too low to pay that particular amount would be unjust. In the case of a military draft, every sector of society must be involved and equally affected. Therefore, all laws must not only be applied fairly, but must take into consideration the capacities and limitations of the individual members of society.

All authority comes from God. As we said earlier, civil laws ought to express some facet of the natural law. If this is not the case, civil law ceases to have binding power. In the case of the Church, the ecclesiastical laws express and apply in legal terms some aspect of Catholic Tradition originating with Christ himself.

Because all authority is ultimately derived from God, every law must transmit, at least in small part, what God has eternally established. No one can place upon himself or herself the authority to issue any law outside the scope of God's law. The legislation of law is an application of the Divine Law through human authority.

No human authority may declare what God reveals as morally evil to be morally good. For this reason, laws permitting slavery, abortion, euthanasia, and "marriages" between persons of the same gender are immoral. Therefore, they have no authority and must not be obeyed.[10]

Dr. Martin Luther King Jr. (1929-1968) dedicated his life to overturning unjust laws through nonviolent methods. His efforts helped bring about the Civil Rights Act of 1964, landmark legislation in the United States that outlawed racial segregation in schools, public places, and employment. The bill was amended prior to passage to protect women of all races.

CONFLICTS BETWEEN CONSCIENCE AND CIVIL LAW

It is normal for a good conscience, one that is well-formed in the moral law, to seek and to find clarity in what ought to be done and not done. Because civil law, to be valid, must be based on Divine Law, and since a true conscience is rooted in the laws of God, there should be no conflicts between conscience and the civil law.

Unfortunately, however, unjust civil laws do exist. In these cases, how is a Christian to respond? This is a question that is raised frequently throughout the country—on behalf of pharmacists who do not want to dispense birth control or abortifacient drugs; soldiers who do not want to fight what they believe is an unjust war; medical students who do not want to learn to do abortions; and justices of the peace who do not want to certify homosexual partnerships, to name a few. It even comes up in corporate contexts involving the rights of Catholic hospitals, schools, and charitable organizations—adoption agencies that do not want to hand children over to homosexual couples, and Catholic institutions that defy state laws requiring that health benefits offered to their employees include coverage for morally objectionable services such as abortion, contraceptives, vasectomies, and tubal ligations.

Given that Christians have an obligation to bear witness to the truth, one is not bound in conscience to cooperate with an unjust law. In fact, there may be times when a Christian is called upon by his or her conscience to actively oppose such a law. Moreover, if authority is usurped from God through the enactment of an unjust civil law, a good and true conscience will reject that law.

A well-formed conscience will clearly indicate the obligation to obey God's law over and beyond any kind of legislation that would undermine the natural law. For example, a physician would be obligated in good conscience to disobey any law stating that doctors must prescribe contraceptives upon request. A Catholic athlete, for instance, whose team's schedule of practices, meetings, and games leaves no realistic opportunity for attending a Mass to fulfill the Sunday obligation, should not comply with that policy.

St. Jerome by Bellini. In this painting St. Jerome, a hermit and Doctor of the Church, represents the highest point of spiritual life, that of mystical exaltation and revealed science. Beside him the fig tree symbolizes that he has been chosen by the Lord to understand his supreme law.

Disobedience to an unjust civil law should only occur after careful deliberation. However, a law that is glaringly evil, like abortion-on-demand, must be opposed.

In situations of conscience in lesser matters, it may be prudent to consider the possible consequences that opposition would bring: "In what would a greater evil consist, submission to the law or the scandal and disturbance that would follow resistance to it?" Or, put another way, "Which is the lesser of these two evils?"

ANALYSIS OF THE HUMAN ACT

Every human act can be evaluated from three distinct perspectives—the *object* or the act itself; the *end in view* or *intentions* of the person performing the act; and the *circumstances* surrounding the act.

The *Catechism of the Catholic Church* clearly details the components which must be present in order for a particular human act to be considered good.

> A *morally good* act requires the goodness of the object, of the end, and of the circumstances together....The object, the intention, and the circumstances make up the three "sources" of the morality of human acts. (CCC 1755, 1757)

For a human act to be considered morally good, all three aspects must be morally good. All three principles must function together toward the enhancement of the goodness of the act itself. Likewise, all three elements must be carefully evaluated in order to determine whether an act is morally good or evil.

These three facets of the human act must be analyzed according to an established order of importance. First, the *morality* of the object itself must be judged, then the *intention*, and lastly the *circumstances*.

First, the object or act itself. Of the three sources of the morality of an action, the object itself carries the most weight for the simple reason that the object determines the objective morality of an action. Therefore, a sinful object or act can never be justified even with the most laudable intentions or "exceptional circumstances." Simply put, a wrong action can never be made right.

Intrinsic evil refers to those actions that are opposed to the will of God or to proper human fulfillment. Intrinsically evil actions are judged to be so by their object, independent of the intention or the circumstances that surround them, i.e., these acts are evil regardless of the circumstances. Intrinsically evil acts would include those that are hostile to life itself, such as murder, genocide, abortion, and euthanasia, and those that violate the integrity of the human person, such as mutilation and physical and mental torture.

Parable of Plucking Grain on the Sabbath by Valckenborch. "But some of the Pharisees said, 'Why are you doing what is not lawful to do on the sabbath?'...And he said to them, 'The Son of man is lord of the sabbath.'" (Lk 6:1-5) First, the morality of the object itself must be judged, then the intention, and lastly the circumstances.

Acts can also be good per se, although not intrinsically good in the same way that an act can be intrinsically evil. A good action must always include the goodness of the object, the end, and the circumstances together. Almsgiving is an act that is good per se, but could be done for the wrong intentions or in the wrong circumstances.

Some erroneously believe that identifying an immoral act with a name is tantamount to an unfair judgment of a person. However, the judgment of a person and the judgment of an action are certainly not identical. Only God can judge the disposition of the human heart, but everyone can morally categorize a type of act, be it good or bad, moral or immoral.[11]

Second, the end in view or intention for the act. A good action can be morally tainted or even become sinful through the wrong intention or from particular circumstances that detract from the morality of the action. For instance, it is good to kneel down and pray, but, if it is done strictly for the reason of being noticed and praised, then the action loses its merit.

What would it be like if every act was judged morally good or bad based on the intention alone? It would be a frightening world indeed. This false position would open a Pandora's Box allowing even the vilest actions to be considered good provided there was a good intention. In fact, some would try to justify abortion, euthanasia, adultery, or genocide under the guise of good motives. Recent history regarding oppressive political regimes, racism, and unjust wars clearly conveys the message that so-called good motives cannot be the sole criteria in determining the morality of actions, laws, or rules of government.

A good intention may diminish the gravity of a sinful action, but can never turn a sinful object into a good one. A woman might lie about her previous employment experience in order to secure a job that will better provide for her family, or a teenager might borrow his father's car without permission so that he could participate in a charitable activity with his youth group. In spite of these edifying intentions to help others, those actions are still sins of lying and stealing.

Though a good motive can never transform a sinful action into a virtuous one, a poor motive can make a good action bad. For instance, it is never right to cheat on a school exam in order to please one's parents with good grades, nor is it justifiable to use profane language in order to be accepted by one's peers. This is an erroneous way of thinking that often is described as "the ends justify the means." In reality, evil and sin cannot be used even to achieve a good and positive goal.

Parable of the Blind Leading the Blind by Bruegel the Elder. "He [Jesus] answered, '…Let them alone; they are blind guides. And if a blind man leads a blind man, both will fall into a pit.'" (Mt 15: 13-14)
A good intention may diminish the gravity of a sinful action, but can never turn a sinful object into a good one.

Likewise, a good deed of being friendly and kind would be lessened or even nullified if it were solely done to secure a favor—for example, if a daughter were to voluntarily clean the kitchen and vacuum the carpets only because she wanted to ask her parents if she could go out with her boyfriend that evening past curfew. Even though some good is accomplished—her taking on the chores means less work for others to do—the moral goodness of her act is diminished somewhat because of the daughter's ulterior motive. The act of helping around the house is done not out of love or duty, but as a bargaining chip for getting what she wants.

St. Paul succinctly puts intentions as a secondary source of moral action with the following, "Why not do evil that good may come?—as some people slanderously charge us with saying."[12] Intentions can never take the lead in determining the morality of an action.

Third, consider the circumstances of the act. Circumstances also play a role in determining the morality of an act. It is part of charity, for instance, to correct someone who is making a mistake that could have negative effects on that person or others. However, if it is done in front of other people and causes the person humiliation, the circumstances will have made the action wrong.

Circumstances usually influence the morality of an act in distinct ways. Some circumstances actually lessen the gravity of a sin. To steal a bottle of water from a well-stocked grocery store, for example, is a lesser sin than to steal the last supply of water from a person stranded in the desert. But *no circumstances can make a wrong action good*. Every intrinsically evil act will stay evil regardless of the circumstances.[13]

For an act to be morally good, the object of the act, the intention behind it, and the circumstances surrounding it must all be good.[14]

THE PRINCIPLE OF DOUBLE EFFECT

Not every human action can be classified as having only good effects or only bad effects. Some bring about some bad results even though all three criteria of object, intention, and circumstances are good. Moral theologians have applied the "principle of double effect" to determine whether or not actions that have both good and evil effects are permissible.

The principle is this: The decision to carry out an action which, as a consequence, has unintended bad results may be made only when the good effect cannot be reasonably brought about in any other way and when certain conditions have been met.

1. **The action must be good in itself.** As we have seen, for an action to be morally sound, it must be good in itself, or at least morally indifferent. This means that the object or immediate purpose of the act must fall in line with objective morality. It is never permissible to perform an immoral act under the pretext of achieving a good and salutary outcome.

Under a very misguided notion of the principle of double effect, some would hold that an abortion is morally licit when the health of the mother is endangered or simply to avoid bringing an unwanted child into the world. This position can never fall under the principle of double effect since the action consists of the direct killing of an innocent person.

2. **The agent must have the right intention.** The good effect must be directly sought and the evil effect, although foreseen, must not be intended, but only permitted or tolerated. One can never directly wish an evil. We may allow the evil to occur because it cannot be separated from the overriding good to be intended and accomplished. For example, a physician who proceeds to amputate a limb to avoid the spread of cancer must have the intention of stopping the cancer. He knows he will cripple the patient, but it is for the sake of the greater good of preserving the person's life.

Under a very misguided notion of the principle of double effect, some would hold that an abortion is morally licit when the health of the mother is endangered or simply to avoid bringing an unwanted child into the world.

3. **Good action must be the means of good effect.** An evil action can never be morally justified even if it results in a good outcome. Again we refer to the moral adage based on centuries of Judeo-Christian tradition, "The end does not justify the means." This statement is at the heart of moral theology and philosophical ethics.

A bad result will always come out of an immoral action even if the impression may be otherwise. For example, it is never morally justified to stage a military operation that targets innocent people who wield no military role or advantage—even if it is thought the action will bring about the end of the war. The principle of double effect would not apply in the case of sterilization of a woman who wants to limit the size of her family for financial or even health reasons. An evil action can never be a means for a good end. The act itself must be morally good in order to invoke this principle.

4. The good effect must be proportional to the evil effect. The good effect of the action taken must at least be equal to or, ideally, outweigh the evil effect. In other words, when there is a foreseeable evil effect of an action, there must be a proportionately or greater good effect for the respective act to be considered moral.

ERRORS IN MORAL THEOLOGY

Parable of the Good Samaritan by Feti.
"But a Samaritan, as he journeyed,
came to where he was; and when he saw him,
he had compassion…" (Lk 10: 33)
Proponents of moral relativism hold that moral standards are determined by personal dispositions and circumstances.

Proponents of moral relativism argue that moral actions can be judged from a purely subjective perspective. This is a way of stating that moral standards are determined by personal dispositions and circumstances, and that the natural law no longer should serve as the ultimate litmus test for human behavior.

These positions strike at the heart of the Church's teaching on morality. If an action does not reflect the standards of the objective and changeless moral law, then no subjective disposition can ever salvage the integrity of the human act.

This section will briefly discuss some of the more common errors of an essentially subjective view of moral action: *situation ethics*, *consequentialism*, and *proportionalism*.

a. Situation ethics maintains that the goodness or evil of a given action is determined by the particular situation. The circumstances of an individual, according to this opinion, form the prevailing criteria concerning the morality of an action.

A common example of the application of situation ethics takes the form of cohabitation of a man and woman for the sake of financial advantages. Some will admit, as a general rule, that living together outside of marriage is wrong, but financial situations or the need "to know one another better" would warrant or at least allow unmarried couples to live together in a sexual relationship as if they were married. This is a clear claim of the situation overriding the standard guidelines of natural law in the area of sexual morality.

This branch of moral relativism does not summarily reject the natural law but rather holds that the circumstances are the main determining factor of the corresponding moral act. Pope Pius XII responded very convincingly to this erroneous adherence to situation ethics as he explained the objection that had motivated the error: How is it possible to apply a universal law to each person when they are all in different circumstances? [15]

> It will be asked in what way can the moral law, which is universal, apply to and even be obligatory for a particular case, which in its concrete situation is always unique and happens only once. It can and it does because, precisely as a result of its universality, the moral law comprehends necessarily and intentionally all of the particular cases in which its concepts are verified. And in these innumerable cases it acts with such conclusive logic that even the conscience of simple faith perceives immediately and with full certainty the decision that must be made. (Pope Pius XII, *Discourse*, June 18, 1952, n. 9.)

b. Consequentialism developed as a theory not long after situation ethics was condemned by Pope Pius XII. Consequentialists judge an action to be good or evil from the consequences that follow and not by whether or not the objectivity of the act reflects the natural law.

For the consequentialists, an act is good if the subject perceives a good outcome, while an act is evil if an evil result is anticipated. This is the clearest expression of the philosophy that "the ends justify the means." It also is seen in the notion that an otherwise evil act is permissible if "nobody gets hurt" or "if I can get away with it."

Whether the act corresponds to objective truth for human behavior becomes at best a secondary consideration. In many instances, consequentialism defies St. Paul's teaching that one can never do evil to bring about a good.[16]

Consequentialism exhibits two main flaws in its moral thinking. First, objective morality takes a back seat to the subjective standards of end results and outcomes. According to this opinion, adultery is an evil action only if the end result has a harmful effect on a marriage and children. However, adultery could also be considered a morally sound form of behavior if somehow it brings about a certain fulfillment that helps the adulterer become an ostensibly better person.

The second error is the false belief that circumstances can change the moral quality of an objectively evil action. In fact, circumstances "can make neither good nor right an action that is in itself evil.[17] In many instances those so-called positive results are euphemisms for selfish satisfactions that very often inflict much harm and pain on others.

There is a general appeal to consequentialism in the area of life issues. Some declare that assisted suicide in the case of someone suffering from a painful terminal illness is a kind and merciful act since the patient is relieved of his or her misery. However, in addition to the fact that euthanasia is objectively a

Parable of the Workers at the Eleventh Hour by Feti. "Friend, I am doing you no wrong;...Take what belongs to you, and go; I choose to give to this last as I give to you." (Mt 20:13-14)

In consequentialism, objective morality takes a back seat to the subjective standards of end results and outcomes.

murderous act, the true consequences have a devastating effect on the perception of human dignity. The divine right to give and take away life is shifted from objective natural law to the subjective decisions of doctors, family members, and legislators.

c. **Proportionalism** is an expression of moral relativism that measures the moral goodness of an action according to a comparison between its good and evil effects. In this view, an action is good when the good effect proportionately exceeds the evil effect. On the other hand, an action is wrong when the evil effect is proportionately greater than the good effect. In practice, the proportionalist will maintain that an individual can disregard the natural law for a proportionately good reason.

Suppose that a young man pressures his girlfriend into having an abortion because they are both young, have very little money to support a child, and have discovered through prenatal tests that the child will be born severely disabled. The proportionalist would argue that it is better to abort the child so that the child would not suffer a life of pain, their families would not be burdened by the child's handicap, and they would not have to face the huge financial burden of caring for a disabled child.

The consequentialist would view abortion as morally justified because he or she judges the consequences that will result from his or her actions to be good. The individual who advocates proportionalism would justify the action because, in his or her opinion, the positive effects proportionately outweigh the negative ones.

Pope John Paul II addressed this proportionalist approach to the morality of abortion in the following words:

> It is often claimed that the life of an unborn child or a seriously disabled person is only a relative good: According to a proportionalist approach or one of sheer calculation, this good should be

compared with and balanced against other goods. It is even maintained that only someone present and personally involved in a concrete situation can correctly judge the goods at stake: Consequently, only that person would be able to decide on the morality of his choice. The state, therefore, in the interest of civil coexistence and social harmony, should respect his choice, even to the point of permitting abortion and euthanasia. (*Evangelium Vitæ*, 68)

The self-evident consequences of these errant perspectives demonstrate that the ethical criteria defended by these systems are not valid. These errors are rejected by the *Catechism of the Catholic Church*:

It is therefore an error to judge the morality of human acts by considering only the intention that inspires them or the circumstances (environment, social pressure, duress or emergency, etc.) which supply their context. There are acts which, in and of themselves, independently of circumstances and intentions, are always gravely illicit by reason of their object; such as blasphemy and perjury, murder and adultery. One may not do evil so that good may result from it. (CCC 1756)

He Sent Them Out Two By Two by Tissot. "And he called to him the twelve, and began to send them out two by two, and gave them authority over the unclean spirits." (Mk 6:7)

CONCLUSION

God communicates his infinite love to every person by inscribing some of his eternal wisdom into the human heart. This eternal wisdom was fully manifested in the witness and teachings of the Son of God made flesh.

If we seriously examine the effects of living by the Ten Commandments and the teachings of Jesus Christ, we will be led to the overwhelming conclusion that God's laws are the path toward profound personal fulfillment and intense happiness. Therefore, civil laws should reflect the eternal wisdom of God as found in the moral law. Especially in democratic societies, each citizen has a responsibility to work toward the creation of a more just society.

However, there are laws which are in violation of the natural law and which inflict serious injury upon the members of society. These are not true laws. They must be opposed, and lawful means to overturn them must be sought. It is always important that a concern for justice and resistance to evil be balanced with Christian love for all people and a genuine respect for civil authority.

Three sources of morality must always be present when any moral act is scrutinized. In doing so, we must analyze the three components of all moral action: the act itself (object), the ultimate aim (intention), and the different conditions surrounding the act (circumstances). All three must be morally good for the act itself to be morally good.[18]

Decisions, choices, and actions guided by moral truth are what best serve and reinforce the common good and the dignity of the person. The tragedies that have marked both present and past centuries offer an overwhelming case for embracing God's eternal moral law.

SUPPLEMENTARY READING

1. True Law is Right Reason in Agreement with Nature

True law is right reason in agreement with nature; it is of universal application, unchanging and everlasting....It is a sin to try to alter this law, nor is it allowable to attempt to repeal any part of it, and it is impossible to abolish it entirely. We cannot be freed from its obligations by senate or people, and we need not look outside ourselves for an expounder or interpreter of it. And there will not be different laws at Rome and at Athens, or different laws now and in the future, but one eternal and unchangeable law will be valid for all nations and at all times, and there will be one master and ruler, that is, God, over us all, for he is the author of his law, its promulgator, and its enforcing judge. Whoever is disobedient is fleeing from himself and denying his human nature, and by reason of this very fact he will suffer the worst penalties, even if he escapes what is commonly considered punishment.

—Cicero, *De Republica*, III, 22

2. Deep within his Conscience Man Discovers a Law

Deep within his conscience man discovers a law which he has not laid upon himself but which he must obey. Its voice, ever calling him to love and to do what is good and to avoid evil, tells him inwardly at the right moment: do this, shun that. For man has in his heart a law inscribed by God.

His dignity lies in observing this law, and by it he will be judged.

—*Gaudium et Spes*, 16

3. Civil Law Cannot Take the Place of Conscience

The real purpose of civil law is to guarantee an ordered social coexistence in true justice, so that all may 'lead a quiet and peaceable life, godly and respectful in every way' (1 Tm 2:2). Precisely for this reason, civil law must ensure that all members of society enjoy respect for certain fundamental rights which innately belong to the person, rights which every positive law must recognize and guarantee. First and fundamental among these is the inviolable right to life of every innocent human being. While public authority can sometimes choose not to put a stop to something which—were it prohibited—would cause more serious harm, it can never presume to legitimize as a right of individuals—even if they are the majority of the members of society—an offense against other persons caused by the disregard of so fundamental a right as the right to life. The legal toleration of abortion or of euthanasia can in no way claim to be based on respect for the conscience of others, precisely because society has the right and the duty to protect itself against the abuses which can occur in the name of conscience and under the pretext of freedom.

—*Evangelium Vitæ*, 71

Christ with the Virgin Mary and St. John the Evangelist by Weyden. The New Law is a law of love, a law of grace, a law of freedom.

SUPPLEMENTARY READING Continued

4. Goodness and Justice

The problem of truth to which I have briefly alluded is only a single example. The same situation arises in the case of the moral and juristic standard, which is supposed to regulate our wills, as truth regulates our thought. Goodness and justice, if they are what they claim to be, must necessarily be unique. Justice which is only just for a certain time, or for a certain race, cancels its own meaning. In ethics and law, then, too, the principles of relativism and rationalism arise, as they do also in art and religion. This is as much as to say that the problem of truth is dispersed throughout all the spiritual orders which we imply when we use the word, culture.

— Jose Ortega y Gasset, *The Modern Theme*, 37

5. The Fundamental Option

In reality, it is precisely the fundamental option which in the last resort defines a person's moral disposition. But it can be completely changed by particular acts, especially when, as often happens, these have been prepared for by previous more superficial acts. Whatever the case, it is wrong to say that particular acts are not enough to constitute mortal sin.

— *Persona Humana*, 10

6. Private Conscience and Public Conduct

In any case, in the democratic culture of our time it is commonly held that the legal system of any society should limit itself to taking account of and accepting the convictions of the majority....Hence every politician, in his or her activity, should clearly separate the realm of private conscience from that of public conduct. As a result we have what appear to be two diametrically opposed tendencies. On the one hand, individuals claim for themselves in the moral sphere the most complete freedom of choice and demand that the State should not adopt or impose any ethical position but limit itself to guaranteeing maximum space for the freedom of each individual, with the sole limitation of not infringing on the freedom and rights of any other citizen. On the other hand, it is held that, in the exercise of public and professional duties, respect for other people's freedom of choice requires that each one should set aside his or her own convictions in order to satisfy every demand of the citizens which is recognized and guaranteed by law; in carrying out one's duties, the only moral criterion should be what is laid down by the law itself. Individual responsibility is thus turned over to the civil law, with a renouncing of personal conscience, at least in the public sphere.

— *Evangelium Vitæ*, 69

Pope John Paul II: "The morality of acts is defined by the relationship of man's freedom with the authentic good. This good is established, as the eternal law, by Divine Wisdom which orders every being towards its end: this eternal law is known both by man's natural reason (hence it is 'natural law'), and—in an integral and perfect way—by God's supernatural Revelation (hence it is called 'divine law')." *Veritatis Splendor*, 72

VOCABULARY

CIRCUMSTANCES
The condition or state of affairs surrounding a moral decision; these include the consequences of an action. Circumstances can increase or diminish the responsibility of a person, but they cannot change the moral quality of the acts themselves; they never make good an act which is in itself evil.

CIVIL GOVERNMENT
The proper authority for governing and enforcing laws at the local, municipal, state, or national level.

CIVIL LAW
A rule of conduct imposed by civil authority; the body of such rules binding on members under control of the authority whether from formal enactment or custom.

COMMON GOOD
The total of social conditions that will allow both individuals and groups to reach their human and spiritual fulfillment more easily.

CONSEQUENTIALISM
An ethical system that determines the level of goodness or evil from the effect or result of an act.

ECCLESIASTICAL GOVERNMENT
The Church's own governing body, such as a diocese, national bishops' conferences, or the Holy See.

END (of an action)
The primary goal of the intention and the purpose pursued in an action.

EQUALITY OF PROPORTION
Principle that the burden of law must be shared by all.

ETERNAL LAW
God's wisdom as manifested in the nature of acts and movements.

FUNDAMENTAL OPTION
The free and responsible choice a person makes to orient, in a radical manner, his whole existence in a moral direction toward good or evil.

HUMAN LAW
Law promulgated by human authority, either civil or ecclesiastical. In order to be legitimate, human law must be consistent with laws of God, conform to the natural law, and promote the good of society.

INTENTION (of an action)
A movement of the will toward an end.

JUST LAW
An ordinance of reason that exists for the common good, having been made by legitimate authority and legislated through an appropriate and recognized process.

LAW
An ordinance of reason that exists for the common good, having been made by legitimate authority and legislated through an appropriate and recognized process.

LAW OF GRACE
The New Law ushered in by Christ.

LAWS OF NATURE
Descriptions of the behavior of the material universe.

LEGITIMATE AUTHORITY
A recognized and official authority in civil or ecclesiastical law.

OBJECT (of an action)
That toward which the will directs itself. This is distinct from the intention that a person has when performing the act.

VOCABULARY Continued

POSITIVE LAWS
Laws created by the proper authority that enjoin specific obligations upon individuals and bind in conscience insofar as they conform to the dictates of the divine and natural laws.

PRINCIPLE OF DOUBLE EFFECT
An act may be performed, even if accompanied by an unintended bad effect, if the act itself is good or indifferent, the good effect far outreaches the bad effect, and the intention of the act is the good effect.

PROPORTIONALISM
An ethical system that deduces the moral value of an act from the proportion of its good and evil effects.

SITUATION ETHICS
An ethical system that determines the good or evil nature of an act from the circumstances.

UNIVERSALITY
The ability to be applied to everyone in every situation.

UNJUST LAW
A human law that contradicts or otherwise fails to conform to divine and natural law. Such a law is never binding on a person's conscience and must be opposed.

Mary and Elizabeth by Bloch.

"And when Elizabeth heard the greeting of Mary, the babe leaped in her womb; and Elizabeth was filled with the Holy Spirit and she exclaimed with a loud cry, 'Blessed are you among women, and blessed is the fruit of your womb!'" (Lk 1: 41-42)

STUDY QUESTIONS

1. What is the purpose of law? Explain what is meant by "law is an ordinance of reason."

2. Choose five laws that exist in our society. Explain how they meet (or do not meet) the purpose of laws as outlined in the chapter.

3. What would happen if laws were made by someone who did not have the proper authority, or if laws were not formulated in an officially recognized way?

4. How can our observation of the material world lead us to conclude that there is an eternal law?

5. How can our human experience show us that the natural law is inscribed on our hearts? Give an example.

6. What is the relationship between reason and natural law?

7. What is the primary difference between physical laws and natural laws?

8. Define "moral relativism." What is its fundamental error?

9. List two of the totalitarian regimes of the twentieth century and describe their violations of the natural law.

10. Explain why, in enacting true laws, lawmakers cannot just make any law that they wish.

11. What is sanctifying grace, and what is the "Law of Grace"? What is its purpose?

12. According to St. Thomas Aquinas, what is required for a law to be valid?

13. How would we look upon a law that fails to meet the requirements specified in the *Catechism of the Catholic Church* (CCC 1925)? Explain your answer.

14. According to St. Thomas Aquinas, when must a law not be obeyed?

15. What is required before a person decides to disobey an unjust law?

16. In what manner may a person seek to overthrow an unjust law?

17. What makes a human act good or evil?

18. Define object, intention, and circumstances in relation to "human acts."

19. What is the established order by which the morality of an act must be analyzed? Why must it be analyzed in this order? Why is the "object" the most important element in determining the morality of an act?

20. How is judging an act different from judging a person? Why is it legitimate to judge an act but not a person?

21. Explain how intention can transform an act for better or for worse. Give an example of each.

22. Why is it that intentions can never be the primary factor in determining the morality of an action? Explain.

23. What would you say to someone who believes that morality depends on the circumstances?

24. Name an otherwise good action. What circumstances might make it a bad action? Now name a morally wrong action, and explain why no imaginable circumstance could make it a good action.

STUDY QUESTIONS Continued

25. Describe a good action that might have unintended bad effects.

26. Why is an evaluation of the object of an act the first step in the Principle of Double Effect?

27. How can it ever be moral to allow an unintended evil to occur? What is the difference between this and intending to perform a bad act?

28. "The end does not justify the means." Explain why a good end can never come from evil means.

29. If the object and intention are good, why must a proportionality between the good and bad effects be considered?

30. Explain moral relativism.

31. Explain how living a "moral" life can benefit a person psychologically or physically.

32. What does it mean to judge something from a subjective perspective?

33. What happens to universal moral laws when situation ethics are applied?

34. How is it possible for the moral law to apply to all situations?

35. Explain consequentialism.

36. How does proportionalism render moral concepts of good and evil meaningless?

Moses Receiving the Tables of the Law (detail) by Tintoretto.
If we seriously examine the effects of living by the Ten Commandments and the teachings of Jesus Christ, we will be led to the overwhelming conclusion that God's laws are the path toward profound personal fulfillment and intense happiness.

PRACTICAL EXERCISES

1. Make a list of the "true goods" of the human person. Does our society have laws which protect these goods?

2. Imagine a society with no laws. Write ten laws to promote the common good of society. (See the *Catechism of the Catholic Church* 1925.)

3. Choose one law that you know of which does not reflect the moral law. Draft a letter to your congressman explaining why this does not meet the standards of a moral law and should be overturned.

4. Summarize and explain the characteristics of the natural law, according to Cicero.

5. List the characteristics of the natural law as described by the *Catechism of the Catholic Church* (CCC 1954-1960).

6. Why does the Magisterium have the authority and duty to interpret the natural law?

7. Some people claim that law and freedom are mutually exclusive. How would you persuade them that law and freedom complement each other?

8. In 1857, the U.S. Supreme Court decided that Dred Scott, a slave, was not a human being, but the property of his "owner." What arguments would you use to refute this decision? Would you appeal to a positivist understanding of law? Would you appeal to the natural law? What other decisions of the Supreme Court neglect to consider the natural law?

9. In the story of Original Sin, determine the object, the end, and the circumstances that surround the case.

10. Explain behavior occurring today that is excused by some because "the ends justify the means."

11. Determine the object, the end, and the circumstances of the actions in Luke 21:1-4.

12. Write a brief essay discussing the similarities, differences and connections between situation ethics, proportionalism, and consequentialism.

Dred Scott (1799-1858) was a slave in the United States who sued unsuccessfully for his freedom in the Dred Scott vs. Sandford case of 1857. His case was based on the fact that he had traveled to "free states" with his master, Dr. John Emerson, who was in the U.S. Army and often relocated. Scott's extended stay with his master in Illinois, a free state, gave him the legal standing to make a claim for freedom, as did his extended stay at Fort Snelling in the Wisconsin Territory, where slavery was also illegal. The United States Supreme Court ruled 7 to 2 against Scott, finding that neither he, nor any person of African ancestry, could claim citizenship in the United States, and therefore Scott could not bring suit in federal court under "diversity of citizenship rules."

FROM THE CATECHISM

417   Adam and Eve transmitted to their descendants human nature wounded by their own first sin and hence deprived of original holiness and justice; this deprivation is called "original sin."

1750   The morality of human acts depends on:
- the object chosen;
- the end in view or the intention;
- the circumstances of the action.

The object, the intention, and the circumstances make up the "sources," or constitutive elements, of the morality of human acts.

1761   There are concrete acts that it is always wrong to choose, because their choice entails a disorder of the will, i.e., a moral evil. One may not do evil so that good may result from it.

1873   The root of all sins lies in man's heart. The kinds and the gravity of sins are determined principally by their objects.

1976   "Law is an ordinance of reason for the common good, promulgated by the one who is in charge of the community." [19]

1977   Christ is the end of the law; [20] only he teaches and bestows the justice of God.

1978   The natural law is a participation in God's wisdom and goodness by man formed in the image of his Creator. It expresses the dignity of the human person and forms the basis of his fundamental rights and duties.

1979   The natural law is immutable, permanent throughout history. The rules that express it remain substantially valid. It is a necessary foundation for the erection of moral rules and civil law.

1985   The New Law is a law of love, a law of grace, a law of freedom.

Agony in the Garden by Bellini.
"The root of all sins lies in man's heart." (CCC 1873)

ENDNOTES – CHAPTER THREE

1. Cf. Jn 19:11.
2. Cf. CCC 1953.
3. St. Thomas Aquinas, *Summa Theologiæ*, I-II, q. 93, a. 1.
4. St. Thomas Aquinas, *Summa Theologiæ*, I-II, q. 91 a. 2.
5. Cf. CCC 1955.
6. Cf. CCC 1956.
7. CCC 1952-1972.
8. Jn 15:15; cf. Jas 1:25; 2:12; Gal 4:1-7, 21-31; Rom 8:15.
9. CCC 1925.
10. Cf. St. Thomas Aquinas, *Summa Theologiæ*, I-II, q. 96, a. 5.
11. Cf. *VS* 79.
12. Rom 3:8.
13. Cf. CCC 1754.
14. Cf. CCC 1760.
15. Cf. Pope Pius XII, *Discourse*, June 18, 1952, n. 4.
16. Cf. Rom 3:8.
17. CCC 1754.
18. *VS* 81.
19. St. Thomas Aquinas, *Summa Theologiæ*, I-II, 90, 4.
20. Cf. Rom 10:4.

Sin and
the Commandments

CHAPTER 4

Sin and the Commandments

> Behold, one came up to [Jesus] saying, "Teacher, what good deed must I do, to have eternal life?" And he said to him, "Why do you ask me about what is good? One there is who is good. If you would enter life, keep the commandments." He said to him, "Which?" And Jesus said, "You shall not kill, You shall not commit adultery, You shall not steal, You shall not bear false witness, Honor your father and mother, and, You shall love your neighbor as yourself." The young man said to him, "All these I have observed; what do I still lack?" Jesus said to him, "If you would be perfect, go, sell what you possess and give to the poor, and you will have treasure in heaven; and come, follow me." (Mt 19:16-21)

The question that the rich young man puts to Jesus of Nazareth rises from the depths of his heart. It is an essential and unavoidable question for the life of every person: What must we do to attain eternal life? The young man senses that there is a connection between making good moral choices and being found worthy of eternal salvation. He is a devout Israelite, raised as it were in the shadow of the Law of the Lord.[1]

In his reply to the young man, Jesus expresses the nucleus and spirit of Christian morality. Through this dialogue, Christ reveals "the essential elements of revelation in the Old and New Testament with regard to moral action."[2]

The answer to the question about moral goodness and its connection to eternal life can be found only in God. One cannot know what is good without knowing goodness itself. For the believer, God is "the One who 'alone is good'; the One who despite man's sin remains the 'model' for moral action."[3] To become good is to become like God. People need to turn to Christ, for it is from him that they will receive "the answer to their question about what is good and what is evil."[4] Essential to all morality is the recognition of God's sovereignty over the moral order, for "acknowledging the Lord as God is the very core, the heart of the Law."[5]

FOR DISCUSSION

- ✠ What is the meaning of sin? Are there different types of sin?
- ✠ How did sin originate, and why is it an offense against God and others?
- ✠ What personal responsibility do we bear for committing a sin?
- ✠ What are the means to conversion and the forgiveness of sin?
- ✠ What are the Last Things?
- ✠ What are the Ten Commandments?
- ✠ Are the Ten Commandments still relevant guides for life in the modern world?
- ✠ How do the Ten Commandments and the Beatitudes guide us in forming and fulfilling the dictates of conscience?
- ✠ How does a moral life lead to eternal salvation?

INTRODUCTION

"If you would enter life, keep the commandments"[6] is Jesus' reply to the rich young man. If sin is the illness, then the commandments are the prescribed remedy.

The commandments were not part of God's original plan, but rather were necessitated by the introduction of sin into the world. The entire existence of mankind since Adam and Eve must be oriented toward overcoming sin and the tendency to sin that separates us from God. Just as sin is an evil act that is freely chosen, it takes an act of will also to remain faithful to the commandments. The struggle of good versus evil takes place in every human heart, and it is only with God's help that we can hope to triumph over the influence of sin.

In this chapter, we will examine the nature of sin in the first section and the importance of the Ten Commandments in the second section.

The Creation of Adam by Michelangelo. Adam and Eve were created without sin and were the recipients of a sanctifying grace that gave them a close relationship and intimacy with God.

SECTION I: THE NATURE OF SIN

We must begin our study of sin by considering what constitutes a sin and what Scripture has to say about sin—beginning with Original Sin.

ORIGINAL SIN AND ITS EFFECTS

The Book of Genesis reveals that the first man and woman, Adam and Eve, were created in the image and likeness of God and enjoyed a state of original holiness and justice.[7] This original state of holiness and justice enabled our first parents to have an existence that none of their descendants would ever enjoy, with the exception of Jesus and Mary.

Adam and Eve were created without sin and were the recipients of a sanctifying grace that gave them a close relationship and intimacy with God. This union and habitual conformity with God's will resulted in an ongoing happiness and total control of the intellect and will over their appetites and passions. Moreover, the original state of justice made them immune to sickness and death. Part of this exalted existence of the first man and woman was a complete dominion over creation. Man was right with God, and the rest of creation in turn was subject to man.

This ideal situation that gratified our first parents would come to an end. God clearly specified that they could eat of every tree in the garden, except for the tree of knowledge of good and evil. If they ate of this tree, they would lose their life of intimacy with God.

The story is familiar. Tempted by the serpent, Eve partook of the fruit of the forbidden tree and persuaded Adam to do likewise. This blatant act of disobedience and violation of God's prohibition ushered sin into the world.

With this first sin, called Original Sin, the original state of holiness and justice dramatically ended. Adam and Eve lost their special relationship with God and, consequently, the perfect self-control over their passions. Their minds would be clouded and their wills would be weakened with regard to the fulfillment of God's will. They would now be subject to the toil of work, sickness, and eventually death. The devil would, as it were, have a greater influence in tempting man to sin. With Original Sin, evil officially entered the world with all its sad and tragic consequences. With the exception of Mary, the Mother of Jesus, no human being would ever enjoy original holiness and justice. This means that every person conceived is deprived of the original holiness and justice enjoyed by our first parents.

Adam and Eve transmitted to their descendants human nature wounded by their own first sin and hence deprived of original holiness and justice; this deprivation is called "original sin." (CCC 417)

Cain Murders Abel by Titian. The tragic consequences of sin are a compelling appeal for the merciful healing power and saving graces of Jesus Christ's Redemption.

But God did not abandon us. As Genesis foretold, God would send a Redeemer to free man from sin and its destructive effects. Jesus Christ, through his Death and Resurrection, would restore what had been lost by Original Sin and offer all people a superabundance of grace and the opportunity to be healed of their sins and to become participants in the divine life of God.

St. Peter Chrysologus wrote that Adam was made by Christ who stamped his image on man.[8] This image of God in which man was created became disfigured by Original Sin, but through Christ it can be restored. For this reason, the proper end of the Christian life is to become conformed to the image of Christ, God made man, who is the head of his Body the Church.[9]

The Original Sin of Adam and Eve did more than just inflict spiritual and moral damage on their souls. This injury to the harmony between God and man disrupted the harmony between human inclinations and appetites and a person's mind and will. Furthermore, because of the linear connection between God, man, and the rest of creation, this first sin disrupted the original harmony that existed between the world and the human person.

As a result of this first sin, every human being, as a descendant of Adam and Eve, inherits Original Sin upon conception.[10] The effects of Original Sin are automatically transmitted through human generation. All of human nature is thus wounded and inclined to sin, and is now susceptible to sickness, toil, hardship in work, and the decline of the body, which ultimately results in death. It is common personal experience that there is an internal struggle in one's inclinations, attitudes, feelings, and emotions.

The damaged nature caused by Original Sin consists of limitations of the intellect in discerning good and evil. It also shows itself in a weak and sometimes malicious will that fails to control selfish passions like lust and anger, a will that is inclined to inflict harm on others through gossip, insults, resentment, hatred, even violence. The tragic consequences of sin are a compelling appeal for the merciful healing power and saving graces of Jesus Christ's Redemption.

The existence of evil and suffering in the world is a mystery that is illuminated by the suffering, Death, and Resurrection of Jesus Christ, who vanquished evil. Through faith we understand that God allows evil to occur because an ultimate good will come from it and that in Heaven we will someday come to fully understand its purpose.

WHAT IS SIN?

Physical evil entered the world with Original Sin. Civil wars, political corruption, and atheistic totalitarian regimes in many occasions cause the populace to suffer poverty, famine, and starvation.

Sin is an offense against God. There are three classical definitions of sin which are offered by two of the Church's greatest theologians, St. Augustine and St. Thomas Aquinas.

a. Sin is any deed, word, or desire that violates eternal law. (St. Augustine) Eternal law is the divine wisdom that directs all of creation. Part of this eternal law includes the natural law, which applies to human beings. A transgression of the natural law, whether through a desire, word, or deed, is considered a sin.

Any violation of the natural law robs man of his dignity, reduces his freedom and self-control, and creates a distance between himself and friendship with Christ. Therefore, desires, thoughts, words, and actions must always be consistent with the natural law, which is a stepping stone for a close relationship with Christ.

b. Sin is a violation of the moral law. (St. Thomas Aquinas) This definition of sin focuses on the actual infraction of the Ten Commandments or one of its immediate applications. Put simply, any violation of the moral law, which always reflects the mind and will of God, is an offense against God.

It would be erroneous to view an action as a sin only in the case of a direct malicious affront against God. Many parents, for instance, feel offended when their children deceive them with the lie that they are at a friend's house when in reality they are at an unsupervised party. Upon discovering the deception, parents understandably are hurt because of this outright lie, even though it was not told out of malice toward the parents. Thus, even without direct malice toward God, the violation of any law which is derived from God's commandments is an offense against God.

For example, the obligation to attend Sunday Mass is an expression of the Third Commandment, which directs us to keep the Lord's Day holy. As a day reserved for God, the Sunday obligation is a Precept of the Church and therefore a serious obligation for all Catholics. Cooperation with God's loving plan of salvation, personal holiness, and true happiness requires faithfulness to his laws, whether transmitted directly or through his Church.

c. Sin is a disordered love for created things over God. (St. Thomas Aquinas) A person sins by violating God's law, not necessarily out of a personal desire to directly offend God. In most instances, sin arises from an inordinate attachment to created goods, which alienates, to some degree, oneself from God.

Whether it pertains to robbery, lying, or physical abuse, the common element is the pursuit of selfish goals which take precedence over the will of God. Sins of the flesh especially reflect this particular definition of sin.

These types of sin consist in giving priority to lustful gratification in a manner that involves a rejection of God's will and brings about a consequent diminution of personal dignity. In a certain sense, all sins manifest a form of idolatry in that the person places some other thing before God.

These three definitions of sin are implicitly stated in the *Catechism of the Catholic Church*.[11]

> Sin, as an offense against God, neighbor, and self, is the only evil that man can commit, and the only thing that we must bear in life. "...for you on earth there is but one evil, which you must fear and avoid with the grace of God: sin."[12]

SIN IN SACRED SCRIPTURE

Sin in the Old Testament

Throughout the Old Testament, the overriding notion of sin is infidelity to a loving Father who lavishes his blessings on his people. In every phase in the history of God's Chosen People, God wants his people to enjoy a healthy, peaceful, and long life—he wants them to be happy. Fidelity to his commandments demonstrates love of God and, in turn, ensures God's promises of protection and generous assistance. However, disobedience or rejection of his laws is not taken merely as an infraction of a law, but as infidelity to God's covenant and ingratitude for his unmitigated love.

Especially in the books of Isaiah and Hosea, Israel's sins are likened to marital infidelity. This image is quite striking because God, through the prophetic writings, discloses his own dispositions toward the Chosen People. His love for them is equated with the all-consuming devotion of a loving husband for his wife. It follows that the sins of God's people are put on the same par as adultery. The expected response to adultery is the automatic cancellation of the benefits connected with the marriage covenant, banishment from the household, and, according to Old Testament Law, death.

Jeroboam Offering Sacrifice for the Idol by Fragonard. As written in 1 Kings 12-13, Jeroboam was the first king of the breakaway ten tribes from the Kingdom of Judah ruled by King Rehoboam, the son of King Solomon. As a means to strengthen the division of the kingdom, Jeroboam set up two altars with golden calves for worship, one at Dan and one at Bethel, and said to the people, "'You have gone up to Jerusalem long enough. Behold your gods,...' And this thing became a sin,..." (1 Kgs 12:28, 30)

Jesus and the Adulterous Woman by Rembrandt. "...he stood up and said to them, 'Let him who is without sin among you be the first to throw a stone at her.'" (Jn 8: 7)

Nevertheless, God cannot persist in his anger and mercifully takes back his wayward wife—his Chosen People—time and again. As demonstrated by this allegorical image of God's covenant with his people, sin is an action that abuses God's love and prevents him from lavishing his loving care upon his sons and daughters.

Sin in the New Testament

In the New Testament, sin is much more divinely personalized than in the Old Testament. Human sin is the essential reason for the Incarnation of Jesus Christ, which fully reveals the love of the Father. Though a mystery, the Redemption from sin begins with Jesus' conception in Mary's virginal womb and culminates with his Death and Resurrection.

The reparation and Redemption from sin lead the Son of God in his human nature to undergo unparalleled suffering, humiliation, and anguish. Jesus, who is God the Son, suffers on account of sin—more from our loss of dignity, happiness, and, in certain cases, salvation than from any personal offense to himself. Since man is ruined and damaged by sin, Jesus suffers out of love and compassion toward the one who has injured himself. The high price for our sins required Jesus' Crucifixion and Death. In other words, our sins are directly connected and intrinsically linked to the suffering and Death of Jesus on the Cross.

Both Testaments show how sin damages man, and how God ardently wants to forgive the sinner. The analogy that began as an offended lover culminates with the love of Jesus Christ demonstrated by his Death on the Cross.

MORTAL AND VENIAL SINS

As we have seen in previous chapters dealing with moral acts, every sin (other than Original Sin) is a personal and willful act of one's thoughts, desires, or actions. The choice of acting in contradiction to God's moral law and Jesus' teachings for holiness constitutes a sin. It is committed at the moment the subject, through a deliberate act of the will, implicitly or explicitly rejects God's will.

We have seen, too, that a sin is a personal act, because a sin is always the result of a free decision. It is precisely because a person freely chooses that he or she personally bears the guilt of his or her sin. Although there may be mitigating circumstances lessening the degree of guilt, each person is ultimately responsible for his or her own actions.

Sacred Scripture shows that sins are not all of the same kind, nor are all immoral acts equally sinful. The most common classification of sin is according to whether it is a mortal *sin* or a *venial sin*.

Mortal sin is a grave offense against God that destroys our relationship with him. In committing a mortal sin, we willingly choose a disordered act which separates us from God and his divine love.[13] Our relationship with God can be restored through the Sacrament of Reconciliation.

The *Catechism of the Catholic Church* lists three conditions for a sin to be considered a mortal sin: The act in question must involve a *grave matter* that is carried out with *full knowledge* and with complete *consent of the will*:

✤ *Grave matter* "is specified by the Ten Commandments," that is, it must be a serious violation of the Divine Law; (CCC 1858)

✤ *Full knowledge* "presupposes knowledge of the sinful character of the act, of its opposition to God's law"; (CCC 1859)

✤ *Complete consent* "implies a consent sufficiently deliberate to be a personal choice." The deliberate violation of a prohibition is sufficient for a person to have complete consent. (CCC 1859)

Allegory of Freewill and Sin.
Miniature Illustration (ca. 1475-80) for *City of God* by St. Augustine.

If even one of these three conditions is not met, then the sin is not mortal, but venial.[14] Because it requires full knowledge and complete consent, there is no way to commit a mortal sin "by accident." It is possible, however, to commit a mortal sin without a desire to offend God directly or explicitly.

Venial sin is a less serious act that offends the love of God. While it does not separate us from God the way a mortal sin does, venial sin weakens our relationship with him. It is recommended that we confess venial sins frequently in order to avoid mortal sin.

One commits *venial sin* when, in a less serious matter, he does not observe the standard prescribed by the moral law, or when he disobeys the moral law in a grave matter, but without full knowledge or without complete consent. (CCC 1862)

The repetition of sins—even venial sins—can lead to the commission of mortal sins and a life of vice. Recall the discussion in a previous chapter about the gradual loss of conscience and the habitual sins that can occur when even small sins and indiscretions accumulate or are repeated without being confronted through prayer, the Sacrament of Reconciliation, spiritual direction, and other spiritual efforts.

CAUSES OF THE LOSS OF THE SENSE OF SIN

Pope Pius XII commented in 1946 that "the sin of the century is the loss of the meaning of sin."[15]

For various reasons, many people refuse to acknowledge sin as the source of evil's presence in the world, in the family, or in their personal lives. Among many people, violations of personal dignity through infractions of the moral law do not even enter the realm of consideration as barriers between God and man. Others choose to reject the idea of sin or even God himself in their lives.

With the loss of the meaning of sin comes the loss of the sense of sin. Many consider sin as no more than an idea that puts a label on certain actions based on arbitrary norms of moral conduct. This insensitivity to both the nature and evil of sin has led to major problems. What would have been unthinkable in other times has now become widely accepted. Legalized abortion, assisted suicide, homosexual activity, and the availability of pornography all reflect this sad state of affairs.[16]

The loss of the sense of sin has many contributing causes. The primary causes include moral relativism, faulty psychology, confusion between what is "moral" and what is "legal," and secular humanism.

Moral relativism, which we have touched upon in earlier chapters, is the belief that there are no objectively good or evil actions, that there exist no moral standards that apply to all situations and circumstances. According to some, morality is relative to the person, the circumstances, the times, the culture, and the prevailing opinions.

In moral relativism, the notion of sin becomes irrelevant since it is defined as an infraction of a law that does not really exist. Violations of sexual morality abound under the guise of prevailing trends or the expectations of the majority, and these violations are commonly portrayed as acceptable behavior in many television programs, movies, and in popular music.

Faulty psychology occurs when the inferences and theories of this otherwise valid behavioral science go against the moral law. Psychology is a valid science that has made wonderful inroads in assisting the human person to overcome emotional and mental difficulties. Like any other discipline, however, it must base its

Las Vegas, Nevada has the nickname of "Sin City" because of its tolerance for adult entertainment and human vices. Las Vegas is the most populous American city founded in the twentieth century. Viewed from space, Las Vegas is the brightest city on earth.

premises and conclusions on objective truth. When the object of science deals directly with human actions, its moral contents fall within the purview of the moral teachings of the Church.

In some psychological circles, however, self-control over one's passions or appetites is labeled as an unhealthy repression resulting in self-imposed guilt. Certain thinkers characterize the experience of guilt and shame as an objective evil, when in fact the sense of guilt and shame is often a product of conscience and therefore a reliable indicator of sin. A psychology that encourages the expression of anger, self-absorption, or immoral sexual behavior would be a false psychology because it would contradict moral truth coming from God himself.

Other psychologists dismiss the concept of sin, attributing disordered choices to insecurity, trauma, poor upbringing, lack of parental concern, or other factors. Though these factors can be valid mitigating circumstances, in themselves they do not exonerate the individual from the culpability of sin.

For these psychologists, the effects of sin are seen as psychological disorders that find their remedy not in the healing graces of Jesus' Redemption, but in the ventilation of negative feelings and thoughts and the

Pope Pius XII (1876-1958) reigned as the 260th pope from 1939-1958. His forty-one encyclicals and almost 1,000 speeches and radio broadcasts are part of the Church's Magisterium. "That which seems to Us not only the greatest evil but the root of all evil is this: often the lie is substituted for the truth, and is then used as an instrument of dispute.... public and private atheism is exalted in such a way that God and His law are being abolished, and morals no longer have any foundation. The Press also too often vulgarly reviles religious feeling, while it does not hesitate to spread the most shameful obscenities, agitating and with incalculable harm leading into vice tender childhood and betrayed youth." *Anni Sacri*, 3. (delivered March 12, 1950)

application of certain mental techniques. While psychology has a very important role in remedying emotional and personality disorders, it can never serve as a substitute to heal the effects of sin.

Confusion between what is moral and what is legal: True laws must in some way reflect God's eternal law. A law that is derived on some level from the natural law binds us in conscience. Unfortunately, what is legal is not always morally correct. Therefore, when a civil law violates or opposes the fundamental tenets of natural law, it must be rejected or disobeyed. The legalization of abortion constitutes a glaring example of a civil law that contradicts the law of God and warrants opposition.

Secular humanism is a philosophy that seeks the improvement of human society through purely human means, such as scientific advancement, efficient social work, and material welfare. However, this view of reality rejects any reference to God, religion, or objective moral values.

A secularistic attitude ignores the spiritual component of the human person and therefore has no concern for moral rectitude and development. The rise in popularity of secular humanism in some segments of society has also contributed to the loss of the meaning of sin.

The very life of the Church is affected by this loss of the sense of sin,[17] as Pope John Paul II indicated:

Even in the field of the thought and life of the Church certain trends inevitably favor the decline of the sense of sin. For example, some are inclined to replace exaggerated attitudes of the past with other exaggerations: from seeing sin everywhere they pass to not recognizing it anywhere; from too much emphasis on the fear of eternal punishment they pass to preaching a love of God that excludes any punishment deserved by sin; from severity in trying to correct erroneous consciences they pass to a kind of respect for conscience which excludes the duty of telling the truth. (*Reconciliatio et Pænitentia*, 18)

The loss of the meaning of sin invariably leads to a misunderstanding and neglect of the role of Christ in his work of salvation.

COOPERATION IN EVIL

One may never explicitly or implicitly cooperate in the sin of another. Cooperation in the sin of another is the help afforded to another in the execution of a sinful purpose. Cooperation may be *formal*, *implicitly formal*, or *material*.

Formal cooperation is deliberate cooperation in an evil action or practice. Explicit formal cooperation is a willing cooperation in the evil act, such as a doctor who assists another doctor in performing an abortion.

Implicit formal cooperation does not involve a direct participation in the evil deed, but rather identifies with the sinful actions by willfully facilitating them. Advising a friend on how best to shoplift from a store, driving a friend to an abortion facility, allowing friends to have a wild drinking party in your house, and so on. Though the agent of implicit cooperation does not have a direct hand in the actual execution of the sin, the consent and cooperation implicate the person in that same evil action.

Material cooperation consists of an action that has a role to play in the accomplishment of the evil deed but lacks the deliberate consent to that same cooperative action. For example, the cashier in a large store that sells a wide assortment of items may need to collect payment for contraceptives, and thereby cooperate with the evil action of selling something that violates the sacredness of human sexuality. In this case, the cashier has no role to play in the decision to make contraceptives available, and thus would have no authority or influence in stopping their sales. On the contrary, a cashier in a sporting goods shop would not be morally permitted to sell a handgun to an individual who looked suspicious and showed signs of anger or instability. In this instance, due to the suspicious circumstances, the material cooperation would be wrong. Although the cashier does not intend a possible murder, the sale of a handgun is essential to act. As seen by these examples, each case needs to be analyzed separately, and a person under certain conditions may or may not be morally responsible for the material cooperation in an evil action.

Material cooperation in evil is only permissible when there are sufficiently serious reasons, when the cooperation is not essential to the evil action, and when the agent's intention is in contradiction to the same evil deed. The culpability of this kind of cooperation in evil depends on the proximity of the cooperative act to the actual evil action.

The Capture of Christ by Bouts. "Now the betrayer had given them a sign, saying, 'The one I shall kiss is the man; seize him and lead him away under guard.'" (Mk 14:44)
Formal cooperation in the sin is deliberate cooperation in an evil action or practice.

We may cooperate in an action that has unintended evil consequences if three conditions are fulfilled: First, the evil must not be a direct result of the cooperator's act; second, the cooperator must not intend the evil that occurs; and third, there must be no possibility of scandal.

A bus driver whose route passes an abortion facility knows from experience that at least some of the women he has picked up or dropped off at the bus stop nearest the facility probably have had abortions. The driver disapproves of abortion, and his contribution to the abortions is not a direct result of his employment as a bus driver. In this case, the bus driver is not committing a sin, although there is a very remote level of cooperation in evil. The more remote the cooperation in evil, the less culpable the act.

EFFECTS OF SIN

Concerning the effects of mortal and venial sins, the *Catechism of the Catholic Church* states the following:

> *Mortal sin* destroys charity in the heart of man...; it turns man away from God, who is his ultimate end and his beatitude....

> *Venial sin* allows charity to subsist, even though it offends and wounds it. (CCC 1855)

Effects of mortal sin. The principal effect of mortal sin is the loss of sanctifying grace together with the theological virtue of charity. Someone who has committed mortal sin has turned away from God in such a way that he has lost friendship with God. If an individual persists in this state, he incurs upon himself eternal damnation. The person in the state of mortal sin by his dispositions and actions has at least implicitly opted for eternal punishment which essentially consists in a permanent separation from God.

While a person is in the state of sanctifying grace, his good deeds merit an increase in sanctifying grace. The graces gained by these meritorious acts are lost upon committing mortal sin. This loss of grace occurs because the sanctifying grace merited through holy actions is completely relinquished through this choice of turning away from Jesus Christ.

It follows, then, that while an individual is in a state of mortal sin, he cannot merit any more grace until his or her mortal sin is remitted through the Sacrament of Penance. Upon being reconciled with God, the previous state of grace acquired through Baptism and augmented through meritorious deeds is fully restored.

An interior emptiness and profound disillusionment visit the person in mortal sin. With mortal sin comes a loss of freedom, where one becomes

The Flagellation by Pacher. "Pilate therefore said to him, '…Do you not know that I have power to release you, and power to crucify you?' Jesus answered him, 'You would have no power over me unless it had been given you from above; therefore he who delivered me to you has the greater sin.'" (Jn 19: 10-11)

enslaved to the passions and falls under the sway of the Evil One. Worst of all, the individual finds himself alienated from God and the everlasting life that awaits him.

Like a cancer that spreads throughout the body unless removed, mortal sin acts like an aggressive malignant tumor, quickly eating away at the subject's moral life. It is regretfully common that a person who persists in a mortally sinful state will commit other mortal sins before long, and even more serious ones. For example, a person who views impure images or watches immoral programs is more readily prompted to drink immoderately, become self-centered, lose ability for prayer, and become angry and cruel. Heinous crimes and heartrending family strife find their origins in the loss of union with God through mortal sins.

Only a sincere Confession of all mortal sins can restore the individual to the state of grace.

Effects of venial sin. One of the effects of deliberate venial sin is lukewarmness regarding the practice of the Gospel message. Venial sin dulls charity and interest in following Christ and renders the practice of the new commandment to love as Christ loved virtually impossible. If left unchecked, venial sin prepares the way to committing mortal sin by gradually eroding the love of God.

THE SACRAMENT OF RECONCILIATION

"The grace of the Holy Spirit confers upon us the righteousness of God."[18] Since the grace of conversion is a gift of God, *"no one can merit the initial grace* of forgiveness and justification."[19] Our justification was earned by the suffering, Death, and Resurrection of Jesus Christ and is bestowed freely in Baptism. Through grace, we receive the forgiveness of sin and sanctification and become adopted sons and daughters of God.

> Like conversion, justification has two aspects. Moved by grace, man turns toward God and away from sin, and so accepts forgiveness and righteousness from on high. (CCC 2018)

God comes to us and offers us his gift of redemption. God, however, in his plan of salvation, has chosen to associate us with his work of grace. By responding to his call and by cooperating with him, we can merit graces for ourselves and others. This includes not only spiritual goods, but temporal goods such as health and friendships.[20] In this manner, we can say that any merit we receive from our good works is due, first and foremost, to the grace of God, and only secondly to our active collaboration with him.[21]

GOD FORGIVES, SO WHY CONFESS?

Many have raised the question: "Why can God not forgive us without having to go to confession?"

It is true that God can forgive sins however he pleases. He is not constrained by the sacraments that he himself instituted through Christ. However, as followers of Christ, Christians cannot pick and choose how to be forgiven according to their own personal interests. Instead, they must follow those means given to them by Christ himself.

Jesus instituted the Sacrament of Reconciliation by instructing his apostles to forgive sins (Jn 20:23). This means that the penitent must seek God's forgiveness through his appointed ministers. The priest will absolve the penitent as long as there is sufficient repentance over the confessed sins and sufficient resolve to sin no more.

In addition to the spiritual benefits, this personal confession corresponds to the needs of the human person. We all have the need to unburden ourselves and to open our hearts, especially regarding actions that inflict painful guilt and regret of conscience. What better way is there of gaining the assurance of forgiveness and the knowledge that we are loved unconditionally by God than in hearing the words of Christ himself, spoken by the priest, "Your sins are forgiven"?

In light of the marvelous benefits of sacramental Confession to the spiritual life, individuals should avail themselves habitually and frequently of this Sacrament—monthly or even weekly. Joy, peace of mind, preparation for Holy Communion, and greater sensitivity of conscience are a few of the benefits that will result from the reception of

Justification involves the removal of the offense of sin by reason of Christ's sacrificial offering on the Cross. Before his redemptive Death and Resurrection, Original Sin, together with personal sins, left every individual alienated from God. This rift caused by sin was removed by Christ's suffering, Death, and Resurrection. The merits gained by Christ restored the relationship intended by God in creation. Justice or justification has been achieved because a supreme and acceptable sacrifice was offered for us. In Baptism, we are justified, receiving sanctifying grace and new life in Christ.

The call to conversion was a key theme in Jesus Christ's public ministry.[22] The many conversion accounts found in the Gospel beautifully attest to God's infinite mercy revealed by the heart of Christ. The Lord is offended by sin not because he incurs pain, but rather because of the damage brought upon ourselves. The power of Christ's Death and Resurrection are such that every sin, no matter how grievous, can be forgiven and taken away. All sins committed after Baptism can be forgiven through the Sacrament of Reconciliation through those same merits Christ won on the Cross.

> **He breathed on them, and said to them, "Receive the Holy Spirit. If you forgive the sins of any, they are forgiven; if you retain the sins of any, they are retained." (Jn 20: 22-23)**

The forgiveness of mortal sin and the subsequent removal of its destructive effects require recourse to the Sacrament of Reconciliation. For this Sacrament to restore a person to a state of grace, the person must have contrition and purpose of amendment, confessing all mortal sins, both in kind and number.

The confession of the specific kind of sin would involve giving enough of a description for the priest to assess the proper gravity and accountability for the sin. For example, there is a difference in gravity between confessing, "I didn't respect my parents as I should," and to say that, "I shouted and insulted my parents." Again, there is a difference between saying, "I lacked purity," and, "I looked at pornographic images." The person should also give a number or estimate the frequency of a specific mortal sin, since it is not the same to do something only once as opposed to many times or habitually.

> A member of the Christian faithful is obliged to confess in kind and number all grave sins committed after baptism and not yet remitted directly through the keys of the Church nor acknowledged in individual confession, of which the person has knowledge after diligent examination of conscience. (CIC, 988 §1)

Since venial sin does not sever one's friendship with Christ, its forgiveness or removal does not require the Sacrament of Reconciliation *per se*. This means that personal acts of contrition or efforts to follow Christ's teachings with implicit repentance can serve as a means for forgiveness. Nevertheless, the frequent confession even of venial sins is highly recommended.

The opportunity to be cleansed from sin through the Sacrament of Reconciliation is a great blessing and consolation. Many attest to the great relief and happiness of receiving forgiveness and having one's relationship with God restored. It is wonderful to realize that God will always give us his forgiving and healing embrace as long as we are contrite in the Sacrament of Reconciliation. Not only is it spiritually salutary to go to Confession, but it is also rewarding to experience the positive effects of unburdening oneself and having personal dignity restored.

CONTRITION

The forgiveness of sins results directly from God's gratuitous mercy. Without the Son of God becoming man and dying on the Cross, we would be mired in sin without hope of liberation or salvation.

Nevertheless, as illustrated in the Parable of the Prodigal Son, the Lord needs our sorrow or contrition in order to forgive us. It was only when the prodigal son approached his Father, saying, "Father, I have sinned against heaven and before you; I am no longer worthy to be called your son,"[23] that reconciliation and restoration of his sonship took place.

We will also recall from the story that the father never stopped looking for his son, and that once the son appeared, the father ran out to meet him. Likewise, God never stops loving us and giving us the grace to return to him. But, he leaves us free and asks that we take a step toward forgiveness.

Scenes from the Life of Christ: 19. Crucifixion by Giotto.
Without the Son of God becoming man and dying on the Cross, we would be mired in sin
without hope of liberation or salvation.

In the process of reconciliation, God's grace is indeed the most vital element. Nevertheless, personal sorrow for sin and the willingness to try to sin no more are indispensable. This sorrow for having offended God along with the firm purpose of avoiding sin is called *contrition*. Without contrition, a person cannot be forgiven, even in the Sacrament of Reconciliation.

There are two types of contrition: *perfect contrition* and *imperfect contrition*.

Perfect contrition is sorrow that springs from a perfect love for God and therefore sins are forgiven, even before we go to Confession—although, naturally, a perfect contrition will always include the intention to confess one's sins as soon as possible. However, because no one can be certain that he or she has perfect contrition, it is necessary to go to Confession anyway.

Imperfect contrition is sorrow for our sins not out of perfect love, but because we fear God's punishment. It is not true contrition if we are merely ashamed of our dishonor, or sorry only for the punishment we may incur from other persons, or just sorry that we got caught. Imperfect contrition does not forgive sins immediately, but is sufficient to obtain forgiveness when accompanied by sacramental absolution.

Included in the spirit of contrition is the commitment to avoid *near occasions of sin*. Near occasions of sin are situations and circumstances that will most likely entice an individual to sin.

These occasions of sin can be certain persons, places, or things that can easily prompt one to sin. Occasions may include going to a party where alcohol is known to be available, when one has a tendency to drink to excess; a boyfriend and girlfriend spending time alone, when privacy makes sexual temptation more likely to arise; hanging around with a certain group of friends whose foul language and bad habits may have a negative moral influence through peer pressure.

Common sense tells us that avoiding situations where sin is more likely to occur is the best way to reduce temptations and maintain virtue. A firm resolve to avoid sin warrants greater attention to staying away from opportunities for trouble. Contrition is not completely genuine and honest if it does not include a purpose of amendment and a willingness to stay out of harm's way, when overpowering temptations abound.

THE LAST THINGS

The Christian life is a journey towards God. It begins with Baptism, when we are incorporated into Christ and become adopted sons and daughters of God. It continues as we grow in the Faith, which is a process of progressive identification with Jesus Christ. Through prayer and the sacraments, our relationship with God continues to be nurtured. Through the work of the Holy Spirit, we are strengthened to follow the moral teachings of Christ, our moral compass, who guides us toward salvation.

The friendship or communion with God that a Christian experiences in this life fulfills the desires of the human heart and gives tremendous joy. This, however, is but a foretaste of the complete happiness that awaits us in Heaven, the proper destination and goal of the Christian journey. The ultimate hope of a child of God, therefore, is not glory and prosperity in this world, but eternal communion and happiness with God in Heaven.

"By his glorious Cross Christ has won salvation for all men."[24] The salvation that Christ won for us is offered to all people. However, this gift of salvation requires a response on our part. We respond by our faith and works. In creating our first parents, God endowed them with the gift of free will. While God calls each person into his friendship, each person is given the freedom to accept God's gift of salvation or to ignore or reject it.

The personal decision to accept the salvation offered by God and to follow the moral teachings of Jesus Christ must be made in this life, for at death, the time in which we have to choose is ended.

> *Death is the end of earthly life.* Our lives are measured by time, in the course of which we change, grow old and, as with all living beings on earth, death seems like the normal end of life. That aspect of death lends urgency to our lives: remembering our mortality helps us realize that we have only a limited time in which to bring our lives to fulfillment. (CCC 1007)

Particular Judgment

> Every man receives his eternal recompense in his immortal soul from the moment of his death in a particular judgment by Christ, the judge of the living and the dead. (CCC 1051)

At the moment of death, Christ will judge each person for the choices and actions he or she made in his or her life. This is referred to as the *particular judgment*. If we die seeking God, in a state of grace, we shall enjoy his friendship for all eternity. If we die having rejected God, in a state of mortal sin, then we shall be separated from him for all eternity.

It is sometimes easy to become focused only on the things of this life. Our responsibilities, cares, and worries often occupy our days, preventing us from keeping the true goal of the Christian life in the forefront of our minds. By reflecting on the truth that each of us shall one day stand before Christ in the particular judgment to answer for each of our thoughts, words, and deeds, should lead us to better evaluate the choices we make in this life.

The best preparation for the particular judgment is to realize that we are continually in the presence of God, who sees our actions, hears our words, and knows our thoughts. Through a daily examination of conscience, we can evaluate our lives and make the required spiritual changes. Through the frequent

The Last Judgment, Altarpiece by Master of the Bambino Vispo.

The Last Judgment by Lochner. At the moment of death, Christ will judge each person for the choices and actions he or she made in his or her life.

reception of the Sacrament of Reconciliation, a person, in a certain sense, anticipates the particular judgment that he or she will receive after death.[25] "In converting to Christ through penance and faith, the sinner passes from death to life and 'does not come into judgment.'"[26]

At the moment of the particular judgment, the eternal fate of our souls is decided. We will be destined for eternal communion with God in Heaven, either directly or following the purification of our soul in Purgatory, or for eternal separation from God in Hell.

Heaven

> Those who die in God's grace and friendship and are perfectly purified live for ever with Christ. They are like God for ever, for they "see him as he is," face to face.[27] (CCC 1023)

Those who have responded to God's gift of salvation, die in a state of grace, and have been perfectly purified, either in this life or in Purgatory, will live in the company of God forever. *Heaven* is the state of eternal happiness in which a person shares in the life and love of the Blessed Trinity. In communion with the angels and saints, a soul enjoys a state of perfect happiness,[28] and in the Kingdom of God, the saints will reign with Christ forever.

This perfect communion with God in Heaven is a mystery of the Faith that is beyond human understanding. "Scripture speaks of it in images: life, light, peace, wedding feast, wine of the kingdom, the Father's house, the heavenly Jerusalem, paradise."[29]

However, these analogies pale in comparison to the joy that actually awaits the blessed in Heaven. In this life, we cannot see God in his magnificence. His presence is veiled. Only through Divine Revelation received in faith can we have an understanding of the happiness that will be enjoyed in Heaven.

What no eye has seen, nor ear heard, nor the heart of man conceived, what God has prepared for those who love him. (1 Cor 2: 9)

In Heaven, the blessed will see God face-to-face and contemplate him in the fullness of glory. This is called the "beatific vision."

Purgatory

All who die in God's grace and friendship, but still imperfectly purified, are indeed assured of their eternal salvation; but after death they undergo purification, so as to achieve the holiness necessary to enter the joy of heaven. (CCC 1030)

Sin has a *double consequence*. Grave sin deprives us of communion with God and therefore makes us incapable of eternal life, the privation of which is called the "eternal punishment" of sin. On the other hand every sin, even venial, entails an unhealthy attachment to creatures, which must be purified either here on earth, or after death in the state called Purgatory. This purification frees one from what is called the "temporal punishment" of sin.[30] (CCC 1472)

St. Francis Rescuing Souls From Purgatory.
The Church reminds us of our obligation to pray for the holy souls in Purgatory and offer masses on their behalf.

Those who die in a state of grace (in God's friendship) are assured of eternal life with God in Heaven. If, however, there is any remaining temporal punishment due to sin not yet remitted, it must be purified before entering Heaven. This purification of the temporal punishment due for sins, after death, is called *Purgatory*. By purifying us of all imperfections before we enter his presence in Heaven, God is showing us not only his justice but also his great love and mercy.

Since all temporal punishment due to sin must be satisfied before a soul, in the state of grace, may enter into the presence of God in Heaven, we should strive to repair the damage caused by sin in this life. God provides us this opportunity through works of mercy and charity, prayer, the sacramental life, mortification, and other penitential practices.[31]

The faithful are also offered the possibility of gaining indulgences, which is the remission of the temporal punishment due to sins already forgiven. A partial indulgence remits part of the temporal punishment due to sin, while a plenary indulgence remits all of the temporal punishment due to sin.[32] The prescribed conditions for gaining an indulgence require that a person have the proper disposition. For a plenary indulgence, this includes being free from all attachment to sin, including venial sin.

Indulgences may be applied by a person to remit his or her own temporal punishment due to sin, or may be applied for the benefit of the holy souls in Purgatory, who are greatly aided by the prayers and sacrifices that are offered for them.

From the beginning the Church has honored the memory of the dead and offered prayers in suffrage for them, above all the Eucharistic sacrifice, so that, thus purified, they may attain the beatific vision of God.[33] (CCC 1032)

The practice of praying and offering sacrifice for the dead finds its origin in the Old Testament. "Therefore [Judas Maccabeus] made atonement for the dead, that they might be delivered from their sin."[34]

The Church reminds us of our obligation to pray for the holy souls in Purgatory and offer masses on their behalf. This spiritual practice is especially remembered in the masses of All Souls Day (The Commemoration of all the Faithful Departed), celebrated on November 2, and is found in the spiritual works of mercy, which remind us to pray for the living and the dead. Believing in the communion of saints, we can be assured that when they enter the presence of God in Heaven, they will remember those who offered prayers for them.

Hell

To die in mortal sin without repenting and accepting God's merciful love means remaining separated from him for ever by our own free choice. This state of definitive self-exclusion from communion with God and the blessed is called "hell." (CCC 1033)

All souls in Hell suffer the loss of eternal communion with God and also suffer punishments according to the sins they committed here on earth. This state of separation from God is eternal, and there can be no repentance. Just as the blessed will enjoy eternal love and joy, those in Hell will suffer eternal hatred and unhappiness. With Satan and his demons, as well as the other lost souls, those in Hell will only be able to express hatred and despair for turning away from God.

Jesus often speaks of "Gehenna," of "the unquenchable fire" reserved for those who to the end of their lives refuse to believe and be converted, where both soul and body can be lost.[35] Jesus solemnly proclaims that he "will send his angels, and they will gather... all evil doers, and throw them into the furnace of fire,"[36] and that he will pronounce the condemnation: "Depart from me, you cursed, into the eternal fire!"[37] (CCC 1034)

The Last Judgment and the Kingdom of God

When the Son of man comes in his glory, and all the angels with him, then he will sit on his glorious throne. (Mt 25:31)

In the Creed, we profess the belief that Christ will come again to judge the living and the dead. This is known as the *General* or *Last Judgment*. When Christ returns, all shall rise in their own bodies, and all things shall be revealed. At that time, we shall see with clarity God's mercy and justice. We shall see the secret disposition of our hearts and the effects

The Rich Man [Dives] in Hades. The story of the sinful and unrepentant rich man and Lazarus is told in Luke 16:19-31. "The rich man...in Hades, being in torment,...lifted up his eyes, and saw Abraham far off and Lazarus in his bosom."

Christ Pantocrator and the Last Judgment, mosaic in the Baptistry of St. John in Florence.
The saved are shown leaving their tombs in joy at Christ's right hand and the damned are shown facing their
punishments at Christ's left hand.

of all of our good and bad deeds. Each person shall be rewarded or punished according to what he or she has done in this life "according to his acceptance or refusal of grace."[38] The faithful shall be glorified in body and soul and shall reign with Christ in the Kingdom of God.[39]

> "We believe that the souls of all who die in Christ's grace . . . are the People of God beyond death. On the day of resurrection, death will be definitively conquered, when these souls will be reunited with their bodies."[40] (CCC 1052)

God's plan of redemption to establish the *Kingdom of God* on earth will come to its fullness at the end of time.[41] The Church will be perfected and the universe transformed into a heavenly city, a New Jerusalem, and God will live among his people.[42]

Keeping our eye on our eternal destination helps us to choose the correct course while on earth. Christ has shown us the way, but we must respond to his gift of salvation and follow him.

> The affirmations of Sacred Scripture and the teachings of the Church on the subject of hell are a *call to the responsibility* incumbent upon man to make use of his freedom in view of his eternal destiny. They are at the same time an urgent *call to conversion*: "Enter by the narrow gate; for the gate is wide and the way is easy, that leads to destruction, and those who enter by it are many. For the gate is narrow and the way is hard, that leads to life, and those who find it are few."[43] (CCC 1036)

SECTION II:
THE COMMANDMENTS AND THE BEATITUDES

THE TEN COMMANDMENTS AND THE TEACHING OF CHRIST

The Mosaic Law, which took the form of the Ten Commandments, set the Jewish people apart from the rest of the ancient world. For the Israelites, the Commandments were the basic guidelines governing every aspect of human conduct—directives on the pursuit of moral good and the avoidance of evil.

Book of Deuteronomy Frontispiece from the Bible of San Paolo Fuori le Mura (St. Paul's Outside the Walls in Rome), ca. 870. It is the most extensively illustrated surviving Carolingian Bible. The Book of Deuteronomy reiterates and synthesizes God's commandments which are known in Judaism as the "Ten Words" or the Decalogue.

In the New Testament, Jesus Christ teaches that the moral law revealed to the Chosen People through Moses is a stepping stone for a higher morality. The New Covenant includes the Mosaic Law but exceeds it and thus perfects it, finding its eloquent expression in the Beatitudes and the Sermon on the Mount. The moral law transmitted to Moses serves as a preparation to fulfill the baptismal mandate of the universal call to holiness.

The chapters on the Commandments will analyze the meaning of these moral directives that were explicitly and directly revealed by God. They will also examine the applications of the Ten Commandments in the preaching of Jesus and his Great Commandment of love.

When Moses went up to Mount Sinai to pray, God manifested himself and asked Moses to prepare the Israelites for the Covenant he was going to establish with them. This Covenant would make the Israelites his Chosen People. Through this Covenant, God would give his people a clear code of conduct.

The Revelation of the Ten Commandments is a clear expression of the moral law written on every human heart. For this reason, the *Catechism of the Catholic Church* states:

The Decalogue contains a privileged expression of the natural law. It is made known to us by divine revelation and by human reason. (CCC 2080)

The Israelites knew that their destiny—for better or worse—was tied to the fulfillment of the commandments. This was their history. When the people of Israel worshiped God with fidelity, they prospered; but when they were not faithful, God permitted them to suffer.

We do not necessarily see ourselves suffering when we do wrong and prospering when we do good, but this does in fact happen to us—remember, a moral act always changes us for the better or for the worse. When we keep God's commandments, we affirm our faithfulness and open ourselves up to the grace of the Holy Spirit. In effect, we tell God that we accept his will in our lives.[44]

The Old Law, which is summarized in the Ten Commandments, was the first stage of God's Revelation to his people. Its precepts convey many of the truths contained in the natural law, i.e., the law written on the human heart, accessible to all people. However, because of Original Sin, mankind did not fully understand

THE TEN COMMANDMENTS

1. I am the LORD your God: you shall not have strange gods before me.

2. You shall not take the name of the LORD your God in vain.

3. Remember to keep holy the LORD'S Day.

4. Honor your father and your mother.

5. You shall not kill.

6. You shall not commit adultery.

7. You shall not steal.

8. You shall not bear false witness against your neighbor.

9. You shall not covet your neighbor's wife.

10. You shall not covet your neighbor's goods.

Moses on Mount Sinai by Gérôme. As expressions of the natural law, the obligations revealed in the Ten Commandments are grave and apply universally to all people.

the natural law and needed God's Divine Revelation. Additionally, the Old Law was a preparation for the New Law that would be revealed by Jesus Christ.[45]

As expressions of the natural law, the obligations revealed in the Ten Commandments are grave and apply universally to all people. However, these obligations apply not only to serious moral issues, but to matters which, in themselves, are light.[46] For example, while the Fifth Commandment specifically states that it is wrong to kill, abusive language is also forbidden, "but would be a grave offense only as a result of circumstances or the offender's intention."[47]

This "New Law," also known as the "law of love," is the grace of the Holy Spirit and aims at reforming the very heart of man. In this manner, it surpasses and fulfills the precepts of the Old Law. Its teachings are found primarily in the message of Christ in the Sermon on the Mount, and its grace is communicated to us through the sacraments.[48]

Despite the novel message preached by Jesus, he did not come to abolish the law, but to perfect it. "Think not that I have come to abolish the law and the prophets; I have come not to abolish them but to fulfill them. For truly, I say to you, till heaven and earth pass away, not an iota, not a dot, will pass from the law until all is accomplished."[49] Following the teachings of Christ, Christians have always been admonished to keep the precepts found in the Decalogue. In the second century, St. Irenæus of Lyons stated:

> The Lord prescribed the love of God and taught justice towards our neighbor so that man might not be unjust, or unworthy of God. Thus, with the Decalogue, God was preparing man to be his friend and to have the same heart for his friend....The words of the Decalogue persist also among us. Far from being abolished, they have received an amplification and development in the Incarnation of the Lord.[50]

The Ten Commandments are enriched by the life and teachings of Jesus Christ and given life by the Holy Spirit. For example, the acceptance and worship of one God is enhanced by acknowledging the love of God as Father and God as a Trinity of Divine Persons. Respect for life is enriched by the new commandment to love all people, including our enemies, as Christ loved us.

Christ's teachings on human sexuality go beyond the simple prohibition of adultery, but seek interior chastity of thoughts and desires.[51] Likewise, they no longer merely forbid injuring one another through malicious acts, but seek a spirit of charity and an active love of neighbor to be played out in word and deed. Seen in this light, the Ten Commandments become the framework upon which the rich moral teachings of Jesus can be better understood.

THE PRECEPTS OF THE CHURCH

Closely linked to the Ten Commandments as well as the teachings of Christ are the Precepts of the Catholic Church. The Magisterium of the Church, with the guidance of the Holy Spirit, has provided applications to the summary of the Ten Commandments expressed in the two greatest commandments—to love God with your whole heart, and to love your neighbor as yourself.

1. You shall attend Mass on Sundays and Holy Days of Obligation and rest from servile labor. This precept directs the faithful to keep holy the day of the Lord's Resurrection, to worship God by participating in Mass every Sunday and Holy Day of Obligation, and to avoid activities that would hinder renewal of soul and body on the Lord's Day—such as needless work and business activities or unnecessary shopping.

2. You shall confess your sins at least once a year. This precept encourages the faithful to receive the Sacrament of Reconciliation regularly—minimally, to receive the Sacrament at least once a year. Annual Confession is obligatory only if a mortal or grievous sin has been committed.

3. You shall receive the Sacrament of the Eucharist at least during the Easter season. This precept encourages the faithful to lead a sacramental life by receiving Holy Communion frequently—minimally, to receive Holy Communion at least once a year, between the First Sunday of Lent and Trinity Sunday.

4. You shall observe the days of fasting and abstinence established by the Church. Encouraging the faithful to a life of penance and self-denial the Church asks that they abstain from meat and fast from food on the appointed days. Ash Wednesday and Good Friday are obligatory days of fasting and abstinence. Fridays in Lent are obligatory days of abstinence. Fridays throughout the year, unless they fall on a feast day or solemnity, are designated as days of penance left to the discretion of the individual.

5. You shall help to provide for the needs of the Church. This assistance given to the Church includes one's own parish community and parish priests, the universal Church, and the pope.

The Resurrection of Christ by Veronese.
Closely linked to the Ten Commandments as well as the teachings of Christ are the Precepts of the Catholic Church.

In addition to these precepts, the Church instructs the faithful to study Catholic teaching in preparation for the Sacrament of Confirmation, to be confirmed, and to continue their studies afterward in order to better advance the mission of Christ. Those persons who wish to become Catholic receive instruction in RCIA (Rite of Christian Initiation for Adults) and are encouraged to continue their religious education after receiving the Sacraments of Initiation. Married couples are asked to observe the marriage laws of the Church, to give

THE BEATITUDES

✣ Blessed are the poor in spirit, for theirs is the kingdom of heaven.

✣ Blessed are those who mourn, for they shall be comforted.

✣ Blessed are the meek, for they shall inherit the earth.

✣ Blessed are those who hunger and thirst for righteousness, for they shall be satisfied.

✣ Blessed are the merciful, for they shall obtain mercy.

✣ Blessed are the pure in heart, for they shall see God.

✣ Blessed are the peacemakers, for they shall be called sons of God.

✣ Blessed are those who are persecuted for righteousness' sake, for theirs is the kingdom of heaven. (Mt 5: 3-12)

✣ Blessed are you when men revile you and persecute you and utter all kinds of evil against you falsely on my account. Rejoice and be glad, for your reward is great in heaven.

religious training (by example and word) to their children, and to use parish schools and catechetical programs. By nature of their Christian vocation, all Catholics are asked to join in the missionary spirit and apostolate of the Church.

In the Precepts of the Catholic Church, the Church acknowledges that the origin of the moral life is the grace of God, which is given to us by the Holy Spirit through the sacraments. For this reason, the precepts encourage the frequent reception of the sacraments, especially the Sacraments of the Eucharist and Reconciliation.

THE BEATITUDES AS THE PERFECTION OF THE MORAL LAW

God created us to be happy, both here on earth and in eternity. True happiness on earth is only possible through union with Jesus Christ, who gives us a share in his very life. His life is manifested by a deep love for God and loving service to others. The Beatitudes exemplify this spirit of love and self-giving, which will bring us "bliss"—the meaning of "beatitude," as we noted in a previous chapter. In this way, the Beatitudes respond to the desire for happiness placed within the human heart by God himself.[52] As great as this bliss may be, however, it is only a small anticipation of the perfect happiness which he has prepared for us in Heaven.

In the Old Testament, Abraham was assured that he would be blessed with fruitful lands and innumerable descendants. However, the promises made to Abraham are mere figures of the inexhaustible blessings of God's Kingdom, which are spiritual. The Beatitudes fulfill God's promises by ordering them to the Kingdom of Heaven.[53] The possessions promised by the Beatitudes transcend any material goods. Self-renunciation and discipleship with Christ are what bring us that joy and peace that the world cannot give.

> The Beatitudes take up and fulfill God's promises from Abraham on by ordering them to the Kingdom of heaven. They respond to the desire for happiness that God has placed in the human heart. (CCC 1725)

The Beatitudes are the perfection of the moral law. The divine mandate for proper moral conduct is a means to living a higher law. The commandments provide an indispensable level of freedom from falsehood, dishonesty, anger, deceit, resentment, lust, and other sinful dispositions so that the subject is enabled to follow Jesus Christ.

In a sense, the Beatitudes are directives aimed at the human spirit so that it is conformed to the heart of Christ himself, enabling us to have a heart that is capable of loving as God loves. Detachment from material possessions, a humble disposition, and a pure and meek heart are the components of the new commandment to love as Christ loved. In fact, it is the practice of these Beatitudes that brings about a profound union with Christ and the ability to reflect his light and joy.

> It is precisely those who are poor in worldly terms, those thought of as lost souls, who are the truly fortunate ones, the blessed, who have every reason to rejoice and exult in the midst of their sufferings. The Beatitudes are promises resplendent with the new image of the world and of man inaugurated by Jesus, his "transformation of values"....When man begins to see and to live from God's perspective, when he is a companion on Jesus' way, then he lives by new standards....Jesus brings joy into the midst of affliction. (Pope Benedict XVI, *Jesus of Nazareth*, 71-72)

"It is precisely those who are poor in worldly terms, those thought of as lost souls, who are the truly fortunate ones, the blessed, who have every reason to rejoice and exult in the midst of their sufferings."
—Pope Benedict XVI, *Jesus of Nazareth*

The Mount of Beatitudes and the Church of the Beatitudes by the Sea of Galilee in modern time.
Built in 1938, the Roman Catholic Chapel has an octagonal shape to represent the eight blessings of the Beatitudes.

In *Veritatis Splendor*, Pope John Paul II taught that the Beatitudes proclaimed in the first part of the Sermon on the Mount paint a verbal portrait of Christ. These Beatitudes command a disposition of the heart that radically breaks new ground in moral teaching. The word *blessed* is included in all of the Beatitudes, and its meaning is at the heart of Christ's entire message.

The practice of the Beatitudes requires the powerful assistance of the Holy Spirit together with a genuine struggle to respond to their demands. The Beatitudes essentially describe the call to holiness, an invitation to be a light of the world through the love of Christ.

Blessed are the poor in spirit, for theirs is the kingdom of Heaven. The first beatitude sets the stage for the next seven. This spirit of poverty and detachment is an essential part of the Gospel message. To possess the Kingdom of God, we need to be liberated from inordinate and unhealthy attachment to material possessions, popularity, comfort, and even personal plans.

Blessed are those who mourn, for they shall be comforted. An inevitable side effect of finding true joy and peace is a sorrow for so many who are deprived of the riches of the Gospel, "like sheep without a shepherd." Living the Gospel sometimes brings suffering in the form of rejection and scorn. The Lord promises that such sadness will be turned into joy.

Blessed are the meek, for they shall inherit the earth. In light of the understanding that the Kingdom of God is not of this world, this verse falls in line with Christ's assurance of ultimate victory. It is through the lived example of a kind and meek heart along with a selfless spirit of service that the Christian can draw others to Christ's way of life.

Blessed are those who hunger and thirst for righteousness, for they shall be satisfied. Idealism and magnanimity characterize the disposition of someone closely united to the Lord. Hunger and thirst for righteousness serve as the driving force of a true Christian life. The apostle of the Gospel longs to see many people enjoy the peace, happiness, justice, and healing promised by Christ. The Lord promises that in spite of hostility toward the Gospel message, the desire and zeal to bring Christ to others will eventually find fulfillment.

Blessed are the merciful, for they shall obtain mercy. The individual who practices mercy not only will obtain mercy from God for himself or herself, but also will be loved by others. Anyone with a merciful attitude will enjoy a special credibility when speaking about Jesus Christ.

Blessed are the pure in heart, for they shall see God. Many people lose their capacity to pray and to see the image of God in others because they are leading a self-centered and carnal life. The self-control brought about by the virtue of purity allows the person to see Christ in prayer, in suffering, and in the lives of others.

Blessed are the peacemakers, for they shall be called sons of God. Jesus promises peace to all who truly follow him. A person united to Jesus will spread peace to everyone around him or her. In imitation of the Son of God, the perfect peacemaker, those who radiate peace are considered children of God.

Blessed are those who are persecuted for righteousness' sake, for theirs is the kingdom of Heaven. The final beatitude says that those who encounter suffering through their Christian witness will be blessed with the ultimate glory of everlasting life. Suffering for Christ and with Christ is the secret power of the Christian evangelizer. The Cross transforms those who lovingly embrace it and, in turn, transforms the world.

The *Catechism of the Catholic Church* offers these insights into the Beatitudes:

> The Beatitudes depict the countenance of Jesus Christ and portray his charity. They express the vocation of the faithful associated with the glory of his Passion and Resurrection: they shed light on the actions and attitudes characteristic of the Christian life: they are the paradoxical promises that sustain hope in the midst of tribulations; they proclaim the blessings and rewards already secured, however dimly, for Christ's disciples; they have begun in the lives of the Virgin Mary and all the saints. (CCC 1717)

CONCLUSION

Today, in a period of history in which the reality of sin is being denied and a general indifference to moral evil prevails, it is particularly important that the Christian strive to be Christlike in his or her conduct among family, friends, and acquaintances.

Christians, by virtue of Baptism, have a mission to be witnesses to the truth. Sin has always existed, and Christ will always be there to forgive sinners and bring them back. The surest way to evangelize others is to strive to imitate Christ in all one's actions. Through God's grace, personal holiness is possible for all faithful members of the Church.

Christians know that when they obey the Ten Commandments and live according to Christ's teachings in the Beatitudes, they do more than just fulfill the moral content that fortifies them. They also live in union with Jesus Christ by the power of the Holy Spirit.

The Church, in presenting the Decalogue and the Beatitudes to every culture, performs a great service for all of humanity. At times, people lose their direction in life and forget or obscure the fundamental elements of the moral life. According to some theologians, this was precisely the moral situation of humanity at the time of God's Revelation to Moses:

> [Because so many of the Israelites were] in the state of sin, a full explanation of the commandments of the Decalogue was necessary because of the obscurity of the light of reason and the deviation of the will. (St. Bonaventure, *Commentaries on the Four Books of Sentences of Master Peter Lombard*, IV, 37, 1-3)

Additionally, there is need for the Church to remind people of every age that simply avoiding evil and satisfying our duties to our neighbors in a minimalist way can never be acceptable if we wish to have a truly just society. Here lies the importance of the Beatitudes: they point the way to a truly free, happy, and peaceful existence based on the love of Christ.

SUPPLEMENTARY READING

1. All Sin is an Offense against God

It is not difficult to see how certain sins—idolatry, for example—offend God. But all immoral acts offend God. Treating one's neighbor unfairly is an offense against God. But why? How is it that every kind of immorality concerns God?

In considering this question, it is necessary to put aside anthropomorphic notions. God is not offended as we are. He does not get angry in the way we do, his feelings are not hurt, he does not suffer wounded pride. Yet our sins do offend him. How?

We begin by considering our relationship with God in the context of the covenant. God offers us the covenant for our good, for the sake of our human well-being. When we do moral evil, we act against God's love, contrary to his will. Even apart from the covenant, moreover, one who sins sets aside reason and so implicitly sets aside God, the source and meaning and value in creation. Sinners, as it were, declare their independence of anything beyond themselves, including God. In that sense, too, sin is an offense against God.

—Germain Grisez and Russell Shaw, *Fulfillment in Christ*, p. 154.

2. The Abandonment of the Moral Law

Sin has become almost everywhere today one of those subjects that is not spoken about. Religious education of whatever kind does its best to evade it. Theater and films use the word ironically or in order to entertain. Sociology and psychology attempt to unmask it as an illusion or a complex. Even the law is trying to get by more and more without the concept of guilt. It prefers to make use of sociological language, which turns the concept of good and evil into statistics and in its place distinguishes between normative and non-normative behavior. Implicit here is the possibility that the statistical proportions will themselves change: what is presently non-normative could one day become the rule; indeed, perhaps one should even strive to make the non-normative normal.

In such an atmosphere of quantification, the whole idea of the moral has accordingly been generally abandoned. This is a logical development if it is true that there is no standard for human beings to use as a model—something not discovered by us but coming from the inner goodness of creation.

—Joseph Cardinal Ratzinger, *In The Beginning*, pp. 78-79

3. Sin is a Personal Act

Sin, in the proper sense, is always a *personal act*, since it is an act of freedom on the part of an individual person, and not properly of a group or community. This individual may be conditioned, incited, and influenced by numerous and powerful external factors. He may also be subjected to tendencies, defects, and habits linked with his personal condition. In not a few cases, such external and internal factors may attenuate, to a greater of lesser degree, the guilt. But it is a truth of faith, also confirmed by our experience and reason, that the human person is free. This truth cannot be disregarded in order to place the blame for individuals' sins on external factors such as structures, systems, or other people. Above all, this would be to deny the person's dignity and freedom, which are manifested—even though in a negative and disastrous way—also in this responsibility for sin committed. Hence there is nothing so personal and untransferable in each individual as merit for virtue or responsibility for sin.

As a personal act, sin has its first and most important consequences in the *sinner himself*: that is, in his relationship with God, who is the very foundation of human life; and also in his spirit, weakening his will and clouding his intellect.

—*Reconciliatio et Pænitentia*, 16

4. On the Cardinal Virtues and Theological Virtues

Here one discerns how the account of the cardinal virtues (prudence, temperance, fortitude, justice) and the theological virtues (faith, hope, and charity) provides the context to understand spiritual growth. One prays and strives to develop virtue so as not to fall beneath that minimal threshold of charity indicated by the final six

SUPPLEMENTARY READING Continued

negative precepts of the Decalogue—but virtue is ordered far beyond this minimal threshold. One needs virtue not merely to avoid sin (and surmount obstacles), but to enable one to move powerfully and joyously toward the ends of a good life—to blossom in enacting the love of God and neighbor. The moral virtues aid the moralist and the catechist to enumerate in concrete and specific ways the right way to fulfill the commandment of love.

— Augustine DiNoia, OP; Gabriel O'Donnell, OP; Romanus Cessario, O.P.; Peter John Cameron, OP *The Love that Never Ends* (Huntington, IN: Our Sunday Visitor, 1996), p. 119.

5. The Personal Invitation of God's Love

If man, then must be a personal spirit able to exist and act on the foundation of a natural structure and reality, he must also be open to the personal invitation of God's love. He must have the capacity for the infinite; he must be a being not closed in upon himself but able to go out in knowledge and love to a personal encounter with the personal God. The natures of created beings lesser than man are not open in this way to God, for lower creatures cannot transcend themselves; they are enclosed, in a sense, in their own natural being. But by his nature, man is capable of going out of himself to meet God. He is created in such a way as to be able to enter into relationship with the divine persons. Not only is man capable of this in an absolute sense; he is so constituted that he can welcome God in virtue of his own deepest longings and desires.

— P. Gregory Stevens, OSB. *The Life of Grace* (Englewood Cliffs, NJ: Prentice-Hall, 1963), p. 69.

"Blessed are the meek, for they shall inherit the earth."

Mosaic in the early tenth century Monastery of Hosios Loukas, on the slopes of Mount Helicon, Greece.
"If I then, your Lord and Teacher, have washed your feet, you also ought to wash one another's feet. For I have given you an example, that you also should do as I have done to you." (Jn 13:14-15)

VOCABULARY

ABSTINENCE
Refers to the obligation to abstain from something, typically food or drink. Every Friday is a day of penitence in the Catholic Church; and Catholics are specifically obliged to abstain from meat on Ash Wednesday and every Friday of Lent.

ACTUAL SIN
A thought, word, deed, or omission contrary to God's eternal law. It is a human act that presumes (a) knowledge of wrongdoing, (b) awareness of malice in one's conduct and (c) consent of the will. It damages a person's relationship with God.

BEATITUDE
Happiness or blessedness, especially the eternal happiness of Heaven, which is the vision of God and partaking of the divine nature. This is the greatest human desire.

BEATITUDES
The teachings of Jesus in the Sermon on the Mount on the meaning and way to true happiness (cf. Mt 5: 3-12). These are at the heart of Jesus' preaching and fulfill the promises of God starting with Abraham.

COMMANDMENT
A norm of moral or religious action. The Ten Commandments were given by God through Moses.

CONCUPISCENCE
Human appetites or desires remain disordered due to the temporal consequences of Original Sin. This remains even after Baptism and constitutes an inclination to sin. This term is often used to refer to desires resulting from strong sensual urges or attachment to created things.

CONVERSION
A radical reorientation of one's whole life away from sin and evil and toward God. This is a central element of Christ's preaching, of the Church's ministry of evangelization, and of the Sacrament of Reconciliation.

COVENANT
A solemn agreement between people or between God and man involving mutual commitments and guarantees.

DECALOGUE
From the Greek for "ten sayings," the Ten Commandments given by God through Moses.

DIVINE REVELATION
Divine Revelation is primarily God's communication of his divine life, so that man can know him and thereby respond to his love. The culmination of Divine Revelation centers on Jesus Christ, the Son of God made man. The truths of Divine Revelation are transmitted through Scripture and Tradition.

FASTING
Mortification by deprivation of food. This is an ancient religious practice that denies the desires of the flesh in order to strengthen the spirit.

FORMAL COOPERATION
A deliberate assistance to another person in the commission of evil.

FORMAL SIN
Sin that is freely and deliberately committed. It involves knowledge of the evil of the act and freedom to avoid it.

HABITUAL SIN
A permanent state of culpability caused by the frequent commission of actual sins.

HOLY DAYS OF OBLIGATION
A Sunday or other feast day of importance that Christians are obliged to keep holy. Minimally, attending Mass and refraining from activities that impede the worship of God are expected.

IDOLATRY
The worship or adoration due God alone paid to images "made with hands" or any created object; this is forbidden by the First Commandment. This is distinct from veneration given to saints and holy objects implicitly allowed by the Incarnation as defined at the Seventh Ecumenical Council (Nicæa II, AD 787).

VOCABULARY Continued

IMPERFECT CONTRITION
Attrition. Sorrow of the soul and detestation for the sin committed together with the resolution not to sin again as a result of being sorry for sins due to fear of God's punishment.

INTRINSIC EVIL
An act that is evil in and of itself and never justifiable, regardless of situation or circumstance.

JUSTICE
One of the four cardinal virtues, this refers to observance of the divine law. This virtue is used to administer to God and each person his due.

KINGDOM OF GOD
There are two senses to this term. There is the heavenly kingdom of God, Heaven itself; there is also the call to establish the kingdom of God on earth, which means to work toward a world of complete love, harmony, peace, and justice.

MAGISTERIUM
The name given to the ordinary and universal teaching authority of the pope and the bishops in communion with him, who guide the members of the Church without error in matters of faith and morals through the interpretation of Sacred Scripture and Tradition.

MATERIAL COOPERATION
An action that plays a role in an evil deed but lacks the deliberate consent to that same cooperative action.

MORTAL SIN
A grave offense against God that destroys a person's relationship with him by severing that person from divine love. It destroys charity in the heart of man; it turns man away from God, who is his ultimate end and his beatitude, by preferring an inferior good to him.

NEW COVENANT
The new "dispensation" or order, established by God in Jesus Christ, to succeed and perfect the Old Covenant.

OCCASION OF SIN
A person, place, thing, or situation that generally leads to temptation.

OLD COVENANT
The Mosaic Law, encapsulated as the Ten Commandments, and its stipulation from God to the Israelites that "I will be your God, and you will be my people."

PERFECT CONTRITION
Sorrow of the soul and detestation for the sin committed together with the resolution not to sin again as a result of being sorry for sins due to a love for God above all else.

PERSONAL SIN
Sin that results from deliberation and an act of the will with knowledge.

PHYSICAL EVIL
An evil that is committed by an act as opposed to an interior attitude.

REDEMPTION
The possibility of spending eternity in Heaven, made possible by the Incarnation, Death, and Resurrection of Christ.

REPENTANCE
True sorrow for one's own sins and the firm resolution to avoid all sin in the future.

RIGHTEOUSNESS
Justice; uprightness; conformity of life to the requirements of the divine or moral law; virtue; integrity.

SACRAMENT OF RECONCILIATION
Also called Penance or Confession. The Sacrament by which Christ forgives sins. Jesus gave his Apostles—who passed it on to their successors down to this day—the power to forgive and retain sins. This Sacrament is administered only by bishops and priests.

VOCABULARY Continued

SALVATION
The Redemption and the promise of Heaven brought about by the Death and Resurrection of Jesus, our discipleship in Christ, and our commitment to seeking holiness and avoiding sin.

SIN
A transgression of the Divine Law and an offense against God involving the individual's knowledge and will.

SIN OF COMMISSION
Sin by means of committing an evil act such as theft or murder.

SIN OF OMISSION
Sin by means of failure to commit a good act such as the failure to forgive someone who wronged us.

VENIAL SIN
An offense against the law and love of God that does not deprive the soul of sanctifying grace, but weakens a person's love for God and neighbor.

Return of the Prodigal Son by Tissot.
The moral emptiness which results from the pursuit of selfish goals and the rejection of God's will is wonderfully depicted in the Parable of the Prodigal Son as told in Luke 15: 11-32.

STUDY QUESTIONS

1. In what way were Adam and Eve created differently from any of their descendants except for Jesus and Mary?

2. What was the Original Sin? In what way are the sins that we commit today comparable to Original Sin?

3. What are the effects of Original Sin in our lives? What are some concrete manifestations of this sin?

4. If God knew that Adam and Eve would sin, introducing evil into the world, why would he create us?

5. Explain the terms "physical evil" and "moral evil."

6. What is St. Augustine's definition of sin? Explain Original Sin in terms of this definition.

7. What is the "natural law"?

8. What are the effects of violating natural law?

9. What is the "moral law"? Where can one find the "moral law"?

10. Explain how one can sin without the direct intent to offend God.

11. What does it mean that all sin is a form of idolatry?

12. How does placing God second in our lives affect the human person?

13. How was sin viewed in the Old Testament? Explain the analogy.

14. Explain how viewing sin as a "simple infraction of some moral guideline" misses the true meaning of sin.

15. Explain how sin is a personal act.

16. What does it mean that "one cannot sin by accident"?

17. How might one's environment mitigate a person's culpability for sin? Can it ever remove one's culpability for sin? Explain.

18. What is the primary difference in the effects of mortal and venial sins?

19. What elements are necessary for a sin to be considered a mortal sin? Using these guidelines, explain why, or why not, an adulterous affair would be a mortal sin.

20. Should a Christian really be concerned about venial sins? Explain.

21. A mortal sin is a turning away from God. What is the ultimate result of persistence in mortal sin?

22. What is the means given to us for the forgiveness of mortal sins?

23. Explain the faulty reasoning behind the statement, "This is the twenty-first century," which is sometimes used to explain why a "sin" is actually acceptable.

24. What would be the result of each person deciding for himself or herself what is "moral" for them?

25. Some psychologists claim that in order to avoid guilt and shame we must convince ourselves that the underlying actions causing them are not wrong. Following this idea to its logical conclusion, what would happen to society if this attitude was adopted by everyone?

STUDY QUESTIONS continued

26. Some people attribute every wrongdoing to bad circumstances (e.g., a bad upbringing). While circumstances do affect our behavior, what would happen if no one was ever held accountable for his or her actions?

27. What is the obligation of Christians in a society where a particular law contradicts moral law?

28. Explain why internal sins (e.g., impure thoughts, etc.) are wrong.

29. When might a person not be culpable for material cooperation in a sin?

30. What is repentance? Why is it necessary for forgiveness?

31. What is the source of forgiveness?

32. What is the means used by Jesus Christ to infuse the sanctifying grace lost through Original Sin? What is the means instituted by Christ to restore sanctifying grace lost by mortal sins committed after Baptism?

33. Venial sins may be forgiven by good works based on personal contrition. What, then, is the value of confessing venial sins?

34. List several of the spiritual benefits which come from the Sacrament of Reconciliation.

35. If God can forgive us in any manner that he chooses, why must we go to Confession?

36. What is contrition, and why is it necessary for forgiveness?

37. What is the difference between imperfect contrition and perfect contrition?

38. If sins can be forgiven by "perfect contrition," then why go to Confession?

39. What does it mean that the commandments are within the "rational grasp" of every human being? Why is this so?

40. How are the Ten Commandments perfected?

41. Where can one find the teachings of the New Covenant?

42. Did Jesus' teaching mean that we are no longer bound by the Ten Commandments? Explain. List some examples of how Jesus enriched the Ten Commandments.

43. If we already have the Ten Commandments, why do we need the Precepts of the Catholic Church?

44. If the Precepts of the Catholic Church are about living the Ten Commandments, why do they recommend the frequent reception of the sacraments? Why fasting and abstinence?

45. How does a person find true joy and peace?

46. The Beatitudes are a verbal portrait of Christ. Explain.

47. What does "poor in spirit" mean? Why must we be poor in spirit to find Christ?

48. When our own sufferings are united to those of Christ, they are elevated and take on redemptive value. Explain.

49. In what way do the meek inherit the earth?

50. Explain how purity is a positive affirmation rather than a negative proscription.

51. According to the eighth Beatitude, how does a person transform the world?

PRACTICAL EXERCISES

1. Read the Parable of the Prodigal Son. In parables, Jesus used people or things as analogies. Who are the characters in the parable, and who do they represent? What does the parable teach us about God and freedom? In the parable, what would be the definition of sin? What are the results of sin? What does it tell us about forgiveness from both the point of view of God and a sinner? What does it tell us should be the attitude of Christians toward a sinner who seeks forgiveness?

2. "Sin is much more divinely personalized in the New Testament." In the movie *The Passion of the Christ*, the director, Mel Gibson, appeared only once. It was his hand that hammered the nail into Jesus' hand. How can it be said that we do the same every time we sin? How might our actions be different if we consider this truth?

3. Read the Parable of the Sheep and the Goats (cf. Mt 25:1-48). What are the things that a Christian must not omit if he or she wants to be a follower of Christ? Think of others which might be added to the list. According to the Parable, what is the true motive of Christian behavior toward others? Why do you think that Jesus concentrated more on sins of omission than sins of commission? What would be the result if all Christians followed Christ's teachings as found in this parable?

4. A Catholic says, "I just tell God my sins and he forgives me. I do not need to go to Confession." How would you respond?

5. List the sins that can be found in the following texts of St. Paul:

- Rom 1:29-31; 13:13
- 1 Cor 5:10-11; 6:9-10
- 2 Cor 12:20-21
- Gal 5:19-21
- Eph 4:31; 5:3-5
- Col 3:5-8
- 1 Tm 1:9-10; 6:9-11
- 2 Tm 3:2-5
- Ti 3:3

6. Comment on the following words of Socrates:

- "But if it were necessary for me either to do or to suffer injustice, I'd elect to suffer injustice rather than do it." (Plato, *Gorgias*, 469 c)
- "Then we ought not to retaliate or render evil for evil to any one, whatever evil we may have suffered from him." (Plato, *Crito*, 49 c-d)

7. Resolve the following case: John and his friend Patrick are discussing the human sins of passion, namely the sins of lust, anger, and gluttony. John holds that actions such as blasphemy against God and grave social injustices are sins, but he denies that premarital sex is a sin. "How can you call it a sin if a man and a woman by mutual consent decide to have sexual relations, when children are starving in Africa and being murdered in wars all over the globe?" he asks. Patrick argues that any evil consists in an offense against God, and since extramarital relations are serious disorders of the human passions and contrary to the express purpose for which God created human sexuality, they offend the dignity of the person, who is made in the image of God.

8. Explain why, according to the text, people like John tend to reduce sin to blasphemy and social crimes. According to Scripture, why are the most serious sins those that offend human dignity? What criteria can be given to determine both what is sinful and the gravity of the sin?

9. The new commandment of love perfects the Ten Commandments. For each of the commandments, take the negative proscription and turn it into a positive commandment based on love. While the Fourth Commandment is already in positive form, it can also be expanded.

10. Make a list of the ten most important rules in society. Compare this list to the Ten Commandments. How are they similar? How are they different?

PRACTICAL EXERCISES Continued

11. What would be some additional examples of servile behavior which might be avoided on Sunday? What are some activities that we might engage in that would help us live out the purpose of the Lord's Day in a better way?

12. List some examples of how the fifth precept of the Church could be put into practice.

13. Give some concrete examples of ways that you could live out the missionary spirit and apostolate of the Church.

14. Do you think the Beatitudes are easier to live than the commandments? Why?

15. Write an essay regarding the practical consequences for social order if a majority of people lived the Beatitudes.

16. Write a comment on this statement from the *Catechism*: "The Beatitudes depict the countenance of Jesus Christ and portray his charity. They express the vocation of the faithful associated with the glory of his Passion and Resurrection; they shed light on the actions and attitudes characteristic of the Christian life; they are the paradoxical promises that sustain hope in the midst of tribulations; they proclaim the blessings and rewards already secured, however dimly, for Christ's disciples; they have begun in the lives of the Virgin Mary and all the saints" (CCC 1717).

Zacchaeus in the Sycamore Awaiting the Passage of Jesus by Tissot. The story of the conversion of the rich, chief tax collector Zacchaeus is told in Luke 19: 2-10: "For the Son of man came to seek and to save the lost."

FROM THE CATECHISM

324 The fact that God permits physical and even moral evil is a mystery that God illuminates by his Son Jesus Christ who died and rose to vanquish evil. Faith gives us the certainty that God would not permit an evil if he did not cause a good to come from that very evil, by ways that we shall fully know only in eternal life.

1490 The movement of return to God, called conversion and repentance, entails sorrow for and abhorrence of sins committed, and the firm purpose of sinning no more in the future. Conversion touches the past and the future and is nourished by hope in God's mercy.

1492 Repentance (also called contrition) must be inspired by motives that arise from faith. If repentance arises from love of charity for God, it is called "perfect" contrition; if it is founded on other motives, it is called "imperfect."

1724 The Decalogue, the Sermon on the Mount, and the apostolic catechesis describe for us the paths that lead to the Kingdom of heaven. Sustained by the grace of the Holy Spirit, we tread them, step by step, by everyday acts. By the working of the Word of Christ, we slowly bear fruit in the Church to the glory of God.[54]

1726 The Beatitudes teach us the final end to which God calls us: the Kingdom, the vision of God, participation in the divine nature, eternal life, filiation, rest in God.

1728 The Beatitudes confront us with decisive choices concerning earthly goods; they purify our hearts in order to teach us to love God above all things.

1857 For a *sin* to be *mortal*, three conditions must together be met: "Mortal sin is sin whose object is grave matter and which is also committed with full knowledge and deliberate consent."[55]

1868 Sin is a personal act. Moreover, we have a responsibility for the sins committed by others when *we cooperate in them*:

- by participating directly and voluntarily in them;
- by ordering, advising, praising, or approving them;
- by not disclosing or not hindering them when we have an obligation to do so;
- by protecting evil-doers.

1873 The root of all sins lies in man's heart. The kinds and the gravity of sins are determined principally by their objects.

1874 To choose deliberately—that is, both knowing it and willing it—something gravely contrary to the divine law and to the ultimate end of man is to commit a mortal sin. This destroys in us the charity without which eternal beatitude is impossible. Unrepented, it brings eternal death.

1875 Venial sin constitutes a moral disorder that is reparable by charity, which it allows to subsist in us.

2018 Like conversion, justification has two aspects. Moved by grace, man turns toward God and away from sin, and so accepts forgiveness and righteousness from on high.

2075 "What good deed must I do, to have eternal life?"—"If you would enter into life, keep the commandments."[56]

2077 The gift of the Decalogue is bestowed from within the covenant concluded by God with his people. God's commandments take on their true meaning in and through this covenant.

"Blessed are the merciful, for they shall obtain mercy."

Mother Teresa's Home for the Dying in Calcutta. The Missionaries of Charity is a Roman Catholic religious order established in 1950 by Mother Teresa of Calcutta. It consists of over 4,500 nuns and is active in 133 countries. They have 19 homes in Calcutta, India which include homes for women, for orphaned children, for the dying, an AIDS hospice, a school for street children, and a leper colony. These services are provided to people regardless of their religion or social caste.

ENDNOTES – CHAPTER FOUR

1. *VS* 8.
2. *VS* 28.
3. *VS* 10.
4. *VS* 8.
5. *VS* 11; J. Michael Miller, C.S.B., The Encyclicals of Pope John Paul II, p. 654.
6. Mt 19:17.
7. Cf. CCC 375.
8. Cf. St. Peter Chrysologus, Sermo 117; PL 52, 520-521.
9. Cf. CCC 380.
10. Cf. Ps 51:5.
11. Cf. CCC 1849-1850.
12. St. Josemaria Escriva, *The Way*, 386.
13. *RP* 17.
14. Cf. *VS* 70.
15. Pope Pius XII, *Radio message to the United States National Catechetical Congress*, October 26, 1946.
16. Cf. *RP* 18; 1 Jn 1:8.
17. Cf. *VS* 88.
18. CCC 2017.
19. CCC 2010.
20. Cf. CCC 2008-2010.
21. Cf. CCC 2025.
22. Cf. *VS* 112.
23. Lk 15:21.
24. CCC 1741.
25. Cf. CCC 1470.
26. CCC 1470; Jn 5:24.
27. 1 Jn 3:2; cf. 1 Cor 13:12; Rev 22:4.
28. Cf. CCC 1023-1025.
29. CCC 1027.
30. Cf. Council of Trent (1551): DS 1712-1713; (1563): 1820.
31. Cf. CCC 1473.
32. Cf. CCC 1471.
33. Cf. Council of Lyons II (1274): DS 856.
34. 2 Mc 12:46.
35. Cf. Mt 5:22, 29; 10:28; 13:42, 50; Mk 9:43-48.
36. Mt 13:41-42.
37. Mt 25:41.
38. CCC 682.
39. Cf. CCC 272.
40. Paul VI, *CPG* § 28.
41. Cf. CCC 1042.
42. Cf. CCC 1042-1044.
43. Mt 7:13-14.
44. Cf. CCC 2061-2062.
45. Cf. CCC 1980-1982.
46. Cf. CCC 2081.
47. CCC 2073.
48. Cf. CCC 1983-1986.
49. Mt 5:17-18.
50. St. Irenæus, *Against Heretics*, IV, 15, 1.
51. Cf. Mt 5:17-48.
52. Cf. CCC 1725.
53. Cf. CCC 1725.
54. Cf. Mt 13:3-23.
55. *RP* 17 § 12.
56. Mt 19:16-17.

The First Three Commandments:
Our Obligations to God

CHAPTER 5

The First Three Commandments: Our Obligations to God

eter was raised Catholic and had attended a Catholic grade school. He received a good education in general but never reached a meaningful understanding of the Faith. When he went to college, he began to date Rebecca, a nonpracticing Christian. As Peter began spending more and more time with Rebecca, he became less diligent in the practice of his Faith. He often neglected to attend Sunday Mass in order to spend more time with Rebecca.

After several years, Peter and Rebecca realized that they had fallen in love and began to consider marriage seriously. Peter recalled that as a Catholic it was his responsibility to ensure that the children they might have should be baptized and raised as Catholics.

Rebecca was very skeptical about the Catholic Faith and refused to agree to raise her future children as Catholics. As Peter tried to persuade Rebecca to accept his position, he began to realize how important his Faith was to him. He regretted his recent laxity in religious matters. He re-evaluated his relationship with God and realized that he owed everything to his Creator. He had a serious duty to carry out his obligations as a Christian. He decided to return to the serious practice of his Catholic Faith.

Now Peter faced more of a dilemma than ever. He truly loved Rebecca, but he also knew his love of God prevented him from marrying a woman who would not agree to raise their children in the Faith. Although he did his utmost to persuade Rebecca, she remained adamant in her opposition. After much careful thought and prayer, Peter came to the conclusion that he must break up with Rebecca and end their relationship.

> **The Sabbath day, which had an enormous importance throughout the history of Israel, became the Christian Sunday. The redeeming Death of Jesus Christ, his Resurrection on the first day of the week, and the descent of the Holy Spirit on Pentecost were decisive events for the faith of the Apostles, who were witnesses to these events. From the beginning of the Church, the Apostles worshipped on Sunday,[1] and the day of worship in the Roman Empire was officially transferred to Sunday by the emperor Constantine in the fourth century.**

FOR DISCUSSION

✠ What does the Catholic Church teach about the obligation to worship God?

✠ How does the Christian's relationship with God differ from that of followers of other religions?

✠ What is the connection between love of God and love of neighbor?

✠ Did Peter do the right thing in breaking up with Rebecca?

✠ What does this story illustrate about the importance of the compatibility of Faith perspectives in dating relationships and in marriage?

God Resting After Creation, Byzantine Mosaic. By worshiping on Sunday,
we celebrate the completion of the first creation and the new creation in Christ
signified by the Resurrection of Jesus, which occurred on a Sunday.

The Lord's Day—as Sunday was called from apostolic times—has always been accorded special attention in the history of the Church because of its close connection with the very core of Christ's Redemption. In fact, in the weekly reckoning of time, Sunday recalls the day of Christ's Resurrection. It is Easter which returns week by week, celebrating Christ's victory over sin and death, the fulfillment in him of the first creation and the dawn of "the new creation."[2] It is the day which recalls in grateful adoration the world's first day and looks forward in active hope to "the last day," when Christ will come in glory[3] and all things will be made new.[4]

The Resurrection of Jesus is the fundamental event upon which Christian faith rests.[5] It is an astonishing reality, fully grasped in the light of faith, yet historically attested to by those who were privileged to see the Risen Lord. It is a wondrous event which is not only absolutely unique in human history, but which lies *at the very heart of the mystery of time*. In fact, "all time belongs to [Christ] and all the ages," as the evocative liturgy of the Easter Vigil recalls in preparing the Paschal Candle. Therefore, in commemorating the day of Christ's Resurrection not just once a year but every Sunday, the Church seeks to indicate to every generation the true fulcrum of history, to which the mystery of the world's origin and its final destiny leads.[6] (Pope John Paul II, *Dies Domini*, 1, 2)

Adoration of the Golden Calf by Poussin. "And as soon as he came near the camp and saw the calf and the dancing, Moses' anger burned hot, and he threw the tables out of his hands and broke them at the foot of the mountain." (Ex 32: 19)

INTRODUCTION

One of the chief distinctions of the Jewish religion as seen in the Old Testament is a belief in one God who completely transcends the material world. This obligation to worship and love the one true God was especially apparent after Moses received the Ten Commandments on Mount Sinai. Among these commandments, the first one sets the tone for the rest and conveys the supreme importance of God in the life of every person.

> **Hear, O Israel: The LORD our God is one LORD; and you shall love the LORD your God with all your heart, and with all your soul, and with all your might. (Dt 6: 4-5)**

The other version of the First Commandment stresses the absolute duty to adhere to the one true God and shun every form of idolatry.

> **You shall have no other gods before me. (Ex 20: 3; Dt 5: 7)**

The Ten Commandments are an elaboration of the two great commandments that Jesus himself strongly recognized in his public life: We must love God above all things and love our neighbor as ourselves.

> **In acknowledging the centrality of love, Christian faith has retained the core of Israel's faith, while at the same time giving it new depth and breadth. The pious Jew prayed daily the words of the Book of Deuteronomy which expressed the heart of his existence: 'Hear, O Israel: the Lord our God is one Lord, and you shall love the Lord your God with all your heart, and with all your soul and with all your might.'[7] Jesus united into a single precept this commandment of love for God and the commandment of love for neighbour found in the Book of Leviticus: 'You shall love your neighbour as yourself.'[8] Since God has first loved us,[9] love is now no longer a mere 'command'; it is the response to the gift of love with which God draws near to us. (*Deus Caritas Est*, 1)**

The first three commandments regard our relationship with God, while the last seven pertain to the treatment of one's neighbor.

SECTION I: THE FIRST COMMANDMENT

I am the LORD, Your God;
You Shall Not Have Strange Gods Before Me

WORSHIP

The First Commandment obliges everyone to acknowledge the existence of God and give him worship. This need to worship God with mind, body, and soul becomes especially clear through the life and words of Jesus Christ.

> God has loved us first. The love of the One God is recalled in the first of the "ten words." The commandments then make explicit the response of love that man is called to give to his God. (CCC 2083)

The worship of God obliges everyone to believe in God, trust in God, and love God. Sanctifying grace enables the believer to know, trust, and love God beyond his natural powers. The theological virtues of faith, hope, and charity are gratuitously given to us at the moment of Baptism. It is through these virtues that the Christian is empowered to worship God (cf. CCC 1813, 1840).

We will examine these three theological virtues and how they pertain to the worship of God one at a time.

FAITH

> Faith is the 'substance' of things hoped for; the proof of things not seen....Faith is a *habitus*, that is, a stable disposition of the spirit, through which eternal life takes root in us and reason is led to consent to what it does not see. (*Spe Salvi*, 7)

Faith is a gratuitous gift that accompanies sanctifying grace. It supernaturally enlightens the mind and moves the will beyond its natural capacities. Through the work of the Holy Spirit, the intellect is given a supernatural light to know, as true, the contents of Divine Revelation.

> Faith is a supernatural gift from God. In order to believe, man needs the interior helps of the Holy Spirit. (CCC 179)

At the same time, the will is moved to embrace these truths, and live by them. Faith is also "a personal adherence of the whole man to God,"[10] and through faith, we enter into a personal relationship with him.

> "Before this faith can be exercised, man must have the grace of God to move and assist him; he must have the interior helps of the Holy Spirit, who moves the heart and converts it to God, who opens the eyes of the mind and 'makes it easy for all to accept and believe the truth.'"[11] (CCC 153)

The virtue of faith enables the person to know truths revealed by God that exceed the light of

Christ and the Canaanite Woman by Carracci. "'Have mercy on me, O Lord, Son of David; my daughter is severely possessed by a demon.'...Then Jesus answered her, 'O woman, great is your faith! Be it done for you as you desire.'" (Mt 15: 22-28)

natural reason. This virtue allows the intellect to see the truth in Divine Revelation. At the same time, it impels the will to accept those divine teachings as true on God's authority.

> Faith is the theological virtue by which we believe in God and believe all that he has said and revealed to us, and that Holy Church proposes for our belief, because he is truth itself. (CCC 1814)

It is common for non-Catholic Christians to convert to the Catholic Faith as a consequence of recognizing as true what the Church teaches about Christ's Real Presence in the Holy Eucharist. Many will unabashedly declare that in a given moment they were enlightened to recognize the truth of this great mystery of faith.

God offers the gift of faith to all, but it is up to the individual to freely accept this gift. Though faith is a supernatural gift, it requires a willing acceptance of Divine Revelation as interpreted and taught by the Catholic Church. Given the fact that salvation consists of believing in Christ and following the path marked out by his teachings, faith is absolutely necessary for salvation.

It is even available to non-Christians, for whom the Lord in some fashion offers the possibility to know him even within the limitations and boundaries of culture, religion, and formation.

> Every man who is ignorant of the Gospel of Christ and of his Church, but seeks the truth and does the will of God in accordance with his understanding of it, can be saved. It may be supposed that such persons would have *desired Baptism explicitly* if they had known its necessity. (CCC 1260)

Divine Revelation often transcends human logic and understanding. The faithful believer who has difficulty understanding a point of doctrine must nevertheless accept it as truth through humble submission, trusting the teaching authority of the Church as the infallible source of doctrinal and moral truth. A Christian should make the effort to understand the Faith more thoroughly through diligent prayer and study. The *Catechism of the Catholic Church* is an invaluable tool for cultivating love and knowledge of Catholic teaching.

Our interior life will be directly impacted by how we worship God. The many divisions in Christianity show how well-meaning Christians often disagree on points of doctrine, which in many cases resulted in the fragmentation of Christianity into denominational

St. Athanasius (ca. 296-373). Almost the entire Eastern Church had fallen to the heresy of Arianism in the fourth century. In spite of five forced exiles, St. Athanasius marshaled the necessary orthodox forces to defeat the Arian heresy in the Church. It was a fight for the heart and soul of Christianity. At the First Council of Nicæa (325), St. Athanasius proposed a statement of Catholic belief resulting in the Nicene Creed.

churches. Some individuals may lose interest in the Faith, convert to another church or religion, or perhaps stop practicing the Faith or worshiping God altogether. Since free will is involved with the practice of faith and the worship of God, it is possible to commit sins against faith.

Sins against faith. There are five primary forms of sin against faith: voluntary doubt, schism, heresy, apostasy, and atheism. *Voluntary doubt* intentionally calls into question at least some aspect of Divine Revelation out of an unwillingness to accept a point of doctrine or moral teaching. *Schism* is a refusal to submit oneself to the authority of the pope or to the bishops in communion with him, though no formal rejection of a truth of Faith occurs. *Heresy* is committed through the obstinate denial or obstinate doubt by a baptized person of one or more tenets of the Catholic Faith. *Apostasy* is worse than heresy in that it implicitly or explicitly consists in a total repudiation of the Christian Faith. Finally, *atheism* is one of the deadliest sins against faith as it denies the very existence of God along with any personal relationship with him. While atheists may claim to hold to an objective morality, a denial of God is ultimately a rejection of objective morality itself.

HOPE

The virtue of hope instills in the person the capacity to trust in God's mercy. Specifically, the person who lives by hope will enjoy a deep confidence that God will give him or her all the graces not only to reach salvation, but also to reach full union with Jesus Christ.

This theological virtue involves a voluntary effort to use all the means at one's disposal and at the same time a strong reliance on God's assistance to faithfully live by Christ's teachings.

> The virtue of hope responds to the aspiration to happiness which God has placed in the heart of every man; it takes up the hopes that inspire men's activities and purifies them so as to order them to the Kingdom of heaven; it keeps man from discouragement; it sustains him during times of abandonment; it opens up his heart in expectation of eternal beatitude. Buoyed up by hope, he is preserved from selfishness and led to the happiness that flows from charity. (CCC 1818)

> Redemption is offered to us in the sense that we have been given hope, trustworthy hope, by virtue of which we can face our present: the present, even if it is arduous, can be lived and accepted if it leads towards a goal, if we can be sure of this goal, and if this goal is great enough to justify the effort of the journey. (*Spe Salvi*, 1)

Sins against hope. The First Commandment indicates that the Christian must freely hope in God's mercy but at the same time not take it for granted. *Despair* involves the loss of trust in God's mercy and love, usually on account of one's past sins, personal weaknesses, unworthiness, or sinfulness. *Presumption* occurs when an individual counts on God's mercy without any attempt to avoid sin and remain faithful to a Christian life, or when a person believes he or she can be saved by personal effort alone.[12]

The virtue of hope instills in the person the capacity to trust in God's mercy.

In addition to the certainty that God is faithful to his promises of mercy, hope also includes the fear of punishment on account of God's justice. A child's loving trust of his father in no way negates the fear of his just punishment.

CHARITY

Charity "is the theological virtue by which we love God above all things for his own sake, and our neighbor as ourselves for the love of God," says the *Catechism of the Catholic Church* (CCC 1822).

The theological virtue of charity challenges the Christian to love as Jesus Christ loves his Father and every human being. As so movingly stated in the Gospel, Christ loved to the point of laying down his life for his friends (cf. Jn 15:13).

The virtue of charity commands a love of God and neighbor with the very heart of Jesus Christ. This obligation to love God above all things comes first from the fact that he is our Creator and Father. God the Son took on a human nature and became our Savior suffering and dying on the Cross for every person. As St. John states, we ought to love God "because he first loved us" (1 Jn 4:19).

The Charity of St. Elizabeth of Hungary by Leighton. St. Elizabeth (1207-1231) was the daughter of King Andrew II of Hungary. She was married at the age of 14 and widowed at 20. She relinquished her wealth to the poor and built hospitals. Elizabeth not only gave food and clothing to the poor, she also personally cared for them when they were sick. She became a symbol of Christian charity after her death at the age of 24.

Though we can never begin to repay God for his bountiful love for us, in justice, every individual should strive to love him above all things.

When the moral life is embraced out of love of God and love of neighbor, a person is enabled to enjoy the spiritual freedom for which he or she was intended as a child of God. Far from an intolerable burden or a service rendered out of fear, the Christian enters into a loving relationship with the heavenly Father.

Which love should be given priority—love of God, or love of neighbor? The First Commandment clearly commands that everyone love God more than anyone else and above all else. However, a genuine love of God, since he is the source of love itself, necessarily leads to a love of neighbor. St. John makes this abundantly clear when he states, "If anyone says, 'I love God,' and hates his brother, he is a liar."[13] Therefore, since love for God automatically extends to love of neighbor, love for others will always serve as a measuring rod for love of God.

This certainly does not mean that Christ wishes to put the love of neighbor higher than, or even set it apart from, the love of God. This is evident from his conversation with the teacher of the Law...

These two commandments, on which "depend all the Law and the Prophets" (Mt 22:40), are profoundly connected and mutually related. *Their inseparable unity* is attested to by Christ in his words and by his very life: his mission culminates in the Cross of our Redemption.[14] (*Veritatis Splendor*, 14)

Sins against charity. There are five categories of sins against charity: indifference, ingratitude, spiritual sloth, lukewarmness, and hatred of God. *Indifference* is a lack of commitment in the exercise of the Catholic Faith. *Ingratitude* is a failure to recognize and acknowledge God's love exhibited in his generous blessings, as in the gift of physical health, a loving family, and most of all the Faith itself. *Spiritual sloth*, or "acedia," is a sadness or dejection of the will regarding the spiritual goods received from God. Often the individual flees from God and takes up the pursuit of worldliness that becomes a distraction from spiritual matters. *Lukewarmness* is a lackluster, lazy, or perfunctory fulfillment of the Catholic Faith. *Hatred of God*, though not a common sin, can certainly occur on account of distaste for his laws, resentment over the consequences of personal sin, or because of some severe or tragic suffering.

VIRTUE OF RELIGION

Since the First Commandment reminds us explicitly of our duty to love God above all things, it directly follows that we try to give him proper worship. The prayerful actions of offering God praise, honor, and atonement which in justice he deserves, fall under the *virtue of religion*. A significant part of giving God glory in response to his exalted and transcendent dignity and for his infinite love for us, involves generous prayer.

Types of prayer. Four kinds of prayer are specified by the virtue of religion: prayers of adoration, thanksgiving, contrition, and petition. *Prayer of adoration* is an expression of love through heartfelt fervor and verbal expression of loving praise in acknowledgement of God's absolute dominion over all creation. *Prayer of thanksgiving* is essential because we are obliged to show thanksgiving and gratitude to God for his generosity with us. *Prayer of contrition*, reflecting our sorrow for our sins, should be a frequent prayer of ours as we appeal to the mercy of Jesus and ask for forgiveness. *Prayer of petition* is a matter of presenting our needs and desires to the Lord.

Sins against religion. Appeals for divine intervention must include an appreciation and respect for God's infinite dignity and power. Proper worship and prayer must recognize the one true God as the only source of supernatural life. Any deviation from that constitutes a sin against religion.

The more common sins against religion and worship include *idolatry*, *superstition*, *divination*, *magic*, *irreligion*, and *satanic worship*.

Catholic veneration of statues and other images is completely different from idolatry. The statuary, stained glass, and artistic renderings of God, Jesus, and the saints are meant to lead us ultimately into a deeper relationship with Christ.

Idolatry involves dealing with or addressing a finite being as if it were divine. The stereotypical notion of idolatry is the primitive worship and veneration of the sun, trees, animals, or artifacts. Nevertheless, there are contemporary versions of idolatry that could take the form of an obsession with professional work, wealth, power, celebrity, achievement, sports, or even obsession with another person. Whenever we give our primary allegiance to anyone or anything other than God, we fall into idolatry.[15]

The veneration of statues and art renderings of God, Jesus, Mary, or the saints in Catholic tradition is not idolatry. These images are meant to lead us to a deeper relationship with Christ. We honor the person represented, but our worship is directed to God alone.

Superstition consists of any belief or practice that offers improper worship to God—for example, believing that a certain number of prayers to a particular saint will guarantee good health, or using certain trinkets, mantras, or actions designed to secure a supernatural effect or to avoid bad luck. The use of these superstitious devices or actions indicates a belief that these objects have secret powers. Seeking supernatural assistance through external rituals without recourse to God's infinite goodness goes against the proper worship of God.

Divination is the use of occult powers in an attempt to predict the future or to obtain information which cannot be discovered through normal channels. Only God can know the future and the mysteries of the world, both material and spiritual. It is up to God to reveal the future or provide knowledge in a preternatural way if he so wills. Any attempt to learn about the future or gain knowledge unobtainable through natural means without reference to God or his revelation is sinful. If God is not involved for supernatural assistance, then dangerous demonic powers may be at work.[16]

Magic involves seeking occult forces through rituals or formulas as a means to obtain either a good or evil effect. For example, the recitation of an incantation accompanied by gestures or the application of exotic substances would fall under the evil of magic. These practices must be distinguished from the sleight-of-hand tricks, optical illusions, etc., that make no claim to occult forces and can be understood as legitimate forms of entertainment. Witchcraft is probably its most common manifestation. Today, some "new age" philosophies that promise self-fulfillment and physical well-being through actions or beliefs that release hidden "energies" would also fall under the category of magic.[17]

Satan Carries Jesus to the Pinnacle of the Temple by Tissot
The direct worship of the devil, is one of the most dreadful sins against the virtue of religion.
Venerating a being that radically contradicts the Gospel and whose aim is to undermine Christ's
redemption is a horrific sin.

Irreligion consists of disrespect and, in many instances, mockery of God's goodness and sacred dignity. Such offenses against the sacredness of religion include sacrilege, which shows serious disrespect, insensitivity, desecration, or malicious action toward the sacraments, sacred persons, places, or objects. The reception of Holy Communion while in the state of mortal sin is one example of sacrilege. Another manifestation is called simony, the buying or selling of spiritual goods like indulgences or the administration of a sacrament.

Satanic worship, the direct worship of the devil, is one of the most dreadful sins against the virtue of religion. Dealing with the Prince of Darkness through perverse or violent rituals that characterize Satanism is terribly destructive to the human person in both soul and body. Venerating a being that radically contradicts the Gospel and whose aim is to undermine Christ's redemption is a horrific sin.

God the Father, Raphael's Stanza, the Vatican.
It is the duty of every Christian to avoid the irreverent use of God's name, to use the name of God only with devotion and praise.

SECTION II: THE SECOND COMMANDMENT
You Shall Not Take the Name of the LORD your God in Vain

THE GRANDEUR OF GOD'S NAME

An important aspect of recognizing a person's dignity is addressing him or her by name. Out of a special deference to that person, one will always refer to his or her name with respect. While this holds true in all human relations, this manner of respecting a person's name pertains especially to God.

In the Old Testament, we read how God revealed his name to his people. When Moses asked whom he should say sent him, God answered, "I AM WHO I AM." Out of a sincere reverence for the almighty and transcendent God, the Israelites of the Old Testament refused to speak this name. Instead, they referred to God as LORD, the "Name," YHWH (Yahweh), or JHVH (Jehovah), the latter two being initialisms that represent the first letter of each part of God's name, "I AM WHO I AM."

This great respect for the name of God continued for Christians in the New Testament. St. Paul emphasized the importance and power of God's name in the Person of Jesus Christ. Moreover, he showed how the invocation of Jesus' name is a most effective means of prayer. As any person is pleased when his name is used respectfully, addressing Jesus Christ by name with affection and humility is most pleasing to him.[18]

> **Therefore God has highly exalted him and bestowed on him the name which is above every name, that at the name of Jesus every knee should bow, in heaven and on earth and under the earth, and every tongue confess that Jesus Christ is Lord, to the glory of God the Father. (Phil 2: 9-11)**

OATHS

An oath is the invocation of the Divine Name as witness to the truth. It "cannot be taken except in truth, in judgment, and in justice."[19]

To take an oath is to call upon God as a witness to a truth or a promise. Expressions like "God is my witness," "I speak before God," and "As God is my Judge" are often repeated in everyday conversation. On some occasions, they are spoken spontaneously. Ordinarily, such statements are not true oaths because the speaker has no intention of making an oath. Nevertheless, it is good to avoid calling upon God's testimony in unimportant matters. To use such words demands the greatest possible discretion, and it would be wrong to trivialize the invocation of God's name.

We can distinguish two kinds of oaths: *assertory* and *promissory*. An *assertory oath* is taken when God is called upon as a witness to the truth of what is being said. A *promissory oath* calls upon God as a witness to what a person intends to do in the future.

A promissory oath is one taken by a public official who solemnly swears before God to fulfill the duties of his office.

In order to take a true oath, one must call upon God as a witness. When one mentions God but does not call him as witness to testimony, it is not considered to be an oath. For this reason, formulas like "only God knows" do not constitute oaths.

In the Old Testament, God swears an oath to David: "When your days are fulfilled and you lie down with your fathers, I will raise up your offspring after you,... and I will establish his kingdom." (2 Sm 7:12)

Oaths in Scripture. Oaths are frequently mentioned and spoken throughout Scripture, in both the Old and New Testaments.

When Yahweh dictated the moral code to his people, he forbade them to use his name in vain. The two expressions of this commandment in the Old Testament fully agree on this point: "You shall not take the name of the LORD your God in vain; for the LORD will not hold him guiltless who takes his name in vain."[20] The phrase *in vain* means "uselessly."

The Old Testament relates promises made by God to his people that are accompanied by oaths. For example, God promises his blessings with this oath:

"By myself I have sworn, says the LORD, because you have done this, and have not withheld your son, your only son, I will indeed bless you, and I will multiply your descendants as the stars of heaven and as the sand which is on the seashore. And your descendants shall possess the gate of their enemies." (Gn 22:16-17)

This oath is remembered by Moses, recorded in the *Magnificat*, and mentioned in the Letter to the Hebrews.[21] Later, God swears an oath to David that he will have a successor.[22] The psalmist also recalls this oath, and St. Peter mentions it in his first discourse, in which he acknowledges Christ as God of all humanity.[23]

The Book of Numbers regulates the use of oaths.[24] Later, the Book of Sirach cautions against making oaths before God too frequently or needlessly.[25]

The Second Commandment is a practical application of the *virtue of religion*, which guides our conversations with God, demands respect for his name and Person, and promotes refinement in the use of holy things. But the words of Jesus are restrictive:

> Again you have heard that it was said to the men of old, "You shall not swear falsely, but shall perform to the Lord what you have sworn." But I say to you, Do not swear at all, either by heaven, for it is the throne of God, or by the earth, for it is his footstool, or by Jerusalem, for it is the city of the great King. And do not swear by your head, for you cannot make one hair white or black. Let what you say be simply "Yes" or "No"; anything more than this comes from evil. (Mt 5:33-37)

Despite initial impressions, Jesus does not condemn every kind of oath. For example, in the Gospel of St. Matthew, Jesus does not rebuke the high priest who demands a response under oath.[26] Rather than forbid oaths, Jesus intends to purify the practice, which was corrupt in his time.

> Following St. Paul,[27] the tradition of the Church has understood Jesus' words as not excluding oaths made for grave and right reasons (for example, in court). (CCC 2154)

Nevertheless, the *Catechism* indicates some limitations on the legitimate use of an oath:

> The holiness of the divine name demands that we neither use it for trivial matters, nor take an oath which on the basis of the circumstances could be interpreted as approval of an authority unjustly requiring it. When an oath is required by illegitimate civil authorities, it may be refused. It must be refused when it is required for purposes contrary to the dignity of persons or to ecclesial communion. (CCC 2155)

Lawful use of oaths. Since taking an oath is a most serious and solemn act, it cannot be taken except in *truth*, *judgment*, and *justice*.[28] To do otherwise would constitute a grave insult to God and his name.

Truth is essential because an oath may not be taken to support a lie, for when one takes an oath and lies, he commits the very grave sin of perjury. *Judgment* is required because we should never call upon God as a witness for superficial reasons. *Justice* must be the motivation because an oath can be taken only for something morally good; an oath to violate the moral law is unjust and therefore meaningless.

The Oath of St. Hedwig (Jadwiga) the Queen by Simmler. An oath is a promise made to another person with God as a witness, a vow is a promise made to God with another person as the witness.

VOWS

Whereas one takes an oath to another person with God as the witness, one makes a vow to God with another person as the witness (cf. CIC, 1191).

Vows in religious life consist of promises made to God to live the evangelical counsels of poverty, chastity, and obedience. When entering into the Sacrament of Matrimony, a couple makes vows before God. A vow can be made regarding any kind of good deed as a way of giving glory to God and serving him.

The validity of a vow depends on the completion of the conditions that define it. These conditions include the commitment to fulfill what is promised, recognition of a serious obligation, and a free choice of the will.

SINS AGAINST THE SECOND COMMANDMENT

Besides giving appropriate guidelines for oaths and vows, the Second Commandment forbids any irreverent use of God's name. Two forms of this sin are *blasphemy* and the *ridicule of the Faith*.

Blasphemy is the act of speaking contemptuously of God or his perfections. It may also be contempt directed toward the saints and is particularly grievous when directed against the Most Holy Virgin Mary. St. Thomas Aquinas states:

> Even as God is praised in his saints, insofar as praise is given to the works that God does in his saints, so does blasphemy against the saints, redound, as a consequence, against God. (St. Thomas Aquinas, *Summa Theologiæ*, I-II, q. 13, a. 1 ad 2)

Improper use of the name of God may take the form of a wide variety of abuses. The Tradition of the Church has underlined the gravity of blasphemy by classifying it as an intrinsically evil act.

In the Old Testament, blasphemy was punished by death. The Book of Leviticus narrates how a son of an Egyptian and an Israelite were put to death because they "blasphemed the Name."[29] With this severe punishment, God tries to root out this grave sin, which was quite common in neighboring towns.[30]

The Sistine Madonna by Raphael. Blasphemy is particularly grievous when directed against the Most Holy Virgin Mary.

In the New Testament, the awareness of the serious nature of this sin continues. For example, the Jews try to stone Jesus to death by accusing him of blasphemy, since "it is not for a good work that we stone you but for blasphemy; because you, being a man, make yourself God."[31]

St. Paul considered himself a blasphemer when he hunted down Christians.[32] Later, the Apostle laments that "the name of God is blasphemed among the Gentiles because of you."[33] In the New Testament, the seriousness of blasphemy is shown by the fact that it appears in lists of sins that merit condemnation.[34]

The *Catechism* shows the diverse forms that blasphemy may take:

> *Blasphemy* is directly opposed to the Second Commandment. It consists in uttering against God—inwardly or outwardly—words of hatred, reproach, or defiance; in speaking ill of God; in failing in respect toward him in one's speech; in misusing God's name. St. James condemns those "who blaspheme that honorable name [of Jesus] by which you are called."[35] The prohibition of blasphemy extends to language against Christ's Church, the saints, and sacred things. It is also blasphemous to make use of God's name to cover up criminal practices, to reduce peoples to servitude, to torture persons or put them to death. The misuse of God's name to commit a crime can provoke others to repudiate religion. (CCC 2148)

Ridicule of the Faith involves irreverent dispositions that come in the form of sarcastic remarks or ridiculous caricatures with respect to Christian customs or moral behavior. So-called humorous imitations of the Sign of the Cross, confession of sins, devotion to Mary, or the practice of chastity are just a few examples of public irreverence toward God.

The media and the arts can be egregious offenders against sacred names and customs as well. Movies have portrayed Christ in an offensive way, and at times artwork has displayed and depicted the Mother of Jesus in a humiliating manner. These irreverent and disrespectful actions are terribly insulting to the grandeur and goodness of God.

In light of the fact that many offend the good name of God and all that is connected with God, it is crucial that Christians defend and profess faith in his name by reacting in a peaceful and reasonable way through letters to editors, editorial pieces, signed petitions, demonstrations, and other appropriate means. Through these kinds of responses, conscientious Christians can use these lamentable occasions to spread the truth and show that blasphemy is unacceptable even in a pluralistic society.

WHY IS IT NECESSARY TO PRAY?

Through prayer, an individual encounters God and enters into communion with each Person of the Blessed Trinity. As a consequence, the individual receives God's grace, enabling him or her to live a moral life and to love God and neighbor as Christ intended. One's relationship with God, founded on a life of prayer, is the very basis for Christian morality. For this reason, we are called, both as individuals and as a faith community, to "pray constantly."[36]

> [Prayer] is commonly held to be a conversation. In a conversation there are always an "I" and a "thou" or "you." In this case the "Thou" is with a capital "T." If at first the "I" seems to be the most important element in prayer, prayer teaches that the situation is actually different. The "Thou" is more important, because our prayer begins with God....
>
> In prayer, then, the true protagonist is God. The protagonist is Christ, who constantly frees creation from slavery to corruption and leads it toward liberty, for the glory of the children of God. The protagonist is the Holy Spirit, who "comes to the aid of our weakness." We begin to pray, believing that it is our own initiative that compels us to do so. Instead, we learn that it is always God's initiative within us, just as Saint Paul has written. This initiative restores in us our true humanity; it restores in us our unique dignity. (John Paul II, *Crossing the Threshold of Hope*, [New York, New York: Alfred A. Knopf, Inc., 1994], 16-17)

The Lord's Prayer

In the Sermon on the Mount, Christ gave his disciples the basic teachings of the New Law. As a vital part of his message, he taught them how to pray, giving them an example to follow, and directing them to call upon God as "Father." The prayer that he left them, known as the Lord's Prayer, is sometimes referred to as the "most perfect of prayers"[37] for it serves as a model for all Christian prayer.

> Our Father who art in Heaven,
> hallowed be thy name.
> Thy kingdom come.
> Thy will be done on earth, as it is in Heaven.
> Give us this day our daily bread;
> and forgive us our trespasses,
> as we forgive those who trespass against us;
> and lead us not into temptation,
> but deliver us from evil. Amen.

It is important to note at the outset that the Lord's Prayer is spoken in the plural—"Our Father who art in heaven."[38] As Christians, we exist as members of a faith community. Through Baptism, we enter into a life of faith and are incorporated into the Church, the Mystical Body of Christ. In communion with Christ, we can call upon God and speak with him in an entirely new way. He is a loving Father—a personal God, who wishes to establish a relationship with his children.

> We can adore the Father because he has caused us to be reborn to his life by *adopting* us as his children in his only Son: by Baptism, he incorporates us into the Body of his Christ; through the anointing of his Spirit who flows from the head to the members, he makes us other "Christs." (CCC 2782)

Christ Teaches "The Lord's Prayer" by Tissot.
In the Sermon on the Mount, Jesus instructed his disciples how to pray, as told in Mt 6: 5-15.

"Pray then like this:..."

While the Christian life is communal by its very nature, each individual is called to a personal and unique relationship with God. "God tirelessly calls each person to this mysterious encounter with Himself,"[39] and it is through a life of prayer that each person responds to his or her Christian vocation.

> God knows us by name and he calls us by name. (Pope Benedict XVI, *Jesus of Nazareth*, 177)

Different Forms of Prayer

In teaching his disciples the Lord's Prayer, Christ gave us the perfect example of how we should pray. In this prayer, we find all of the basic forms of prayer that should be offered to God: blessing and adoration, petition, intercession, thanksgiving, and praise.[40]

Prayers of *blessing and adoration* are an acknowledgement of the blessings that God has bestowed on us, both as individuals and as members of all of creation. "*Adoration* is the first attitude of man acknowledging that he is a creature before his Creator."[41] In praying "hallowed be thy name," we recognize the holiness of God's Name, thus fulfilling, in a positive manner, the precept given to us in the Second Commandment.

Through worship, we give adoration to each Person of the Blessed Trinity. We adore God the Father, God the Son, and God the Holy Spirit. While angels and saints, as well as relics and holy images, are given special veneration in Christian tradition, adoration is offered to God alone, and the most perfect act of adoration that can be given to God is the offering of the most Holy Sacrifice of the Mass. The Mass is, therefore, the most perfect prayer that can be offered to God.

> The Eucharist contains and expresses all forms of prayer: it is "the pure offering" of the whole Body of Christ to the glory of God's name[42] and, according to the traditions of East and West, it is *the* "sacrifice of praise." (CCC 2643)

Adoration is offered to God in the worship of the Blessed Sacrament (the Eucharist)-the Body, Blood, Soul, and Divinity of Christ-both in the liturgy of the Mass and in Eucharistic devotion outside of Mass.

> *Worship of the Eucharist.* In the liturgy of the Mass we express our faith in the real presence of Christ under the species of bread and wine by, among other ways, genuflecting or bowing deeply as a sign of adoration of the Lord. "The Catholic Church has always offered and still offers to the sacrament of the Eucharist the cult of adoration, not only during Mass, but also outside of it, reserving the consecrated hosts with the utmost care, exposing them to the solemn veneration of the faithful, and carrying them in procession."[43] (CCC 1378)

The prayer of *petition* is the recognition that we depend upon God, and that, as a loving Father, he gives us everything that is good.[44] When we ask for "our daily bread," we are acknowledging the right relationship between Creator and creature. As members of God's family, we depend upon him for all things both material and spiritual.

One particular form of petition is the prayer of *intercession*. In intercessory prayer, a person asks for the benefits of God on behalf of others. This form of prayer is a recognition of the communion that exists among the members of the Church. This communion,

St. Christopher with the Infant Christ and St. Peter by Cima. As the patron saint of travelers, a prayer of intercession is often said to St. Christopher to ensure a safe journey. His name means Christ-bearer. There are several legends about him including one in which he was crossing a river when a child asked to be carried across. When St. Christopher put the child on his shoulders he found the child was very heavy. The child, according to the legend, was Jesus Christ carrying the weight of the whole world.

known as the communion of the saints, extends not only to the faithful on earth, but also to those who have gone before us and are now in Heaven and in Purgatory.

As Catholics, we have a special responsibility to pray for all in need, which includes praying for the holy souls in Purgatory. This is summarized in the spiritual works of mercy, which admonish us to pray for the living and the dead. Intercessory prayer also occurs in the "General Intercessions" in the Liturgy of the Mass.

In the same manner that we are called to pray for others, we also rely on the other members of the Church to pray for us. This includes the prayers of the saints in Heaven (called the intercession of the saints) and, in a special way, the prayers of Our Lady.

The prayer of *thanksgiving* is an expression of our gratitude for all of the benefits that God has bestowed on us. This prayer is expressed most fully in the Liturgy of the Eucharist (from the Greek word meaning "thanksgiving"), which is a sacrifice of praise and thanksgiving. It is also expressed each time that we show our gratitude to God for his great gifts, such as when we pray before meals.

In the prayer of *Praise*, we give glory to God for his own sake, for his marvelous works, and, in particular, for his work of salvation. One example of a prayer of praise is the *Te Deum*, which begins:

> We praise you, O God,
> we acknowledge you to be the Lord.
> You, the Father everlasting,
> all the earth does worship.
> To you all the angels,
> to you the heavens, and all the powers,
> To you the cherubim and seraphim
> cry out without ceasing:
> Holy, Holy, Holy,
> Lord God of hosts.

TYPES OF PRAYER

Prayer in the events of each day and each moment is one of the secrets of the kingdom revealed to "little children," to the servants of Christ, to the poor of the Beatitudes. It is right and good to pray so that the coming of the kingdom of justice and peace may influence the march of history, but it is just as important to bring the help of prayer into humble, everyday situations; all forms of prayer can be the leaven to which the Lord compares the kingdom.[45] (CCC 2660)

But do not imagine that prayer is an action to be carried out and then forgotten. The just man "delights in the law of the Lord and meditates on his law day and night. Through the night, I meditate on you" and "my prayer comes to you like incense in the evening." Our whole day can be a time of prayer-from night to morning and from morning to night.[46]

The tradition of the Church has generally recognized three different types of prayer in the Christian life:[47]

✤ *Vocal prayer* is speaking to God through word, whether in the silence of one's heart or audibly in the presence of others. A vocal prayer may be a memorized or formula prayer, such as the "Our Father" or "Hail Mary," or may take the form of a prayer that arises spontaneously from the heart.

✤ In *meditation*, a person generally focuses or thinks about a particular event in salvation history or an aspect of the Faith. For example, a person might read the Gospel account of the Crucifixion and, entering into the scene, reflect on the meaning of our Lord's Passion, Death, and Resurrection in his or her own life. The Rosary is a good example of a prayer of meditation. While the person is praying the Our Father or Hail Mary (vocal prayer), he or she is meditating on the lives of Jesus Christ and the Blessed Virgin Mary (meditative prayer).

✤ "*Contemplative prayer* is the simple expression of the mystery of prayer. It is a gaze of faith fixed on Jesus, an attentiveness to the Word of God, a silent love. It achieves real union with the prayer of Christ to the extent that it makes us share in his mystery."[48]

THE BATTLE OF PRAYER[49]

The battle of prayer is inseparable from the necessary "spiritual battle" to act habitually according to the Spirit of Christ: we pray as we live, because we live as we pray.

"It is always possible to pray. It is even a vital necessity." (CCC 2757)

The principal difficulties that we often encounter in prayer are the following:

✤ We "don't have the time." Prayer, in this view, is considered as an occupation incompatible with all the other things we have to do.

The remedy: "Make the time" for your personal prayer, knowing that nothing can excuse your failing to do so.

✤ We "get distracted." Concentration becomes really difficult and we easily give up.

The remedy: Turn your heart back to God, offering him the distractions with humility and without discouragement.

✤ We "feel dry." It seems that the heart is separated from God, with no taste for thoughts, memories, and feelings, even spiritual ones.

The Madonna by Bartolomeo.
We pray to "Our Lady" in an intercessory prayer, asking for the benefits of God's grace on our behalf or on the behalf of others including prayers for the holy souls in Purgatory.

The remedy: Remember that "unless the grain of wheat falls into the earth and dies, it remains alone; but if it dies, it bears much fruit."[50] Through dryness the Holy Spirit purifies us, so that we seek God's glory and not just the spiritual consolations that can come from prayer at times.

There are also two frequent temptations that threaten prayer:

✤ Lack of faith. Prayer is not the first priority.

The remedy: Ask our Lord with a humble heart, "Lord, increase my faith."

✤ Acedia. This is a form of depression stemming from lax ascetical practice, which leads to discouragement.

The remedy: Trust God more and hold fast in constancy.

SECTION III: THE THIRD COMMANDMENT
Remember to Keep Holy the LORD's Day

THE SABBATH IN THE OLD TESTAMENT

On the universal calendar, Sunday has always constituted a special reference point for all social activities. Some non-Christian religions have their own day of worship—Saturday for Jews, Friday for Muslims. But in Western culture, Sunday is the day of rest and—for Christian believers—worship.

In the Old Testament, God himself, through his Revelation to Moses, outlined the norms that people should follow in worshiping him. A very detailed set of laws was established that included the institution of a priesthood, the construction of a temple, principal feasts, practices of worship, and above all, the celebration of the Sabbath.

By worshiping on Sunday, we celebrate the completion of the first creation and the new creation in Christ signified by the Resurrection of Jesus, which occurred on a Sunday.

From the very beginning of the Bible, one can see the importance of the seventh day. It is widely believed that the narration of creation as happening in seven days meant to highlight the importance of the seventh day and the obligation to dedicate this day to divine worship.

The heavens and the earth were finished, and all the host of them. And on the seventh day God finished his work which he had done, and he rested on the seventh day from all his work which he

had done. So God blessed the seventh day and hallowed it, because on it God rested from all his work which he had done in creation. (Gn 2:1-3)

Later, when God had made the Israelites his people, he made laws concerning the observance of the Sabbath.

Remember the Sabbath day, to keep it holy. Six days you shall labor, and do all your work; but the seventh day is a sabbath to the LORD your God; in it you shall not do any work, you, or your son, or your daughter, your manservant, or your maidservant, or your cattle, or the sojourner who is within your gates; for in six days the LORD made heaven and earth, the sea, and all that is in them, and rested the seventh day; therefore the LORD blessed the sabbath day and hallowed it. (Ex 20: 8-11)

Jesus Unrolls the Scroll in the Synagogue by Tissot.

"He went to Nazareth, where he had been brought up, and on the Sabbath day he went into the synagogue, as was his custom. And he stood up to read. The scroll of the prophet Isaiah was handed to him. Unrolling it, he found the place where it is written:

"The Spirit of the Lord is on me, because he has anointed me to preach good news to the poor. He has sent me to proclaim freedom for the prisoners and recovery of sight for the blind, to release the oppressed, to proclaim the year of the Lord's favor." (Lk 4: 16-19) NIV

In this passage, we see rest as the primary purpose of the Sabbath and divine worship as secondary. But soon after, Scripture gave the Sabbath a dual purpose. It was also a day consecrated to God. The Book of Leviticus prescribed:

> **Six days shall work be done; but on the seventh day is a sabbath of solemn rest, a holy convocation; you shall do no work; it is a sabbath to the LORD in all your dwellings.** (Lv 23:3)

The bread of proposition—the ritual twelve loaves kept by the Jewish high priests for use as a sacrificial offering according to the Mosaic Law—would be renewed on the Sabbath,[51] and specific sacrifices were to be celebrated.[52]

Consequently, from Mosaic times, the Sabbath included rest and the obligation of sacrifice. Both requirements showed the recognition of the power of God over his entire creation and over all people.

The Gospels speak of the arguments between Jesus and the religious authorities of Israel in relation to the observance of the Sabbath. Jesus declared that the care of the sick comes before the Sabbath.[53] Jesus proclaimed the true meaning of the Sabbath with these words: "The Sabbath was made for man, not man for the Sabbath."[54]

THE LORD'S DAY IN THE NEW TESTAMENT

The Resurrection of the Lord on the first day of the week introduced notable changes in the practice of divine worship, but this did not come about immediately. In fact, we know that the first Christians practiced the Jewish form of worship in the Temple or the synagogue and then celebrated the liturgy of the Eucharist in their private homes. Sts. Peter and John likewise went up to the Temple at the customary hour of prayer and then celebrated the Eucharist in their homes.[55] During this early period, they were already talking about the "Lord's Day."[56]

Likewise, on "the first day of the week," they "gathered together to break bread."[57] On the Lord's Day, they also took up a collection for the poor.[58]

The Resurrection by Bloch.
"...toward the dawn of the first day of the week,...And for fear of him [an angel] the guards trembled and became like dead men. But the angel said to the women, 'Do not be afraid; for I know that you seek Jesus who was crucified. He is not here; for he has risen, as he said.'" (Mt 28:1-6)

At the beginning of the second century, St. Ignatius, bishop of Antioch, spoke of Sunday as the day of Christian worship.

> If then they who walked in ancient customs came to a new hope, no longer living for the Sabbath, but for the Lord's Day, on which also our life sprang up through him and his death—though some deny him—and by this mystery we received faith, and for this reason also we suffer, that we may be found disciples of Jesus Christ our only teacher. (St. Ignatius of Antioch, *Letter to the Magnesians*, IX, 1)

The change of the day of worship also brought about a variation of name: The "Sabbath" was substituted by the "first day of the week,"[59] or the "day of the sun,"[60] and more generally, "the Lord's Day."

Communion of the Apostles by Fra Angelico.
Sunday is the day on which the Church celebrates the victory of Christ's redemptive mission.
For this reason, it occupies the center of a Christian's life.

THE HISTORY OF THE CHRISTIAN SUNDAY

From the beginning of the Church, the Eucharist was celebrated on Sundays. The *Didache* (an anonymous first-century text) and the *First Apologia* (written by St. Justin Martyr) relate the details of the celebration of Christian worship on the Day of the Lord. These two writings even include some of the actual ceremonies that accompanied this celebration.

These celebrations took place in private homes as Sunday lacked a public character until AD 314, one year after Emperor Constantine recognized the Christian religion. He enacted laws forbidding servile work on Sunday, and on July 3 of that same year, he forbade other public activities (such as judicial action). Gradually, as much work as possible was suspended on that day. During this period, Eucharistic worship went together with a day of rest. For that reason, any work that impeded attendance at the Mass was forbidden. The first and third councils at Orleans (AD 511 and 538) emphasized the importance of attending Mass and made laws prohibiting servile work on Sunday.

Together with Sunday, the custom of celebrating other Solemnities such as Christmas and other feasts commemorating important events in the life of our Lord was very quickly introduced. Additionally, some of the days celebrating the martyrdom of saints were made Solemnities. In this way, the Christian calendar would be punctuated by the important Mysteries of Faith and feasts of Mary and the saints. However, Sunday stands out above all feasts because it commemorates the Death and Resurrection of Jesus Christ. The Second Vatican Council reminds us:

> By a tradition handed down from the apostles, which took its origin from the very day of Christ's Resurrection, the Church celebrates the Paschal mystery every eighth day, which day is appropriately called the Lord's Day or Sunday. For on this day Christ's faithful are bound to come together into one place. They should listen to the word of God and take part in the Eucharist, thus calling to mind the Passion, Resurrection, and glory of the Lord Jesus, giving thanks to God who "has begotten them again, though the Resurrection of Christ from the dead, unto a living hope"

(1 Pt 1:3). The Lord's Day is the original feast day, and it should be proposed to the faithful and taught to them so that it may become in fact a day of joy and of freedom from work. Other celebrations, unless they be truly of greatest importance, shall not have precedence over Sunday, which is the foundation and kernel of the whole liturgical year. (*Sacrosanctum Concilium*, 106)

THE OBLIGATION TO ATTEND HOLY MASS

The obligation for Catholics to attend Holy Mass on Sundays and Holy Days of Obligation is first derived from the Third Commandment of the Decalogue, which requires us to keep the Sabbath holy.

The second reason for this requirement concerns the importance of the Eucharistic sacrifice, the unbloody and sacramental re-presentation of Jesus' redemptive sacrifice on the Cross, which makes present the one sacrifice of Christ, and the celebration of his Resurrection from the dead. The Mass is called a "*Holy Sacrifice*, because it makes present the one sacrifice of Christ the Savior and includes the Church's offering."[61] In her maternal care for the faithful, the Church makes attendance at Sunday Mass obligatory because of the tremendous spiritual benefits for those who participate.

The Immaculate Conception by Tiepolo.
Holy Days of Obligation are days on which the Church commemorates the important events in the life of Christ and his Mother, or which are dedicated to celebrating important mysteries of the Faith.

Sunday is the day on which the Church celebrates the Lord's work of Redemption known as the Paschal Mystery, which includes Christ's Passion, Resurrection from the dead, and his Ascension into Heaven.[62] Therefore, the center and high point of a Christian's life consists in participating in the liturgical celebration of the Paschal Mystery.[63] As the Second Vatican Council teaches, the Eucharist is "the summit toward which the activity of the Church is directed; it is also the fount from which all her power flows."[64] The many graces that can be obtained through the liturgical participation in the Eucharistic sacrifice and reception of Communion, have a very powerful effect on the moral life. It is precisely this union with the Paschal Mystery that strengthens the individual to live the moral law and share more deeply in the life of Christ.

It is this mystery of Christ that the Church proclaims and celebrates in her liturgy so that the faithful may live from it and bear witness to it in the world. (CCC 1068).

The *Code of Canon Law* declares the importance of Sunday in Christian life and, secondly, proclaims the obligation of attending Sunday Mass and refraining from servile work.

Sunday, on which by apostolic tradition the Paschal mystery is celebrated, is to be observed in the universal Church as the primary Holy Day of Obligation. On Sundays and other Holy Days of Obligation, the faithful are obliged to participate in the Mass. They are also to abstain from such work or business that would inhibit the worship to be given to God, the joy proper to the Lord's Day, or the due relaxation of mind and body. (CIC, 1246-1247)

Holy Days of Obligation, on the other hand, are days on which the Church commemorates the important events in the life of Christ and his Mother, or which are dedicated to celebrating important mysteries of the Faith.

Our Blessed Mother was an example of faith and a model of Christian discipleship. By the grace of God, she was preserved from the stain of Original Sin (the Immaculate Conception) and remained sinless throughout her life. As a fruit of the Redemption earned by her Son, she was taken body and soul to Heaven at the moment of her death (the Assumption).

Over the course of the centuries, the Church has established these obligatory celebrations to recall the love of God the Father through his Son Jesus Christ with the close cooperation of Mary, his Mother. Not only are these events called to mind, but they serve as an example for us to follow. These Holy Days of Obligation serve as an occasion for the Church to teach the faithful about the most important mysteries of the Faith.

Canon law lists ten days as Holy Days of Obligation for the universal Church: *Christmas; the Epiphany; the Body and Blood of Christ; the Ascension; Mary, Mother of God; the Immaculate Conception; the Assumption; St. Joseph; Sts. Peter and Paul;* and *All Saints Day*. However, not all of these Solemnities are Holy Days of Obligation in every country. The *Code of Canon Law* permits the bishops' conferences of individual nations, with the prior approval of the Holy See, to suppress certain Holy Days or to transfer their observance to a Sunday.[65] This is ordinarily the case when the observance of the Holy Day would create a burden on the faithful in that particular country.

Assumption of the Virgin by Cabezalero.
The solemnity of the Assumption of the Blessed Virgin Mary is a Holy Day of Obligation, August 15.

In the United States, there are six Solemnities that are Holy Days of Obligation:

✢ The Solemnity of Mary, Mother of God (January 1);

✢ The Solemnity of the Ascension (Thursday of the Sixth Week of Easter, i.e., forty days after Easter);

✢ The Solemnity of the Assumption of the Blessed Virgin Mary (August 15);

✢ The Solemnity of All Saints (November 1);

✢ The Solemnity of the Immaculate Conception (December 8); and

✢ The Solemnity of the Nativity of Our Lord Jesus Christ (December 25).

Whenever January 1, the solemnity of Mary, Mother of God, or August 15, the solemnity of the Assumption, or November 1, the solemnity of All Saints, falls on a Saturday or on a Monday, the precept to attend Mass is abrogated.

The bishops of the United States have transferred the solemnities of the Epiphany and the Body and Blood of Christ to the Sundays that follow these feasts on the calendar, and have suppressed the solemnities of St. Joseph and Sts. Peter and Paul as Holy Days of Obligation in the U.S. calendar. In most U.S. dioceses, the Ascension of Jesus has also been transferred to the following Sunday (the Seventh Sunday of Easter). While remaining Solemnities, Catholics are encouraged, although not obligated to attend Mass on these days.

FULFILLMENT OF THE PRECEPT OF ATTENDING MASS

To fulfill the precept to attend Mass is a grave obligation. It serves as a means for instruction in the Faith and for obtaining graces coming from the Eucharistic sacrifice and reception of Holy Communion. Therefore, whoever does not fulfill this precept commits a grave sin, except in situations where there is a serious reason to miss Mass or in cases where it is impossible to be present at its celebration.

The only circumstance that excuses someone from attending the Sunday Eucharist or a Holy Day of Obligation is qualified in the law of the Church with the adjective "serious."

The only circumstance that excuses someone from attending the Sunday Eucharist (i.e., the Sunday liturgy) or a Holy Day of Obligation is qualified in the law of the Church with the adjective "serious." Consequently, any reason for not attending Mass that is not serious can never be justified. The *Catechism* mentions illness and the care of infants as "serious reasons."[66] For other situations, the individual should consult his or her pastor.[67]

By virtue of the natural law, the closer the relationship, the greater the duty to love. God, who is the source of our being, established his relationship with us by his creative act of love. We show that love in return by setting aside proper time to worship and give thanks to God. In this way, the requirement to designate a regular time or day, dedicated to God, finds its origin in the natural law.

The Sunday requirement can be fulfilled by attending the Vigil Mass on Saturday evening (in some dioceses, this may include a wedding Mass or a funeral Mass). Similarly, one may attend Mass on the evening before a Holy Day of Obligation instead of the Holy Day itself.[68] This practice of beginning the celebration of the Lord's Day on the evening before finds its origin in the Jewish custom of beginning the commemoration of the Sabbath after sundown on the eve of the Sabbath. This extension also affords people a greater opportunity to fulfill their Sunday or Holy Day precept, especially if certain commitments or time constraints require a wider range of possible choices.

Since attending the celebration of the Eucharist on Saturday evening is a universal norm, one may opt for it whenever desired. But one must still make sure that the meaning of the Day of the Lord is not lost. For this reason, if the obligation is fulfilled on a Saturday, one should keep in mind that there is still the obligation to observe the directives regarding work on Sunday.

THE OBLIGATION TO REST

It is clear from the very beginning of our salvation history that the Lord's Day also included rest from normal daily occupations. There is a twofold reason for this. Rest facilitates the worship of God by eliminating the expenditure of energy and distractions connected to work; it also is a requirement of the human condition because it replaces lost energies and makes time for other activities along with the enrichment of the human spirit and the deepening of fraternity and friendship.

Work that is required for the welfare and safety of the individual and for the common good is permissible on Sunday. Some of the following lines of work, though not exhaustive, would fall into that category—health care workers, restaurant workers, police, firefighters, pharmacists, and gas station attendants. However, work that habitually impedes attendance at Sunday Mass, whether on Saturday evening or Sunday, must be curtailed. For example, an athlete who is involved with a basketball tournament is not dispensed from attending Mass on Saturday evening or on Sunday. Part of being a witness to the importance of the Gospel is that Catholics insist with their employers or supervisors that they be allowed to attend Mass.

It is important that one's colleagues, friends, and family see that God comes before anything else, expressed by the firm commitment to attend Mass. The spirit behind the prohibition of work is that there be a greater focus on God and on deeds of charity. Furthermore, a day of rest contributes to both bodily and mental health.

> Sharing in the Eucharist is the heart of Sunday, but the duty to keep Sunday holy cannot be reduced to this. In fact, the Lord's Day is lived well if it is marked from the beginning to end by grateful and active remembrance of God's saving work. This commits each of Christ's disciples to shape the other moments of the day—those outside the liturgical context: family life, social relationships, moments of relaxation—in such a way that the peace and joy of the Risen Lord will emerge in the ordinary events of life. For example, the relaxed gathering of parents and children can be an opportunity not only to listen to one another but also to share a few formative and more reflective moments. Even in lay life, when possible, why not make provision for special times of prayer—especially the solemn celebration of Vespers, for example—or moments of catechesis, which on the eve of Sunday or on Sunday afternoon might prepare for or complete the gift of the Eucharist in people's hearts? (*Dies Domini*, 52)

Part of the new evangelization of re-Christianizing society needs to include restoring the observation of Sunday and Holy Days as the Lord's Day.

CONCLUSION

Though it is not humanly possible to do justice to God's infinite love for us, everyone should make a serious effort to show appreciation and gratitude for everything God the Father has done for us through his Son Jesus Christ by the Holy Spirit. In essence, the First Commandment invites us to love God above all things through Jesus by the assistance of the Holy Spirit in response to his unfailing love for us.

Often we think of prayer in the context of petition, asking God for those favors that we want to receive or those which we believe we need. That kind of prayer is perfectly acceptable, for God invites us to turn to him with our petitions. What is lacking sometimes in the spirituality of individual Christians is the practice of outright praise and thanksgiving to God. It is an excellent practice to make all four forms of prayer part of our regular spiritual life on a daily basis.

God's name should be given the highest respect. Therefore, any use of God's name must be in the context of worship and veneration. For this reason, many people have adopted the custom, when they hear his name abused, of saying a prayer of reparation to make up for the offense committed. The best rule for respecting God's name is to use it only to give him honor and adoration.

A Christian has a serious obligation to ensure that Sundays and Holy Days of Obligation are especially devoted to the Lord. Making holy the Lord's Day invokes the twofold duty of participation in the celebration of the Eucharist and abstention from work that would hinder the worship owed to God, the joy proper to the Lord's Day, and the appropriate relaxation of mind and body.[69] For Christians, this commandment of the Decalogue is meant to cultivate a greater union with Jesus Christ through prayer and love for one's neighbor.

Keeping the Sabbath holy enables us to indicate the importance of the Lord in our lives; and worshiping God on Sunday is a sign of our love for him as well as an example to others in a world that needs the witness of believers.

SUPPLEMENTARY READING

1. On Matters of Faith and Morals

What the Church has decided definitively on matters of faith and morals, all Catholics must accept. On what has not been decided definitively, you may follow what theologian seems most reasonable to you. On matters of policy you may disagree, or on matters of opinion. You do not have to accept everything your particular pastor says unless it is something defined by the whole Church, i.e., defined or canon law. We are all bound by Friday abstinence. This does not mean that the sin is in eating meat but that the sin is in refusing the penance; the sin is in disobedience to Christ who speaks to us through the Church; the same with missing Mass on Sunday...

— Flannery O'Connor [70]

2. The New Age

The New Age is...appropriated by its disciples and is presented to its proselytes as a salvific wisdom. In this, it approximates to the Gnostic enthusiasm which have troubled the Church from her inception, and which in fact ground all heresy. Gnosticism consists, in all its varied presentations, in a reversion to paganism under pseudo-Christian auspices. This camouflaging of an absolute and comprehensive antagonism to Christianity has characterized Gnosticism from its origins, as it did in the flower children in the Age of Aquarius, and as it does in the New Age disciples today. The New Age movement is only the current Western version of this perennial perversion of the Christian faith....In the end, the New Age is no more than one more pagan soteriology: it looks to the extinction of the good creation that is in Christ, the Image of God, in order that one may image Nothing.

— Archbishop Francis J. Stafford [71]

3. The Eucharistic Prayer

At the Eucharist, offer the Eucharistic prayer in this way. Begin with the chalice: "We give thanks to thee, our Father, for the holy Vine of thy servant David, which thou hast made known to us through thy servant Jesus." "Glory be to thee, world without end." Then over the particles of bread: "We give thanks to thee, our Father, for the life and knowledge thou hast made known to us through thy servant Jesus." "Glory be to thee, world without end." "As this broken bread, once dispersed over the hills, was brought together and became one loaf, so may thy Church be brought from the ends of the earth into thy kingdom." Assemble on the Lord's Day, and break bread and offer the Eucharist; but first make confession of your faults, so that your sacrifice may be a pure one.

—*Didache*, 9, 14

4. On the Day Called Sunday

And on the day called Sunday, all who live in cities or in the country gather together to one place, and the memoirs of the apostles or the writings of the prophets are read, as long as time permits; then, when the reader has ceased, the president verbally instructs, and exhorts to the imitations of these good things. Then we all rise together and pray, and, as we before said, when our prayer is ended, bread and wine and water are brought, and the president in like manner offers prayers and thanksgiving, according to his ability, and the people assent, saying Amen.

— St. Justin Martyr, *The First Apology*, Chapter 67

VOCABULARY

ACEDIA
Spiritual sloth. A form of spiritual laziness due to relaxed vigilance and a lack of custody of the heart. This is one of the seven capital sins.

ADORATION
Worship. This is the humble acknowledgment by human beings that they are creatures of the thrice-holy Creator. By obeying the First Commandment, people acknowledge and respond to the Revelation of the glory and power of God.

APOSTASY
The total repudiation of the Christian Faith. This is forbidden by the First Commandment and is against the theological virtue of faith.

ASSERTORY OATH
A type of oath in which God is called upon as a witness to the truth of what is being said, as when a person takes an oath in court.

ATHEISM
Rejection of the existence of God, founded often on a false conception of human autonomy. This is forbidden by the First Commandment.

BLASPHEMY
Words or insulting gestures against God, the Virgin Mary, the saints, or the Church.

CHARITY
Love. The theological virtue by which a Christian loves God above all things for his own sake, and loves his neighbor as himself for the love of God.

CONTRITION
True sorrow for and hatred of sin committed, coupled with the firm purpose to sin no more. This is necessary to make a good confession and for the priest to absolve a penitent in the Sacrament of Penance.

DESPAIR
The loss of hope in God because of doubt in his fidelity, care for people, or power to save a sinner. This is a sin against the theological virtue of hope.

DIDACHE
An early Christian work (ca. AD 60) of unknown authorship, it summarizes morality as a choice between the path of life and the path of death, and includes liturgical practice and disciplinary norms.

DIVINATION
The practice of foretelling future events or discovery of what is hidden, by supernatural or magical means. This is forbidden by the First Commandment.

EVANGELICAL COUNSELS
The vows of poverty, chastity, and obedience often taken upon entrance to religious life.

FAITH
The theological virtue by which one believes in all that God has said and revealed to man and that the Church proposes for belief.

HATRED OF GOD
The sin against charity opposed to the love of God, denying his goodness and cursing him as the one who forbids sin and inflicts punishment.

HERESY
The obstinate denial or obstinate doubt by a baptized person of some truth that must be believed with divine faith.

HOPE
Hope is the theological virtue by which one desires the happiness of eternal life with God by placing his trust in Christ's promises and relying on the grace of the Holy Spirit.

INDIFFERENCE
Making no decision between conflicting parties or ideas. This leads to a refusal to reflect on the goodness and power of divine charity.

INGRATITUDE
The refusal to acknowledge divine charity or return God's love.

VOCABULARY Continued

INVOLUNTARY DOUBT
The sin against faith that hesitates in believing or overcoming difficulties connected with the Faith and fails to attempt to dispel it.

IRRELIGION
Disrespect and, in many instances, mockery of God's goodness and sacred dignity. The more common sins of irreligion are tempting God, sacrilege, and simony.

LEISURE
Temporary freedom from occupations in order to enjoy and enrich oneself and celebrate the good things God has created, such as family, culture, society, and religion.

LORD
A title for God and for Jesus that recognizes divine sovereignty.

LUKEWARMNESS
Having little depth of feeling or zeal; indifference. A lukewarm person fails or hesitates to respond to divine love.

MAGIC
The pretended art of influencing the course of events and producing physical phenomena by processes attributed to spiritual beings.

MASS or LITURGY OF THE EUCHARIST
Also called the Eucharist or Lord's Supper. This name is derived from the Latin dismissal of the faithful, "*Ite, missa est.*" The principal sacramental celebration of the Church, established by Jesus at the Last Supper, in which the mystery of salvation through participation in the sacrificial Death and glorious Resurrection of Christ is renewed and accomplished.

OATH
The calling of God as a witness to the truth of what is being said.

PERJURY
To make a promise without any intention of completing it, or to lie under oath.

PETITION
Form of prayer asking God to aid oneself or others.

PRESUMPTION
The sin by which one expects salvation without personal effort or trusts solely in his efforts without God's aid.

PROMISSORY OATH
A type of oath in which God is called upon as a witness to something that will be done in the future, as when a public official solemnly swears to fulfill the duties of his office.

REAL PRESENCE
The presence of Jesus Christ—Body and Blood, Soul and Divinity—in the Eucharist under the appearance of bread and wine.

RELIGION
Probably from the Latin for "to bind," the virtue that enables a Christian to render God the worship, honor, devotion, and service he deserves. It involves a set of beliefs and practices followed by those committed to the service and worship of God.

SABBATH
The Sabbath—or seventh day—on which God rested after the work of the six days of creation was completed. In honor of Christ's Resurrection, Sunday, or the Lord's Day, must include rest from labor and the worship of God as required by the Third Commandment.

SATANIC WORSHIP
Worship of Satan, the Prince of Darkness, or any other evil demons.

SCHISM
A breach of the unity of the visible Church; the refusal to submit to the pope or be united with the Church in communion with him.

VOCABULARY Continued

SIMONY
The buying or selling of ecclesiastical offices, sacraments, grace, benefices, or other sacred things.

SUPERSTITION
An irrational religious belief or practice founded on fear or ignorance. Various forms such as good-luck charms, omens, divination, and magic are forbidden by the First Commandment.

THANKSGIVING
A form of prayer praising God for the good he has given.

THEOPHANY
A manifestation or appearance of God to man. This can be in the form of his glory, a medium such as a storm or fire, or in the Person of Jesus Christ on earth.

VAIN
Empty, worthless, hollow; having no genuine substance, value, or importance.

VOLUNTARY DOUBT
The sin against faith that disregards or refuses to hold what God has revealed as true.

VOW
A promise made freely and deliberately to God concerning something that is better than its opposite.

WORK
To actively exert oneself (mentally or physically) by operating upon a part of creation in order to do or make something more useful than the materials used.

WORSHIP
Adoration paid to God or the actions, rites, or ceremonies associated with such adoration. In an archaic sense, the condition of being rightly esteemed.

YHWH (Yahweh)
The shorthand initialism (Tetragrammaton) used by the Israelites for the name of God, "I AM WHO AM," which out of great respect for God could not be uttered.

Adoration of the Shepherds by Murillo.
The solemnity of the Nativity of Our Lord Jesus Christ is a Holy Day
of Obligation, December 25.

STUDY QUESTIONS

1. How does the First Commandment set the tone for the rest?

2. How can the Ten Commandments be summed up in the two great commandments of Christ?

3. How does Christ's Revelation differ from revelation in all other faiths?

4. What are the theological virtues, and how are they received?

5. Define faith. What is the response that is required on the part of man?

6. What is the relationship between humility and the Faith? What is the relationship between reason and the Faith?

7. Give examples of voluntary doubt, schism, and heresy.

8. Give an example of how a person might fall into despair. Give an example of presumption.

9. Explain how loving God leads naturally to a love of neighbor.

10. Is ingratitude a common sin? Explain.

11. Explain how a person can sin against love? What do you think is the root cause of these sins?

12. Explain each of the four types of prayer.

13. Give an example of idolatry in modern society. Explain how the example meets the definition given in the *Catechism*.

14. If idols are wrong, then why are Catholics allowed, or even encouraged, to have pictures, icons, and religious symbols?

15. Select three violations against proper worship and explain why they are violations against the First Commandment.

16. What name did God reveal to Moses? How did the Israelites refer to God, and why?

17. Explain how respect for God's name continued in the New Testament.

18. When is it most appropriate to refer to the name of God?

19. What is an oath? What are some instances in which God himself swore an oath?

20. What is the difference between an assertory oath and a promissory oath?

21. List and explain the conditions which are necessary in taking an oath.

22. What is the difference between a vow and an oath?

23. What are two circumstances when vows are taken? What is the meaning of taking these two vows?

24. List and explain the three requirements for taking a vow.

25. What is blasphemy? List three examples.

26. What are some examples from modern society that would indicate that blasphemy has become acceptable among some people?

27. What is the origin of the seventh day or the Sabbath as a day of rest?

28. What was the double purpose of the Sabbath in the Old Testament?

29. Under Mosaic Law, what were the Israelites obliged to do on the Sabbath?

30. How did the earliest Christians, as indicated in the Book of Acts, keep the Lord's Day?

31. What is a Holy Day of Obligation?

32. List the reasons why Sunday worship is an obligation for Christians.

33. List the ten Holy Days of Obligation for the universal Church, and summarize the meaning of each celebration.

34. Why may the Sunday or Holy Day obligation be fulfilled on the evening before?

35. When may a Catholic miss Mass?

36. Why is there an obligation to rest on Sunday? What would be an example of permitted work that is not listed in the text?

37. List several activities which would help an individual or a family to keep the meaning of the Lord's Day.

PRACTICAL EXERCISES

For each of the following situations (numbers 1 through 6), indicate whether it describes a sin against faith, a sin against hope, a sin against charity, or a sin against religion. Then identify the specific type of sin within that category.

1. Daniel does not go to Mass or pray very much at all. When his friends ask him why, he tells them: "God is supposed to be all about love and mercy. If he is really that loving and merciful, he would not send anyone to Hell. In fact, I will bet that hell does not really exist. Everyone ends up in Heaven."

2. Vivian considers herself to be Catholic, but she does not believe that Christ rose from the dead. She thinks the Resurrection was a story made up by the disciples in order to gain new followers.

3. Jeremy prays to God for all the things he wants in life—a good career, a nice home, and general success. When he does not feel that God is hearing him, he gets angry with God. He never takes time to consider all the gifts that God has given him, so he never even thinks of thanking God for anything.

4. Bart and Emily went to a psychic to have a séance. Emily was very close to her late uncle and wanted to contact him so that he could advise her on some issues that were happening in her family.

5. Although they consider themselves members of St. Dominic Parish, Anna and her parents do not make it to Mass every Sunday. Once or twice a month is all they seem to be able to handle. Anna's father says that Sunday is his only day off, and so he would rather rest, watch football games, and spend time with the family.

6. Evan has led a very sinful life. He has gotten hooked on hallucinogenic drugs and alcohol; he has stolen cash from his employer; he has had a series of sexual relationships even though he has never been married. Now and then he comes to realize how wrong and sinful he has been, but he decides that he has done so much sinning and has sunk so low that God would never be able to forgive him.

For numbers 7 through 10, name the type of prayer indicated—adoration, petition, thanksgiving, or contrition. (Some arguably may reflect more than one type.)

7. "Jesus Christ, Son of God, have mercy on me, a sinner."

8. "We give you glory, almighty God, for your goodness and mercy."

9. "Lord, I come to you with gratitude for all the gifts you have given me today."

10. For all those who are sick, especially my grandmother, we pray to the Lord."

11. Write out the words of the Lord's Prayer (the Our Father). How many different types of prayer do you find? Put slash marks between each type of prayer and write above each segment what type of prayer is indicated.

12. Read and take note of the principles found in the following Scriptural passages that condemn superstition:
   - Lv 19: 26; 19: 31; 20: 6; 20: 27
   - Dt 13: 2-4

13. Discuss and enumerate several classes of superstition. Analyze and assess their plausibility. Do these superstitions describe what is real in any way? Why would anyone believe them?

14. What is the difference between wearing amulets or good-luck charms and wearing devotional medals, such as the Miraculous Medal or a patron saint medal? What is the difference between divination with the dead and prayers to the saints?

PRACTICAL EXERCISES Continued

Evaluate the following situations in numbers 15 through 17. Are the statements made oaths or vows? If so, what type of oath or vow is it? Would this use of an oath or vow be acceptable according to the Second Commandment?

15. In the film *Gone with the Wind*, Scarlett O'Hara at one point stands alone in a field with her fist upraised and says, "As God is my witness, I'll never be hungry again!"

16. An older sister says to a younger brother: "If you touch my bike again, I swear to God I'll slug you."

17. A daughter says to her mother, "I promise to do the dishes just as soon as I get home from the game."

In the following cases in numbers 18 through 21, to what degree are the oaths or vows obligatory, and why?

18. Mark's sister Carrie recently married Allen, her boyfriend of four years. Things appeared to have been going well until Mark accidentally discovered one day that Allen had concealed from his sister the fact that he had been previously married and is the father of a six-year-old child. The situation is further complicated when Mark learns that Allen has not obtained a legal divorce or a declaration of nullity from the Church. This means that his sister's marriage is invalid. When Mark confronted Allen about this information, Allen denied the charges, and a terrible argument ensued. The next morning, Allen was gone. Mark feels that his family's honor has been destroyed by Allen's actions, and has personally vowed to take revenge on him. Does this vow bind Mark? Why, or why not?

19. Laura and her sister Theresa have not spoken to one another for seven years as a result of a fight over some antiques that their grandmother left behind when she died. Because he was angry with Laura at the time of her argument with Theresa, their father supported Theresa and gave all of the property to her, an action he later deeply regretted. Although he apologized to Laura and asked Theresa to share the property with her sister, Theresa refused to do so, resulting in the rift between the sisters. Their father recently decided to rewrite his will, and Laura demanded that he swear to name her as his sole heir, leaving her sister out of his will. Because he still feels guilty about what occurred before, her father has done so, but his conscience is bothering him. Must he do what he swore to do?

20. Peter promised to give his friend Sara a ring that he won in a contest and she liked very much. Although he believed the ring to be of little value, he later discovered that it is actually worth quite a lot of money. Now he doesn't want to give Sara the ring. Must he?

21. Because he had been only an average student for the first three years of high school, David had found it difficult to be accepted to the extremely competitive premedical program at the college he had chosen at the beginning of his senior year. His family was poor and could not afford to send him to the school, and it was not very likely that he was going to get a scholarship because of his past academic performance. But David had thought and prayed about it, and he wanted to be a doctor. He worked hard during his senior year, and had succeeded in earning straight A's both semesters. In addition, he had gone to a local community college for one year, where he had also earned straight A's. The entire time that he was working on his lately-developed dream of attending medical school, he had prayed to God to help him and to grant him the favor of becoming a doctor. At one point, after careful consideration, he had even vowed that if God would help him gain admittance to medical school, he would devote his first two years as a doctor to serving as a missionary doctor with a lay volunteer program in a poor country in Asia or Africa. Now that he has graduated at the top of his class from medical school, David has been offered a position at one of the most prestigious research hospitals in the U.S. He remembers the vow that he made, but this is a chance that he may not get again for a long time. What should he do?

PRACTICAL EXERCISES Continued

Read the situations described in numbers 22 to 24. For each, state whether you believe the person has a legitimate excuse for missing Mass.

22. The Duncan family was on its way to church when they witnessed a terrible car accident. Since Mrs. Duncan is a doctor, the family stopped to render aid to those injured. By the time the police and ambulances arrived, Mass was nearly over.

23. Catherine is a college student at St. Anne's University. During the school year, she likes to attend the Mass that is held in the campus chapel at 8 p.m. on Sundays—the latest Mass in the city. After spring break, when she moved back into her dorm room on the Sunday just before classes began again, she planned to attend the 8 p.m. Mass. When she got to the chapel, she saw a note that there would not be a Mass that evening. The schedule change had been announced before spring break, but Catherine did not hear about it.

24. Jacob is a big fan of the Green Bay Packers. He worked at the pizza parlor until midnight on Saturday night and didn't get up in time for either the 8 a.m. Mass or the 10 a.m. Mass. The Packers game was on television starting at 1:30 p.m., and he felt sure the game would be over in time for him to make the 5 p.m. Mass. But the score was tied after regulation play, and the teams had to have a sudden-death overtime. When the Packers finally won, it was already 5:25 p.m. Jacob had missed Mass. He knew there was one more Mass that evening, at 6 p.m., but it was on the other side of town, 11 miles away. He decided that was too far, and God would understand.

25. Sunday Mass has the character of a community experience that strengthens the life of faith. Formulate a response to these common objections:

- "I don't want to go to Mass every Sunday because I don't get anything out of it."
- "I think that a person can pray just as well at home as in Church."

26. Discuss and explain the problems that surround the requirement for Sunday rest. What can be done on Sundays, and what ought to be avoided? In your opinion, does modern culture facilitate or inhibit the Christian observance of Sundays? Provide examples to support your statements.

27. Make a list of activities that families can do on Sunday that would facilitate a return to the festive character of Sunday.

Christ Falls on the Way to Calvary by Raphael. The subject of Raphael's altarpiece is the mutual gaze of Christ, stumbling beneath the weight of the Cross, and his distraught mother, who reaches out her arms in vain.

In meditation, a person generally focuses or thinks about a particular event in salvation history or an aspect of the Faith. For example, a person might read the Gospel account of the Crucifixion and, entering into the scene, reflect on the meaning of our Lord's Passion.

FROM THE CATECHISM

1260 "Since Christ died for all, and since all men are in fact called to one and the same destiny, which is divine, we must hold that the Holy Spirit offers to all the possibility of being made partakers, in a way know to God, of the Paschal mystery."[72] Every man who is ignorant of the Gospel of Christ and of his Church, but seeks the truth and does the will of God in accordance with his understanding of it, can be saved. It may be supposed that such persons would have *desired Baptism explicitly* if they had known its necessity.

1842 By faith, we believe in God and believe all that he has revealed to us and all that the Holy Church proposes for our belief.

1843 By hope we desire, and with steadfast trust await from God, eternal life and the graces to merit it.

2138 Superstition is a departure from the worship that we give to the true God. It is manifested in idolatry, as well in various forms of divination and magic.

2139 Tempting God in words or deeds, sacrilege, and simony are sins of irreligion forbidden by the First Commandment.

2140 Since it rejects or denies the existence of God, atheism is a sin against the First Commandment.

2142 The Second Commandment *prescribes respect for the Lord's name.* Like the First Commandment, it belongs to the virtue of religion and more particularly it governs our use of speech in sacred matters.

2147 *Promises* made to others in God's name engage the divine honor, fidelity, truthfulness, and authority. They must be respected in justice. To be unfaithful to them is to misuse God's name and in some way to make God out to be a liar.[73]

2162 The Second Commandment forbids every improper use of God's name. Blasphemy is the use of the name of God, of Jesus Christ, of the Virgin Mary, and of the saints in an offensive way.

2163 False oaths call on God to be witness to a lie. Perjury is a grave offense against the Lord who is always faithful to his promises.

2189 "Observe the Sabbath day, to keep it holy."[74] "The seventh day is a sabbath of solemn rest, holy to the Lord."[75]

2192 "Sunday...is to be observed as the foremost holy day of obligation in the universal Church."[76] "On Sundays and other holy days of obligation the faithful are bound to participate in the Mass."[77]

2193 "On Sundays and other holy days of obligation the faithful are bound...to abstain from those labors and business concerns which impede the worship to be rendered to God, the joy which is proper to the Lord's Day, or the proper relaxation of mind and body."[78]

2194 The institution of Sunday helps all "to be allowed sufficient rest and leisure to cultivate their familial, cultural, social, and religious lives."[79]

2195 Every Christian should avoid making unnecessary demands on others that would hinder them from observing the Lord's Day.

The Widow's Mite by Tissot.
"Truly I tell you, this poor widow has put in more than all of them; for they all contributed out
of their abundance, but she out of her poverty put in all the living she had." (Lk 21: 3-4)

ENDNOTES – CHAPTER FIVE

1. Cf. Acts 20: 7.
2. Cf. 2 Cor 5: 17.
3. Cf. Acts 1: 11; 1 Thes 4: 13-17.
4. Cf. Rev 21: 5.
5. Cf. 1 Cor 15: 14.
6. *DD* 1, 2.
7. Dt 6: 4-5.
8. Lev 19: 18; cf. Mk 12: 29-31.
9. Cf. 1 Jn 4: 10.
10. CCC 176.
11. *DV* 5; cf. DS 377; 3010.
12. Cf. CCC 2091-2092.
13. 1 Jn 4: 20.
14. Jn 3: 14-15.
15. Cf. CCC 2113.
16. Cf. CCC 2116.
17. Cf. CCC 2117.
18. Cf. CCC 2144-2145.
19. CIC, 1199.
20. Ex 20: 7; Dt 5: 11.
21. Cf. Dt 6: 3; Lk 1: 73; Heb 6: 13-17.
22. Cf. 2 Sm 7: 11-13.
23. Cf. Ps 132: 11; Acts 2: 30.
24. Nm 30: 2.
25. Sir 23: 9-11.
26. Cf. Mt 26: 63-64.
27. Cf. 2 Cor 1: 23; Gal 1: 20.
28. Cf. CIC, 1199.
29. Lev 24: 14-16.

30. Cf. 2 Mc 8: 4; 9: 28; Ez 35: 12-15.
31. Jn 10: 33.
32. Cf. 1 Tm 1: 13.
33. Rom 2: 24.
34. Cf. 2 Tm 3: 2; Col 3: 8.
35. Jas 2: 7.
36. 1 Thes 5: 17.
37. St. Thomas Aquinas, *STh* II-II, 83, 9.
38. Mt 6: 9.
39. CCC 2591.
40. Cf. CCC 2644.
41. CCC 2628.
42. Cf. Mal 1: 11.
43. Paul VI, *MF* 56.
44. Cf. CCC 2629.
45. Cf. Lk 13: 20-21.
46. St. Josemaria Escriva, *Christ Is Passing By*, (Princeton, N.J.: Scepter Publishers, 1974), 119.
47. Cf. CCC 2721-2724.
48. CCC 2724.
49. Cf. CCC 2752, 2755.
50. Jn 12: 24.
51. Cf. Lev 24: 8.
52. Cf. Nm 18: 9-10.
53. Cf. Lk 13: 10-16; 14: 1-5; Jn 5: 9-10.
54. Mk 2: 27.
55. Cf. Acts 2: 46.
56. Cf. Rev 1: 10.

57. Acts 20: 7.
58. Cf. 1 Cor 16: 2.
59. Acts 20: 7.
60. St. Justin Martyr, second century.
61. CCC 1330.
62. Cf. CCC 1067.
63. Cf. CCC 1067.
64. *SC* 10.
65. Cf. CIC, 1246.
66. Cf. CCC 2181.
67. Cf. CIC, 1245.
68. Cf. CIC, 1248.
69. Cf. CCC 2185.
70. Flannery O'Connor, *Collected Works: Letter to Cecil Dawkins*, December 23, 1959, p. 1117
71. Archbishop Francis J. Stafford, "The 'New Age' Movement: Analysis of a New Attempt to Find Salvation Apart from Christian Faith," Catholic Position Papers, March 1993
72. *GS* 22 § 5; cf. *LG* 16; *AG* 7.
73. Cf. 1 Jn 1: 10.
74. Dt 5: 12.
75. Ex 31: 15.
76. CIC, 1246 § 1.
77. CIC, 1247.
78. CIC, 1247.
79. *GS* 67 § 3.

The Fourth Commandment:
Honor Your Father and Your Mother

CHAPTER 6

The Fourth Commandment: Honor Your Father and Your Mother

*J*ack, a 15-year-old, arrived home one night with his eyes blurry and his balance obviously affected. It was clear that he had been drinking. His family had never seen him like this before and was very concerned. Jack's older brother, Mike, was as worried as his mother. Mike knew what the problem was: He had been a bad example, and Jack was simply imitating him. Mike knew that he had never actually become intoxicated himself, but he suspected he had undermined the authority of his parents by his actions and attitudes.

Mike had returned home after finishing college at the beginning of the summer. He had come with the attitude that he did not have to obey his parents the way he was expected to before he went to college. But because he was living at home, his parents laid down the rules of the house: Mike's parents wanted him to come home at a certain time, not smoke in the house, and to do certain chores.

Mike had grown accustomed to living with his roommates at college where he did not have to do chores and could come and go as he pleased. So Mike stayed out late many nights and, at times, smoked in the house around Jack and his other brothers and sisters. Mike's parents warned him that he was giving a bad example to the rest of the family. They had begun to notice that Jack especially had begun to disregard their authority by neglecting his homework and small jobs around the house.

The night Jack came home drunk, it hit Mike like a bad dream. He had been an influence for the worse in his disregard for his parents' rules. He realized that even as an adult he had the responsibility to honor his father and mother and to abide by the rules established in their home, and, more importantly, that his example as the eldest could influence his brothers and sisters who were still dependent on their parents' guidance and direction.

FOR DISCUSSION

✠ How does the Fourth Commandment protect the integrity of family relationships?

✠ What are some of the specific obligations that are enjoined upon parents and children by this commandment?

✠ What obligations does the Fourth Commandment set for human relations outside the family?

Christ Returning to His Parents by Simone.
"'Son, why have you treated us so? Behold, your father and I have been looking for you
anxiously.' And he said to them, 'How is it that you sought me? Did you not know
that I must be in my father's house?'...And he went...with them and came to Nazareth,
and was obedient to them...'" (Lk 2:48-51)

INTRODUCTION

Millennia of history attest to the fact that a person's upbringing and moral and physical support find their ideal setting within the context of the family. A newborn entering into the world is best served in terms of protection, physical development, and eventual education under the care and supervision of a loving mother and father. The vital importance of the family for the well-being of the person explains why the Fourth Commandment takes pride of place among the commandments referring to the person.

Since every human being depends first on his or her parents for physical, emotional, and moral health, there are many important ramifications derived from the words, "Honor your father and mother." This chapter will discuss the duties of parents toward their children—and the duties of children toward their father, mother, and anyone else who has rightful authority over their development.

THE FAMILY AS A COMMUNITY OF LOVE

The vital importance of the family for the well-being of the person explains why the Fourth Commandment takes pride of place among the commandments referring to the person.

Relationships flow from the social nature of every human being. An essential aspect of the divine image each person carries within his or her intimate self is the inclination to love others and to seek their good. This love for others is not some kind of generic love, but rather a relational and hierarchical love. We must love first those closest to us by reason of family ties, especially in the case of spouses, parents, and siblings. By virtue of natural law, the closer the relationship, the greater the duty to love.

By reason of marriage, a husband and wife must show their greatest and most intense love for each other. Linked to spousal love is the very close bond they must have with their children, the fruit of their intimate love for each other. Because a person's existence, in cooperation with God's creative power, is a direct consequence of his or her parents' love, children must honor, obey, respect, and love their mother and father as representatives of God's authority over them.

Due to the close natural ties between parents and their children, every household should be an oasis of happiness and charity. For this vision to become a reality, each family member must have a strong relationship with Jesus Christ. The practice of family prayer, especially the Rosary, helps to maintain an atmosphere of love. Both parents and children should have as a priority and goal the imitation of Christ's affection, kindness, and spirit of service toward those closest to them.

Unfortunately, our activity-driven culture, together with the craze to achieve and succeed, has harmed family life. This often occurs when the focus is not on spending time with one another and serving each other's needs, but rather on work, sports, and recreation. There is a need today to restore family life, where parents have meals with their children, and where there is a daily interaction and growth in love among family members.

A healthy family environment ultimately contributes good citizens to society, while the opposite situation has left many people psychologically and emotionally wounded. The *Catechism of the Catholic Church* summarizes these ideas well:

> The Fourth Commandment is addressed expressly to children in their relationship to their father and mother, because this relationship is the most universal. It likewise concerns the ties of kinship between members of the extended family. It requires honor, affection, and gratitude toward elders and ancestors. Finally, it extends to the duties of pupils to teachers, employees to employers, subordinates to leaders, citizens to their country, and to those who administer or govern it.

> This Commandment includes and presupposes the duties of parents, instructors, teachers, leaders, magistrates, those who govern, all who exercise authority over others or over a community of persons. (CCC 2199)

OBSERVANCE IN THE OLD TESTAMENT

There are several places in the Old Testament where the Fourth Commandment is repeated. Two of these formulas are presented in the Books of Exodus and Deuteronomy:

> Honor your father and your mother, that your days may be long in the land which the LORD your God gives you. (Ex 20: 12)

> Honor your father and your mother, as the LORD your God commanded you; that your days may be prolonged, and that it may go well with you, in the land which the LORD your God gives you. (Dt 5: 16)

The Old Testament is filled with exhortations and considerations concerning the obligations to honor father and mother. God promises many blessings for those who respectfully love, serve, and revere their parents. The idea behind the powerful encouragement to truly love father and mother is that human life, a priceless gift, comes from them. No matter how solicitous and grateful children are, they can never repay their parents for the gift of life and upbringing.

This passage from the Book of Sirach conveys accurately both the duty to honor one's parents and the benefits resulting from fidelity to the Fourth Commandment.

Listen to me your father, O children; and act accordingly, that you may be kept in safety. For the Lord honored the father above the children, and he confirmed the right of the mother over her sons. Whoever honors his father atones for sins, and whoever glorifies his mother is like one who lays up treasure. Whoever honors his father will be gladdened by his own children, and when he prays he will be heard. Whoever glorifies his father will have long life, and whoever obeys the Lord will refresh his mother; he will serve his parents as his masters. Honor your father by word and deed, that a blessing from him may come upon you. For a father's blessing strengthens the houses of the children, but a mother's curse uproots their foundations.

Do not glorify yourself by dishonoring your father, for your father's dishonor is no glory to you. For a man's glory comes from honoring his father, and it is a disgrace for children not to respect their mother. O son, help your father in his old age, and do not grieve him as long as he lives; even if he is lacking in understanding, show forbearance; in all your strength do not despise him. For kindness to a father will not be forgotten, and against your sins it will be credited to you; in the day of your affliction it will be remembered in your favor; as frost in fair weather, your sins will melt away. Whoever forsakes his father is like a blasphemer, and whoever angers his mother is cursed by the Lord. (Sir 3: 1-16)

St. Joseph and the Christ Child by El Greco.
The family is the domestic church; a man and a woman united in marriage, together with their children; a community of faith, hope, and charity.

DUTIES OF PARENTS TO THEIR CHILDREN

St. Paul profoundly summarizes the duties of good Christian parents: "Fathers, do not provoke your children to anger, but bring them up in the discipline and instruction of the Lord."[1] These words exhort parents to love their children with the love of Jesus Christ. This love involves kindness, mercy, and affection, but also fortitude and courage in imparting discipline in their education and formation of their children. This Pauline teaching addressed to mothers and fathers of all times touches on three principle aspects of Christian parenting—*fairness and understanding*, *discipline*, and *instructions in the Christian Faith*.

Fairness and understanding: The phrase "do not provoke your children to anger" conveys the message that parents must try to earn and maintain the respect of their children. There is a happy medium between laxity in leadership and guidance on one extreme and abusive tyranny on the other. In an absolute sense, children belong to God, and God has entrusted those children to the care of their parents. Each child is a child of God redeemed by Jesus Christ and must be treated as such. Humiliating reprimands, for example, let alone the use of physical violence, would be totally incompatible with Christian parenting.

Though infants, children, and even adolescents are not adults, Christian charity requires that parents treat them with the respect owed to children of God. If there is genuine concern and desire to truly help them, the children will quickly perceive that discipline and guidance spring out of a deep love.

Christian charity requires that parents treat children with the respect owed to children of God.

> Children—even those who seem intractable and unresponsive—always want this closeness, this fraternity, with their parents. It is a question of trust. Parents should bring up their children in an atmosphere of friendship, never giving the impression that they do not trust them. They should give them freedom and teach them how to use it with personal responsibility.[2]

Discipline: Discipline is a crucial component in raising children to become good citizens as well as followers of Christ. Children do not reach the age of reason until about seven years of age, which means that the capacity for true self-control requires consistent discipline that paves the way for virtuous actions.

As in most facets of human development, formation in the proper use of freedom, self-control, and sense of responsibility rests in large part on the parent's success in instilling discipline. Insensitivity to the needs of others, habitual laziness and idleness, and an inability to fulfill tasks reasonably betrays in many instances a lack of parental discipline.

There is a special urgency for parents to genuinely play the role of mother and father and avoid the common pitfall of limiting themselves to simply being "friends" of their children. Regrettably, there is a generalized fear of exercising a certain tough love when it comes to forming children in a spirit of sacrifice typified by hard work, good manners, selflessness, and sobriety in creature comforts. The virtue of self-giving generosity as a way of sharing and advancing the Kingdom of God always presupposes the conscientious sense of responsibility that comes from discipline.

The Letter to the Hebrews expresses well the importance of discipline in the formation and education of children.

And have you forgotten the exhortation which addresses you as sons?—"My son, do not regard lightly the discipline of the Lord, nor lose courage when you are punished by him. For the Lord disciplines him whom he loves, and chastises every son whom he receives."

It is for discipline that you have to endure. God is treating you as sons; for what son is there whom his father does not discipline?...For the moment all discipline seems painful rather than pleasant; later it yields the peaceful fruit of righteousness to those who have been trained by it. (Heb 12:5-11)

Parents have a serious obligation to form and educate their sons and daughters in the Catholic Faith.

Instruction in the Catholic Faith: In addition to overseeing the physical well-being of their children, parents have a serious obligation to form and educate their sons and daughters in the Catholic Faith. They simply cannot pass this responsibility on to schools, parishes, or supplementary educational programs.

A Catholic education is much more than learning the facts and information about the Catholic Faith. A key component of Christian upbringing involves training in charity, kindness, compassion, and service. For instance, all children should contribute to the upkeep of the house, share their possessions with others, and learn how to care for anyone who is suffering, beginning with members of their own family.

Given our consumerist culture, it is very important for parents to train and form their children to be happy with what is necessary to lead a simple and sober life, and not to accumulate so many possessions that the child becomes self-centered and distracted from other people and from God.

Another aspect of religious instruction involves cultivating friendship with Jesus Christ. Studying the four Gospels and displaying images of Christ and Our Lady—especially crucifixes in bedrooms—are a few means of fostering a real relationship with Christ and his Mother. Parents must coach their children in speaking habitually with the Lord and listening to his voice on a very personal level.

Beyond the regular reception of the sacraments, children should be taught simple prayers to be said at bedtime with the parents participating. As the child grows, the child should be instructed in the *Catechism* and in the lives of the saints. Many resources are available today to aid parents in the fulfillment of this task.

Although both parents must attend to this especially grave obligation, studies have shown that fathers play an especially important part in the formation of their children's religious habits. Parents must remember there is a direct connection between their own personal religious practices and that of their children.

Instructing children in the Faith does not mean, however, that parents have the right to choose the manner in which their children will live their faith in the future. On the contrary, parents must respect and encourage the vocational choices of their children, whether they choose the married state or celibacy for the Kingdom of God.

Studies have shown that fathers play an especially important part in the formation of their children's religious habits.

DUTIES OF CHILDREN TO THEIR PARENTS

Besides honoring their parents, children are also expected to obey them. The Apostle adds a Christian motive for obedience: it is desired by Christ. St. Paul writes to the Colossians, "Children, obey your parents in everything, for this pleases the Lord" (Col 3: 20).

The *Catechism* states:

> Respect for parents (*filial piety*) derives from *gratitude* toward those who, by the gift of life, their love and their work, have brought their children into the world and enabled them to grow in stature, wisdom, and grace....
>
> As long as a child lives at home with his parents, the child should obey his parents in all that they ask of him when it is for his good or that of the family...Children should also obey the reasonable directions of their teachers and all to whom their parents have entrusted them. But if a child is convinced in conscience that it would be morally wrong to obey a particular order, he must not do so. (CCC 2215, 2217)

In principle, parents have a divinely bestowed authority over their offspring. Independent of their own character flaws, natural law reinforced by the Fourth Commandment requires that children honor, respect, and obey their parents in all that is not sinful.

Nevertheless, it is important that parents win the respect of their children by being effective role models in the Christian life. Habitual anger, impatience, and irritability, among many other defects, cause parents to

Implementing the command to love as Christ loves in every particular circumstance means making the needs of family members a top priority, especially the elderly or disabled parents and grandparents.

quickly lose their moral authority. Parents effectively direct and guide their children not only by verbal command, but especially by their good example. Behind the lives of many of the contemporary saints are the holy lives of their parents.

The commandment "honor your father and your mother" indirectly tells parents: Honor your sons and daughters. They deserve this because they are alive, because they are who they are, and this is true from the first moment of conception.

The Fourth Commandment then, by expressing the intimate bonds uniting the family, highlights the basis of its inner unity. (Pope John Paul II, *Letter to Families*, 15 [1994])

Even when a parent does not act in an honorable way, his or her position as parent requires respect. Children in such situations need to be reminded that they have an obligation to honor their parents with charity and support, without condoning their wrongdoing.

RELATIONS WITH EXTENDED FAMILY

Blood ties go beyond the immediate family of parents and children. They include grandparents, aunts, uncles, and cousins. Identity and contact with the extended family have significantly changed over the past decades. In previous times, it was expected that a home would house not just parents and children, but also grandparents and single aunts and uncles. This practice has largely been lost, given the nature and demands of a highly developed modern industrialized society.

However, busy schedules, demanding working hours, and frequent changes in domiciles still should not dispense anyone from living Christ's commandment of charity. Implementing the command to love as Christ loves in every particular circumstance means making the needs of family members a top priority, especially the elderly or disabled parents and grandparents.

Whenever possible, unless professional assistance is required, the disabled and the aged should have the security and care of a home. The opportunity to take care of debilitated family members brings out the best in a family and makes the presence of Christ more evident through such selfless service.

THE IMPORTANCE OF SPOUSAL UNITY

The Lord's teaching on the permanence of marriage has tremendous importance for the emotional, psychological, and spiritual health of the children. Both boys and girls need guidance and love from both a father and a mother. The faithful love, commitment, and dedication of the spouses to each other presents to the children a clear reflection of the love of God for each person.

The tragedy of separation and divorce can often cause confusion or even psychological problems in children by depriving them of a focused fatherly and motherly love. A consequence of this common, lamentable state of affairs is the infliction of emotional wounds that become obstacles to respect and love for parents and those in authority. In some cases, parental disunity causes so much insecurity and anxiety that the children rebel against their parents and come to harbor deep seated bitterness and resentment that carries over into their adult lives.

Because a healthy spousal relationship encourages respect and devotion from the children, this facet of family life is connected to the Fourth Commandment. The spousal love between a husband and a wife has a direct bearing on their children's ability to obey and honor their parents.

The spousal love between a husband and a wife has a direct bearing on their children's ability to obey and honor their parents.

CIVIC OBLIGATIONS OF CITIZENS

No human being is an isolated entity. It is human nature to interact with others at home, work, and recreation. The social character of every human being requires that there be an established authority to facilitate harmonious relationships among members of society as well as to protect their rights as citizens. Therefore, the Fourth Commandment extends to the authority of the state and the duties of citizens with regard to those in positions of authority.

From the writings of the Old Testament to the teachings of St. Paul, it is made abundantly clear that all legitimate authority comes from God. Though some rulers established in authority have been flawed both in morals and in leadership, their authority still comes from God. Therefore, they must be obeyed in everything that is not immoral. Part of abiding by the Fourth Commandment consists of seeing the will of God in the directives and legitimate laws of the heads of state. The following passage transmits the proper Christian attitude towards those in positions of authority:

> Let every person be subject to the governing authorities. For there is no authority except from God, and those that exist have been instituted by God. Therefore he who resists the authorities resists what God has appointed, and those who resist will incur judgment. For rulers are not a terror to good conduct, but to bad. Would you have no fear of him who is in authority? Then do what is good, and you will receive his approval, for he is God's servant for your good. But if you do wrong, be afraid, for he does not bear the sword in vain; he is the servant of God to execute his wrath on the wrongdoer. Therefore one must be subject, not only to avoid God's wrath but also for the sake of conscience. For the same reason you also pay taxes, for the authorities are ministers

The Tribute Money by Tissot.
"And they brought him a coin. And Jesus said to them, 'Whose likeness and inscription is this?' They said, 'Caesar's.' Then he said to them, 'Render therefore to Caesar the things that are Caesar's, and to God the things that are God's.'" (Mt 22:19-21)

of God, attending to this very thing. Pay all of them their dues, taxes to whom taxes are due, revenue to whom revenue is due, respect to whom respect is due, honor to whom honor is due. (Rom 13:1-7)

This teaching from St. Paul specifies guidelines for a citizen's duties toward civil authority:

Authority has a divine origin. God wills that an established ruler with his collaborators govern society well. However, God does not specify how this authority should govern. For example, authority can take the form of a monarchy or a democracy.

Christians, therefore, must obey authority. Because authority has a divine origin, the Christian has the obligation in conscience to obey the established ruler and his representatives and the laws of the state.

Christians, however, must use moral discretion. A Christian must disregard any mandate to act immorally. Unjust laws that violate the moral standards of natural law must not be obeyed.

Disregard for just civil law warrants reprimand. Disobedience to the just laws of the state merits a just punishment by the civil authorities.

Authority may impose taxes. Because the governing body of the state must care for the common good of society, it is at liberty to impose taxes to finance the required measures to competently and effectively oversee the well-being of society.

Authority deserves respect. Because authority ultimately comes from God, rulers and their representatives merit respect and obedience.

An unjust law fails to meet the basic requirements of a true law. For instance, laws that legislate the option of destroying unborn life or usurp parental rights in the education of their children should be challenged and resisted with measures taken to overturn them. The *Catechism* clearly states that the laws of the state only obligate in conscience when they coincide with the natural law given to us by God:

The citizen is obliged in conscience not to follow the directives of civil authorities when they are contrary to the demands of the moral order, to the fundamental rights of persons or the teachings of the Gospel. *Refusing obedience* to civil authorities, when their demands are contrary to those of an upright conscience, finds its justification in the distinction between serving God and serving the political community. "Render therefore to Caesar the things that are Caesar's, and to God the things that are God's."[3] "We must obey God rather than men."[4] (CCC 2242)

GOVERNMENTAL OBLIGATIONS TO CITIZENS

Authority is a service to the common good of society and also a help to each one of its citizens. The nature of civil authority itself is not simply power, but rather service. The authority has *power* precisely because it must serve the community.

Public authority is obliged to respect the fundamental rights of the human person as well as to guarantee the conditions that make the exercise of these rights possible. In effect, because human nature requires us to live in a society, authority is necessary for both the preservation and advancement of the common good of all in society.

The principle that guides the relations in society is the *principle of subsidiarity*. It states that the higher authority must not interfere with the lower authority without necessity. For example, the state must not intervene in the role of parents to raise their children unless there is a serious necessity.

The fundamental reality that must inspire and guide the exercise of authority is the dignity of the human person. Therefore, laws, institutions, and the state itself exist to facilitate dignified lives for their citizens. Furthermore, government has the responsibility of exercising its authority in accord with the moral law. This includes protecting the dignity of the human person and the sanctity of life, as well as guaranteeing the conditions for the exercise of freedom. If the objective of the state is to obtain true common good, then it will pursue only morally acceptable means to help its citizens reach and live according to their dignity.

CONCLUSION

The success of all societies is based on the success of the family. Just as each organ of the body is crucial to the functioning of the entire body, so does the health of particular families contribute to the functioning of the body of society. It is necessary that all members of society make a concerted effort to promote the well-being of the family. In this way, the well-being of society will be promoted.

The *Catechism* offers the following summary:

> The Fourth Commandment *illuminates other relationships in society*. In our brothers and sisters we see the children of our parents; in our cousins, the descendants of our ancestors; in our fellow citizens, the children of our country; in the baptized, the children of our mother the Church; in every human person, a son or daughter of the One who wants to be called "our Father." In this way our relationships with our neighbors are recognized as personal in character. The neighbor is not a "unit" in the human collective; he is "someone" who by his known origins deserves particular attention and respect.

> Human communities are *made up of persons*. Governing them well is not limited to guaranteeing rights and fulfilling duties such as honoring contracts. Right relations between employers and employees, between those who govern and citizens, presuppose a natural good will in keeping with the dignity of human persons concerned for justice and fraternity. (CCC 2212-2213)

As taught by Jesus in his *Parable of the Good Steward*[5] and reaffirmed in St. Paul's Letter to the Romans,[6] the exercise of human authority is always a sharing in the authority of God our Father. It is therefore necessary that this power be exercised with care. God will call everyone to account for its use or misuse.

SUPPLEMENTARY READING

Christian Marriage and the Christian Family

1. Christian marriage and the Christian family build up the Church: for in the family the human person is not only brought into being and progressively introduced by means of education into the human community, but by means of the rebirth of Baptism and education in the Faith the child is introduced into God's family, which is the Church.

The human family, disunited by sin, is reconstituted in its unity by the redemptive power of the Death and Resurrection of Christ. Christian marriage, by participating in the salvific efficacy of this event, constitutes the natural setting in which the human person is introduced into the great family of the Church.

The commandment to grow and multiply, given to man and woman in the beginning, in this way reaches its whole truth and full realization. The Church thus finds in the family, born from the sacrament, the cradle and the setting in which she can enter the human generations, and where these in turn can enter the Church.

— *Familiaris Consortio*, 15

2. The family, which is founded and given life by love, is a community of persons…Its first task is to live with fidelity the reality of communion in a constant effort to develop an authentic community of persons. The inner principle of that task, its permanent power and its final goal is love: without love the family is not a community of persons and, in the same way, without love the family cannot live, grow and perfect itself as a community of persons. What I wrote in the encyclical *Redemptor hominis* applies primarily to and especially within the family as such: "Man cannot live without love. He remains a being that is incomprehensible to himself, his life is senseless, if love is not revealed to him, if he does not encounter love, if he does not experience and make it his own, if he does not participate intimately in it."

— *Familiaris Consortio*, 18; cf. *Redemptor Hominis*, 10

3. The Church is deeply convinced that only by the acceptance of the Gospel are the hopes that man legitimately places in marriage and the family capable of being fulfilled. Willed by God in the very act of creation, marriage and the family are ordained to fulfillment in Christ and have need of his graces in order to be healed from the wounds of sin and restored to their "beginning," that is, to full understanding and the full realization of God's plan.

— *Familiaris Consortio*, 3

There is a need today to restore family life, where parents have meals with their children, and where there is a daily interaction and growth in love among family members.

VOCABULARY

CIVIL AUTHORITY
The power to enforce obedience to dictated laws in the realm of public actions within a defined territory; those persons who exercise this power.

EXTENDED FAMILY
Grandparents, aunts, uncles, and other relatives who are not in the immediate family.

FAMILY
The domestic church; a man and a woman united in marriage, together with their children; a domestic church; a community of faith, hope, and charity. Each member, in accord with his own role, exercises the Baptismal priesthood and contributes toward making a community of grace and prayer, a school of human and Christian virtue, and the place where the Faith is first proclaimed to children.

MANDATE
A command or order, usually from a superior. Jesus' mandate on Holy Thursday followed the washing of the Apostles' feet: "A new commandment I give to you, that you love one another; even as I have loved you" (Jn 13:34).

POLITICS
The science and art dealing with the form, organization, administration, and government of people within a state or between states.

PRINCIPLE OF SUBSIDIARITY
The principle that guides the relations in society. It states that the lower authority must not be interfered with by the higher authority without necessity. When the higher authority does intervene, it should be for the legitimate common good. Therefore, the Church opposes all forms of collectivism or nationalism.

SOCIETY
The condition of living in harmonious association and company with others for mutual benefit, defense, and other needs.

STATE
A defined geographic region comprised of people who are under the same governmental structure.

The Holy Family with the Infant St. John by Frangipane.

STUDY QUESTIONS

1. Explain the hierarchical or relational aspect of human love.

2. The first three commandments relate to our relationship with God. Why do you think the commandment to honor your father and mother is placed first among the commandments relating to other people? Hypothesize what might happen to society if people did not honor their fathers and mothers.

3. A family which expresses love must be centered on Christ. Explain this statement. What are some practical ways in which families can live the Fourth Commandment?

4. The Fourth Commandment is the only commandment with a promise. What is the promise? Explain what it means.

5. List the blessing promised in the Book of Sirach for those who honor their father and mother.

6. In what ways might a parent provoke his or her child to anger? Give examples.

7. Explain why discipline is necessary in the upbringing of children. In what ways might God discipline us?

8. Why is it not sufficient for parents to simply send their children to Catholic schools or to the parish for a religious education?

9. List the obligations that parents have toward their children.

10. Children must obey their parents no matter what. True or False? Explain.

11. Why is it essential for parents to be good role models for their children? If they are not good role models, do their children no longer have an obligation to respect them? Explain.

12. Define *extended family*. What changes occurred that make the extended family less common today? What obligations do families have to the extended families?

13. What benefits does the unity of the parents give to their children?

14. What is the basis for the obligation to respect the authority of the state?

15. What does it mean that all authority comes from God?

16. Under what circumstances might the laws of a state be opposed to the moral law?

17. What is the primary reason for the power of the government?

A healthy spousal relationship encourages respect and devotion from the children, this facet of family life is connected to the Fourth Commandment.

PRACTICAL EXERCISES

1. Marriage presents the opportunity for the children to observe interactions between the parents. Write an essay describing some ideas regarding marriage you have learned by observing your parents.

2. Discuss some of the material benefits possessed by families in modern Western civilization and the positive and negative effects you think they have on family life. Do you think family life in less fortunate countries is generally better, or do you think that things are generally the same everywhere? Support your answer with specific examples.

3. Comment on each of the following situations, evaluating each person's attitude, actions, or decisions in light of the Fourth Commandment:

- Susan says that she should be allowed to live according to her own rules at home, since she is 18 years old.

- Peter's father arrives at home drunk on a regular basis, and starts screaming at family members. Peter plans to throw his father out of the house on the next occasion.

- Danny doesn't want to tell his parents that his brother has been hanging out with kids who are known to sell drugs at school because he doesn't want to be a squealer.

4. Imagine that you are a parent with four children. Discuss steps that can be taken to avoid or reduce sibling disagreements.

5. List ten rules that are essential for a Catholic home.

6. Discipline does not mean punishment, although it may involve punishment. "Discipline" comes from the same root as "disciple," which involves training a person in the right direction. List five specific things that parents can do to "discipline" their children.

The Child Jesus Going Down with His Parents to Nazareth by Dobson.
"And Jesus increased in wisdom and in stature, and in favor with God and man." (Lk 2: 52)

FROM THE CATECHISM

1918 "There is no authority except from God, and those authorities that exist have been instituted by God."[7]

1923 Political authority must be exercised within the limits of the moral order and must guarantee the conditions for the exercise of freedom.

2234 God's Fourth Commandment also enjoins us to honor all who for our good have received authority in society from God. It clarifies the duties of those who exercise authority as well as those who benefit from it.

2247 "Honor your father and your mother."[8]

2248 According to the Fourth Commandment, God has willed that, after him, we should honor our parents and those whom he has vested with authority for our good.

2249 The conjugal community is established upon the covenant and consent of the spouses. Marriage and family are ordered to the good of the spouses, to the procreation and the education of children.

2251 Children owe their parents respect, gratitude, just obedience, and assistance. Filial respect fosters harmony in all of family life.

2252 Parents have the first responsibility for the education of their children in the faith, prayer, and all the virtues. They have the duty to provide as far as possible for the physical and spiritual needs of their children.

2253 Parents should respect and encourage their children's vocations. They should remember and teach that the first calling of the Christian is to follow Jesus.

2254 Public authority is obliged to respect the fundamental rights of the human person and the conditions for the exercise of his freedom.

2256 Citizens are obliged in conscience not to follow the directives of civil authorities when they are contrary to the demands of the moral order. "We must obey God rather than men."[9]

The Virgin Child with Parents, Sts. Anne and Joachim by Mancini

---

ENDNOTES – CHAPTER SIX

1. Eph 6:4.
2. St. Josemaria Escriva, *Conversations*, 100.
3. Mt 22:21.
4. Acts 5:29.
5. Cf. Lk 12:42-48.
6. Cf. Rom 13:1-5.
7. Rom 13:1.
8. Dt 5:16; Mk 7:10.
9. Acts 5:29.

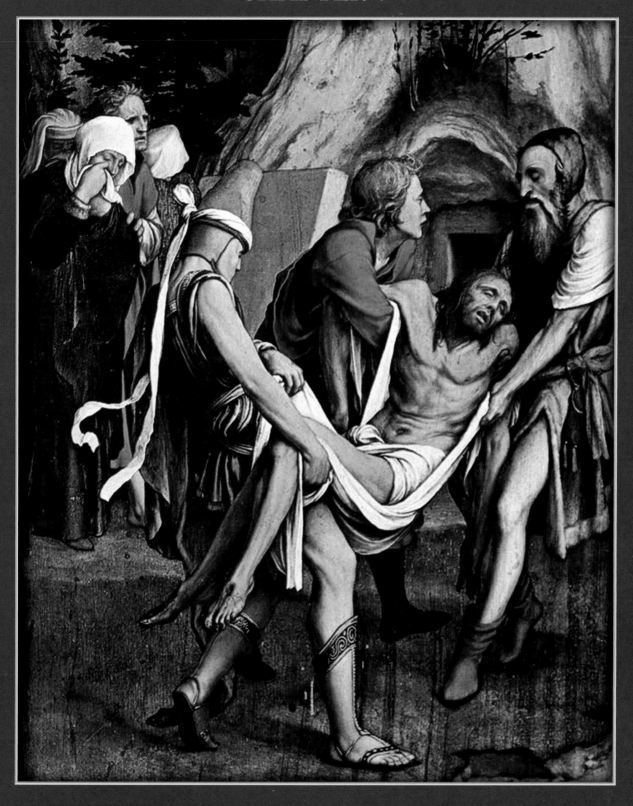

The Fifth Commandment:
You Shall Not Kill

CHAPTER 7

The Fifth Commandment: You Shall Not Kill

Now Abel was a keeper of sheep, and Cain a tiller of the ground. In the course of time Cain brought to the Lord an offering of the fruit of the ground, and Abel brought of the firstlings of his flock and of their fat portions. And the LORD had regard for Abel and his offering, but for Cain and his offering he had no regard. So Cain was very angry, and his countenance fell. The LORD said to Cain, "Why are you angry, and why has your countenance fallen? If you do well, will you not be accepted? And if you do not do well, sin is crouching at the door; its desire is for you, but you must master it."

Cain said to Abel his brother, "Let us go out to the field." And when they were in the field, Cain rose up against his brother Abel, and killed him. Then the LORD said to Cain, "Where is Abel your brother?" He said, "I do not know; am I my brother's keeper?" And the LORD said, "What have you done? The voice of your brother's blood is crying to me from the ground. And now you are cursed from the ground, which has opened its mouth to receive your brother's blood from your hand. When you till the ground, it shall no longer yield to you its strength; you shall be a fugitive and a wanderer on the earth." Cain said to the LORD, "My punishment is greater than I can bear. Behold, thou hast driven me this day away from the ground; and from thy face I shall be hidden; and I shall be a fugitive and a wanderer on the earth, and whoever finds me will slay me." Then the LORD said to him, "Not so! If anyone slays Cain, vengeance shall be taken on him sevenfold." And the LORD put a mark on Cain, lest any who came upon him should kill him. Then Cain went away from the presence of the LORD, and dwelt in the land of Nod, east of Eden. (Gn 4: 2-16)

The story of Cain and Abel is one of the most dramatic and instructive in Scripture. Along with the Decalogue, it forms the biblical foundation for the Church's absolute insistence on the inviolability and sacredness of innocent human life.

FOR DISCUSSION

✠ Does God's Revelation forbid all killing, or only some types of killing?

✠ In light of the biblical prohibition against murder, can war ever be truly justifiable?

✠ Can the desire to prevent suffering ever justify taking someone's life?

✠ Why does the Church teach that a person's stewardship over his own life does not include the right to end it?

✠ What is the meaning of human suffering?

Cain Kills Abel by Novelli.
The story of Cain and Abel forms the biblical foundation for the Church's absolute insistence
on the inviolability and sacredness of innocent human life.

INTRODUCTION

In the creation account in Genesis, man, having been made in the image and likeness of God, is given stewardship over the material world. God has ultimate dominion over man and absolute power over human life. He alone has the authority to grant life and to take it away. Therefore, every human life is sacred and must be protected and nurtured. As the *Catechism* clearly states:

> Every human life, from the moment of conception until death, is sacred because the human person
> has been willed for its own sake in the image and likeness of the living and holy God. (CCC 2319)

In recent decades, the sacredness of human life has been called into question in the political arena, in academic circles, and in popular culture. Some people believe the human being is nothing more than an object—a very sophisticated being, but nonetheless one whose value is measured subjectively. The failure to recognize the human person as a son or daughter of God makes us extremely vulnerable to manipulation or actual destruction, if the whims of society or convenience so dictate.

Unless God is acknowledged as having exclusive dominion over human life, each person's well-being and safety will be in great peril.

RESPECT FOR HUMAN LIFE

The admonition "You shall not kill" is synonymous with "murder" or the deliberate and immoral taking of "human" life. The main thrust of the Fifth Commandment is the absolute duty to respect, defend, and protect human life. The commandment "You shall not kill" essentially means that killing an innocent person is a flagrant violation of natural law and, therefore, a most grievous sin. Intimately linked to this prohibition against taking innocent life is the dignity of the human person, a dignity that transcends the value of all material creation. The value of each person is particularly indicated by Jesus Christ, who became man, suffered, and offered his own life in sacrifice for our sins so that we might be redeemed.

Under the New Covenant, this commandment has still deeper connotations. In his Sermon on the Mount, Jesus stipulates a merciful heart as the proper attitude toward all people, particularly those steeped in sin. In this same discourse, the Lord maps out what it means to have a heart of mercy. We as Christians are expected to love everyone, even those who may injure or hate us. The Lord commands that anger has no place in the hearts of his followers. Moreover, our general disposition must be marked by a habitual meekness.

Jesus goes on to describe this unconditional love to which he calls us:

> **"You have heard that it was said to the men of old, 'You shall not kill; and whoever kills shall be liable to judgment.' But I say to you that every one who is angry with his brother shall be liable to judgment; whoever insults his brother shall be liable to the council, and whoever says, 'You fool!' shall be liable to the hell of fire. So if you are offering your gift at the altar, and there remember that your brother has something against you, leave your gift there before the altar and go; first be reconciled to your brother, and then come and offer your gift." (Mt 5: 21-24)**

Christ and the Child by Bloch.
"Whoever humbles himself like this child, he is the greatest in the kingdom of heaven." (Mt 18: 4)

The words of Christ introduce a new element about love of neighbor not included in the Old Testament. As followers of Christ, we must be willing to love, serve, and forgive others. Our hearts must be completely free of resentment and rancor if we are to worship God properly. A forgiving heart, free of enmity, is necessary for any meaningful relationship with God.

SINS AGAINST HUMAN DIGNITY

If we were to live our lives in accordance with the Sermon on the Mount and the Beatitudes, we would fulfill the commandments and become faithful followers of Christ. This cannot be done in its entirety, however, without the grace of God. The challenge to love everyone as Jesus loves requires a serious prayer and sacramental life. These supernatural measures give the disciples of Christ the necessary strength and assistance to reach the levels of love and charity required of every Christian.

Christ's deeper teaching on the Fifth Commandment is enriched with the proclamation of the commandment of love. The precept of not killing is understood in the light of the new commandment of Jesus: "This is my commandment, that you love one another as I have loved you."[1] This commandment of charity thus enriches the Fifth Commandment—as it does all commandments—beyond its Old Testament interpretation.

Christians should lead lives that give good example to others. In the Gospels, Jesus constantly reminds his followers that they will be judged by the fruits of charity that their conduct produces. Moreover, they must be prepared to forgive one another if they wish to receive the Father's forgiveness. Finally, others will know that they are his followers by the love they show toward one another.[2]

In equally forceful terms, however, Jesus also warns his followers about the sin of scandal:

> [W]hoever causes one of these little ones who believe in me to sin, it would be better for him to have a great millstone fastened round his neck and to be drowned in the depth of the sea. Woe to the world for temptations to sin! For it is necessary that temptations come, but woe to the man by whom the temptation comes! (Mt 18:6-7)

Scandal is an attitude or behavior that leads another to do evil. Not only does the person damage his own virtue and integrity, but his or her example may draw another person into sin. The sin of scandal is grave when it leads others to mortal sin by deed or omission.[3] Those in authority have a particular responsibility to avoid scandal.

Causes of scandal take on many forms. Laws that fail to respect human life, dishonesty among political or religious leaders, and the prevalence of immoral entertainment and immodest fashions are among the many causes of scandal today.

To counteract the many occasions of scandal, it is of paramount importance that individual Christians aspire to a genuine holiness of life. A true reflection of Christ's life in all its dimensions is much more powerful than the innumerable occasions of sin caused by scandal.

RESPECT FOR OUR OWN LIVES

Excesses of the Prodigal Son by Honthorst.
A serious violation of human dignity is excessive consumption of alcoholic beverages which can result in offensive and risky behavior.

Only God has absolute dominion over human life. Therefore, by natural law, every individual is obligated to respect his or her own life as well as the lives of others. God has blessed us by giving us life and made us stewards of human life. Our responsibility as stewards of life includes cultivating good health, avoiding physical injury to oneself or others, treating all human persons with the utmost respect, and defending human dignity.

Some of the sins that show a lack of respect for one's own life include *suicide, cult of the body, gluttony,* and *substance abuse.*

Suicide: The Fifth Commandment strongly commands that we respect our own lives. Objectively speaking, it would be a grievous sin for someone to kill himself or herself. Suicide, which is the willful termination of one's own life, usurps God's exclusive right to call us out of this present life.

However, there are many attenuating circumstances that could diminish the subjective gravity of this kind of tragic action. Many people who think seriously about committing suicide simply lack the nurturing love and attention required for healthy emotional and psychological growth and development. Also, severe psychological problems may significantly diminish responsibility for suicide.

Temptation to commit suicide can also develop when we replace God with an idolatry of achievement, money, physical appearance, or success. When these poor substitutes fail to satisfy us or bring meaning to our lives, we can develop a sense of emptiness that can lead us to despair. The only element that brings ultimate meaning to our lives is the love of God, the commitment to love and service to others, and the humble acceptance of God's forgiveness and Redemption.

Cult of the body: It is immoral to disfigure or mutilate one's body. Enhancement of the beauty of the body that contributes to human elegance is a natural way of emphasizing human dignity. When ordinary attention to sound health and well-being give way to obsession, we call it the *cult of the body*. Excessive food deprivation, inordinate body piercing and tattooing, extreme efforts at bodybuilding, and radical and unnecessary plastic surgery violate the Fifth Commandment as offenses against the human body.

Gluttony: The sin of gluttony, which consists of eating to an excess beyond the purpose of proper nourishment, is incompatible with human dignity. Instead of serving as a means of replenishing the body and restoring energy, overeating turns the pleasure of eating into an end in itself. This intemperance has unhealthy and even life-shortening effects on the body. Moderation in eating, along with some attention to physical exercise, shows respect for the body and results in significantly better health.

Substance abuse: Substance abuse is always seriously sinful. The Fifth Commandment also strongly urges prudence and moderation in drinking alcoholic beverages. Excessive consumption of alcoholic beverages causes intoxication and inebriation, which is objectively sinful as a serious violation of human dignity. The state of intoxication relinquishes self-control and impairs proper judgment and use of reason, which can give way to offensive and even tragic situations, including automobile accidents, acts of violence, abusive behavior, and inappropriate sexual contact—not to mention the potential for sullying one's reputation, scandal to others, and the embarrassment caused to oneself and to one's family.

RESPECT FOR THE LIVES OF OTHERS

The Good Samaritan by Tissot. In many of Christ's parables, the sins were by omission, not by commission. The sinners had failed to come to the aid of the needy among them.

Because of the innate sacredness of every human person, violations against human dignity go far beyond *murder* and *violence* resulting in physical injury inflicted upon another. The more common sins against the Fifth Commandment specified by Jesus include *anger, hatred, abusive language, resentment, omissions in service, racism, and failures to treat an enemy or oppressor with love. Revenge* or *vindictiveness* also has no place in the heart of a Christian.

Murder, violence, anger, hatred, abusive language, resentment: In precise terms, the Fifth Commandment prohibits the taking of human life. Murder, or homicide, constitutes the termination of the life of another through violence.

The Sermon on the Mount, however, extends this commandment to encompass the root causes of murder. Any preliminary actions or attitudes that could lead to the destruction of the life of another are also severely prohibited, including hatred, physical violence, and uncontrollable anger. Recall that Jesus spoke of other commandments in the same way—for example, that a man who entertains lustful thoughts for a woman who is not his wife has already committed adultery in his heart.[4]

The question of the morality of violent acts and the killing of other persons is central to a number of

The Flagellation of Our Lord Jesus Christ by Bouguereau.
"But I say to you, offer no resistance to someone who is evil." (Mt 5: 39)

today's most debated moral issues, including abortion, capital punishment, just war, self-defense, embryonic stem-cell research, and euthanasia.

Omission of service: The rich teachings contained in the twenty-fifth chapter of St. Matthew's Gospel, and in particular the Parable of the Sheep and the Goats, amply illustrate the sin of failing to serve others. As we have noted already, those who were sent to eternal punishment had sinned not by commission, but by omission. They had failed to feed the hungry, give drink to the thirsty, clothe the naked, shelter the homeless, visit the imprisoned, free the captive, or instruct the ignorant.

To provide these basic necessities to fellow human persons who do not have them is to recognize Christ in the faces of the poor; conversely, failure to provide these basic necessities is a failure to serve Christ.

Racism: Another sin against the Fifth Commandment is racism, a hatred or lack of respect for other persons because of their skin color, ethnicity, or national origin. This attitude historically has led to terrible injustices and untold suffering by those so oppressed. Racial prejudice contradicts in a dramatic way the unconditional love that Jesus has for every person. God wills that we regard everyone as equal because we are equal in his eyes, each having been made in his image and likeness.

Revenge, vindictiveness, poor treatment of oppressors: The Old Law in the Old Testament provided for a system of justice based on "an eye for an eye, a tooth for a tooth." Jesus explicitly brought this simplistic law to a much higher level with his commandment of love:

> "You have heard that it was said, 'An eye for an eye and a tooth for a tooth.' But I say to you, Do not resist one who is evil. But if any one strikes you on the right cheek, turn to him the other also...You have heard that it was said, 'You shall love your neighbor and hate your enemy.' But I say to you, Love your enemies and pray for those who persecute you...For if you love those who love you, what reward have you? Do not even the tax collectors do the same?" (Mt 5:38-39, 43-44, 46)

The sense of the text here is not that disciples of Christ must be pacifists or allow themselves to become victims of violence and wrongdoing, but that our response to our enemies should be grounded in love. We must never lose sight of the presence of God in every human person—for the moment we do, we fail to recognize that person's dignity and status as a child of God.

ABORTION

The unborn child developing in his or her mother's womb is the most innocent and defenseless of all human persons. It is at the very moment of conception that a new human person, made in the image and likeness of God, comes into existence. There is no basis in truth, scientifically or morally, to claim that the embryo or fetus is not a person because he or she has not yet reached full development. From a strictly biological perspective, the fertilized egg in the womb is a completely new organism with its unique genetic code, the blueprint of a fully developed person.

Study of an Embryo in the Womb by Leonardo da Vinci. Regardless of the classification, every induced abortion is the intentional destruction of a human life and is therefore gravely sinful.

Because one becomes a human person at the moment of conception, any intentional termination of unborn life is a violation of the Fifth Commandment. Some abortion supporters try to soften this grievous crime by calling it "termination of pregnancy" or lumping it into a sanitized category of "family planning" or "reproductive services" instead.

Those who fail to recognize or respect human life from conception fail to see the intrinsic value of the human person. Since the unborn life is seen as having no real value, abortion enters the picture as a way to sidestep moral responsibility and to resolve the inconvenient and sometimes painful situation of an unwanted pregnancy.

The reasons women give for having an abortion are many. Some find pregnancy as an obstacle to their career or educational goals. A woman may not want others to find out about the pregnancy. Parents, boyfriends, or husbands sometimes pressure the woman into having an abortion to avoid their own responsibility for the child. A woman may believe she is too young, or too old; she might not want any more children than she already has because she cannot handle the burden emotionally or financially. A child may present an undesired change of lifestyle. In some cases, the fetus may have been diagnosed with some kind of birth defect; or the pregnancy may have been the result of rape or incest.

While we must be sympathetic and willing to help those who find themselves in difficult circumstances, none of the reasons above can ever justify an abortion. The unborn child is neither a commodity, nor a possession, let alone an obstacle or a disruption that can be discarded if unwanted or inconvenient. Even in the case of moral tragedies, such as rape or incest, the fetus is an innocent person willed into existence by a loving God and made in his image. It is important to separate the sinful actions, which resulted in

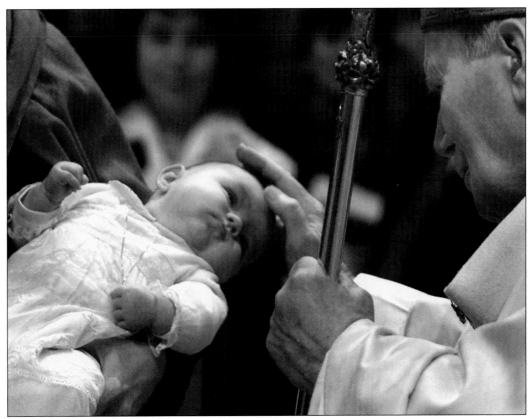

Pope John Paul II blesses an infant. Pope John Paul II stated clearly the gravity of the sin of abortion in *Evangelium Vitæ*. "…abortion willed as an end or as a means, always constitutes a grave moral disorder, since it is the deliberate killing of an innocent human being."

conception, from the reality of the newly-created human being, who deserves all the rights and safeguards intrinsic to human dignity. Likewise, physical or mental deformity does not detract from the dignity of being a person created in the image of God. Every child, from the moment of conception, is a human person created by God and endowed with all the human rights and dignity of any other person.

Abortion has wreaked untold emotional and psychological pain in women. Many have come to realize that what they had conceived in their womb can never be considered as a "something," but a "someone." In addition to the deep psychological wounds, abortion can have severe adverse effects on the woman, including sterility and eventual cancer, not to mention the harm done by the actual abortive procedure. Entire counseling ministries reach out to women who have aborted one or more children and have come to regret those choices and are in need of healing and compassion. The same is true of the fathers of these aborted children, who often are opposed to the abortion or regretful for not standing up for their child. The Church and all Christians need to extend the utmost compassion to post-abortive women and men and to affirm and reflect for them the love and forgiveness of Jesus.

There are three classifications of induced abortion: *eugenic abortion*, performed because of a malformation of the fetus; *therapeutic abortion*, performed because of a danger to maternal health; and *psychological* or *psychosocial abortion*, done for psychological, economic, or social reasons. Regardless of the classification, every induced abortion is the intentional destruction of a human life and is therefore gravely sinful.

The Magisterium of the Church has proclaimed the grievously sinful nature of abortion throughout Christian history. The Fathers of the Church condemned this frequent practice in the ancient Greco-Roman world. One such condemnation is found in the *Didache*, a first-century Christian text (ca. AD 80) which told Christians: "You shall not procure abortion. You shall not destroy a newborn child."

This condemnation has been repeated often in recent times by the Church's Magisterium as found in the works of the Second Vatican Council, Pope Paul VI, and Pope John Paul II.

> Some people try to justify abortion by claiming that the result of conception, at least up to a certain number of days, cannot yet be considered a personal human life. But in fact, "from the time that the ovum is fertilized, a life is begun which is neither that of the father nor the mother; it is rather the life of a new human being with his own growth. It would never be made human if it were not human already. This has always been clear, and...modern genetic science offers clear confirmation. It has demonstrated that from the first instant there is established the program of what this living being will be: a person, this individual person with his characteristic aspects already well determined. Right from fertilization the adventure of a human life begins, and each of its capacities requires time...to find its place and to be in a position to act.[5] Even if the presence of a spiritual soul cannot be ascertained by empirical data, the results themselves of scientific research on the human embryo provide "a valuable indication for discerning by the use of reason a personal presence at the moment of the first appearance of a human life: how could a human individual not be a human person?" (*Donum Vitæ*, 1, 1)

> Furthermore, what is at stake is so important that, from the standpoint of moral obligation, the mere probability that a human person is involved would suffice to justify an absolutely clear prohibition of any intervention aimed at killing a human embryo. Precisely for this reason, over and above all scientific debates and those philosophical affirmations to which the Magisterium has not expressly committed itself, the Church has always taught and continues to teach that the result of human procreation, from the first moment of its existence, must be guaranteed that unconditional respect which is morally due to the human being in his or her totality and unity as body and spirit. (*Evangelium Vitæ*, 60)

Pope John Paul II stated clearly the gravity of the sin of abortion:

> Therefore, by the authority which Christ conferred upon Peter and his Successors, in communion with the bishops—who on various occasions have condemned abortion and who in the aforementioned consultation, albeit dispersed throughout the world, have shown unanimous agreement concerning this doctrine—*I declare that direct abortion, that is, abortion willed as an end or as a means, always constitutes a grave moral disorder*, since it is the deliberate killing of an innocent human being. This doctrine is based upon the natural law and upon the written Word of God, is transmitted by the Church's Tradition and taught by the ordinary and universal Magisterium. (*Evangelium Vitæ*, 62)

The gravity of abortion is reflected in the *Code of Canon Law*, which excludes those participating in an abortion from the sacramental life of the Church. One who knows that abortion is condemned and performs it anyway is automatically excommunicated from the Church. All those who formally cooperate in procuring an abortion are also subject to automatic excommunication.[6]

IN VITRO FERTILIZATION

In vitro fertilization (IVF) is a medical technique which today is commonly used by couples who are unable to conceive children. The term *in vitro* means "in glass," referring to the fertilization of the egg which takes place in a test tube or petri dish. The procedure involves the removal of a number of eggs from the woman, which are then fertilized in the laboratory with sperm taken from the man. The embryo or embryos are then inserted into the woman's uterus. As the process must often be repeated, excess embryos are created and later discarded or frozen for possible use in the future.

This procedure raises a number of moral issues. The conception of human life in a laboratory setting is a gravely sinful act, contrary to the moral law, because it opposes the dignity of the person, who should be the fruit of the loving conjugal union between husband and wife—an issue we will examine in more detail when we discuss the Sixth and Ninth Commandments.

Where IVF involves a sin against the Fifth Commandment is in the selection and final disposition of the fertilized embryos, each of which is a human person. Fertility specialists may produce as many as one or two dozen fertilized embryos for a particular couple. By genetic testing, they may eliminate those embryos that seem weaker or that may have discernible defects. When they finally implant one of the embryos into the mother's womb, the remaining embryos are either destroyed or frozen according to the wishes of the parents. They may return a few years later for another embryo implantation when they decide they want another child, but inevitably some embryos will not be used. Many thousands of such frozen embryos are presently being held in fertility clinics throughout the Western world. Most of these embryos, frozen in a limbo made by human hands, will likely be disposed of or used for experimentation.

Many thousands of frozen embryos are being held in fertility clinics throughout the Western world. Most embryos will likely be disposed of or used for experimentation.

Medicine which seeks to be ordered to the integral good of the person must respect the specifically human values of sexuality. The doctor is at the service of persons and of human procreation. He does not have the authority to dispose of them or to decide their fate.

A medical intervention respects the dignity of persons when it seeks to assist the conjugal act either in order to facilitate its performance or in order to enable it to achieve its objective once it has been normally performed. On the other hand, it sometimes happens that a medical procedure technologically replaces the conjugal act in order to obtain a procreation which is neither its result nor its fruit. In this case the medical act is not, as it should be, at the service of conjugal union but rather appropriates to itself the procreative function and thus contradicts the dignity and the inalienable rights of the spouses and of the child to be born. (*Donum Vitæ*, II, B, 7)

EMBRYONIC STEM-CELL RESEARCH

Another procedure that takes the life of the unborn takes place in embryonic stem-cell research. Some scientists believe that stem cells—cells that are "pluripotent," meaning they have the capacity to adapt and repair any human organ—may someday provide a cure for presently incurable conditions such as Parkinson's disease, juvenile diabetes, certain neuromuscular disorders, and spinal cord injuries.

Some researchers insist they need stem cells from human embryos in order to conduct the experiments and research necessary to find these cures. They either create a fertilized egg in the laboratory or accept donated embryos from fertility clinics for this purpose. These newly formed human embryos are then "harvested" so that their stem cells can be used in research. When the stem cells are extracted from the embryo—usually at eight to twenty-one days of age—the embryo dies.

The Catholic Church does not oppose all stem-cell research, but only the kind of stem-cell research that uses human embryos. Stem cells can readily be obtained through a number of sources other than human embryos—such as umbilical-cord blood, adult skin cells, and bone marrow—all of which involve no harm to the donor and are therefore morally licit.

Recent studies show that stem cells from non-embryo sources have as much potential for finding cures as embryonic stem cells. Research announced in late 2007 revealed that stem cells taken from the skin of human adults show the same "pluripotence" as cells from embryos. These adult cells have another distinct advantage. They can be taken from the very person who will benefit from the cells, eliminating any chance of incompatibility from getting genetically different cells from another person.

> *If the embryos are living, whether viable or not, they must be respected just like any other human person; experimentation on embryos which is not directly therapeutic is illicit.* No objective, even though noble in itself, such as a foreseeable advantage to science, to other human beings or to society, can in any way justify experimentation on living human embryos or fetuses, whether viable or not, either inside or outside the mother's womb.... To use human embryos or fetuses as the object or instrument of experimentation constitutes a crime against their dignity as human beings having a right to the same respect that is due to the child already born and to every human person. (*Donum Vitæ*, I, 4)

EUTHANASIA AND ASSISTED SUICIDE

The dignity of the human person and therefore the right to life remains, as the saying goes, from "womb to tomb." The value of our lives as human beings is determined not by our fame, skills, wealth, or accomplishments, but by the simple fact that we are children of God who were created in his image.

Just as the size or stage of development of an unborn child can never serve as a measuring stick for his or her worth, an incapacitating sickness or severe suffering does not diminish the value of a person. A terminal illness or a debilitating physical condition is never an occasion to usurp God's exclusive right to call someone out of this world through death.

Euthanasia involves the decision by doctors, family members, or public officials to end the life of a person who has been given little or no chance of recovery and is thought to have a poor quality of life.

The word *euthanasia* itself comes from the Greek *euthanatos*, which means "a good or sweet death," and the traditional phrase for this violation of the Fifth Commandment is "mercy killing."

Euthanasia was officially implemented in Nazi Germany between 1939 and 1941. During this period, the Nazi government euthanized between 75,000 and 250,000 non-Jewish German citizens who had mental or physical disabilities—a precursor to the eventual execution of six million Jews and others also deemed unfit for life during the Holocaust.

At present, euthanasia is legal in the Netherlands under some circumstances, but anecdotal evidence suggests that it has been practiced quietly to some degree there and in other Western nations for quite some time.

An April 1945 photo of the cemetery at Hadamar where victims of Nazi Germany's euthanasia killings (1939-1941) were buried.

Assisted suicide is distinct from euthanasia in that the person who is suffering requests help from doctors, nurses, family members, or friends in ending his or her own life. This request is often made when the person lacks the strength and the means to perform this action without help. This form of killing is another egregious offense against God's love and a violent disruption of his plan for each person and his or her eternal life.

Regrettably, physician-assisted suicide has legal status in the state of Oregon. Elsewhere, the notorious Dr. Jack Kevorkian aided the suicides of several dozen persons before he was finally arrested and imprisoned.

Euthanasia and assisted suicide are both grave violations of the Fifth Commandment and must not be condoned in any form.

The question often arises as to why people—even good people—must suffer. The power of the Cross and the Redemption brought about by Jesus unlock the mystery of suffering and give ultimate meaning to incapacitating sickness and injuries. Those who shoulder these special crosses, whether through Alzheimer's, terminal cancer, physical paralysis, or other causes, carry within themselves the power of God.[7] Only from the perspective of the crucified Christ can we realize that human dignity reaches its finest hour when suffering is joined to the Cross of Christ.

Someone who suffers from an illness or a condition that will end in death or render him extremely incapacitated must receive special care and the necessary medical treatment to stay alive. However, the Church also teaches that the sufferer can refuse what are called *extraordinary or disproportionate means* of sustaining life when there is virtually no hope for recovery.[8]

Measures that were quite extraordinary in the past have now become standard procedure for medical practice. In light of these great strides in medical science, the Church has indicated that extraordinary means, which only prolong the imminent dying process, or that impose an odious burden on the patient and family, do not need to be taken.

The spirit behind this guideline rests on the fact that God's will to call someone out of this world must be respected. Respect for the person in a terminal situation will involve allowing him or her to suffer and die in the most dignified way possible.

On the other hand, ordinary medical treatment of nourishment, hydration, and medication to sustain life are always required. At times, trustworthy people need to be consulted regarding the right moral course of action to be taken in these matters.

The well-publicized case a few years ago of Terri Schiavo, a Florida woman who had been diagnosed as in a *persistent vegetative state* due to a sudden illness thirteen years before, gave the nutrition-hydration issue unprecedented national attention. While some doctors considered Terri as brain dead and incurable, family members and some other doctors disagreed, stating that they recognized some cognitive response in her. Terri's husband, who had denied Terri any rehabilitative therapy for most of her convalescence, ultimately prevailed in a long legal dispute with Terri's parents over his wish to remove Terri's feeding tube. Terri thus was starved and dehydrated to death in 2005.

St. Thomas Aquinas by Crivelli.
The first theologians of the "just war doctrine" were St. Augustine and St. Thomas Aquinas. The spirit behind the Church's teachings on "just war" is that the objective is self-defense and not simply to destroy or punish the enemy.

JUST WAR

War is always a terrible tragedy. When nation rises against nation or opposition forces revolt within their own nation, the pain and suffering for the dead, the wounded, their families, and the nations as a whole are immense and incalculable.

War on the whole is never a desirable option. Under certain conditions, however, a nation's participation in a war can be morally justified. The spirit behind the Church's teachings on just war is that the objective is self-defense and not to destroy or punish the enemy. The mere fact that a country is engaged in a war does not grant it license to disregard the moral law, especially the Fifth Commandment.

The Magisterium of the Catholic Church has established several principles on just war, commonly called the "just war doctrine." For a nation's participation in war to be morally just, it must fulfill the principles of *self-defense*, *last resort*, *probability of success*, and *proportionality*. In the course of actually conducting the war, the nation in addition must *never deliberately target non-combatants*.[9]

a. Self-defense: Combat against an opposing force does not violate the Fifth Commandment when this course of action consists in self-defense against an unjust aggressor. The damage inflicted by the aggressor on the nation or community of nations must be "lasting, grave, and certain."[10]

b. Last resort: Recourse to war must be viewed only as a last resort. Diplomacy, negotiations, persuasion, even trade restrictions and embargos, and all other nonviolent options must be exhausted before war can become a moral option. With the development of weapons of mass destruction, there is a greater urgency than ever to resolve misunderstandings and tensions through peaceful means.

c. Probability of success: In some ways, this may be the most difficult of the just-war criteria. For a military action to be justified, it must have a reasonable chance of victory. If defeat is almost certain to take place, it is morally wrong to wage a war that will only result in more casualties, no matter how heroic the effort might seem.

d. Proportionality: A military response to an enemy attack must not be greater than that required for self-defense. For example, if an aggressor enters another nation's domain and attacks with tanks and ground troops, it would be far out of proportion for the nation to defend itself by dropping a nuclear bomb on the aggressors.

e. Non-combatants: Even if a country is justified by all the above criteria and thereby chooses to attack, the moral considerations do not end there. Each battle or military action within that war must also fulfill the just-war criteria. In addition, it is always morally wrong for a military force to target non-combatants and unarmed citizens.

Contemporary history recounts horrific violations of human dignity with indiscriminate bombings of residential areas and massacres of innocent people. While certainly not the only example taking place in the twentieth century, a very dark episode in the history of warfare occurred with the mass destruction of human life by Allied forces through the firebombing of Dresden, Germany and the use of atomic bombs on Hiroshima and Nagasaki, Japan at the end of World War II. These acts were not aimed at military targets; rather, they were meant to exert pressure on the opposing governments to surrender. The fact that the Japanese surrendered within days of dropping two atomic bombs does not legitimize the attacks on civilian targets. Grave violations of human rights were also perpetrated against millions of innocent civilians by Communist China, the Soviet Union, and many other nations throughout much of the twentieth century.

On Monday, August 6, 1945, the atomic bomb "Little Boy" was dropped on Hiroshima directly killing an estimated 80,000 people. In the course of the twentieth century, this and numerous other atrocities were committed by many of the world's nations resulting in the deaths of hundreds of millions of innocent civilians.

The Gospel of love articulated by Catholic teaching is radically opposed not only to targeting innocent people, but also to kidnapping, torture, hostage-taking, and terrorism. A war policy that allows for such violent abuse of both the innocent and the guilty is a flagrant violation of the Fifth Commandment. The imposition of justice or the effort to win a war can never take the forms of barbaric inflictions of pain and of fearful dread.

SELF-DEFENSE

Christ Taken Prisoner by Cesari.
"Then they came up and laid hands on Jesus and seized him...one of those who were with Jesus...drew his sword and struck the slave of the high priest,...Then Jesus said to him, 'Put your sword back into its place; for all who take the sword will perish by the sword.'" (Mt 26: 50-52)

The right to self-defense is an extension of the inalienable right to life. Every individual is justified in defending and protecting himself or herself and others against an unjust aggressor. The act of self-defense, even though it may involve harm and injury inflicted upon the assailant, is compatible with the Fifth Commandment. The spirit behind the commandment is to respect and protect innocent life.

The criteria for a moral use of self-defense parallels the criteria for just war. It must be a true act of self-defense, and that defense must be used only in proportion to the aggression sustained. It would be terribly wrong, for example, to injure someone severely in response to an unprovoked push or shove. It would also be grievously sinful to purposely do serious bodily harm or even take a life in reaction to someone initiating an unjustified altercation. The purpose of self-defense is not to harm the aggressor; rather, one must use the minimum amount of force necessary to protect oneself and others.

The use of proportionate means to protect the common good of society applies to police forces and any other authorized security agency. Brutal violence that causes serious injury or even loss of life in response to violations of the law that would not endanger someone's life or cause physical harm to another is gravely sinful.

An individual responsible for maintaining security is authorized to use all the measures at his disposal to protect the lives of others as long as they maintain the principles of proportionality and last resort. Unfortunately, serious physical injury and even death sometimes result from these protective efforts. The idea behind imposing law and order is to only respond with extreme measures as a last resort, even though physical force may sometimes be the only option to establish safety for the common good.

THE ARMS RACE

Following the Second World War, many nations began to build weapons of mass destruction as a preventive measure against attack from other countries. This resulted in an arms race, in which nations invested much of their economic resources in the stockpiling of weapons. The Second Vatican Council addressed this issue in its pastoral document entitled *Gaudium et Spes*.

In short, the Council stated that an arms race is not a safe way to preserve a sure and authentic peace in the world. Furthermore, the money spent on these weapons contributes to the economic miseries that afflict the modern world. It called on society to look for new approaches to promote peace and to free themselves from the slavery to war.[11]

CAPITAL PUNISHMENT

Christ Before Pilate by Multscher. "But they shouted all the more, 'Let him be crucified.' So when Pilate saw that he was gaining nothing, but rather that a riot was beginning, he took water and washed his hands before the crowd, saying, 'I am innocent of this righteous man's blood; see to it yourselves.'" (Mt 27: 22-24)

Pope John Paul II's encyclical on the dignity of human life, *Evangelium Vitæ*, formally confirmed the Church's resistance to the use of the death penalty. The encyclical did not declare that capital punishment is intrinsically morally wrong; rather, it stated that the death penalty should be used only as an extreme measure when it is absolutely necessary to protect society from the one convicted. Given the prisons and security systems available in most parts of the world, the instances in which capital punishment would be an "absolute necessity," the Pope noted, "are very rare if not practically nonexistent."[12]

Governmental authorities have the right to impart just punishments after due process in proportion to particular crimes. The various levels and branches of government enact laws, issue judicial verdicts, and enforce the determined sentences for infractions of the law. According to strict justice, the state has the option to hand down even the death penalty for crimes involving the murder of innocent persons or high treason. Nevertheless, there is a law that is higher than that of strict justice, and that is the law of compassion and charity based upon the inherent dignity of human life.

From the perspective of the Gospel, the purpose of the imposition of justice is not so much retribution as it is to seek the spiritual and moral rehabilitation of the person guilty of the crime. Capital punishment, although it sometimes may satisfy the demands of strict justice, often does not serve as a deterrent from future crime. It may even serve to perpetuate a lessened view of the value of human life in society that leads to capital crimes in the first place. Capital punishment is often opposed on the grounds that the criminal justice system is fallible and innocent people will inevitably be executed by mistake. In such situations, capital punishment excludes the possibility of reversal and reparation of damages wrongly inflicted.

The *Catechism of the Catholic Church* reflects the teaching of *Evangelium Vitæ*. It explains that while the Church does not absolutely exclude the death penalty, non-lethal means are preferred when they are sufficient to defend public safety.

> Assuming that the guilty party's identity and responsibility have been fully determined, the traditional teaching of the Church does not exclude recourse to the death penalty, if this is the only possible way of effectively defending human lives against the unjust aggressor.
>
> If, however, non-lethal means are sufficient to defend and protect people's safety from the aggressor, authority will limit itself to such means, as these are more in keeping with the concrete conditions of the common good and more in conformity with the dignity of the human person.
>
> Today, in fact, as a consequence of the possibilities which the state has for effectively preventing crime, by rendering one who has committed an offense incapable of doing harm—without definitively taking away from him the possibility of redeeming himself—the cases in which the execution of the offender is an absolute necessity "are very rare, if not practically nonexistent."[13] (CCC 2267)

INTEGRITY OF THE HUMAN BODY

The human person, composed of both body and soul, must be given the utmost respect. It is the soul, a reflection of divine life that enlivens the body and expresses itself through it as well. The fact that God the Son assumed a human nature to carry out his redemptive work indicates that the human body must be considered sacred as it is both an integral part of the human person and an instrument of salvation, sanctification, and evangelization.

Among the issues regarding the integrity of the human body that are linked to the Fifth Commandment are *organ removal*, *organ transplant*, *sterilization*, and *human cloning*.

Organ removal: The human body is so intimately united to the soul and connected to the dignity of the person that it should not be degraded or disfigured by mutilation or abuse. Any type of mutilation or disfigurement of the body is contrary to the moral law. As St. Paul pointed out, "Do you not know that your body is a temple of the Holy Spirit within you, which you have from God? You are not your own."[14]

At certain times, however, it may be necessary to remove an organ or limb to save the life of a seriously ill person. Such surgery is morally permissible.

Organ transplant: In recent years, organ transplants have been performed with increasing frequency. Organ transplants are permitted when both the donor and the recipient (or those who speak for them) give informed consent and the physical and psychological dangers and risks are proportionate to the good sought. With these criteria satisfied, the donation of an organ is a laudable means of self-giving in order to restore health to the recipient.

It is a grievous violation of human dignity to bring about the disabling mutilation or death of a human being by removing an organ, even in order to save the life of another person.[15] Recent moral and scientific discussions regarding the very definition of death, particularly "brain death," must also be considered so that a premature assumption of death does not result in the removal of vital organs from a still-living person for donation to another.

The brain and gonads may not be transplanted because they ensure the personal and procreative identity respectively.[16]

Human cloning: Recent breakthroughs in scientific technology have added yet another dimension to the continuing debate over the dignity of human life. In 1997, genetic scientists in Scotland successfully cloned a sheep—that is, they created a genetically identical sheep by fusing genetic material from a living sheep into an egg cell that has had its cytoplasm removed. Some scientists today are experimenting with cloning humans in a similar manner. Some have even claimed to have done so successfully, although none so far has allowed the cloned human embryo to develop very far. These developments obviously raise new moral and ethical concerns for the Church.

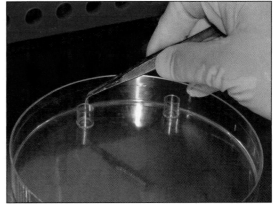

Human cell-line colony being cloned in vitro. The temptation to "play God" is very strong, particularly when human science discovers techniques to manipulate human life.

As many as ten years before the successful completion of the sheep-cloning experiment, however, the Church—aware of the direction in which scientific research was proceeding—had condemned the procedure in regard to human beings in the document *Donum Vitæ*.

Scientists today speak of two varieties of human cloning based on the intended use for the clones. *Therapeutic cloning* would involve the cloning of a human embryo for the purpose of research for medical cures. Embryonic stem-cell research, discussed earlier in this chapter, generally falls into this category. The clones thus developed would be killed at a very early stage of development for the acquisition of their stem cells. *Reproductive cloning* is the name given to the cloning of a human embryo with the intent to allow his or her development and eventual birth—the human equivalent of the sheep experiment.

Some scientists view these two purposes as morally diverse, claiming that therapeutic cloning is permissible because of the potential for life-saving cures, while reproductive cloning would be ethically questionable at the very least. The Catholic Church, however, recognizes both methods as gravely and intrinsically immoral affronts to human dignity and the integrity of God's plan for human reproduction.

All human cloning is gravely sinful and contrary to the moral law because it flagrantly separates procreation from the conjugal union, thereby violating the human dignity of both the parents and their child. Cloning, like artificial insemination, *in vitro* fertilization, and the use of frozen embryos, is a technology that aims at producing human beings selected according to gender or other predetermined quality. It reduces human beings to objects that can be manufactured and manipulated according to whim rather than unique and irreplaceable creations of God, each possessing his or her own integrity and identity.

Sterilization is the alteration of the reproductive organ, depriving a person of his or her procreative capability. As we have no authority to destroy our procreative faculties, Christian morality declares that voluntary sterilization employed toward contraceptive ends is gravely sinful.

The morality of sterilization is dependent in part upon its circumstances, represented by two types:

Direct sterilization is performed with the intention of destroying a person's ability to procreate. It is a sin against the Fifth Commandment not only because it is a mutilation of the body, but also because it is an attack on the integrity of the person. In males, sterilization usually takes the form of a vasectomy; in women, the procedure is generally a tubal ligation, although removal of the ovaries or the entire uterus is sometimes performed.

Indirect sterilization is a secondary and unintended result of a medical procedure directed toward the cure of a patient or as a result of an accident. The Magisterium teaches that indirect sterilization is morally licit *only under necessary medical conditions*—such as, for example, in the case of a woman whose ovaries must be removed because of ovarian cancer. In this situation, the operation is performed for a legitimate medical reason—namely, the prevention of cancer.

The temptation to "play God" is very strong, particularly when human science discovers techniques to manipulate human life. But experience shows us that in the long run the lack of respect for the human being results in serious moral disorders. The Christian should exercise faith and trust in the moral law and the moral teachings of the Catholic Church, which is the sure guide for upholding the dignity and welfare of the human person.

CONCLUSION

God's commandments teach us the way of life. The negative moral precepts, which declare that the choice of certain actions is morally unacceptable, have an absolute value for human freedom: they are valid always and everywhere, without exception. They make it clear that the choice of certain ways of acting is radically incompatible with the love of God and with the dignity of the person created in his image. Such choices cannot be redeemed by the goodness of any intention or of any consequence; they are irrevocably opposed to the bond between persons; they contradict the fundamental decision to direct one's life to God. (*Evangelium Vitæ*, 75)

The moral obligation to respect human life in all its stages has been a basic tenet of natural law since the very beginning of mankind. In recent times, however, there has been a special urgency to protect and promote the right to and dignity of life. Mindsets that uphold a relative morality, coupled with technological advances that can artificially manipulate human life, are indicators that there is an urgent need to cultivate an appreciation of the dignity and unrepeatable value of every person. This means that more than ever, Jesus Christ, who is the Way, the Truth, and the Life, must be clearly evident in the lives of his followers. This witness to the truth and life of Christ is the most compelling testimony to the immeasurable worth of every human life.

SUPPLEMENTARY READING

1. The Distinction Between Physical Suffering and Moral Suffering

Man suffers in different ways, ways not always considered by medicine, even in its most advanced specializations. Suffering is something which is still wider than sickness, more complex and at the same time still more deeply rooted in humanity itself. A certain idea of this problem comes to us from the distinction between physical suffering and moral suffering. This distinction is based upon the double dimension of the human being and indicates the bodily and spiritual element as the immediate or direct subject of suffering. Insofar as the words "suffering" and "pain" can, up to a certain degree, be used as synonyms, physical suffering is present when "the body is hurting" in some way, whereas moral suffering is "pain of the soul."

— *Salvifici Doloris*, 5

2. All Human Beings Belong To God

All human beings, from their mothers' womb, belong to God who searches them and knows them, who forms them and knits them together with his own hands, who gazes on them when they are tiny shapeless embryos and already sees in them the adults of tomorrow whose days are numbered and whose vocation is even now written in the "book of life"…

— *Evangelium Vitæ*, 61

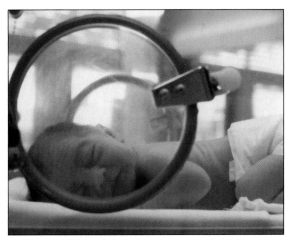

We are children of God who were created in his image.

3. Conscientious Opposition to Abortion in Political Debate

The political debate about abortion has produced much muddled thinking about the possibilities of conscientious dissent from the Church's teaching on the dignity of all human life. It is all too common for Catholic politicians to say they are "personally" opposed to abortion but will nevertheless vote to permit it, and even fund it, out of respect for the consciences of those who hold different views. This "respect" for another's conscience should never require abandoning one's own. Conscientious opposition to abortion, rooted in an understanding of the sanctity of human life, may not be sacrificed to the mistaken consciences of those who would unjustly take the life of an unborn baby.

— Bishop John J. Myers, *Pastoral Statement*, July 1990

4. Biological and Genetic Manipulation of Human Embryos

Techniques of fertilization *in vitro* can open the way to other forms of biological and genetic manipulation of human embryos, such as attempts or plans for fertilization between human and animal gametes and the gestation of human embryos in the uterus of animals, or the hypothesis or project of constructing artificial uteruses for the human embryo.

These procedures are contrary to the human dignity proper to the embryo, and at the same time they are contrary to the right of every person to be conceived and to be born within marriage and from marriage. Also, attempts or hypotheses for obtaining a human being without any connection with sexuality through "twin fission," cloning or parthenogenesis are to be considered contrary to the moral law, since they are in opposition to the dignity of both human procreation and of the conjugal union.

— *Donum Vitæ*, 1.6

VOCABULARY

ABORTION
The destruction of a child after conception but before birth. Direct abortion or cooperation in it is forbidden by the Fifth Commandment. Attached to this sin is the penalty of excommunication because, from the moment of conception, every human being must be absolutely respected and protected in his integrity.

ASSISTED SUICIDE
Any action or omission of action that assists another person in bringing about his own death. Responsibility may be aggravated by the scandal given because every human being must be absolutely respected and protected in his integrity. It is forbidden by the Fifth Commandment.

AUTONOMY
The belief that one is entirely independent and is responsible only to himself for his actions and the direction of his life. A false conception of this can lead to atheism.

BIOETHICS
Derived from the Greek words *bios* (life) and *ethos* (ethics), the discipline dealing with ethical questions related to human life that arise as a result of advances in medicine and biology.

CAPITAL PUNISHMENT
An act by the legitimate authority of a state or nation to put a criminal to death.

CLONING
The process of developing a person or animal from one somatic cell of its parent, thus it is genetically identical to that parent. Because God created man in his image and likeness, human cloning can never be moral.

CULTURE OF DEATH
Term introduced by Pope John Paul II to indicate a society or culture that tolerates or favors acts and ideas that are an affront to the dignity of human life.

DIGNITY OF HUMAN LIFE
The quality of being worthy or honorable; worthiness, nobleness, excellence. Every human person, by reason of his or her creation in the image and likeness of God, has an intrinsic dignity.

EUTHANASIA
From the Greek meaning "good death," an action or omission of an action that, by itself or by intention, causes a person's death in order to eliminate suffering.

EXCOMMUNICATION
Censured by a bishop in response to a grave, habitual, public sin. An excommunicated person is forbidden to have a ministerial role in the celebration of the sacraments and other public ceremonies, to receive the sacraments, or to exercise church offices or ministries (cf. CIC, 1331).

EXTRAORDINARY MEANS
Life-sustaining forms of medical care that are (a) radically painful, (b) excessively expensive, (c) doubtfully able to accomplish their designated objective, or (d) radically burdensome.

JUST WAR
The principle that war may be legitimately waged, under certain specific conditions, for the protection of a nation's rights.

MURDER
The sinful killing of a human being with malice aforethought. This is listed among the sins that cry to Heaven and is forbidden by the Fifth Commandment.

MUTILATION
The action of disfiguring a part of the body, sometimes rendering it useless or wounded.

VOCABULARY Continued

"PRO-CHOICE"

Term commonly used to identify individuals and organizations that favor the availability of legalized abortion—so called because it claims to support a woman's "choice" of whether to give birth to a child or to kill the child in the womb.

"PRO-LIFE"

Term commonly used to identify individuals and organizations that oppose abortion and other affronts to human dignity.

SACRED

Holy, worthy of great respect or veneration.

SCANDAL

An attitude or behavior that leads another to do evil.

STERILIZATION

The destruction of fertility and fruitfulness; the rendering incapable of producing offspring, especially by surgical or chemical procedures affecting the reproductive organs. This is forbidden by the Fifth and Sixth Commandments.

SUICIDE

The act of taking one's own life; self-murder. This is forbidden by the Fifth Commandment.

Cain Flying Before Jehovah's Curse by Cormon.
"Woe to those who call evil good and good evil, who put darkness for light and light for darkness, who put bitter for sweet, and sweet for bitter!" Is 5: 20

STUDY QUESTIONS

1. Why did God create us?

2. What does it mean that human life is "sacred"? What implication does this have on the way that we regard human life? What are the consequences when human life is not held as sacred?

3. What new light did the teachings of Jesus shed on the Fifth Commandment?

4. For Christians, the Fifth Commandment is more than a mere prohibition on the taking of human life. List other acts prohibited by the Fifth Commandment.

5. What enables a Christian to live out this Commandment as Christ intended?

6. God made us stewards of human life. What does this mean, and what are its ramifications?

7. What is meant by the sin of scandal?

8. The severity of the sin of scandal depends on the person giving it and the people offended. Explain.

9. What are some of the causes which might lead a person to suicide?

10. What did Pope John Paul II mean by the "culture of death"?

11. Name three offenses against the human body. Why are they wrong?

12. Everyone agrees that it would be wrong to drive a car while drunk. Why is drunkenness itself an offense against human dignity?

13. Preliminary actions or even dispositions that could lead to the destruction of the life of another are also severely prohibited by the Fifth Commandment. Explain what this means and give examples.

14. When does life begin? What implications does this have for the unborn child?

15. What are the three classifications of abortion? Give an example of each.

16. What is excommunication, and what is its connection with abortion?

17. What is IVF, and what moral questions are raised by its usage?

18. Some claim that embryonic stem cell research promises great cures to alleviate human suffering. Why is embryonic stem cell research wrong?

19. A politician states that although he or she is personally against abortion, he or she believes that everyone should have the right to make up his or her own mind. Explain why this political position is wrong.

20. In what way does the pro-choice position try to avoid the issue of human life?

21. What is euthanasia? What does it say about the value of human life?

22. What are some ways in which euthanasia could be abused by the state?

23. What is assisted suicide, and why does the Church teach that it is wrong?

24. We must use every means available to keep a person alive for as long as possible. True or false? Explain.

25. Explain in your own words the conditions required before a government may legitimately go to war.

26. What are the boundaries placed on the legitimate right to self-defense?

27. Under what circumstances might a state have the moral right to impose the death penalty?

28. How might the sacredness of life be devalued by use of the death penalty?

29. When would an organ transplant be considered wrong?

30. What two organs cannot be transplanted based on moral law? Why?

31. Why is human cloning wrong?

32. Why is direct sterilization an immoral act, while indirect sterilization is sometimes permissible?

PRACTICAL EXERCISES

1. Karen is sixteen-years-old and has been dating Jim for three months. Because she has been taught by her parents to practice her faith, she knows that her parents would be very upset to discover that she has involved herself in a sexual relationship with him. Things are complicated further when she finds out that she is pregnant. Now, Karen is afraid and thinks that she wants to have an abortion so that her parents will not find out that she is pregnant. When her friend Tiffany objects, Karen tries to rationalize her decision by saying, "It is all right because this doctor I saw on TV said that it's not truly human for the first three months, anyway." Imagine that you are Tiffany. What arguments could you offer, drawing upon what you have learned in this chapter, to persuade Karen that having an abortion would be a terrible mistake?

2. Dan has been selling marijuana at school. When confronted by his friend Marco, he justifies his actions by arguing that marijuana is no more addictive than alcohol. Whether or not this is true, why is Dan's argument in defense of his actions irrelevant? Why is it still immoral for Dan to use and sell marijuana?

3. What are some of the moral problems arising out of drug use and the abuse of alcohol?

4. Summarize what the *Catechism* says about the death penalty (2266-2267). In light of the teaching contained in the *Catechism*, can the death penalty ever be legitimately used in the United States? Why or why not?

5. Bearing in mind what this chapter explains about mutilation, what do you think of practices such as tattooing and body piercing? Are these forms of mutilation and, therefore, immoral? Why, or why not?

6. Because Christians are obliged to preserve the lives of others, to protect their dignity, and to do no harm, do you believe that there can ever be a good reason for an individual to fight with another person (i.e., in the case of a young man whose sister's reputation has been damaged by a lie)? Why, or why not? Provide specific examples to support your argument.

And the Earth Shook by Tissot. "And behold, the curtain of the temple was torn in two, from top to bottom; and the earth shook, and the rocks were split..." (Mt 27: 51)

FROM THE CATECHISM

2307 The Fifth Commandment forbids the intentional destruction of human life. Because of the evils and injustices that accompany all war, the Church insistently urges everyone to prayer and to action so that the divine Goodness may free us from the ancient bondage of war.[17]

2318 "In [God's] hand is the life of every living thing and the breath of all mankind."[18]

2320 The murder of a human being is gravely contrary to the dignity of the person and the holiness of the Creator.

2321 The prohibition of murder does not abrogate the right to render an unjust aggressor unable to inflict harm. Legitimate defense is a grave duty for whoever is responsible for the lives of others or the common good.

2322 From its conception, the child has the right to life. Direct abortion, that is, abortion willed as an end or as a means, is a "criminal" practice,[19] gravely contrary to the moral law. The Church imposes the canonical penalty of excommunication for this crime against human life.

2324 Intentional euthanasia, whatever its forms or motives, is murder. It is gravely contrary to the dignity of the human person and to the respect due to the living God, his Creator.

2325 Suicide is seriously contrary to justice, hope, and charity. It is forbidden by the Fifth Commandment.

2326 Scandal is a grave offense when by deed or omission it deliberately leads others to sin gravely.

2327 Because of the evils and injustices that all war brings with it, we must do everything reasonably possible to avoid it. The Church prays: "From famine, pestilence, and war, O Lord, deliver us."

2330 "Blessed are the peacemakers, for they shall be called sons of God."[20]

ENDNOTES – CHAPTER SEVEN

1. Jn 15:12.
2. Cf. Mt 6:14-15; Mt 7:16-20; Jn 13:34-35.
3. Cf. CCC 2284-2285.
4. Cf. Mt 5:28.
5. Cf. Congregation for the Doctrine of the Faith, *Declaration on Procured Abortion*, 12, 13.
6. Cf. CIC, 1398.
7. Cf. 1 Cor 1.
8. Cf. IOE, 4.
9. Cf. CCC 2309.
10. Cf. CCC 2309.
11. *EV* 56.
12. Ibid.
13. 1 Cor 6:19.
14. Cf. CCC 2292-2296.
15. CHCW, 88.
16. Cf. *GS* 81 § 4.
17. Jb 12:10.
18. *GS* 27.
19. Mt 5:9.

The Sixth and Ninth Commandments:
You Shall Not Commit Adultery
You Shall Not Covet Your Neighbor's Wife

CHAPTER 8

The Sixth and Ninth Commandments: You Shall Not Commit Adultery You Shall Not Covet Your Neighbor's Wife

*I*n the story of Genesis, we see that man and woman were created in a state of unity and love that reflected the image and likeness of God. In a partnership of love, they shared in God's friendship and cooperated with him as stewards of creation. Blessed by God, they would start the human family, which would give honor to God and show forth his glory.

This original unity in which man and woman were created became so weakened by Original Sin that many in the time of Christ felt it was impossible for a man and woman to be truly united in a permanent bond of marriage. However, Christ elevated and restored marital love to the place originally intended by God.

> "Have you not read that he who made them from the beginning made them male and female...? 'For this reason a man shall leave his father and mother and be joined to his wife, and the two shall become one flesh'? So they are no longer two but one flesh. What therefore God has joined together, let no man put asunder." (Mt 19: 4-6)

Through the grace of God given in the Sacrament of Matrimony, a man and a woman are joined in a permanent and exclusive union of love. They are given the grace to share their lives, to participate in the creative power of God, and to raise a Christian family, which is the fruit of their love.

INTRODUCTION

God created man and woman with natural sexual differences. One's gender describes not only the constitution of one's body, but also one's very identity. Sexuality affects us at the most elementary level of personhood. Inscribed in one's sexual identity is a profound complementarity to the opposite gender. In addition to insuring the continuation of the human race, this sexual attraction between man and woman includes a personal calling to a community of love. Man and woman, made in God's image, have been inscribed with the vocation of love and communion.

FOR DISCUSSION

✠ What is the purpose of marriage and human sexuality?

✠ Why do Christians view marriage as more than a social or legal contract?

✠ Why is the use of human sexuality outside the context of marriage always a sin?

✠ What are some trends in modern society that tend to undermine marriage?

Creation of Eve by Michelangelo. Blessed by God, Adam and Eve would start the human family, which would give honor to God and show forth his glory.

> "God is love and in himself he lives a mystery of personal loving communion. Creating the human race in his own image..., God inscribed in the humanity of man and woman the *vocation*, and thus the capacity and responsibility, *of love* and communion."[1] (CCC 2331)

Marriage is a fundamental and natural part of human life. Far from being a purely human institution, marriage was created by God in the beginning and "the vocation to marriage is written in the very nature of man and woman."[2]

The Sixth and Ninth Commandments, "You shall not commit adultery" and "You shall not covet your neighbor's wife," encompass a wide range of moral teachings on Christian marriage. They also evidence the authentic nature of human sexuality as revealed by God. These two commandments teach us that human sexuality can only find its true meaning and full expression within the inner sanctum of marriage. The Sixth Commandment teaches that we are called to a vocation of chastity, which is "the inner unity of man in his bodily and spiritual being,"[3] while the Ninth Commandment warns against lust or carnal concupiscence, as well as teaching about the necessity of being pure of heart.

As in all issues that involve the inherent dignity of the human person, the issue of human sexuality, which is a participation in God's creation of a human person, must be viewed with the utmost respect. An important part of this mutual respect is to fully acknowledge and accept the sexual identity of the other as well as one's own.

> By creating the human being man and woman, God gives personal dignity equally to the one and the other. Each of them, man and woman, should acknowledge and accept his sexual identity. (CCC 2393)

It is through marital union that God intervenes and infuses a soul, thereby creating a new person. The virtue of chastity as taught in the Sixth and Ninth Commandments reflects how the gift of human sexuality must be held in the highest esteem and used according to God's plan.

Chastity is a virtue that enables a person to have a loving relationship with God and to see Christ in every human person. "Chastity means the integration of sexuality within the person. It includes an apprenticeship in self-mastery."[4] The self-control taught by the Sixth and Ninth Commandments is directed toward the genuine expression of Christian love, expressed in a true love of God and neighbor. In fact, chastity enables the individual to love as Christ loves, for example, by always seeking the good of others.

The purity of heart called for in the sixth beatitude allows us to affirm our real being, made in the image and likeness of God.

> The organ for seeing God is the heart. The intellect alone is not enough. In order for man to become capable of perceiving God, the energies of his existence have to work in harmony. His will must be pure and so too must the underlying affective dimension of his soul, which gives intelligence and will their direction. (Pope Benedict XVI, *Jesus of Nazareth*, 93)

These ideas will be developed throughout this chapter under three headings: the sacredness and meaning of marital love, sins against marriage and chastity, and Christian formation in the virtue of chastity.

MARRIAGE AND CREATION

In the beginning, man and woman were united as husband and wife. God created them as companions equal in dignity and in a permanent and exclusive union of love. The two creation accounts found in the first two chapters of Genesis convey a wealth of information about the meaning of marriage and marital love as intended by God.

✤ God created man and woman in his image and likeness.

✤ Man and woman are companions and equal in dignity.

✤ Man and woman are destined to form a new social unit-the family. For that reason, man and woman will leave their fathers and mothers to become a new family.

✤ This unity of man and woman is so intimate that, in biblical language, they will form "one flesh." Husband and wife will become "two in one."

✤ The man-woman relationship, united in marriage, has a procreative purpose. God directed his blessing precisely to this purpose.

✤ Man and woman willingly and intelligently cooperate with God in his plan of creation for a new person.

The union between a husband and a wife is a reflection of the union between Christ and his Church.

In the New Testament, Scripture teaches us that the union between a husband and a wife is a reflection of the union between Christ and his Church, which is called the Bride of Christ.[5]

The Catholic Church has always promoted an attitude of deep respect and profound veneration toward human sexuality as something created and blessed by God. The lived reality of marriage and family that touches the lives of every member of the Church makes this aspect of human existence extremely important. The unity of a man and a woman in a faithful Christian marriage is intended for the mutual good of the spouses and the procreation and education of children.

PURPOSES OF MARRIAGE

"The matrimonial covenant, by which a man and a woman establish between themselves a partnership of the whole of life, is by its nature ordered toward the good of the spouses and the procreation and education of offspring; this covenant between baptized persons has been raised by Christ the Lord to the dignity of a sacrament."[6] (CCC 1601)

Children are always a source of joy when they are born out of the parents' love for one another.

Sexuality is not merely an instinct in humans as it is in animals. Human sexuality involves psychological aspects and is subject to the intellect and will. This is why a person can control and direct it. The proper exercise of sexuality should involve a loving self-giving between the husband and wife. The marital act is properly considered a personal and loving "meeting" between the two that reaffirms their total dedication to each other.

For any sexual act or expression between spouses to be morally good, it must fully respect both the unitive and procreative aspects of sexual union. This is the fundamental truth that governs every moral question involving marriage and sexuality. To act in a manner which denies or denigrates either of these two purposes degrades the dignity and the meaning of the marital act itself.

In this context, the term *unitive* means that the marital act must be an act of self-giving love according to God's plan or design that takes place between a validly married husband and wife who are committed to their lifelong union. The term *procreative* in this context means that the marital act must be open to the possibility of conception.

The unitive purpose: The Sacrament of Marriage unites a man and a woman in a permanent and exclusive partnership for life. This union is a most unique gift, for the gift can be received in its proper sense only as a result of its first being given to the other in marriage. Marital union is meant to signify and express spousal fidelity marked by a loving spirit of sacrificial service that reflects Christ's love for his Church.

The love of the spouses requires, of its very nature, the unity and indissolubility of the spouses' community of persons, which embraces their entire life: "so they are no longer two, but one flesh."[7] They "are called to grow continually in their communion through day-to-day fidelity to their marriage promise of total mutual self-giving." (*Familiaris Consortio*, 19)

The sexual union of a husband and wife, referred to as the *conjugal act* (from the Latin *conjungere*, meaning "to join together") or the *marital act*, is sacred in dignity and blessed by God as an integral part of his plan of creation for human beings when it is exercised according to his will. Through the marital act, a unique union is created between a man and a woman. The bodies and spirits of the couple are drawn closer together to represent—or to embody—the union formed when they were joined in marriage. In this manner, the marital act is a renewal of the covenant of marriage analogous to the way that the Eucharistic sacrifice is a renewal of the covenant established by Christ.

The complementarity of man and woman make possible this union between them in much the same way that the pieces of a puzzle fit together to make a complete picture. In a certain sense, each person is completed by the other, both physically and spiritually. This complementarity inherent in the nature of man and woman is one of the principal reasons why there cannot be a marriage between persons of the same gender.

The physical, emotional, and psychological pleasure which is experienced in the marital act, when united to love, affection, and sacrifice, serves to cultivate this joining of the spouses. For this reason, if the marital act is misused as an act of self-gratification rather than a selfless act of love, it loses its inherent dignity, meaning, and purpose. Rather than expressing an act of self-giving, it becomes an act of selfishness.

The expression of conjugal love is a participation in a great mystery that, taken as a whole, results directly in the creation of new life.

The procreative purpose: In the natural order, the reproductive organs found in all life forms are for the purpose of reproducing the species. For human beings, endowed with an intellect, will, and self-awareness, however, this component of procreation takes on a much deeper meaning. The animal order acts only according to instinct, while a man and a woman, in conceiving new life, give expression to their love and willingly cooperate with God in his creation of a new person. Simultaneous to conception, God infuses a soul, thereby creating a human being. God and the spouses are, as it were, partners in bringing new human life into the world.

The expression of conjugal love is a participation in a great mystery that, taken as a whole, results directly in the creation of new life. The couple, united as one, chooses to cooperate with God in the creation of a human person who is made in the image and likeness of both the parents and of God. Thus, the union of a husband and a wife becomes a sacred act blessed by God.

Marriage and conjugal love are by their nature ordained toward the begetting and educating of children. Children are really the supreme gift of marriage and contribute very substantially to the welfare of their parents....Hence, while not making the other purposes of matrimony of less account, the true practice of conjugal love, and the whole meaning of the family life which results from it, have this aim: that the couple be ready with stout hearts to cooperate with the love of the Creator and the Savior. Who through them will enlarge and enrich His own family day by day. (*Gaudium et Spes*, 50)

Children are always a source of joy when they are born out of the parents' love for one another. The Church, following the testimony of Sacred Scripture, has traditionally viewed large families as a sign of God's blessing and the generosity of the parents.[8]

PROPERTIES OF MARRIAGE

The teachings of Christ show us that Matrimony, as the original unity of man and woman created by God, is characterized by two essential properties: *exclusivity* and *indissolubility*.

Exclusivity: Since marriage involves a total self-giving by each spouse, it follows that this gift can never be shared with a third party. Exclusivity means that a person cannot give himself or herself totally to more than one person in the same way. Consequently, adultery (sexual relations with someone other than one's spouse) and polygamy (marriage to more than one spouse) are both grave violations of the nature of marriage.

This total gift of self demands fidelity, not only by one's physical presence, but in giving one's love and affection.

Indissolubility: Marriage demands permanence and stability. Divine Revelation, as found in the teachings of Jesus Christ, teaches us that this stability was intended by God to be permanent. The union created by God in Matrimony cannot be broken by anyone.

By the very nature of the complete gift of self in marriage, the union of the spouses is permanent. Common sense tells us that when a gift is given, the giver no longer has any rights to the gift. It belongs completely to the one to whom it was given. The same holds true of the gift of self in the Sacrament of Matrimony. Each person can truly say, "I belong to the other." This total gift of self demands fidelity, not only physically, but in giving one's love and affection. In this way, the union between the spouses reflects the communion between Christ and his Church. He gave himself completely for us and we belong to him.

Therefore, when a sacramental marriage between a baptized man and a baptized woman is ratified through the marriage vows and consummated through the marital act, God unites them in a permanent bond which is indissoluble by any human power or by a cause other than death. Jesus, when asked about divorce, definitively taught the indissolubility of marriage.[9]

MARRIAGE AND SEXUALITY

A sacrament is a sign instituted by Christ that produces a spiritual effect in the soul through a specific sacramental grace. In the Sacrament of Matrimony, God joins a man and a woman together for life. The marital act is a renewal of the covenant of marriage that created this permanent and exclusive one-flesh union and thus provides a unique occasion for divine intervention. Procreation refers to the conception of a new person, who is the direct consequence of marital relations. It involves God's direct creative action consisting in the infusion of a spiritual soul into the human body at the moment of conception.

During its two-thousand-year history, the Church has dealt with a number of false attitudes toward human sexuality. These can be separated into two categories—the *puritanical approach* and a trivialized or *self-centered approach* that denies the sacredness and dignity of human sexuality.

The puritanical view considers all sexual passions and attractions to be sinful and attributes them to Original Sin. People of this viewpoint find any consideration of human sexuality distasteful and an occasion of sin. They would view the conjugal act, exercised within marriage, as necessary for procreation, but inherently sinful in itself. In certain cases, those holding this viewpoint go so far as to denounce marriage itself as sinful. Fortunately, these views mostly belong to a bygone age.

The self-centered approach, in radical opposition to the puritanical point of view, is the belief that sexuality is designed primarily for self-gratification. For those who tend toward this view, human sexuality has lost its sense of mystery, and respect and has given way to self-indulgence. Human sexuality is discussed irreverently, openly, and casually, and sexual experience itself is sought and carried out just as irreverently, openly, and casually—the sacredness of the act is not respected, there is little or no shame and guilt of living such a lifestyle, and sexual partners are often discarded and replaced rather easily.

The Catholic understanding and teaching of human sexuality stands in opposition to both of these views. The Church teaches that all of God's creation is a reflection of his own infinite love and therefore is inherently good. Human love and sexuality within marriage is a special expression of God's goodness and thus is inherently sacred. The loving marital act is made holy when it is a reflection of God's self-giving love, a physical expression of a profound personal love between husband and wife, and is open or directed toward the creation of new life.

The Fall of Man by Mantegna.
The puritanical view toward human sexuality considers all sexual passions and attractions
to be sinful and attributes them to Original Sin.

The dignity of the marital bond which unites a man and a woman is a reflection of the life of the Blessed Trinity, a community of Persons. The sacredness of the marital act thus requires that it be an expression of a permanent and total loving commitment that is open to new life within marriage.

To understand better the sacred nature of human sexuality, let us use examples of sacred objects. As we know, a crucifix serves as an object of loving reverence whose purpose is to contemplate the love and compassion of Christ. It would be terribly offensive, let alone blasphemous, to violate a crucifix's sublime purpose, by using it as a doorstop or boomerang. Such misuse would degrade the purpose of this sacred object.

By the same token, an individual would degrade the dignity of human sexuality if he or she were to shift its purpose from marriage commitment and self-giving to self-centered sensual gratification. This is the case when the marital act is performed outside of the context of marriage.

THEOLOGY OF THE BODY

During his pontificate, Pope John Paul II explained the beauty of marital relations through his deep insights into the original meaning of marriage as shown in the Book of Genesis. Through his profound meditation on the dignity of man and woman, the pope saw with great clarity that a person must always be given love for his or her own sake and never become an object of use. These considerations formed the underpinnings of his teachings on chastity and human sexuality called the *theology of the body*.

In his catechesis, Pope John Paul II taught that the union between a husband and a wife reveals the image of God. The *communio personarum* ("community of persons") which typifies the union between a man and a woman in marriage reflects the community of persons of the Blessed Trinity.

> "We can then deduce that man became the 'image and likeness' of God not only through his own humanity, but also through the communion of persons which man and woman form right form the beginning. The function of the image is to reflect the one who is the model, to reproduce its own prototype. Man becomes the image of God not so much in the moment of solitude as in the moment of communion." (John Paul II, *By the Communion of Persons Man Becomes the Image of God*, 3)

He further explained that the marital act reveals God's plan for the expression of their total gift of self in an act of spousal love. The marital act is the language of the body that communicates spousal unity and expresses the commitment to serve and love each other for life.

> "Sexuality, by means of which man and woman give themselves to one another through the acts which are proper and exclusive to spouses, is not something simply biological, but concerns the innermost being of the human person as such. It is realized in a truly human way only if it is an integral part of the love by which a man and woman commit themselves totally to one another until death."[10] (CCC 2361)

Pope John Paul II taught that the union between a husband and a wife reveals the image of God.

Since man and woman possess body and soul, the physical, one-flesh union must always mirror the spiritual union expressed in the faithful and total commitment of the marital covenant. The intimacy shared between a husband and a wife reiterates what was said verbally during the marriage ceremony when they entered into a lifelong commitment to a dedicated sacrificial love. In the marital act, the man and the woman express with their bodies what Christ intended to be continually present in their hearts and minds. In this way, the true meaning of the marital act expresses an enduring, exclusive, faithful, and sacrificial love.

For marital relations to maintain their true meaning, a habitual spirit of loving sacrifice must be continually present in the relationship between the husband and wife. If the spouses, therefore, lack kindness, affection, and a spirit of total self-giving and sacrificial service for each other, then their shared intimacy begins to lose its meaning. However, if a truly sacrificial love is present, then the marital act serves as an expression of charity and a way of growing in holiness and true joy.

SINS AGAINST MARRIAGE

Any act that directly violates the marriage covenant—by either failing in the fidelity to the permanent and exclusive nature of marital love or in the misuse of one or both purposes of the marital act—is considered a grave sin. The Church's extensive and clear teachings on marriage and human sexuality offer a wonderful road map for healthy and happy marriages. It is precisely when these guidelines are either rejected or ignored that untold problems arise for marriage, the family, and ultimately society itself.

The main sins against marriage include adultery, polygamy, incest, free union, trial marriage, and divorce.

Adultery involves sexual relations between two people when one or both of them are married to someone else. This act is never justifiable under any circumstances. Adultery not only violates the true meaning of the conjugal act, it also radically betrays the marital commitment and covenant made before God. Anyone who falls into this kind of sin commits a grave injustice against his or her spouse who, in justice, deserves unfailing fidelity.[11]

Marital infidelity, aside from being a grave sin, causes severe emotional and psychological damage to the offended party. In many instances, adultery destroys the marriage itself. The offended party often does not fully recover from the emotional wounds left by this terrible breach of trust and committed love.

Lastly, marital infidelity very often leaves deep and permanent emotional scars on the children, especially during their sensitive formative years when a significant part of their human development depends on the secure knowledge that their parents love each other.

Fidelity requires that spouses keep themselves on guard at all times. There is danger that close friendships outside of marriage can lead to temptation or at very least to a kind of "emotional infidelity" whereby the outside friendship becomes more valued than the friendship with one's own spouse. Perhaps one of the greatest mistakes a spouse can make is to consider himself or herself completely invulnerable to temptation.

Polygamy consists in having more than one wife. This practice is a flagrant violation of the natural law revealed by God, which teaches that marriage by nature is between one man and one woman, who become one flesh.

One of the greatest mistakes a spouse can make is to consider himself or herself completely invulnerable to temptation in the area of infidelity.

> *Polygamy* is not in accord with the moral law. "[Conjugal] communion is radically contradicted by polygamy; this, in fact, directly negates the plan of God which was revealed from the beginning, because it is contrary to the equal personal dignity of men and women who in matrimony give themselves with a love that is total and therefore unique and exclusive."[12] (CCC 2387)

Incest designates intimate relations between relatives or in-laws, within a degree that prohibits marriage between them.

> St. Paul stigmatizes this especially grave offense: "It is actually reported that there is immorality among you...for a man is living with his father's wife....In the name of the Lord Jesus...you are to deliver this man to Satan for the destruction of the flesh...."[13] Incest corrupts family relationships and marks a regression toward animality. (CCC 2388)

Incest destroys family harmony and inflicts in many instances irreparable harm to children and adolescents who form part of a family.

> Connected to incest is any sexual abuse perpetrated by adults on children or adolescents entrusted to their care. The offense is compounded by the scandalous harm done to the physical and moral integrity of the young, who will remain scarred by it all their lives; and the violation of responsibility for their upbringing. (CCC 2389)

Finally, incest violates natural law, in that marriage is intended for a man and a woman who are unrelated or, at worst, distantly related.

Free union usually involves a man and a woman living together, availing themselves of sexual relations with each other, but with no intention of marrying, or only with the remote possibility of marriage. Free union often includes the rejection of the "institution" of marriage.

> The expression covers a number of different situations: concubinage, rejection of marriage as such, or inability to make long-term commitments.[14] All these situations offend against the dignity of marriage; they destroy the very idea of the family; they weaken the sense of fidelity. They are contrary to the moral law. The sexual act must take place exclusively within marriage. Outside of marriage it always constitutes a grave sin and excludes one from sacramental communion. (CCC 2390)

Trial marriage, often referred to as cohabitation, consists of a man and woman living together and having sexual relations, with the intention of marrying each other in the future. The obstensible reason for this arrangement is to "get to know each other" as an aid in making a definitive decision on their compatibility to become husband and wife.

Human love does not tolerate "trial marriages." It demands a total and definitive gift of persons to one another.[15] (CCC 2391)

Divorce, or the civil dissolution of marriage, involves a deliberate intent to break the lifelong commitment of fidelity and spousal love required by the sacred bond of marriage. In many instances, one or both spouses have the intention or willingness to marry again.

Divorce strikes at the dignity of Christian marriage. The *Catechism of the Catholic Church* is very clear and direct in its teaching that divorce is a grave sin against marital fidelity.

> *Divorce* is a grave offense against the natural law. It claims to break the contract, to which the spouses freely consented, to live with each other till death. Divorce does injury to the covenant of salvation, of which sacramental marriage is the sign. Contracting a new union, even if it is recognized by civil law, adds to the gravity of the rupture: the remarried spouse is then in a situation of public and permanent adultery. (CCC 2384)

Divorce has devastating effects on everyone involved. In many cases, it inflicts indescribable suffering on both spouses, especially on the injured party. A person who initiates a divorce after having fully committed oneself to an enduring and exclusive spousal love in marriage betrays himself or herself, his or her spouse, the children, and society as well. Divorce often leaves terrible emotional and psychological scars that can render the spouses and their children emotionally, psychologically, and morally crippled.

The Church recognizes the damage caused by divorce, especially on an innocent party and the children. The Church also recognizes that a valid marriage can take an ugly turn into situations of abuse, abandonment, and adultery, where remaining together becomes unhealthy or dangerous. In such cases, a civil divorce may be necessary to protect the innocent spouse and the children. The Church therefore extends its loving pastoral care to all those who might find themselves in this situation.

Divorce has devastating effects on everyone involved. The Church therefore extends its loving pastoral care to all those who might find themselves in this situation.

> It can happen that one of the spouses is the innocent victim of a divorce decreed by civil law; this spouse therefore has not contravened the moral law. There is a considerable difference between a spouse who has sincerely tried to be faithful to the sacrament of marriage and is unjustly abandoned, and one who through his own grave fault destroys a canonically valid marriage.[16] (CCC 2386)

In cases where an innocent party finds serious grounds for a declaration of nullity—a declaration by the Church, after thorough investigation, that there never was a sacramental marriage due to defect of consent, defect of canonical form, or the existence of an impediment—a legal divorce is recognized as a first step before proceedings for a declaration of nullity can begin.

Contraception is the deliberate intervention by use of mechanical, chemical, or other medical procedures, with the express intention of preventing the conception of new life which might occur through sexual intercourse. Among the many forms of contraception are chemical substances like the birth control pill, which impedes ovulation, and devices such as condoms and diaphragms that block fertilization. Given both its intended objective and the manner in which it functions, the use of contraception is contrary to the purposes of the marital act and therefore gravely immoral.

WORKING WITH GOD:
NATURAL FAMILY PLANNING

While the two primary aspects of the marital act are the unitive and the procreative, nature has determined that each and every marital act does not necessarily result in conception. In such cases, the expression of marital love still remains a reflection of the one-flesh union created by God.

> Periodic continence, that is, the methods of birth regulation based on self-observation and the use of infertile periods, is in conformity with the objective criteria of morality.[17] These methods respect the bodies of the spouses, encourage tenderness between them, and favor the education of an authentic freedom. In contrast, "every action which, whether in anticipation of the conjugal act, or in its accomplishment, or in the development of its natural consequences, proposes, whether as an end or as a means, to render procreation impossible" is intrinsically evil.[18] (CCC 2370)

Refraining from the marital act during those days when a conception would most likely occur does not alter the act of total self-giving nor prevent the complete unity between spouses. On the contrary, when used with the proper intentions, the practice of temporary abstinence in marriage can be a gift of self-sacrifice and can increase the communication and love shared between a husband and a wife.[19] In the case of marital relations when contraception is used, the gift of fertility is intentionally withheld. This is especially the case when, through a surgical procedure (direct sterilization), one or both of the parties is rendered infertile.

The Church teaches that spouses can avail themselves of Natural Family Planning (NFP), which applies the knowledge of the cyclic fertility inherent in nature, allowing the couple to abstain from marital relations when a pregnancy could occur.

NFP permits the married couple to plan the number and spacing of the children, while retaining its natural ordination to life. The proper use of NFP respects and preserves the proper ends of marriage. Natural Family Planning, when used with the proper intentions, helps the spouses grow in their friendship and strengthens their marriage. It may be used if:

WORKING WITH GOD:
NATURAL FAMILY PLANNING Continued

✤ Each and every conjugal act is open to the transmission of life.

✤ The judgment to use NFP is made with an upright conscience—a conscience informed by the teachings of the Church.

✤ There is a serious reason for the decisions determining the number and spacing of the children. (e.g., physical and mental health, financial, the legitimate needs of the existing family, etc.)

Responsible parenthood implies that the spouses fully recognize their own duties towards God, towards themselves, towards their family, and towards society, in a correct hierarchy of values. Their actions must be conformed to the creative intention of God expressed in the very nature of marriage and of its acts, and manifested by the constant teaching of the Church.[20]

Responsible parenthood means knowing and respecting the functions of biological processes, which are a part of the human person. It also means the necessary mastery of the reason and the will over instinct and passion. In relation to physical, economic, psychological, and social conditions, responsible parenthood is exercised either by the generous decision to raise a large family, or by the decision, made with respect for the moral law, to avoid a new birth for the time being, or even for an indeterminate period. Above all, responsible parenthood implies a profound relationship to the objective moral order established by God.

God has a plan for every couple, which includes the number of children which they should offer him through their marriage. He does not force his will on us but wants the couple to freely, generously, and responsibly say "yes" to his plan.

The practice of temporary abstinence in marriage can be a gift of self-sacrifice.

Some of the methods employed to prevent new life can also act as *abortifacients* — drugs or devices that can cause an abortion or prevent a fertilized egg from attaching itself to the lining of the womb. These include the intra-uterine device (IUD), the birth control pill, and the new "morning-after pill" being marketed as "Plan B."

Direct sterilization is a permanent form of contraception, which involves a surgical procedure performed on the man or woman with the intent to render future conception biologically impossible. These surgical modifications of the generative organs violate the sacredness of the human body and are a sin against the openness to life in marriage. Thus, they are gravely immoral. The *Catechism of the Catholic Church* reminds us:

> **Legitimate intentions on the part of the spouses do not justify recourse to morally unacceptable means (for example, direct sterilization or contraception). (CCC 2399)**

As noted earlier, the marital act as created by God is intended to express a complete gift of self which presupposes the unitive and procreative aspects.

> **"By safeguarding both these essential aspects, the unitive and the procreative, the conjugal act preserves in its fullness the sense of true mutual love and its orientation toward man's exalted vocation to parenthood."[21] (CCC 2369)**

Evangelium Vitæ (*The Gospel of Life*) is an encyclical written by Pope John Paul II and issued March 25, 1995. It expresses the Catholic Church's position on the value and inviolability of human life. "Together we all sense our duty to preach the Gospel of life, to celebrate it in the Liturgy and in our whole existence, and to serve it with the various programmes and structures which support and promote life" (*EV* 79).

The marital act is one of total self-giving of which openness to procreation is an integral part. The intentional withholding of one's fertility and the refusal to accept the other in his or her totality as a person through the use of contraception places limitations on this gift of self, degrading the image of God, which this union was designed to reflect.

> The fundamental nature of the marriage act, while uniting husband and wife in the closest intimacy, also renders them capable of generating new life-and this as a result of laws written into the actual nature of man and of woman. And if each of these essential qualities, the unitive and the procreative, is preserved, the use of marriage fully retains its sense of true mutual love and its ordination to the supreme responsibility of parenthood to which man is called. (*Humanæ Vitæ*, 12)

> The direct interruption of the generative process already begun and, above all, all direct abortion, even for therapeutic reasons, are to be absolutely excluded as lawful means of regulating the number of children. (*Humanæ Vitæ*, 14)

Pope John Paul II, in his encyclical *The Gospel of Life*, made it abundantly clear that contraception "contradicts the full truth of the sexual act as the proper expression of conjugal love."[22] The significance of total self-giving inherent in the marital act is lost by the use of contraception.

Over the past decades since this document was issued, attacks on the dignity of human sexuality and human life have reached alarming levels. Laws have been passed permitting the destruction of unborn life, and the divorce rate, out-of-wedlock pregnancies, incidents of sexual promiscuity, and sexually transmitted diseases have skyrocketed. Indeed, many of the moral issues current in society, such as genetic engineering, *in vitro* fertilization, assisted suicide, euthanasia, embryonic stem-cell research, and cloning are at least indirectly connected to the endorsement of contraception and its consequent devaluing of the sanctity of human life.

SINS AGAINST THE INTEGRITY AND DIGNITY OF THE CONJUGAL ACT AND AGAINST THE DIGNITY OF THE CHILD

Artificial insemination, which seeks the conception of new life outside of the marital act, is a grave offense against the unitive dimension of marriage.

Artificial insemination is the name for fertilization outside the conjugal act. This can be performed in two ways. The first, called *in vivo fertilization*, involves a medical procedure which inserts the sperm of a donor (the husband or another person) directly into the uterus of the woman in hopes of fertilization. In some instances, a non-spousal donor is really a "seller," who "donates" sperm to a sperm bank for an agreed-upon fee.

The second method, called *in vitro fertilization* (IVF), involves the taking of a woman's egg and its subsequent fertilization (utilizing the sperm of the husband or other donor) in the laboratory. The fertilized egg (zygote) is then inserted back into the uterus of the woman for implantation. If the future mother is not physically capable of carrying the fetus, the embryo sometimes is carried on her behalf by a surrogate mother.

All of these practices are a violation of the sanctity of life and of the marital act, and they pose several moral difficulties.

The usual means for obtaining sperm from the father for use in the procedure is masturbation, which is a misuse of one's body and a sin against chastity. These modes of conception circumvent marital union as the normal and natural means of procreation.

The dignity of human life requires that the conception of new life be the fruit of the physical expression of marital love and not a biological procedure performed in a laboratory. Additionally, the practice of utilizing non-spousal sperm, egg donors, or surrogate mothers is morally objectionable and could be considered a form of "clinical adultery."

In vitro fertilization, as we have seen in the previous chapter on the Fifth Commandment, commonly involves the creation of multiple embryos. Those which are not ultimately implanted in the uterus are either destroyed or frozen for future use. Since human life begins at conception, this practice results in the

A child is not something *owed* to one, but is a *gift*. The "supreme gift of marriage" is a human person. (CCC 2378)

taking of innocent human life and the treatment of the human person in the embryonic stage as nothing more than a piece of merchandise eventually to be discarded. The procedure also can be used to selectively choose a particular embryo based on predetermined criteria or conditions. This reduces the value of a human being to subjective standards that society determines to be beneficial.

> A child is not something *owed* to one, but is a *gift*. The "supreme gift of marriage" is a human person. A child may not be considered a piece of property, an idea to which an alleged "right to a child" would lead. In this area, only the child possesses genuine rights: the right "to be the fruit of the specific act of the conjugal love of his parents," and "the right to be respected as a person from the moment of his conception."[23] (CCC 2378)

SINS AGAINST CHASTITY

If sexual intercourse occurs outside of the context of marriage, it cannot be an expression of love, and thereby becomes a deception and a misuse of one's sexuality. Therefore, the Sixth and Ninth Commandments forbid the pursuit of those actions proper to marriage when they occur outside of that sacred union.

The *Catechism* states that the marital act "is morally legitimate only when a definitive community of life between a man and woman has been established. Human love does not tolerate 'trial marriages.' It demands a total and definitive gift of persons to one another" (CCC 2391). In light of the teachings of Christ, this includes not only the physical actions of a person, but also his or her thoughts and desires.

When separated from the Sacrament of Marriage, the marital act ceases to express its true meaning and exhibits a deceptive lie that blatantly contradicts its true meaning. In the language of the body, the marital act reflects a complete union of persons. If the true self-giving love, the lifelong commitment in marriage, or the proper openness to procreation is absent, the marital act and the intimacy leading up to it are a lie, because they are the sign of a union that simply does not exist.

Recall the purposes of marriage and sexuality—the unitive and the procreative dimensions. If either one is missing or compromised, then the act is morally wrong. The legitimate pursuit and enjoyment of sexual pleasure must occur within a committed and loving marriage.

The Magisterium of the Church—confirming the teaching of the Old Testament, the New Testament, and Sacred Tradition—has also urged these same teachings throughout history. Some examples of sins the *Catechism* lists as violating the Sixth and Ninth Commandments (in addition to the sins covered in the section "Sins Against Marriage") include *impure thoughts and desires*, *masturbation*, *premarital sex*, *oral or anal intercourse*, *homosexual acts*, and *bestiality*.

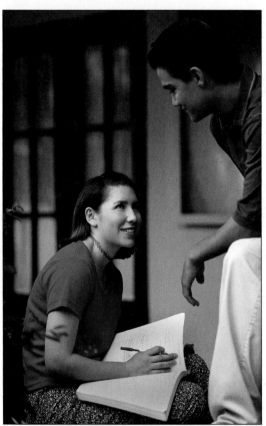

The moral question regarding impure thoughts and desires is in how we respond when we become conscious of these transitory thoughts.

Impure thoughts and desires are temptations that are virtually inevitable, particularly for youths who are going through hormonal and bodily changes. Capitalizing on this general inclination toward sensuality, the devil is always on the lookout for ways to tempt people into sin.

The moral question regarding impure thoughts and desires is in how we handle it when we become conscious of these transitory thoughts. If we recognize the temptation and quickly push it aside, we have made a good moral choice. If we instead give our consent and dwell on these thoughts, willfully entertain them, or go along with these flights of fantasy for even a short while and perhaps even allow ourselves to be aroused by them, then we have committed the sin of impure thoughts and desires. The entire question hinges on whether we consent to these thoughts or not.

We must never willfully *entertain* nor *be entertained* by such thoughts or desires. As a corollary, it is sensible and necessary to avoid sexually provocative images or discussions, whether they are viewed directly or appear in magazines, on television, at the theater, or on the Internet. Applying the appropriate means to guard the eyes and mind is a virtuous practice because it serves to avoid the near occasion of sin.

In raising Christian morality to a higher level, Jesus taught that evil proceeds from the thoughts which come from the heart.[24] In the Sermon on the Mount, he taught that it was not enough for a person not to commit adultery, but that even a lustful look or desirous thought of adultery was a sin.[25] Thus, the standard which Christ calls us to follow begins with aligning our will to the law of love. Once we have given our hearts and minds to Christ and his teachings, our actions will follow.

Pornography involves exhibiting images that expose the human body or show sexual actions for the purpose of lustful gratification. Indulgence in pornography violates the dignity of human sexuality, presents the human person as an object of lustful use, and denigrates the dignity of the viewer.

> *Pornography* consists in removing real or simulated sexual acts from the intimacy of the partners, in order to display them deliberately to third parties. It offends against chastity because it perverts the conjugal act, the intimate giving of spouses to each other. It does grave injury to the dignity of its participants (actors, vendors, the public), since each one becomes an object of base pleasure and illicit profit for others. It immerses all who are involved in the illusion of a fantasy world. It is a grave offense. (CCC 2354)

Christ by Titian (detail from *Noli me Tangere*). In raising Christian morality to a higher level, Jesus taught that evil proceeds from the thoughts which come from the heart.

As cited in *Catechetical Formation in Chaste Living*, the United States Conference of Catholic Bishops states, "Pornography also tends to become addictive. The ready availability of pornography on the Internet and television adds to the spread of this addiction."[26]

Masturbation is a more serious sin to which impure thoughts may lead. The enjoyment of sexual pleasure forms part of God's plan only when it is connected with sexual relations in marriage. Therefore, every act of self-stimulation or self-satisfaction is morally wrong.

The physical expression of human sexuality is innately "other-centered" and "new-life-centered," not "self-centered" or disconnected from spousal love. In the case of masturbation, the individual misuses his or her sexuality by focusing this gift only on himself or herself, completely separated from its purpose.

For this reason, the *Catechism of the Catholic Church* states that "masturbation is an intrinsically and gravely disordered action" (CCC 2352). Its practice easily becomes addictive and can lead to sexual obsession and a greater proclivity to run away from the challenges and problems of real life. Once a person has become addicted to this type of behavior, oftentimes he or she can only overcome this habit with strenuous effort, frequent reception of the Sacraments of Reconciliation and the Eucharist, prayer, penance, and God's abundant grace.

As mentioned above, sometimes arousal takes place unwittingly. Occasionally, particularly with boys, an erotic dream results in sexual stimulation or satisfaction. As long as these acts are neither consented to nor entertained, no moral harm is done. Quite to the contrary, the practice of virtue in fighting these temptations is bound to make a person stronger in the face of all types of temptations.

Premarital sex, or fornication, is a sin because it takes place outside the context of marriage. Here we include not only genital sex, but any act designed to illicit sexual pleasure outside of marriage, such as passionate kissing, sexual petting, or oral intercourse. There are absolutely no circumstances or considerations that would justify any of these sexual activities outside of marriage. They are not justified even if the relationship is "monogamous," even if the partners truly love each other and care for each other, even if they pray together and go to Mass together, or even if they are engaged to be married and already "feel married."

All forms of sexual expression are preliminary actions leading to sexual union in marriage and therefore must be seen as closely connected to the conjugal act. Prudence would insist that we avoid any situations, discussions, or actions that may lead to sexual temptation. Many a young unmarried couple have thrown caution to the wind and ended up crossing lines of sexual intimacy that they had not originally intended.

Oral or anal intercourse as a means of sexual satisfaction offends the moral law even if they occur within the bonds of marriage. To seek or permit sexual climax outside of the genital union is gravely sinful and disordered. Anal acts are particularly disordered and can also cause permanent physiological damage.

Homosexual acts involve sexual actions between members of the same gender. They are in and of themselves unnatural and contrary to the natural sexual expression established by God between persons of the opposite gender. For this reason, the *Catechism* categorizes homosexual acts as "intrinsically disordered"[27] and grievously sinful, since by their very nature they are devoid of both the unitive and procreative dimensions of human sexuality. For example, sexual relations between a man and a woman outside of marriage is always sinful, but not intrinsically disordered, since the act involves a sexual union that corresponds to human nature.

Given the complementarity of the sexes and the direct and intimate connection between sexual union and new life, attraction between members of the opposite gender is clearly derived from human nature. For this reason, the *Catechism* goes on to say, homosexual inclinations are "objectively disordered"[28] for the simple reason that God has established that men and women be attracted to each other for the purpose of a spousal relationship of life-giving love. Therefore, any same sex inclinations would certainly be outside of God's plan of sexual complementarity that leads to the conception of new life. Same sex attraction or inclinations, though disordered, are not immoral or sinful if they are not acted out in willful thought, desire, or action.

The Church makes no judgment on what causes some persons to be attracted to members of the same sex. From a moral perspective, it makes no difference whether the inclination is determined by genetics, psychology, environmental conditioning, or by other influences. Independently of the cause, acting on these homosexual tendencies is always gravely sinful.

As with every person, those with homosexual tendencies are called by Christ to live a life of chastity. Spiritual direction, prayer, and frequent recourse to the sacraments are indispensable aids for everyone to live in accordance with their Christian vocation.

> **Homosexual persons are called to chastity. By the virtues of self-mastery that teach them inner freedom, at times by the support of disinterested friendship, by prayer and sacramental grace, they can and should gradually and resolutely approach Christian perfection. (CCC 2359)**

The Church recognizes that many people in society could have same sex inclinations. With much pastoral concern, the *Catechism* addresses their particular situation and the need for God's love, along with guidance for living a moral life focused on Jesus Christ.

> **The number of men and women who have deep-seated homosexual tendencies is not negligible. This inclination, which is objectively disordered, constitutes for most of them a trial. They must be accepted with respect, compassion, and sensitivity. Every sign of unjust discrimination in their regard should be avoided. These persons are called to fulfill God's will in their lives and, if they are Christians, to unite to the sacrifice of the Lord's Cross the difficulties they may encounter from their condition. (CCC 2358)**

SINS AGAINST CHASTITY IN THE OLD TESTAMENT

Prohibitions against unchaste living are formulated not only by Catholic moral theology but are also found in the Bible and Sacred Tradition. The following is a list of the sins that are condemned in the Old Testament:

- **Adultery** is sexual relations between a married person and someone other than that person's spouse. Exodus clearly formulates this principle: "You shall not commit adultery." (Ex 20:14)

- **Fornication** (or pre-marital sex) is forbidden in a rigorous manner. Besides the moral prohibition, a fine was also included in the Old Testament. (cf. Dt 22: 20-21, 28-29)

- **Onanism** (withdrawal before ejaculation) is condemned in the Old Testament because Onan's intent was contraceptive; he refused to provide offspring for his sister-in-law in his deceased brother's place, as was required by the custom of his time. (cf Gn 38: 4-10)

- **Prostitution** is prohibited because it uses a person for sexual pleasure. (cf. Lv 19: 29)

- **Bestiality** (sex with an animal) is a vice punished with death. (cf. Lv 20: 15-16; Ex 22: 19)

- **Incest** (sexual activity among relatives) is prohibited. (cf. Lv 20: 17)

- **Homosexual acts** are forbidden, as they are contrary to the nature of man and of the sex act itself. (cf. Gn 19: 4-10)

EDUCATION IN CHASTITY

The Supper at Emmaus (detail) by Titian.
A firm commitment to Christ and a sincere desire to make Christ the center of one's life is the first step in leading a successfully clean life.

As challenging as Christian morality may appear in an atmosphere of rampant sensuality, the inner recesses of the human heart desire the holy purity taught by Jesus Christ. Many young people, in spite of so much propaganda to the contrary, experience that chastity is not only possible but also a joyful and liberating virtue.

A person leading a chaste life will have greater freedom to love in sacrificial service to others, will be inclined to have a deep relationship with Christ, and will be able to contemplate God's goodness and beauty in every person.

Effective ways to grow in the virtue of chastity and avoid those occasions that militate against living a pure life include a firm commitment to Christ, fostering a life of piety and Christian virtue, *prudent use of the media*, *modesty in dress, sensible norms for dating*, and certain *spiritual practices*.

A firm commitment to Christ and a sincere desire to make Christ the center of one's life is the first step in leading a successfully clean life. When a person's life is centered on Christ, he or she will naturally want to remove those obstacles that impair a relationship with him and which compromise moral integrity. Given the many temptations and pressures in modern society, it is extremely difficult to honestly pursue chastity without a firm commitment to follow Christ.

The apparent insurmountable difficulties in living the virtue of chastity are usually due to bad habits, a weak commitment, and a lack of love, rather than anything inherently difficult. In his exhortations on avoiding occasions of sin, Christ states that the individual should act decisively. For example, "If your eye causes you to sin, pluck it out and throw it away" (Mt 5: 29). Christ's message, through the use of very graphic imagery, teaches us that we must aggressively rid ourselves of all that would lead us into sin.

Passivity and ambiguity of purpose often prepare the way for major falls in sexual morality. Unless a person has explicitly and seriously decided on reflecting Christ and his teachings in his or her life, the chances for impure conduct are quite high.

However, a person who has wholeheartedly taken the decision to live by Christ's teachings will very seldom be caught by the surprise of an overwhelming temptation. God will always give us the grace to overcome temptations, avoid occasions of sin, and grow in virtue.

Prudent use of the media is a critical measure for guarding one's chastity. Provocative images on the internet, television, magazines, movies, literature, and conversation commonly give rise to temptation. Christ clearly mentions the vital importance of the custody of the eyes to win in the battle for purity. "The eye is the lamp of the body. So, if your eye is sound, your whole body will be full of light; but if your eye is not sound, your whole body will be full of darkness."[29]

An individual who is genuinely serious about chastity needs to avoid looking at those things which are designed to arouse the passions. The true Christian must selectively choose shows and programs that do not contradict the message of the Gospel. Therefore, movies and shows that portray immoral or anti-Christian behavior and which are designed to lead a person into temptation are incompatible with a Christian lifestyle.

Modesty in dress is often an overlooked virtue to cultivate. In many instances, the purpose of fashion has shifted from an emphasis on elegance, which ultimately reinforces the dignity of the person, to immodest attire, which invariably conveys the message that an individual is defined mainly by his or her sexual attractiveness. This trend deceives others into believing that a person of the opposite gender is primarily an

"HOW FAR CAN WE GO BEFORE IT IS A SIN?"

While the Sixth Commandment forbids adultery, the *Catechism of the Catholic Church* reflects Christ's teaching that any action contrary to the expression of genuine love is sinful. In the physical expression of the marital act, there are preliminary actions which as part of God's design are expressions of love and therefore proper to a husband and a wife. However, they involve a level of intimacy that can only be morally sound when they are shared between a husband and a wife and lead to a physical union between them in the marital act.

Classroom and conference discussions about chastity with young people inevitably raise the question: "How far can we go before it is a sin?" Such an attitude indicates a lack of generosity and a lack of love of Christ, of self, and of others. One would not dream of contemplating, "How badly can I treat a friend before it becomes wrong?" It is the same with Christ and with his gift of human sexuality.

A disturbing trend among teenagers is the belief that while sexual intercourse may be forbidden, other acts such as petting, mutual masturbation, and oral sex are permissible outside of marriage. Some reports suggest that these behaviors sometimes occur among casual friends who are not even dating, and among girls who claim a commitment to abstinence and who still consider themselves virgins.

It is not only the marital act itself that must be reserved for marriage, however. The truth of the matter is that *every sexual expression, every moment of sexual pleasure*, and even *every sexual thought or desire* must be reserved for the loving embrace of husband and wife.

If the question of "how far can we go?" begs an answer, it would be this: Any act or touch that is sexual or genital in nature or is immodest is inappropriate; and any sexual arousal, even if it occurs innocently and without being intended, is a danger signal that the couple must stop what they are doing and do whatever it takes to flee the temptation that has confronted them.

There are no moral loopholes: Any deliberate thought, desire, or action directed outside of the aims of marriage is sinful.[30]

object of lustful desire rather than a person to be respected and loved. A person's choice in clothing should reflect the dignity and inestimable value of the human person and should invite respect and admiration.

> Purity requires *modesty*, an integral part of temperance. Modesty protects the intimate center of the person. It means refusing to unveil what should remain hidden. It is ordered to chastity to whose sensitivity it bears witness. It guides how one looks at others and behaves toward them in conformity with the dignity of persons and their solidarity. (CCC 2521)

In addition to dress, the virtue of modesty also forms the way that we conduct ourselves in conversation and in thought, as well as in what we see and hear. Modesty demands discretion, requiring that we sometimes remain silent or keep a healthy reserve, or that we decline to watch or listen to certain types of media, in those circumstances when the dignity of the human person is being degraded. It also warns against an unhealthy curiosity, especially in areas of human sexuality.

Common sense norms for dating should be established by the individual and in the family long before the oldest child enters high school. The contemporary trend among many young people is to establish an exclusive relationship almost from the first date. A "going steady" relationship over a long period of time when marriage is not imminent can make the practice of chastity quite difficult.

It is best to look at these types of relationships as temporary in that they should either lead to marriage or cease to exist if it becomes clear that marriage is not in their near future. A couple should see their steady relationship as a remote marriage preparation, not as an open-ended imitation of an engagement or marriage. When a close or exclusive relationship carries on too long without imminent hope of marriage, it often presents a growing temptation for the man and woman that can soon lead to sexual sins.

The possibility of an imminent marriage often provides a good incentive for the couple to live chastely. The virtue of chastity fosters a deeper friendship that will make the wedding day all the more special. The future husband and wife should realize that sexual restraint in dating and in their engagement promotes a deeper friendship and an exciting romance. The serious observation of chastity in a dating relationship will also help strengthen the couple's capacity for fidelity in marriage.

Particularly during the high school and early college years, steady dating should be discouraged.

Particularly during the high school and early college years, steady dating should be discouraged. The late teens and early twenties are years of rapid development that are very critical to a person's formation as an adult. Socializing among young men and women should not be limited to steady dating. To be tied down to an exclusive relationship cuts off other relationships that might provide insights into what one might want to look for in a future spouse.

Unless a young man or woman is ready to consider marriage, it is better to be "just friends" with people of the opposite gender and arrange group dates rather than pair off into exclusive relationships. Such group dates also have the advantage of limiting "alone time" and thereby avoiding situations where temptation can more likely arise.

Spiritual measures as a means of protecting chastity are a natural outgrowth of a commitment to Christ. When a person has Christ at the center of his or her life, he or she will be given the grace to follow his teachings. The virtue of chastity requires not only the exercise of the will, but also a good relationship with God, which is characterized by a habitual recourse to prayer, self-denial, penance, and the Sacraments of Reconciliation and the Holy Eucharist. These spiritual measures are a source of grace that gives the person the disposition and strength to live a Christian life.

THE SEX-CRAZED MEDIA AND THE CHRISTIAN RESPONSE

It often seems that the various forms of entertainment in modern society attempt to convey the message that expressions of human sexuality are not intimate, spiritual, or sacred aspects of marriage, but simply natural outlets for physical and emotional needs and desires. In television and film, premarital, homosexual, and adulterous relationships are often presented as an acceptable mode of behavior. Movies, advertisements, music, and fashion incessantly but deceptively proclaim that self-indulgence, not self-sacrifice, is the key for true happiness.

The media, following the adage that "sex sells," frequently distorts the true notion of human intimacy and in so doing degrades the moral tone of society. A television viewer watching a ball game cannot avoid commercials designed to arouse the passions in order to sell the newest cologne. Sitcoms convey the message that true comedy must be charged with sexual jokes and innuendoes in order to produce levity and laughter. In many instances, an otherwise excellent movie will invariably include some gratuitous scenes portraying nudity no matter what their relevance to the overall theme of the film. Often television series will portray intelligent, successful, and charming men or women with loose morals as an example of acceptable or even exemplary behavior.

Many modern songs contain lyrics that are explicitly demeaning and offensive to women. In too many cases, fashions, instead of emphasizing the dignity of the person through elegant dress, transmit the false message that the person is primarily an object of sensual gratification.

An even more blatant abuse of the media is the widespread availability of pornography on television, film, and the internet. This deceptively tantalizing escape from reality enslaves the person and forms a distorted attitude toward human sexuality and the sacredness of the human body. Both those who are being lustfully viewed and those who look at them demean and degrade themselves.

The culture in which we live affects us and influences our views and opinions. Christians must remain aware of this influence and its destructive effect on the true meaning of human sexuality and Christian marriage. Christians have the serious responsibility of presenting the authentic meaning of genuine love and the beauty of human sexuality expressed in the sanctity of marriage. In doing so, an authentic culture can be created which manifests the reality of human love, the sacredness of marriage, and the happiness offered us by God.

The Annunciation by Fra Angelico. Devotion to Mary is a powerful means to grow in chastity.

The habit of a nightly examination of conscience serves to bring about a humble recognition of personal sins together with the effort to depart from occasions of sin. This will effectively help us to overcome the temptations with which we are faced.

Devotion to Mary is a powerful means to grow in chastity. Mary, who is the Mother of God and our Mother as well, will not fail in helping her children remain liberated from those things which are contrary to the love of her Son Jesus Christ.

CONCLUSION

The pure heart is the loving heart that enters into communion of service and obedience with Jesus Christ. Love is the fire that purifies and unifies intellect, will, and emotion, thereby making man one with himself, inasmuch as it makes him one in God's eyes. Thus, man is able to serve the uniting of those who are divided. This is how man enters God's dwelling place and becomes able to see him. And that is just what it means for him to be "blessed."[31]

The Church's teaching on chastity is summarized in the phrase, *"Blessed are the pure in heart, for they shall see God"* (cf. Mt 5: 8). This beatitude shows us that a chaste heart empowers the person to see the image of God in every human being.

True love presupposes an appreciation of the exalted dignity of every person regardless of sex, talents, virtues, and social status. Self-mastery in the area of chastity liberates men and women so that they can contemplate the beauty of God in his creation and especially in every human being.

Self-control affords the person the ability to serve, show true affection, and give oneself for the good of the other. Through the practice of love as sacrificial service to the other, the lover discovers God more and more in himself or herself. This experience of love assists in the appreciation of the inestimable worth of every person. It is no mere coincidence that Jesus Christ's first words on purity are positive and presents it as a means to true love and fulfillment.

SUPPLEMENTARY READING

1. Love Must Find its Safeguard in the Stability of Marriage

Experience teaches us that love must find its safeguard in the stability of marriage, if sexual intercourse is truly to respond to the requirements of its own finality and to those of human dignity. These requirements call for a conjugal contract sanctioned and guaranteed by society—a contract which establishes a state of life of capital importance both for the exclusive union of the man and the woman and for the good of their family and of the human community. Most often, in fact, premarital relations exclude the possibility of children. What is represented to be conjugal love is not able, as it absolutely should be, to develop into paternal and maternal love.
Or, if it does happen to do so, this will be to the detriment of the children, who will be deprived of the stable environment in which they ought to develop in order to find in it the way and the means of their insertion into society as a whole. The consent given by people who wish to be united in marriage must therefore be manifested externally and in a manner which makes it valid in the eyes of society.

—*Persona Humana*, 7

2. Homosexuality

In the pastoral field, homosexuals must certainly be treated with understanding and sustained in the hope of overcoming their personal difficulties and their inability to fit into society. Their culpability will be judged with prudence. But no pastoral method can be employed which would give moral justification to these acts on the grounds that they would be consonant with the condition of such people. For according to the objective moral order, homosexual relations are acts which lack an essential and indispensable finality. In Sacred Scripture they are condemned as a serious depravity and even presented as the sad consequence of rejecting God. This judgment of Scripture does not of course permit us to con-clude that all those who suffer from this anomaly are personally responsible for it, but it does attest to the fact that homosexual acts are intrinsically disordered and can in no case be approved of.

—*Persona Humana*, 8

3. Chastity

Whatever the force of certain arguments of a biological and philosophical nature, which have sometimes been used by theologians, in fact both the Magisterium of the Church—in the course of a constant tradition—and the moral sense of the faithful have declared without hesitation that masturbation is an intrinsically and seriously disordered act.[32] The main reason is that, whatever the motive for acting this way, the deliberate use of the sexual faculty outside normal conjugal relations essentially contradicts the finality of the faculty. For it lacks the sexual relationship called for by the moral order, namely the relationship which realizes "the full sense of mutual self-giving and human procreation in the context of true love."[33] All deliberate exercise of sexuality must be reserved to this regular relationship. Even if it cannot be proved that Scripture condemns this sin by name, the tradition of the Church has rightly understood it to be condemned in the New Testament when the latter speaks of "impurity," "unchasteness" and other vices contrary to chastity and continence.

—*Persona Humana*, 9

4. Marriage is Not Just a Social Institution

For a Christian, marriage is not just a social institution, much less a mere remedy for human weakness. It is a real supernatural calling. A great sacrament, in Christ and in the

Church, says St. Paul. At the same time, it is a permanent contract between a man and a woman. Whether we like it or not, the sacrament of matrimony, instituted by Christ, cannot be dissolved. It is a permanent contract that sanctifies in cooperation with Jesus Christ. He fills the souls of husband and wife and invites them to follow him. He transforms their whole married life into an occasion for God's presence on earth.

— St. Josemaria Escriva, *Christ Is Passing By*, 23

SUPPLEMENTARY READING Continued

5. Responsible Parenthood

Conjugal love requires in husband and wife an awareness of their mission of "responsible parenthood," which today is rightly much insisted upon, and which also must be exactly understood. Consequently it is to be considered under aspects which are legitimate and connected with one another. In relation to the biological processes, responsible parenthood means the knowledge and respect of their functions; human intellect discovers in the power of giving life biological laws which are part of the human person.
In relation to the tendencies of instinct or passion, responsible parenthood means that necessary dominion which reason and will must exercise over them.

In relation to physical, economic, psychological and social conditions, responsible parenthood is exercised, either by the deliberate and generous decision to raise a large family, or by the decision, made for grave motives and with due respect for the moral law, to avoid for the time being, or even for an indeterminate period, a new birth.

Responsible parenthood also and above all implies a more profound relationship to the objective moral order established by God, of which a right conscience is the faithful interpreter. The responsible exercise of parenthood implies, therefore, that husband and wife recognize fully their own duties towards God, towards themselves, towards the family and towards society, in a correct hierarchy of values.

In the task of transmitting life, therefore, they are not free to proceed completely at will, as if they could determine in a wholly autonomous way the honest path to follow; but they must conform their activity to the creative intention of God, expressed in the very nature of marriage and of its acts, and manifested by the constant teaching of the Church.

— *Humanæ Vitæ*, 10

6. Relationship Between Love and the Divine

Nowadays Christianity of the past is often criticized as having been opposed to the body; and it is quite true that tendencies of this sort have always existed. Yet the contemporary way of exalting the body is deceptive. *Eros*, reduced to pure "sex," has become a commodity, a mere "thing" to be bought and sold, or rather, man himself becomes a commodity. This is hardly man's great "yes" to the body. On the contrary, he now considers his body and his sexuality as the purely material part of himself, to be used and exploited at will. Nor does he see it as an arena for the exercise of his freedom, but as a mere object that he attempts, as he pleases, to make both enjoyable and harmless. Here we are actually dealing with a debasement of the human body: no longer is it integrated into our overall existential freedom; no longer is it a vital expression of our whole being, but it is more or less relegated to the purely biological sphere. The apparent exaltation of the body can quickly turn into a hatred of bodiliness. Christian faith, on the other hand, has always considered man a unity in duality, a reality in which spirit and matter compenetrate, and in which each is brought to a new nobility. True, *eros* tends to rise "in ecstasy" towards the Divine, to lead us beyond ourselves; yet for this very reason it calls for a path of ascent, renunciation, purification and healing.

— Pope Benedict XVI, *Deus Caritas Est*, 5

VOCABULARY

ABORTIFACIENTS
Chemical substances or mechanical devices that inhibit a fertilized egg's ability to attach itself to the lining of the uterus, thereby destroying the human zygote.

ADULTERY
Sexual relations between a married person and one to whom he or she is not married. Adultery is opposed to the Sacrament of Matrimony because it contradicts the unity and exclusivity of married love.

CHASTITY
The moral virtue that, under the cardinal virtue of temperance, is directed toward the positive integration of sexuality within a person by moderating the sexual appetite. This virtue leads to a correct understanding of human sexuality when integrated into every relationship. Chastity is a gift of God, a grace, and a fruit of the Holy Spirit.

COMPLEMENTARITY
Refers to the compatible and mutually beneficial relationship between man and woman according to the original plan of God.

CONCEPTION
The union of sperm and egg that creates a new life.

CONJUGAL ACT (see Marital Act)

CONTINENCE
Self-restraint of the sexual appetite either by abstinence or moderation. By extension, self-restraint of other appetites.

CONTRACEPTION
Any of a number of barrier or chemical measures used to prevent pregnancy which would result from sexual intercourse.

DIVORCE
A civil dissolution of marriage. A civil divorce does not dissolve a valid marriage before God; thus, an attempted remarriage would be adultery. In addition, divorce introduces disorder into the family and into society. It brings grave harm to the spouses and the children.

EMBRYO
Refers to an unborn child in the first several weeks of life.

EROTICISM
The use of sexually arousing imagery in literature or art. A tendency to become sexually aroused, usually by some stimulus.

FERTILIZATION (see Conception)

FETUS
An unborn child.

FORNICATION
Pre-marital intercourse and other sexual acts.

HEDONISM
The theory of ethics in which pleasure is regarded as the chief good and end of every action.

HUMANÆ VITÆ
Pope Paul VI's 1968 encyclical that reaffirmed and beautifully explained the Catholic Church's condemnation of contraception.

INDISSOLUBILITY
The quality of an entity such that it cannot be divided into its elements. This quality of the Sacrament of Matrimony means the union of marriage cannot be broken except by the death of a spouse.

IN VITRO FERTILIZATION
Morally objectionable fertility technique of fertilizing a woman's egg with a man's sperm in the laboratory and then implanting the fertilized egg into a woman's uterus.

IN VIVO FERTILIZATION
The quality of an entity that it cannot be divided into its elements. This quality of a sacramental and consummated marriage means the union of marriage cannot be broken except by the death of a spouse.

LUST
Sensuous appetite or desire; usually sexual in nature. This lawless and passionate desire of or for some object leads to sin. This is one of the seven capital sins.

VOCABULARY Continued

MARITAL ACT
The genital sexual act proper to marriage, an embodiment of the permanent union of the husband and wife.

MASTURBATION
The deliberate stimulation of the genital organs in order to derive sexual pleasure.

MATRIMONY
The Sacrament by which a man and a woman, in accordance with God's design from the beginning, are joined in an intimate union of life and love, "so they are no longer two but one" (Mt 19: 6). This union is ordered to the mutual benefit of the spouses and the procreation and education of children.

MODESTY
Moderation, freedom from exaggeration, and self-control. This most often refers to propriety of behavior, chastity in thought and speech, and avoidance of clothing that is revealing or otherwise excites the senses or may lead others to sin.

NATURAL FAMILY PLANNING
Any of several Church-approved methods by which a couple may regulate conception by studying the signs of the woman's cycle of fertility.

POLYGAMY
Attempted marriage between more than two people (one man and one woman) at the same time. Polygamy refers to a man attempting marriage with more than one wife; polyandry refers to a woman attempting marriage with more than one husband. This is a sin against the unity of marriage and forbidden by the Sixth Commandment.

PORNOGRAPHY
An offense against the virtue of chastity and the Sacrament of Matrimony; the expression or suggestion of obscene or unchaste subjects in literature or art. This consists in a removal of sexual acts from the intimacy of a married couple in order to display them to third parties.

PROCREATIVE
One of the purposes of marriage and the marital act; indicates an openness to producing children.

PURITANICAL
A perspective that considers all sexual passions and attractions to be sinful and attributes them to Original Sin.

SEXUALITY
The possession of sexual powers and capability of sexual feeling; this includes every aspect of the whole person: physical, psychological, intellectual, emotional, and moral.

THEOLOGY OF THE BODY
A body of teaching by Pope John Paul II on the dignity of the human person and the complementarity of men and women.

UNITIVE
One of the purposes of marriage and the marital act, it refers to the loving sacramental bond between husband and wife and mirrors the unity of Christ and his Church. The quality or condition of being one in number. This can be said of many things, including God, of Christ and his Church, and a man and woman in matrimony.

ZYGOTE
A newly fertilized egg before its implantation in the uterus.

STUDY QUESTIONS

1. Define "chastity."

2. List and explain three concepts about marriage that we can learn from the creation story found in the Book of Genesis.

3. Explain how human reproduction has a different meaning from that found in other species.

4. Explain the analogy between the Eucharist and the marital act in regard to the renewal of a covenant.

5. What is complementarity? How does this apply to marriage?

6. Explain the different ways in which married love is fruitful.

7. Reproduction is an inherent meaning of sexuality common to all species. What additional meaning does sexuality have for human beings?

8. What are the two primary aspects of the marital act?

9. Why is "education of the children" an inherent obligation of marriage?

10. Explain the meaning of "exclusivity" and "permanence." Explain how these concepts can be deduced from the creation story. Explain the significance of the "total gift of self" in marriage.

11. What are two false views of human sexuality? Why are these views false?

12. Explain how sexual relations outside of the context of marriage are a degradation of the sacred.

13. What is the true meaning of the marital act?

14. Explain why the Catholic Church does not recognize civil divorce as the nullification of a sacramental marriage.

15. How is divorce an offense against the dignity of marriage? List the harmful consequences of divorce.

16. What is adultery, and how is it a betrayal of marriage? What are some of its harmful consequences?

17. What is an abortifacient?

18. Why does the Catholic Church teach that the use of contraception is sinful?

19. Explain how removing the procreative intent from the marital act impedes the unitive intent as well.

20. What are some of the consequences which Pope Paul VI warned would occur if the use of contraception became widespread in society? Explain how these warnings were prophetic.

21. How does the use of contraception promote promiscuity and lead to an increase in abortion?

22. How can the use of donated sperm in artificial insemination be considered clinical adultery?

23. How does IVF degrade the sanctity of human life? How does genetic selection (i.e., the choice of an embryo based on predetermined characteristics) undermine the sanctity of life?

24. What is Natural Family Planning, and how does it function?

25. How does NFP uphold the sanctity and dignity of marriage? How is this different from the use of contraception?

26. What are the conditions for the moral use of NFP?

27. List ways in which the media distorts the true meaning of human sexuality.

28. How are we affected by the culture in which we live?

29. How can Christians help to create an authentic culture?

STUDY QUESTIONS Continued

30. What are five violations of the dignity of human sexuality? How can these be considered a lie?

31. List five actions contrary to the Sixth and Ninth Commandments mentioned in the chapter. How are they violations of the true meaning of human sexuality?

32. How can an impure thought be considered a sin? Use the teachings of Christ to explain your answer.

33. Explain how masturbation degrades the true meaning of human sexuality. What does it mean that human sexuality is directed toward the "other"?

34. How do homosexual acts violate the complementarity of human sexuality? How do they violate the inherent meaning of sexuality as found in nature?

35. How does Christ ask his followers to treat others who have homosexual tendencies?

36. What standard of morality does Christ ask of those who have homosexual tendencies?

37. How is a life focused on Christ the first step in living a chaste life?

38. "If your eye causes you to sin, pluck it out and throw it away" (Mt 5:29). Explain.

39. Explain how immodest dress detracts from the dignity of the person.

40. What are some ways to avoid temptations against chastity while dating?

41. How do the Sacraments of Reconciliation and the Eucharist help a person to grow in the virtue of chastity?

Christ Blessing Little Children by Eastlake. The Church's teaching on chastity is summarized in the phrase, "Blessed are the pure in heart, for they shall see God" (cf. Mt 5:8). This beatitude shows us that a chaste heart empowers the person to see the image of God in every human being.

PRACTICAL EXERCISES

1. Comment on the following text from the *Code of Canon Law* which defines Matrimony:

> The marriage covenant, by which a man and a woman establish between themselves a partnership of their whole life, and which of its own very nature is ordered to the well-being of the spouses and to the procreation and upbringing of children, has, between the baptized, been raised by Christ the Lord to the dignity of a sacrament. (CIC, 1055)

2. Analyze Supplementary Reading 5 and outline the principal characteristics of "responsible parenthood," according to the encyclical *Humanæ Vitæ*.

3. Explain why the following statements and ideas are seriously erroneous:

   a. "For me, premarital sex is not a sin because I love my boyfriend and we are planning to get married someday."

   b. "My wife and I do not intend to have any children. The world is overpopulated already, and it would be irresponsible to bring more children into such a situation."

   c. "Masturbation is not wrong because it is normal and does not hurt anyone."

   d. "If a person is not happy with his or her marriage, then he or she should get a divorce. It is stupid to stay with someone when you are unhappy."

   e. "Calling those sex talk numbers is okay because they are just harmless fantasies, and I am not involved in any sexual activity."

4. Kimberly is engaged to Marcus and thinks they should discuss the number of children they will have. Whenever she brings up the subject, he says he does not want to think about children yet, and that they can decide after they are married. Should Kimberly be concerned about his attitude? Explain. Do you think that this is a good approach to marriage in general? Why or why not?

5. Katie has been dating Matt for six months. She feels that their kissing has gone too far but is afraid to say anything out of fear of losing him. At the same time, she is afraid that he will soon try to go farther than simply kissing, although she hopes that this will not happen. She has confided all this to you, and you can see that she is very uncertain about what to do. Do you see any danger signs in this relationship? What do you think are the chances that Matt will try to go too far? What would you advise her to do next?

6. Imagine that you and your boyfriend/girlfriend are double-dating with the following couples. How would you react to the following situations, and what would you say to the people involved?

   • You are at your senior prom with Kevin and Marisa. Kevin suggested they get a hotel room for the night and told Marisa, "Don't worry; there are two double beds in the room. You can sleep in one; I'll sleep in the other."

   • You and your boyfriend/girlfriend have gone to a party at a friend's house with Gino and Anne. Upon arrival, you discover that there is a lot of alcohol making its way around the party. You overhear Gino saying to Anne, "You can drink as much as you like; you're safe with me."

PRACTICAL EXERCISES Continued

7. Steve and Melanie are young newlyweds, married for just over two years. They already have two children and have decided that they do not want to have any more. Since he is skeptical of other methods of contraception, Steve thinks that they should seek sterilization as a solution. Melanie objects, saying that this would be a sin. She proposes that they simply use natural family planning to prevent pregnancy, arguing that because it is a natural method and is approved by the Church, they would not be committing a sin. There are three problems with both Steve's and Melanie's dispositions and their reasoning according to Catholic moral teaching. What are they?

8. Review the discussion about the unitive and procreative purposes of marriage. Then, for each of the acts or situations below, explain whether one or both of these purposes is violated and why:

a. *In vitro* fertilization;

b. masturbation;

c. sexual activity between an engaged couple;

d. oral sex between husband and wife;

e. a person with homosexual inclinations who successfully battles the temptation to act on his inclination.

The Betrothal of Joseph and Mary by Tissot.
For a Christian, marriage is not just a social institution,
it is a great sacrament.

FROM THE CATECHISM

1659 St. Paul said: "Husbands, love your wives, as Christ loved the Church....This is a great mystery, and I mean in reference to Christ and the Church."[34]

2394 Christ is the model of chastity. Every baptized person is called to lead a chaste life, each according to his particular state of life.

2397 The covenant which spouses have freely entered into entails faithful love. It imposes on them the obligation to keep their marriage indissoluble.

2399 The regulation of births represents one of the aspects of responsible fatherhood and motherhood. Legitimate intentions on the part of the spouses do not justify recourse to morally unacceptable means (for example, direct sterilization or contraception).

2400 Adultery, divorce, polygamy, and free union are grave offenses against the dignity of marriage.

2528 "Everyone who looks at a woman lustfully has already committed adultery with her in his heart."[35]

2529 The Ninth Commandment warns against lust or carnal concupiscence.

Christ With the Woman Taken in Adultery by Guercino. The Catholic Church has always promoted an attitude of deep respect and profound veneration toward human sexuality as something created and blessed by God.

ENDNOTES – CHAPTER EIGHT

1. *FC* 11.
2. CCC 1603.
3. CCC 2337.
4. CCC 2395.
5. Cf. Eph 5:25; CCC 808.
6. CIC, can. 1055 § 1; cf. *GS* 48 § 1.
7. Mt 19:6; cf. Gn 2:24.
8. Cf. CCC 1652.
9. Cf. Mk 10:2-9.
10. *FC* 11.
11. Cf. CCC 2380-2381.
12. *FC* 19; cf. *GS* 47 § 2.
13. 1 Cor 5:1, 4-5.
14. Cf. *FC* 81.
15. Cf. *FC* 80.
16. Cf. *FC* 84.
17. *HV* 16.
18. *HV* 14.
19. Cf. CCC 2368-2369.
20. Cf. Cardindal Ugo Poletti, *Avvenire*, March 18, 1988.
21. Cf. *HV* 12.
22. John Paul II, *The Gospel of Life*, 13.
23. CDF, *DoV* II, 8.
24. Cf. Mt 15:19.
25. Cf. Mt 5:27-28.
26. USCCB, *Catechetical Formation in Chaste Living*, p. 11.
27. CCC 2537.
28. CCC 2358.
29. Mt 6:22-23.
30. Cf. CCC 2351.
31. Pope Benedict XVI, *Jesus of Nazareth* (Doubleday: New York, 2007), 95-96.
32. Cf. Leo IX, letter *"Ad spendidum nitentis,"* in the year 1054 DS 687-688, decree of the Holy Office, March 2, 1679: DS 2149; Pius XII *"Allocutio,"* October 8, 1953 AAS 45 (1953), pp. 677-688; May 9, 1956 AAS 48 (1956), pp. 472-473.
33. *GS* 51 AAS 58 (1966), p. 1072
34. Eph 5:25, 32.
35. Mt 5:28.

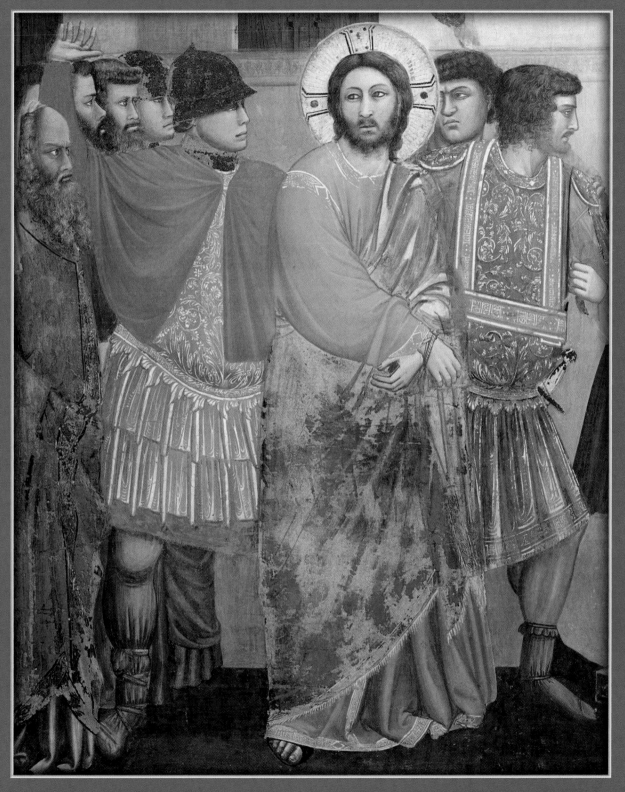

The Seventh, Eighth, and Tenth Commandments:
You Shall Not Steal
You Shall Not Bear False Witness Against Your Neighbor
You Shall Not Covet Your Neighbor's Goods

CHAPTER 9

The Seventh, Eighth, and Tenth Commandments:
You Shall Not Steal
You Shall Not Bear False Witness Against Your Neighbor
You Shall Not Covet Your Neighbor's Goods

here was a rich man, who was clothed in purple and fine linen and who feasted sumptuously every day. And at his gate lay a poor man named Lazarus, full of sores, who desired to be fed with what fell from the rich man's table; moreover the dogs came and licked his sores. The poor man died and was carried by the angels to Abraham's bosom. The rich man also died and was buried; and in Hades, being in torment, he lifted up his eyes, and saw Abraham far off and Lazarus in his bosom. And he called out, "Father Abraham, have mercy upon me, and send Lazarus to dip the end of his finger in water and cool my tongue; for I am in anguish in this flame." But Abraham said, "Son, remember that you in your lifetime received your good things, and Lazarus in like manner evil things; but now he is comforted here, and you are in anguish." (Lk 16: 19-25)

This principle is the starting-point for understanding the great parables of Jesus. The rich man[1] begs from his place of torment that his brothers be informed about what happens to those who simply ignore the poor man in need. Jesus takes up this cry for help as a warning to help us return to the right path. (*Deus Caritas Est*, 15)

The rich man from the Gospel story represents any individual or sector of society that fails to realize that everyone has a right to avail himself or herself of the goods of this world so as to live a dignified life. The Parable of the Sheep and the Goats (cf. Mt 25: 31-46) illustrates the plight of the poor and the evil of ignoring their urgent needs. It also shows how sensitivity and compassion for the underprivileged manifests our love of Jesus Christ.

Catholic teaching has always maintained the right of individuals to own private property. The moral law does not prohibit anyone from being rich. It does, however, require that there be a fair distribution of the goods of this world.

The more we are blessed with wealth and prosperity, the greater the obligation to share that wealth and prosperity with the poor and needy. As Christ said, "Much will be required of the person entrusted with much, and still more will be demanded of the person entrusted with more."[2]

FOR DISCUSSION

✤ What is the relationship of humans to the material goods of this world?

✤ How does one maintain a balance between private ownership of goods and the demands of Christian charity?

✤ What demands do the Seventh and Tenth Commandments make on Christian morality?

✤ What is the value in being "poor in spirit"?

Parable of Lazarus and Dives [Latin for "Rich Man"], illumination from the *Codex Aureus of Echternach*.
Top panel: Lazarus at the rich man's door; *Middle panel:* Lazarus' soul is carried to Paradise by two angels, and Lazarus sits in Abraham's bosom; *Bottom panel:* Dives' soul is carried off by two devils to Hell, and Dives cries out to Abraham.

The more we are blessed with wealth and prosperity, the greater the obligation to share that wealth and prosperity with the poor and needy.

From a moral standpoint, the blessings of an abundance of money, material goods, talents, and social standing bring with them a serious moral obligation to use a significant portion of those blessings to help the poor and suffering.

And yet even those who are powerless and of low means are blessed to share something of what they have with others. Recall the story of the poor widow who gave her meager donation to the temple treasury, and the widow who used the last of her food supplies to serve a meal to the prophet Elijah.[3] It is a sad irony that persons of low means often give to others in far greater proportion than those of wealthier means.

Poverty, wars, and misguided policies in many cases stem from grinding poverty caused in part by a concentration of riches in the hands of the few. The more that Christians follow Christ's teachings to serve those in need, the more they will see crimes, wars, and the sense of despair diminish throughout the world.

INTRODUCTION

We link the Seventh and Tenth Commandments because they both regard moral questions over the right possession and use of goods. These questions are vital both at the interpersonal level and at the international level. Citizens, businesses, and governments have a right to own property and to regulate its use, but the needs of the common good take precedence over such possession. This is a contentious question that is evidenced in how we regard issues such as stewardship, taxation, charitable giving, and private property.

The Eighth Commandment is important because good and trustworthy communication is vital in all human relationships. Whether the communication is between two persons, within a family, or within a larger group or society at large, truth in speech, written language, or any other form of communication makes trusting human interaction possible. When there is miscommunication—particularly in the case of a direct lie, evasive language, or an intentional withholding of the truth—it can create mistrust and discord in human relationships and even sow the seeds of hatred.

In the second section of this chapter, we will examine the moral principles concerning human rights, duties, and injustices with regard to property and truth.

SECTION I:
THE SEVENTH AND TENTH COMMANDMENTS
You Shall Not Steal
You Shall Not Covet Your Neighbor's Goods

PRINCIPLE OF SUBSIDIARITY

Catholic social teaching from Pope Leo XIII through Pope Benedict XVI has been a cry for justice in the economic and moral wilderness of modern society. Time after time, the Church has spoken the truth that economic systems must serve the common good. Social progress is possible only on the basis of sound moral principles.

Both the individual and the family have priority over the state. The state exists to serve the people, not *vice versa*. While individual and private business initiatives should be encouraged, justice and the dignity of the person must supersede pure capitalist competition in decisions concerning the distribution of goods. The achievement of the common good in this life is directly related to the quest for eternal life, which is why the Church makes moral judgments in social and economic matters as they relate to fundamental human rights and ultimately to the salvation of souls.[4]

Dwellings built by the homeless from garbage in Los Angeles. The Church has always spoken the truth that economic systems must serve the common good.

Property must always be used in accordance with what best serves the common good. Wages paid to a breadwinner should be sufficient for the support of a family, so the parents have the opportunity to dedicate themselves wholly to the rearing and education of their children. Human beings have a fundamental right to form and act through their own private associations, including labor unions, unhindered by the power of the state.

The resources of human labor must be recognized and protected as more valuable and more important than capital or material resources. Actions involving social justice should be carried out at the appropriate level—in other words, where possible, the individual should act on behalf of himself, herself, or others through work, family, the local community, and so on. The *principle of subsidiarity*, which we have discussed in a previous chapter, applies here, too. The higher levels of government or society should not usurp the authority of lower and more local government, except when absolutely necessary.

> The teaching of the Church has elaborated the principle of *subsidiarity*, according to which "a community of a higher order should not interfere in the internal life of a community of a lower order, depriving the latter of its functions, but rather should support it in case of need and help to co-ordinate its activity with the activities of the rest of society, always with a view to the common good."[5] (CCC 1883)

The goal of society is to enable its citizens to fulfill their human vocation. For this aim to be achieved there must be a correct ordering in the hierarchy of values held by society. This includes subordinating material values to those that are spiritual. A just society should promote the practice of human virtue rather than prevent its proper exercise.[6] The dignity of the human person must be cultivated rather than viewing individuals simply as a means to achieve a societal end. This goal of society, however, can only be achieved when there is a moral conversion of the individual.

Creation of the Animals by Tintoretto.
Because human beings are made in the image and likeness of God, they enjoy superiority over the rest of creation.

HUMAN DOMINION OVER CREATION

As one called to till and look after the garden of the world,[7] man has a specific responsibility towards the environment in which he lives, towards the creation which God has put at the service of his personal dignity. It is the ecological question—ranging from the preservation of the natural habitats of the different species of animals and other forms to "human ecology" properly speaking—which one finds in the Bible a clear and strong ethical direction leading to a solution which respects the great good of life, of every life....When it comes to the natural world, we are subject not only to biological laws but also to moral ones, which cannot be violated with impunity. (*Evangelium Vitæ*, 42)

According to the stories of creation as found in the Book of Genesis, God created the world along with all of its vegetation and animal life. He gave everything to man, so that he might be lord over it. Human dominion over creation is described in Genesis.[8]

God further explains the purpose of created things. They are destined for the use and service of humanity.

And God said, "Behold, I have given you every plant yielding seed which is upon the face of all the earth, and every tree with seed in its fruit; you shall have them for food." (Gn 1:29)

Using figurative language, Genesis narrates the superiority and dominion of humans over all creation.

So out of the ground the LORD God formed every beast of the field and every bird of the air, and brought them to the man to see what he would call them; and whatever the man called every living creature, that was its name. The man gave names to all cattle, and to the birds of the air, and to every beast of the field. (Gn 2:19-20)

Because man is made in the image and likeness of God, he enjoys a superiority over the rest of creation. As detailed in these early passages of Genesis, the material world is entrusted to man and is meant to serve him. God, however, made every person not only a beneficiary of creation, but also its steward.

In Jesus' time, the person who was in charge of his master's goods was called a "steward." He managed the property but did not own it, and he could be held accountable for its use. To promote the correct attitude in regard to possessions, the Church teaches the concept of *stewardship.*

STEWARDSHIP

> Human beings, created in the image of God, are persons called to enjoy communion and to exercise stewardship in a physical universe. The activities entailed by interpersonal communion and responsible stewardship engage the spiritual—intellectual and affective—capacities of human persons, but they do not leave the body behind. Human beings are physical beings sharing a world with other physical beings. Implicit in the Catholic theology of the *imago Dei* is the profound truth that the material world creates the conditions for the engagement of human persons with one another. (International Theological Commission, *Communion and Stewardship*, 26)

The Church uses the term "stewardship" to remind people that God did not give us an absolute right over creation, but rather has entrusted us with the world to be used responsibly and justly. Stewardship calls for a careful balance between the right to ownership of property and the obligation to distribute one's possessions or wealth for the common good.

Shanty town in the Philippines.
The created goods of the earth are destined to benefit everyone, not just a small segment of the population.

Universal destination of goods: Divine Revelation explicitly tells us that God created the world to serve the needs of humanity. Though we cannot create in the strict sense, we do share in God's creative power through our capacity to work. Put simply, through work, men and women complete what God has started. Because of this ability to produce new things and to dominate the created world, we have a God-given role to cooperate with God in transforming his creation. The material world was intended to be completed through the labors of man, who has the power to modify the things of the natural world to fulfill the various needs of human existence.

Because every person has an innate right to life, nourishment, and shelter, among other things, the created goods of the earth are destined to benefit everyone, not just a small segment of the population. This concept is generally referred to as the "universal destination of goods." Ownership of created goods goes hand-in-hand with the moral obligation to help those in need. These ideas are summarized in the *Catechism of the Catholic Church* when it says, "The goods of creation are destined for the whole human race" (CCC 2402).

Right to own property: In emphasizing that the goods of this world are intended for the benefit of all, the Church also indicates that each person also has the right to his own possessions—a right founded on human nature itself.

This teaching is mentioned in the *Catechism of the Catholic Church*:

> However, the earth is divided up among men to assure the security of their lives, endangered by poverty, and threatened by violence. The appropriation of property is legitimate for guaranteeing the freedom and dignity of persons and for helping each of them to meet his basic needs and the needs of those in his charge. It should allow for a natural solidarity to develop between men. (CCC 2402)

How, then, does the Catholic Magisterium reconcile these two fundamental human rights—the right to own property, and the right to a fair distribution of goods so that the dignity of every human person is respected by having their basic material needs of food, water, and shelter met?

The Seventh Commandment requires that the use of earthly goods and the fruits of people's labor must always be joined to justice and charity.

SEEKING THE COMMON GOOD

Catholic morality teaches that the natural right to private property is subordinate to the universal destination of goods. If there is a dispute between private property and its destination, the social principle prevails over the private because God created goods for the use of all people. When only a few persons possess most of the goods, it becomes impossible for the majority of people to live in accordance with basic human dignity. In such instances, the Father's plan is not fulfilled.

> The *universal destination of goods* remains primordial, even if the promotion of the common good requires respect for the right to private property and its exercise. (CCC 2403)

Catholic morality, while affirming the natural right to private property, has always taught that possessions are nevertheless created by God to help every person. The ownership of private property will not conflict with the common good as long as there is a fair distribution of the goods of creation.

> The goods of creation are destined for the entire human race. The right to private property does not abolish the universal destination of goods. (CCC 2452)

As a rational being with free will, the human person can plan his future destiny in terms of work, establishment of a home, and raising a family. The need for private property is intimately linked to a person's freedom to develop himself through work and care for himself and his family.

If a person lacks basic needs such as shelter, clothing, nourishment, and tools for work, however, he or she cannot function properly as a free being. The Seventh Commandment, therefore, requires that the use of earthly goods and the fruits of people's labor must always be joined to justice and charity, for the human being is the author, center, and goal of all economic life.

In addition, the state can intervene when necessary to ensure that private property not only does not oppose the common good, but also has a positive repercussion for the good of society. In the same way, the state can claim certain goods of special interest for the public. For instance, the state can use the right of *eminent domain*, the principle that states that a government can claim private property—with appropriate payment to the owner—because of a legitimate and overriding public concern, such as when a farmer's land is needed to build an interstate highway.

SOCIAL DOCTRINE OF THE CHURCH

Moral theology has always been concerned with the right use of goods, defending their possession and condemning their abuse. With the start of the industrialized age, however, serious social problems related to poor working conditions began to appear.

To address these problems, a new moral science emerged called the "social doctrine of the Church"—that is, the moral teaching of the Church with regard to the dignity of the person, the basic rights of the person, and the requirements of the common good. The encyclical *Rerum Novarum*, written by Pope Leo XIII in 1891, initiated the Church's social doctrine.

> The Church's social teaching argues on the basis of reason and natural law, namely, on the basis of what is in accord with the nature of every human being. It recognizes that it is not the Church's responsibility to make this teaching prevail in political life. Rather, the Church wishes to help form consciences in political life and to stimulate greater insight into the authentic requirements of justice as well as greater readiness to act accordingly, even when this might involve conflict with situations of personal interest. Building a just social and civil order, wherein each person receives what is his or her due, is an essential task which every generation must take up anew. As a political task, this cannot be the Church's immediate responsibility. Yet, since it is also a most important human responsibility, the Church is duty-bound to offer, through the purification of reason and through ethical formation, her own specific contribution towards understanding the requirements of justice and achieving them politically. (*Deus Caritas Est*, 28.)

The social doctrine of the Church is founded on the belief that labor is for the benefit of man. It is a part of creation that is inscribed in human nature. Created in the image and likeness of God, man is privileged to participate with God in his act of Creation, thus giving our labor an inherent dignity and transforming it into a redemptive act.[9] The inherent dignity of the human person gives urgency to the need of reducing "excessive social and economic inequalities."[10]

> Work honors the Creator's gifts and the talents received from him. It can also be redemptive. By enduring the hardship of work[11] in union with Jesus, the carpenter of Nazareth and the one crucified on Calvary, man collaborates in a certain fashion with the Son of God in his redemptive work. He shows himself to be a disciple of Christ by carrying the cross, daily, in the work he is called to accomplish.[12] Work can be a means of sanctification and a way of animating earthly realities with the Spirit of Christ. (CCC 2427)

The social doctrine of the Church is far-reaching and encompasses virtually every form of human relationship. In its moral teachings, the Church is concerned not only with individual moral conduct, but also with the morality of economic and political systems and the world of labor. The teaching of the Church regarding social life, economics, and politics of all peoples continues to form an important part of moral theology.

Pope Leo XIII worked to encourage understanding between the Church and the modern world. Among the eighty-seven encyclicals written by Pope Leo XIII, none was so widely received, praised, and influential as *Rerum Novarum* (On Capital and Labor), his encyclical on social justice.

> The equality of men concerns their dignity as persons and the rights that flow from it. (CCC 1945)

Catholic social teaching covers work and just wages, private property and its social function, the right to belong to associations and labor unions, the defense of justice, and the social function of economics and political life—everything related to the common good and to social justice.[13]

Closely connected with the obligation to promote the common good, especially regarding the universal right of every person to benefit from the goods of this earth, is the need to influence economic legislation.

The practice of moral virtue requires that solidarity should exist, first and foremost, among the Christian faithful. Pope John Paul II, in his encyclical *Sollicitudo Rei Socialis*, speaks of solidarity as the system of interdependence that determines economic, cultural, political, and religious elements in the modern world. When solidarity is understood in this way, the moral response becomes a virtue.[14] While the goal of solidarity involves the effort to build a more just social order, when it is practiced as a Christian virtue, solidarity also involves "the sharing of spiritual goods even more than material ones."[15]

Each person is called to enter into the life of the Blessed Trinity—Father, Son, and Holy Spirit—which is a communion of Divine Persons. This vocation to enter into the life of God is extended to both the individual and to all people. By responding to this vocation in Baptism, a person becomes a member of the Church, the Mystical Body of Christ, and a community of faith, which reflects the image of God. In a similar manner, the communion that the faithful are called to establish in society, when based on moral principles and centered on Jesus Christ, is a reflection of the image of the Blessed Trinity.

Catholic faithful participating in charitable projects in Mexico.
It is necessary for the conscientious Christian to either directly participate in public life
or establish some role in contributing to a more just society.

ROLE OF THE FAITHFUL

Christian discipleship cannot be satisfied merely with practicing an individual morality, but rather must do whatever possible to create a society based on a fair distribution of goods and solicitous concern for every individual. Not only is it a moral duty to cast votes from a Christian perspective of justice, it is even more necessary for the conscientious Christian to either directly participate in public life or establish some role in contributing to a more just society.

For example, business employers can form associations designed to promote the Church's social teaching. Christian leaders in labor unions can urge employers to pay just wages and organize their companies so that the workers receive proper health benefits and have time for family life and religious practice.

The Church's work of evangelization to create a more just society falls on the shoulders of the Catholic faithful in the workplace, private organizations, and through their involvement in some form of public life. The Second Vatican Council strongly encourages that the Christian faithful take responsibility to cultivate a world that corresponds to man's dignity as a child of God.

> The pace of change is so far-reaching and rapid nowadays that no one can allow himself to close his eyes to the course of events or indifferently ignore them and wallow in the luxury of a merely individualistic morality. The best way to fulfill one's obligations of justice and love is to contribute to the common good according to one's means and the needs of others, even to the point of fostering and helping public and private organizations devoted to bettering the conditions of life. (*Gaudium et Spes*, 30)

The implications of the Seventh Commandment are intimately linked to human dignity, and the equality and rights that flow from this dignity. The Gospel makes it clear that the requirements of justice and charity must extend to the poor and underprivileged. One of the true hallmarks of the Christian is the keen awareness of human misery, coupled with deeds of generosity, exhibited in almsgiving of both a material and spiritual nature.

As Christians, we must realize that the true development of man has spiritual as well as material aspects. People deserve to have sufficient material resources to lead a dignified life, but they also need the riches of the Gospel message brought to them as well. The follower of Christ is called to relieve both material and spiritual poverty, so rampant in the world today. By addressing the development of the whole man, each person is given the means to respond to their Christian vocation.[16]

> "The Church's love for the poor ... is a part of her constant tradition." This love is inspired by the Gospel of the Beatitudes, of the poverty of Jesus, and of his concern for the poor.[17] Love for the poor is even one of the motives for the duty of working so as to "be able to give to those in need."[18] It extends not only to material poverty but also to the many forms of cultural and religious poverty.[19] (CCC 2444)

INTERNATIONAL SOLIDARITY

> At a time of dramatic global changes and challenges, Catholics in the United States face special responsibilities and opportunities. We are members of a universal Church that transcends national boundaries and calls us to live in solidarity and justice with the peoples of the world. We are also citizens of a powerful democracy with enormous influence beyond our borders. As Catholics and Americans we are uniquely called to global solidarity. (*Called to Global Solidarity*, USCCB, p. 1)

Contrary to the views of those who would advocate a national policy of isolation, concern for the common good does not stop at international borders. Catholic social teaching applies also to international relations.

Poverty in Serbia. Richer nations must show solidarity in their international relations and thereby contribute to the material welfare of poorer nations.

Poverty in Soweto, South Africa. The overarching premise of Catholic social teaching is that no people should suffer in squalor while others are able to live quite comfortably.

By virtue of the principle of the universal destination of goods, richer nations must show solidarity in their international relations and thereby contribute to the material welfare of poorer nations. It is an offense against justice and a grievous neglect of basic human rights to ignore groups of people suffering misery and destitution while other nations have a surplus of riches at their disposal.

> **Rich nations have a grave moral responsibility toward those which are unable to ensure the means of their development by themselves or have been prevented from doing so by tragic historical events. It is a duty in solidarity and charity; it is also an obligation in justice if the prosperity of the rich nations has come from resources that have not been paid for fairly. (CCC 2439)**

A globalized economy has potential to help poorer nations, but it also leaves them subject to potential exploitation by multinational corporations that make use of their resources and labor forces without attention to stewardship and human rights. International financial institutions such as the World Bank are called upon to take steps to ease the burden of Third World debtor nations so as to assist them in securing economic independence and paths to true economic and social development.

> **There must be solidarity among nations which are already politically interdependent. It is even more essential when it is a question of dismantling the "perverse mechanisms" that impede the development of the less advanced countries.[20] In place of abusive if not usurious financial systems, iniquitous commercial relations among nations, and the arms race, there must be substituted a common effort to mobilize resources toward objectives of moral, cultural, and economic development, "redefining the priorities and hierarchies of values."[21] (CCC 2438)**

> **Direct aid is an appropriate response to immediate, extraordinary needs caused by natural catastrophes, epidemics, and the like. But it does not suffice to repair the grave damage resulting from destitution or to provide a lasting solution to a country's needs. It is also necessary to reform international economic and financial institutions so that they will better promote equitable relationships with less advanced countries.[22] (CCC 2440)**

In addition to the exploitation of workers, especially in poorer nations, the moral law forbids the enslavement of human beings or to the buying or selling of persons in the manner of merchandise.[23]

While Jesus never spoke directly concerning the topic of slavery, it is clear that the Gospel implicitly condemns slavery as a grave offense against humanity and Christ's call to love as he loved. Slavery undermines the essential dignity of the human person, reducing the human being to the status of a machine or animal that can be bought, sold, and exploited. Such treatment of human beings is entirely inconsistent with Christ's teachings and the two greatest commandments. In fact, slaves were welcomed in the early

Christian community, not as inferior beings, as they were considered by Roman society, but as dignified members of the Christian community.

The solution to helping the poorer countries of the world is admittedly complex. The overarching premise is that no people should suffer in squalor while others are able to live quite comfortably. Although prosperity and its pursuit are not inherently wrong, richer nations and individuals are called in justice to substantially assist less fortunate nations and individuals in a spirit of solidarity and to take some responsibility for their progress.

> It is above all a question of interdependence, sensed as a system determining relationships in the contemporary world, in its economic, cultural, political, and religious elements, and accepted as a moral category. When interdependence becomes recognized in this way, the correlative response as a moral and social attitude, as a "virtue," is solidarity. This then is not a feeling of vague compassion or shallow distress at the misfortunes of so many people, both near and far. On the contrary, it is a firm and persevering determination to commit oneself to the common good; that is to say to the good of all and of each individual, because we are all really responsible for all. This determination is based on the solid conviction that what is hindering full development is that desire for profit and that thirst for power already mentioned. (*Sollicitudo Rei Socialis*, 38)

The *Catechism* recognizes the complexity of the issue of immigration, at once affirming a nation's right to limit immigration while also requiring compassion and generosity for those seeking basic human dignity.

> The more prosperous nations are obliged, to the extent they are able, to welcome the *foreigner* in search of the security and the means of livelihood which he cannot find in his country of origin. Public authorities should see to it that the natural right is respected that places a guest under the protection of those who receive him.
>
> Political authorities, for the sake of the common good for which they are responsible, may make the exercise of the right to immigrate subject to various juridical conditions, especially with regard to the immigrants' duties toward their country of adoption. Immigrants are obliged to respect with gratitude the material and spiritual heritage of the country that receives them, to obey its laws and to assist in carrying civic burdens. (CCC 2441)

ECOLOGY

> Not only has God given the earth to man, who must use it with respect for the original good purpose for which it was given to him, but man too is God's gift to man. He must therefore respect the natural and moral structure with which he has been endowed. (*Centesimus Annus*, 38)

The term *ecology* is derived from the Greek *oikos* (which means "a house or dwelling") and *-logia* (meaning "a discourse"). Ecology, then, deals with the science of studying and protecting the habitat in which human life is nourished, protected, and developed.

Respect for another's goods also extends to the world of nature, which includes both vegetative and animal life. The material world does not have an unlimited supply of resources nor an impenetrable resilience to irresponsible exploi-tation and abuse.

Air pollution blocks the sun at an oil refinery. The material world does not have an unlimited supply of resources nor an impenetrable resilience to irresponsible exploitation and abuse.

The connection between ecology and the Seventh Commandment is based on the universal destiny of goods for the use of all people and of every generation.

> The seventh commandment enjoins respect for the integrity of creation. Animals, like plants and inanimate beings, are by nature destined for the common good of past, present, and future humanity.[24] Use of the mineral, vegetable, and animal resources of the universe cannot be divorced from respect for moral imperatives. Man's dominion over inanimate and other living beings granted by the Creator is not absolute; it is limited by concern for the quality of life of his neighbor, including generations to come; it requires a religious respect for the integrity of creation.[25] (CCC 2415)

Since the environment is the world common to all people, it should be respected. Nevertheless, some ecological interpretations are exaggerated because they forget a basic principle: Mineral as well as plant and animal resources are at the service of humanity. For this reason, people can make use of them, but may not abuse them.

THEFT

Stealing or theft refers to unjustly taking another's possessions against his reasonable will. The sin of stealing includes a wide range of infractions against justice and respect toward a neighbor's goods.

Some of the acts that fall under the category of stealing include vandalism, cheating on exams, reporting more payroll hours than actually worked, wasting time at work, price gouging, shoplifting, and even finding and keeping things of value without an honest attempt to find the rightful owner. In addition, although direct stealing is not involved, failure to pay taxes and bills, overspending the money of another person, failing to put in an honest day's work, and reneging on a business contract all constitute sins against the Seventh Commandment.

Robbery, which is taking the property of another by force, adds malice to stealing. Damage to goods may involve either private or state property, and all who effectively cooperate in doing damage are obliged to make restitution. The complexity of social life nowadays offers different ways of unjustly appropriating the goods of another. The *Catechism of the Catholic Church* proposes the following cases, which are more frequent in today's social life:

Slot Machine in Las Vegas. Excessive gambling involves squandering money that is destined for the support of oneself and one's family.

> The following are also morally illicit: speculation in which one contrives to manipulate the price of goods artificially in order to gain an advantage to the detriment of others; corruption in which one influences the judgment of those who must make decisions according to law; appropriation and use for private purposes of the common goods of an enterprise; work poorly done; tax evasion; forgery of checks and invoices; excessive expenses and waste. Willfully damaging private or public property is contrary to the moral law and requires reparation. (CCC 2409)

Excessive gambling involves squandering money that is destined for the support of oneself and one's family. This vice, then, is also a violation of the Seventh Commandment. In general, any misuse or unjust acquisition of another's goods is at least indirectly linked to stealing and therefore a sin against the Seventh Commandment.

Because everyone has a right to life which involves nourishment, clothing, medicine, and shelter, they have the right to avail themselves of material goods. In the case of extreme necessity, an individual may take some private possessions from another if it is required to preserve life for himself or herself and his or her family.

The *Catechism of the Catholic Church* assures the faithful that when in dire circumstances, people have a right to a part of their neighbor's possessions:

> There is not theft if consent can be presumed or if refusal is contrary to reason and the universal destination of goods. This is the case in obvious and urgent necessity when the only way to provide for immediate, essential needs (food, shelter, clothing…) is to put at one's disposal and use the property of others.[26] (CCC 2408)

COVETOUSNESS

The Tenth Commandment forbids covetousness, meaning the sinful desire for the goods of others. Our natural appetite leads us to desire things that are good in themselves, but an excessive desire leads to sins of *greed*, *avarice*, and *envy*. These sins in some fashion make possession of material things an absolute good.

Parable of the Man Who Hoards by Tissot.
"'…And I will say to my soul, Soul, you have ample goods laid up for many years; take your ease, eat, drink, and be merry.' But God said to him, 'Fool! This night your soul is required of you; and the things you have prepared, whose will they be?' So is he who lays up treasure for himself, and is not rich toward God." (Lk 12:16-21)

Greed is the desire for earthly goods that are not truly needed for a Christian life. It is the act of acquiring things solely to look rich and powerful in the eyes of one's neighbors, or simply for self-gratification.

Avarice is the inordinate desire of accumulating and hoarding wealth. The avaricious person becomes hardhearted, unjust, and deceitful in his effort to hold on to his wealth. Ebenezer Scrooge, the character in Charles Dickens' *A Christmas Carol*, is the enduring model of the avaricious person.

Envy is the wrongful desire for things possessed by another or the unhappiness at another's good fortune. Besides being sinful, it leads directly to hatred and the sinful desire to acquire the desired goods by whatever means available.

By way of distinction, avarice is the sinful desire for wealth, while envy is the sinful desire for the goods of one's neighbor. They are capital sins that easily lead to moral deterioration.

The remedy for greed, avarice, and envy is in taking to heart the Lord's first Beatitude, "Blessed are the poor in spirit, for theirs is the kingdom of heaven."[27] Poverty in spirit involves much more than deprivation of material goods. It also requires a general detachment from the things of this world.

This spiritual poverty encourages the firm conviction that only God can fill the human heart. The human heart is such that it can become overly consumed with material possessions, thereby increasingly suffocating the life of the spirit. Material things have some value in themselves, but they can never be treated as absolute goods and ultimate ends.

The practice of poverty of spirit requires habitual meditation on the life of Christ, examination of conscience regarding any possible disordered attachment to earthly goods, and a general desire for total identification with Christ and imitation of his life of loving service.

Since the dignity of the person made in the image and likeness of God is of direct concern to the Church, she will continue to instruct the world about justice and solidarity, particularly with those in need.

RESTITUTION

Restitution is the remedy for an offense against the Seventh Commandment. It involves either repairing damage unjustly done or repaying the owner a fair price for his stolen or damaged goods.

> *Reparation for injustice* committed requires the restitution of stolen goods to their owner:

> Jesus blesses Zacchaeus for his pledge: "If I have defrauded anyone of anything, I restore it fourfold."[28] Those who, directly or indirectly, have taken possession of the goods of another, are obliged to make restitution of them, or to return the equivalent in kind or in money, if the goods have disappeared, as well as the profit or advantages their owner would have legitimately obtained from them. Likewise, all who in some manner have taken part in a theft or who have knowingly benefited from it—for example, those who ordered it, assisted in it, or received the stolen goods—are obliged to make restitution in proportion to their responsibility and to their share of what was stolen. (CCC 2412)

The person who has unjustly stolen or damaged property not their own must do all in his or her power to restore the stolen items or repair the damage. In some instances, it is impossible to make restitution because the business that was harmed is out of business, or because the injured party is deceased or unable to be found. In these cases, the perpetrator is obligated to give to charity the fair value of the property damaged or goods stolen.

In order to be absolved from sins of stealing or vandalism, self-accusation must be accompanied with a total commitment to making restitution. Such restitution can be made confidentially when possible.

Christ Before the High Priest Caiaphas by Honthorst. After Jesus' capture in the garden at Gethsemane, all the disciples fled and "forsook him." "Then those who had seized Jesus led him to Caiaphas the high priest,...Now the chief priests and the whole council sought false testimony against Jesus that they might put him to death, but they found none, though many false witnesses came forward. At last two came forward...." (Mt 26: 56-60)

SECTION II: THE EIGHTH COMMANDMENT
You Shall Not Bear False Witness Against Your Neighbor

THE IMPORTANCE OF TRUTH

The quest for truth goes back as far as the beginning of the human race. The pursuit and written analysis of what comprises truth can be traced to the Greek philosophers a few centuries before Christ. These philosophers were fascinated with man precisely because he was the only creature who could grasp and communicate the truth. For this reason, man is defined as a *rational animal*.

In the ancient Greco-Roman world, philosophical thought became a tool to explain and penetrate the meaning of Divine Revelation. This merging of pagan philosophy with Judeo-Christian tradition opened up a marvelous perspective regarding the truth about God, the nature of man, and the means to everlasting life.

Truths concerning faith and morals taught by the Catholic Church have the stamp of total certainty because of the promised assistance of the Holy Spirit. It is important always to bear in mind that the ultimate truth that liberates, saves, and fulfills is found exclusively in the life and teachings of Jesus Christ as interpreted and taught by the Church.

Peter Denies Christ by Rembrandt. "Now Peter was sitting outside in the courtyard. And a maid came up to him, and said, 'You also were with Jesus the Galilean.' But he denied it before them all, saying, 'I do not know what you mean.'" Two more times Peter was accused of having been with Jesus and two more times Peter swore he did not know Jesus. "And Peter remembered the saying of Jesus, 'Before the cock crows, you will deny me three times.' And he went out and wept bitterly." (Mt 26:69-75)

THE IDEA OF TRUTH IN SACRED SCRIPTURES

Like the previous commandments which we have studied, the moral prohibition of the Eighth Commandment, when elevated by the teachings of Christ, concerns a sin that implicitly includes a whole range of moral infractions. For example, the Fifth Commandment, "You shall not kill," forbids dispositions of hatred, angry reactions, and mean spirited conduct. The Eighth Commandment, "You shall not bear false witness against your neighbor," although specifying a lie regarding someone's character, prohibits any kind of falsehood.

Truth in the Old Testament. The Old Testament is filled with strong exhortations to speak and act truthfully. Implicitly or explicitly, every book of the Old Testament affirms that truth finds its source in God. God himself reveals in the beginning that man is made in his own image and likeness. It follows that if we are to reflect God's own life, we must also behave in a truthful manner at all times.

God's Chosen People in the Old Testament had a great love of Scripture because it was the Word of God. One of the many privileges they recognized was their ready access to the truth about the world, morality, and God himself. No other people during that period enjoyed such direct communication with God. Living in an age abounding in deceit, dishonesty, and treachery, they had assurance and security in God's Word and the fullness of truth it expressed.

The Book of Numbers repeats the teaching of Yahweh, who testifies to his truthfulness in everything he does and says: "God is not man, that he should lie, or a son of man, that he should repent. Has he said, and will he not do it? Or has he spoken, and will he not fulfill it?"[29]

The Book of Proverbs exults in the truthfulness of Yahweh and honors those who seek knowledge and the love of truth. When one acts in this way, he is on his way to reaching true wisdom.

> Hear, for I will speak noble things, and from my lips will come what is right; for my mouth will utter truth; wickedness is an abomination to my lips. All the words of my mouth are righteous; there is nothing twisted or crooked in them. They are all straight to him who understands and right to those who find knowledge. Take my instruction instead of silver, and knowledge rather than choice gold; for wisdom is better than jewels, and all that you may desire cannot compare with her. I, wisdom, dwell in prudence, and I find knowledge and discretion. (Prv 8: 6-12)

Truth in the New Testament: One of the characteristics that separates mankind from animals is our ability to ask questions and seek knowledge. It is characteristic of the human person to pursue truth and to share it with others. In fact, the very dignity of a child of God requires that every person pursue and speak the truth. Consequently, by virtue of the dignity of the human person, everyone deserves to hear the truth.

This theme of truth lies at the heart of the New Testament. As always, the teachings of the Old Testament are dramatically completed and perfected by Jesus Christ. By including the obligation to speak truthfully and simply, Jesus opens up a new panorama with respect to the truth.

The teachings of Christ show us that the fullness of truth is present when it is articulated with charity. Because God is love,[30] our words and actions can reveal truth in its fullness only when it is accompanied by love.

While explicitly forbidding the spread of false statements, the Eighth Commandment requires us to be truthful in word and deed in all our dealings with others. Truthfulness is a virtue, which demands that we seek the truth and strive to put it into practice in our lives, as well as share it with others.

> Truth or truthfulness is the virtue which consists in showing oneself true in deeds and truthful in words, and guarding against duplicity, dissimulation, and hypocrisy. (CCC 2505)

As followers of Christ, we should always be careful to avoid giving scandal through double-dealing or duplicity by acting or speaking differently depending on the circumstances. Such conduct gives rise to hypocrisy and reduces our effectiveness in spreading the truth of Christ. Christians also have a responsibility to avoid gossip by unnecessarily repeating statements, whether true or untrue, which damage the character of others. Such conversations bring no benefit to anyone involved.

Perhaps the most impressive and surprising disclosure is that Christ himself is the truth. Jesus gives an awe-inspiring definition of truth by declaring, "I am the truth."[31]

The entire New Testament is a powerful reminder that revelation of truth culminates in the life and teachings of Christ. As Christians, we must be familiar with the contents of the Gospels and the other New Testament writings. The individual who most reflects the truth about God and man is the one who incarnates most profoundly the Gospel message.

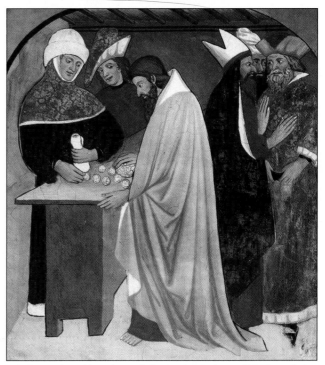

Judas receives thirty pieces of silver to betray Jesus. "And from that moment he sought an opportunity to betray him." (Mt 26:16)

> Offenses against the truth express by word or deed a refusal to commit oneself to moral uprightness: they are fundamental infidelities to God and, in this sense, they undermine the foundations of the covenant. (CCC 2464)

The Pharisees Question Jesus by Tissot. "Jesus then said to the Jews who had believed in him, 'If you continue in my word, you are truly my disciples, and you will know the truth, and the truth will make you free.' They answered him, 'We are descendants of Abraham, and have never been in bondage to any one. How is it that you say, "You will be made free"?' Jesus answered them, 'Truly, truly, I say to you, every one who commits sin is a slave to sin.'" (Jn 8: 31-34)

By virtue of his or her incorporation into the life of Jesus Christ, every Christian has a vocation to witness and communicate the truth. Because Christ incarnates the fullness of the truth, every truth, at least in some small way, reflects his mind. All of creation and all physical and moral laws come from the mind of God. As stated in the Gospel of St. John, "All things were made through him, and without him was not anything made that was made."[32]

The Eighth Commandment compels every person to pursue and practice moral truth and express it to others as well. Knowledge of truths, especially the moral law and the teachings of Christ, are a direct pathway to God as long as these truths are lived out faithfully. Falsehood, on the other hand, is a deviation from the reality God has established. Personal sadness, family strife, and crimes are just some consequences of living by a false moral code.

The words of Jesus concerning the truth are especially meaningful in an age where our world is afflicted with moral relativism. "If you continue in my word, you are truly my disciples, and you will know the truth, and the truth will make you free."[33]

TRUTH AND DISCRETION

The Eighth Commandment obligates every person to learn the truth and to speak truthfully. Jesus reiterates the message of the Eighth Commandment when he says, "Let what you say be simply 'Yes' or 'No'; anything more than this comes from evil."[34]

The first practical way of abiding by this commandment is to speak truthfully at all times. Truth in speech involves expressing what the individual perceives as corresponding to reality. In justice, everyone deserves to receive truthful information and not to be deceived or misled. Therefore, it is an injustice to intentionally transmit false information.

An important aspect of the Eighth Commandment concerns the discretion necessary to uphold and protect someone's good name or in maintaining silence regarding sensitive material. Silence is not only permitted, but it is also a duty when another person does not have a right to certain information or the reputation of another must be upheld.

Not everyone should have access to all information, especially if it is confidential. The public at large has no right to certain kinds of private information, such as the classified information regarding a company, military intelligence, health histories, or how someone votes in a general election.

However, sometimes the protection or welfare of an individual or society may warrant disclosure of classified information. For example, knowledge of drug trafficking, financial fraud, sexual abuse, corruption, or criminal activity must be communicated to the competent authorities. Withholding certain information under the false guise of loyalty, friendship, or discretion could result in terrible tragedies.

Moral issues may also arise from the public diffusion of information. The media provides a wonderful service of information that the public deserves to know. Reporters and writers can violate their natural duty of protecting someone's good name. Scandalous details of celebrities' private lives in many instances offer information that is morally unhealthy for the reader and exposes this personal wrong-doing to an entire population. The writer must consider whether these disclosures will truly benefit the common good or will simply feed on people's weakness for scurrilous sensation, thus contributing to the general lowering of morality in society.

LIES AND THEIR CONSEQUENCES

To articulate a falsehood is a violation of a person's human dignity. A lie is always an injustice because it invites the listener or reader to accept false information as if it were true.

An individual lies when he or she deliberately says something that is contrary to what he or she thinks or knows, or when he or she says something false to someone who has the right to be dealt with truthfully. The intention of a lie is to lead another person into error.

Judas returns the pieces of silver to the chief priests and elders "saying, 'I have sinned in betraying innocent blood.'" (Mt 27:4)

Of course, to transmit erroneous information unintentionally—simply through misspeaking or affirming something that the person erroneously "knows" to be true but is not—is not a lie.

Every lie has consequences. A lie causes the speaker *moral damage.* This vice can easily be rationalized and become a habit that continues to show disrespect for the rights and value of others. Lies *detract from one's own sincerity and credibility*, for as the saying goes, "Fool me once, shame on you; fool me twice, shame on me." The maxim implies that once someone has been found in a lie, he or she should be considered less credible and trustworthy. Æsop's fable about the boy who cried "Wolf!" provides an apt illustration of this effect of lying. Finally, a person who lies breeds *mistrust in human relationships*. As a consequence, he or she tacitly encourages others to lie. That is because habitual lying creates an atmosphere of hostility and separation among family, friends, co-workers, and other social networks.

The *Catechism* reiterates these considerations:

> Since it violates the virtue of truthfulness, a lie does real violence to another. It affects his ability to know, which is a condition of every judgment and decision. It contains the seed of discord and all consequent evils. Lying is destructive of society; it undermines trust among men and tears apart the fabric of social relationships. (CCC 2486)

GRAVITY OF THE SIN OF LYING

Every lie is a sin. Its gravity is determined by the criteria established by the *Catechism of the Catholic Church*:

> The *gravity of a lie* is measured against the nature of the truth it deforms, the circumstances, the intentions of the one who lies, and the harm suffered by its victims. (CCC 2484)

The *Catechism* mentions four points of reference to determine the gravity of a lie: the *nature or object of the lie*, the *intentions*, the *circumstances*, and the *effects* on others.

Nature or object of the lie: The severity of the falsehood and its damaging effects determine the gravity of the sin. As in all evaluations of moral actions, the object or nature of the act must be determined. The gravity of a violation of the Eighth Commandment can be as superficial as a "white lie" (i.e., a lie which a person feels is not serious or has few consequences) or as grievous as *calumny*, in which someone's reputation is damaged or destroyed through false information.

Intentions: Once the object of the lie is established, the intentions need to be considered. One can lie, for instance, simply to avoid giving an embarrassing answer, or one can intend to inflict serious suffering through a false accusation of a crime. In the former case, the intention is a venial sin; in the latter, it is mortally sinful. Although the intention can increase or diminish the gravity of a lie, it can never erase its objective evil.

Circumstances: As in all moral acts, circumstances play an important role in determining the degree of wrongdoing caused by a lie. If the person lies while under duress, it can reduce the gravity of the sin; if he or she lies under oath in a court of law, the seriousness of the deception is significantly intensified. As with intentions, the circumstances of the lie can increase or diminish the culpability of the person who lied, but can never change the object of the act.

Effects: Every moral act affects others in some way. By its nature, lying deceives another person or group of persons. Recommending someone as an honest and virtuous person for a job while realizing the person is dishonest and troublesome, for example, would cause problems for everyone in that person's new place of employment. The overriding consequence of lying and deception is always the creation of mistrust, hostility, and strife among people who are victims of falsehood.

SINS AGAINST THE REPUTATION OF ANOTHER

The Eighth Commandment also covers the sin of sullying the good name or reputation of another person through false information or accusations. These sins include *calumny*, *slander*, *detraction*, and *rash judgment*. Violations of truthfulness and honesty often come in the form of exaggeration expressed in *insincere flattery* and *bragging*.

Calumny or slander involves a lie that falsely accuses another of wrongdoing or a vice. This sinful act is directly forbidden by the Eighth Commandment: "You shall not bear false witness against your neighbor" (Ex 20:16; cf. Dt 5:20).

By virtue of his or her dignity as children of God, every person has a right to a good name. It is an obligation both of justice and charity to protect and, if possible, build up the good reputation of another. Calumny, which often arises out of envy or hatred, is especially ugly because it robs someone of his or her good name through lies and false accusations.

John 18: 38 *"What is truth?"*

Quod est veritas? Pilate Questions Jesus by Nikolai Ge. "Pilate said to him, 'So you are a king?' Jesus answered, 'You say that I am a king. For this I was born, and for this I have come into the world, to bear witness to the truth. Every one who is of the truth hears my voice.' Pilate said to him, 'What is truth?'" (Jn 18: 37-38)

John 19:5 *"Here is the man!"*

Ecce Homo by Ciseri. "Pilate went out again, and said to them, 'Behold, I am bringing him out to you, that you may know that I find no crime in him.' So Jesus came out, wearing the crown of thorns and the purple robe. Pilate said to them, 'Here is the man!'" (Jn 19:4-5)

Detraction involves hurting someone's good name through the disclosure of an incriminating truth. Reference to an individual's mistakes or misbehavior is not a sin of detraction when his personal welfare or the common good requires it. If a person is taking drugs, stealing, or habitually cheating an employer, for instance, justice would require that this misconduct be reported. However, unless it is necessary to eradicate a personal evil or danger to others, someone's defects or mistakes should not be communicated to another party. This kind of talk is often the essence of gossip.

Rash judgment involves a judgment that questions someone's character or concludes a moral defect without sufficient evidence. In rash judgment, the facts do not logically lead to an accusation of guilt. This kind of judgment is sinful because the verdict could very well be false.

Insincere Flattery, though usually not a serious infraction of the Eighth Commandment, is a form of lie that falsely attributes qualities that may not exist or which are exaggerated. The purpose of insincere flattery is to praise in an exaggerated way in order to obtain a favor or to win over someone's affection.

Bragging is a form of self-flattery whereby personal qualities are embellished to impress others. Since insincere flattery and bragging convey a certain degree of falsehood, they are sinful and should be avoided.

THE DUTY TO MAKE REPARATIONS

Lying causes harm, and the person who lies has the obligation to make restitution for it. Calumny always causes great harm, so much so that it is not sufficient to repent or even to ask for forgiveness; the perpetrator must make up for the harm committed. A lie is not a sin only against truth and charity, but also against justice, which by its very nature demands reparation.

If the injury so requires, reparation should be carried out publicly. In other cases, it can be accomplished privately. Reparation is a moral obligation that obliges in conscience and may include monetary restitution. There is no forgiveness of sins if one lacks the intention to make full reparation.

The *Catechism of the Catholic Church* states:

> Every offense committed against justice and truth entails the *duty of reparation*, even if its author has been forgiven. When it is impossible publicly to make reparation for a wrong, it must be made secretly. If someone who has suffered harm cannot be directly compensated, he must be given moral satisfaction in the name of charity. This duty of reparation also concerns offenses against another's reputation. This reparation, moral and sometimes material, must be evaluated in terms of the extent of the damage inflicted. It obliges in conscience. (CCC 2487)

OBLIGATION TO KEEP SECRETS

We are obliged to keep a secret under three conditions—when the good of our neighbor demands it, when we have promised to keep it, or when our profession or office requires it.

Even if we made a promise not to do so, revealing a secret is sometimes necessary in extraordinary cases, when it is the only way to correct a serious wrong or avoid a great harm to the common good. For the correction of faults, it is allowable to tell secrets to parents or superiors who need to know them. For example, in a community, camp, or boarding school, where, by rule, those in charge must protect the common good, it is a serious obligation to reveal grievous disorders that may easily corrupt the innocent.

Professional secrets are the most seriously binding. Even the common good of society is not sufficient reason for a physician, lawyer, or priest, for instance, to reveal a secret impediment to marriage that he may happen to know in the exercise of his office.

The most binding of all secrets is that of the Sacrament of Reconciliation. Under the pain of sacrilege and excommunication, a priest may not reveal for any cause or reason anything that he learns in Confession, even at the cost of his own life. This is called the "Seal of Confession."

TRUTH AND MARTYRDOM

The ultimate love for the truth is to witness it with one's very life. The truth that Jesus is the Savior of the world and the only means to everlasting life must be proclaimed and defended even at the expense of one's own life.

The first Christians preferred torture and execution rather than to withdraw their belief in the truth of the Christian Faith. Though most followers of Christ will not be in a position to sacrifice their lives for the truth, they are called to live the virtue of fortitude and lay down their lives for Christ and his message through the ordinary activities that mark a person's life.

Centering one's daily life around Jesus Christ in an effort to strive for sanctity is the best way of showing love for the truth. The modern-day Christian will have ample opportunity to profess the Gospel in speaking for the rights of the unborn, embracing a chaste lifestyle and evangelizing by both word and example.

> Although martyrdom represents the high point of the witness to moral truth, and one to which relatively few people are called, there is nonetheless a consistent witness which all Christians must daily be ready to make, even at the cost of suffering and grave sacrifice. Indeed, faced with

the many difficulties which fidelity to the moral order can demand, even in the most ordinary circumstances, the Christian is called, with the grace of God invoked in prayer, to a sometimes heroic commitment. In this he or she is sustained by the virtue of fortitude, whereby—as Gregory the Great teaches—one can actually "love the difficulties of this world for the sake of eternal rewards."[35] (*Veritatis Splendor*, 93.)

CONCLUSION

The Seventh and Tenth Commandment involve many complex obligations that arise from the right to own property and relations with others and the whole society. The Church's continuing instruction on the ownership of property and the universal destiny of goods is an invaluable guide in forming a more just society.

The social doctrine of the Church is a moral teaching, not a detailed technical response to problems in social life and politics. It is up to citizens, society, and the state to find practical and specific solutions. The Church offers only the principles and general criteria.

Since the dignity of the person made in the image and likeness of God is of direct concern to the Church, she will continue to instruct the world about justice and solidarity, particularly with those in need. Moreover, when individuals or even nations suffer inequities stemming from an unfair distribution of basic necessities for human dignity, the Church will speak in defense of those most vulnerable and forgotten. The social doctrine of the Catholic Church provides the blueprint for a more just world.

The Catholic Church gives us certain guidelines in following the teachings of Christ in regard to the Seventh and Tenth Commandments:

✤ In creation, mankind was made a steward of the created world. Therefore, each person has an obligation to take care of the world and its moral order.

✤ Christians are called to be "poor in spirit" and to provide for the needs of the poor.

✤ Private property is a gift from God and as such should be used in a spirit of Christian charity. Likewise, Christians have an obligation to use the goods of the world in a wise and charitable manner.

✤ Christians are called to promote the common good both locally, nationally, and internationally, enabling each person to follow the vocation which they are given by God.

✤ Christians must respect the goods of others and avoid the temptations of greed, avarice, and envy.

✤ Restitution must be made if a person's property is stolen or damaged.

Ascent to Calvary (detail) by Tintoretto.
"As the Father has loved me, so have I loved you; abide in my love. If you keep my commandments, you will abide in my love, …These things I have spoken to you, that my joy may be in you, and that your joy may be full." (Jn 15:9-11)

In order for society to function properly, truth must be the keystone of human and social relationships. There can be no true peace and harmony if people cannot trust one another. All people have an obligation to speak the truth themselves and to speak out in defense of the truth. The truth is the glue that not only binds society together, but also binds us to our Savior Jesus Christ who called himself "the Truth."

SUPPLEMENTARY READING

1. Private Goods Subordinated to the Common Good.

In *Rerum novarum*, Leo XIII strongly affirmed the natural character of the right to private property, using various arguments against the socialism of his time. This right, which is fundamental for the autonomy and development of the person, has always been defended by the Church up to our own day. At the same time, the Church teaches that the possession of material goods is not an absolute right, and that its limits are inscribed in its very nature as a human right.

While the Pope proclaimed the right to private ownership, he affirmed with equal clarity that the "use" of goods, while marked by freedom, is subordinated to their original common destination as created goods, as well as to the will of Jesus Christ as expressed in the Gospel.

— *Centesimus Annus*, 30

2. Countries Have a Right to Control their Borders

The Church recognizes the right of a sovereign state to control its borders in furtherance of the common good. It also recognizes the right of human persons to migrate so that they can realize their God-given rights. These teachings complement each other. While the sovereign state may impose reasonable limits on immigration, the common good is not served when the basic human rights of the individual are violated. In the current condition of the world, in which global poverty and persecution are rampant, the presumption is that persons must migrate in order to support and protect themselves and that nations who are able to receive them should do so whenever possible. It is through this lens that we assess the current migration reality between the United States and Mexico.

— *Strangers No Longer: Together on the Journey of Hope. A Pastoral Letter Concerning Migration from the Catholic Bishops of Mexico and the United States (2002)*

3. Forming a Correct Conscience on the Use of the Media

It is essential that all those involved should form a correct conscience on the use of the media, especially with regard to certain issues which are particularly controversial today.

The first of these issues is information, or the search for news and its publication. Because of the progress of modern society and the increasing interdependence of its members on one another, it is obvious that information is very useful and, for the most part, essential. If news or facts and happenings are communicated publicly and without delay, every individual will have permanent access to sufficient information and thus will be enabled to contribute effectively to the common good. Further, all of them will more easily be able to contribute in unison to the prosperity and the progress of society as a whole.

There exists therefore in human society a right to information on the subjects that are of concern to men either as individuals or as members of society, according to each man's circumstances. The proper exercise of this right demands that the content of the communication be true and— within the limit set by justice and charity— complete. Further, it should be communicated honestly and properly. This means that in the gathering and in the publication of news the moral law and the legitimate rights and dignity of man should be upheld. All knowledge is not profitable, but on the other hand "love builds" (1 Cor 8:1).

— *Inter Mirifica*, 5

4. Proper Use of the Media

If they are to obey the moral law, those who use the media ought to keep themselves informed in good time about assessments arrived at by the authorities with competence in this sphere and to conform to them as a right conscience would dictate. They should take appropriate steps to direct and form their consciences so that they may more readily resist less wholesome influences and profit more fully from the good.

— *Inter Mirifica*, 9

VOCABULARY

AVARICE
A passionate desire for riches that leads one to use money to control others.

CALUMNY
False and malicious misrepresentation of the words and actions of another intended to injure his or her reputation.

CENTESIMUS ANNUS
A social encyclical by Pope John Paul II on the occasion of the 100th anniversary of Pope Leo XIII's encyclical *Rerum novarum*.

COMMON GOOD
The general good of all citizens.

DETRACTION
The action of taking away from a person's merit or reputation by disclosing another's true faults or sins. This is a sin against the Eighth Commandment because each person has a right to his good name.

ECOLOGY
From the Greek *oikos* meaning a house or dwelling, this science deals with the relations of living organisms (especially humans) to their surroundings or habitats. This field also studies environmental issues.

EMINENT DOMAIN
The superiority of the civil authority over all property under its control; this principle states that a government can claim private property, with compensation to the owner, because of a legitimate and overriding public concern.

ENVY
Unhappiness at another's good fortune or social status.

FALSEHOOD
That which is contrary to truth; the intentional making of untrue statements.

FLATTERY
Attributes qualities that may not exist or which are exaggerated, usually for personal gain or favor.

GRAVITY
The weight or seriousness of a sin, sometimes influenced by circumstances and intentions.

GREED
The desire for earthly goods without limit.

HONOR
Respect or good reputation that is acquired through the practice of virtue or heroic acts. The quality that brings people to be guided by the most elevated moral norms.

JUSTICE
One of the four cardinal virtues, this refers to observance of the divine law. This virtue is used to administer to God and each person his due.

MARTYRDOM
The act of giving up one's life for the Faith.

OBJECTIVE TRUTH
Reality as it is, even outside a person's intellect and independent of his acknowledgment of its existence.

PRINCIPLE OF SOLIDARITY
The duty of cooperating and harmonizing all of the rights of the individual and the demands that are derived from the sociability of man. It represents the entire, joint effort to reach the good of the individual and of society.

PRINCIPLE OF THE COMMON GOOD
The primacy of that which is beneficial for all people within a community over that of individual(s) within the same community. The term "common good" is applied to the effort to achieve a social good that makes possible the full development of perfection for each member of the community.

PRIVATE PROPERTY
The right of a person or community of persons to own, govern, and otherwise dispose of some part of creation.

RASH JUDGMENT
A judgment that questions someone's character or concludes a moral defect without sufficient evidence.

VOCABULARY Continued

REPUTATION
The good or bad opinion commonly held about a person.

RERUM NOVARUM
Social encyclical of Pope Leo XIII that represented the first comprehensive social teaching of the Catholic Church on issues such as labor and the distribution of goods.

SLANDER
A maliciously false statement or report in order to defame or injure a person; same as calumny, except usually an oral utterance, rather than written.

SOCIAL DOCTRINE OF THE CHURCH
Moral teaching of the Church with regard to the dignity of the person, the basic rights of the person, and the requirement of the common good.

SOCIAL JUSTICE
The mode of action that requires from each person what is necessary for the common good. This should characterize relations among individuals or among diverse groups and social classes in all areas of social interaction.

STEWARDSHIP
The responsible and just use of the world's resources.

SUBJECTIVISM
The philosophical theory that treats all knowledge as merely relative, denying the possibility of objective knowledge.

THEFT (Stealing)
Unjustly taking and keeping the property of another against the reasonable will of the owner.

TOLERANCE
The practice of the virtue of patience with respect to the opinions or practices of others.

TRUTH
The correlation between the idea in one's mind and objective reality.

UNIVERSAL DESTINATION OF GOODS
Biblical principle that the goods of the earth are meant to be used to supply the needs of all human persons in an equitable fashion.

VERACITY
Truthfulness; the disposition of a person to tell the truth.

God did not give us an absolute right over creation, but rather has entrusted us with the world to be used responsibly and justly.

STUDY QUESTIONS

1. Why does the Church issue teachings regarding social and economic life?

2. What is the relationship of the state in regard to the individual and the family?

3. Explain the "principle of subsidiarity."

4. In the story of creation in Genesis, what is the role of man in God's plan of creation?

5. In Genesis, what is the first act of man that establishes his dominion over creation? What is significant about this act?

6. What is stewardship, and what does it mean for Christian morality?

7. How does the restriction of the world's resources in the hands of the few undermine the intentions of God in creation?

8. What is the universal destination for which God created all the goods of this world?

9. What does it mean to say that human beings have a "common stewardship" over the goods of the earth?

10. List four truths deduced from the universal destination of goods.

11. What is the solution between the universal destination of goods and the right to private property?

12. Why is our dominion over nature not absolute?

13. Why is private property subordinate to the social function of property?

14. When may a state legitimately intervene in the inherent right of a person to own private property?

15. Explain why the age of industrialization required a new application of the Church's social doctrine. What Church documents outlined the Church's teaching on social doctrine?

16. What aspects of social life are covered in the Church's teaching on social doctrine?

17. What are some of the responsibilities for Christians in the political life of society?

18. What is the mission of the Christian in public life?

19. What is the purpose of the state?

20. What is necessary for social progress?

21. Explain the responsibilities of wealthier nations toward the poorer nations in the world.

22. What is the basis for responsibility of Christians toward the environment?

23. List five ways in which a person can violate the Seventh Commandment and explain why these are forms of stealing.

24. "The love of money or the envy of another's goods is not really sinful because it doesn't hurt anyone." Explain the fallacy of this line of thinking.

25. Why is restitution an essential part of conversion?

26. In your own words, explain why the communication of truth is essential in society.

27. What did Greco-Roman philosophy add to the understanding of truth?

28. With what type of falsehood is the Eighth Commandment literally concerned? How was this elevated by the teachings of Jesus Christ?

29. What is the source of truth for Christians? How is a Christian to learn the truth?

30. What is the relationship between happiness and truth? Explain.

31. What are some of the things that the Christian vocation involves regarding the truth?

STUDY QUESTIONS Continued

32. What two points are made in Jesus' statement that "the truth will make you free"?

33. "Let what you say be simply 'Yes' or 'No'; anything more than this comes from evil" (Mt 5: 37). Explain the meaning of this verse from the Bible.

34. When might Christian morality require a person to remain silent? Give an example. When might Christian morality require a person to reveal a truth? Give an example.

35. Under what circumstances should truth be affirmed?

36. What is the role of "intention" in regard to a lie?

37. How does "lying" harm society?

38. Explain the four criteria used in evaluating the gravity of a lie.

39. What is the difference between calumny and slander?

40. Explain why it can sometimes be wrong to tell the truth. What is required in these circumstances?

41. How can flattery be a violation of the Eighth Commandment?

42. List three different types of lies and explain how reparation might be made in each case.

43. When might a person be morally obligated to tell a secret?

44. What is the "Seal of Confession"?

45. How is martyrdom one of the chief examples of obeying the Eighth Commandment?

St. John's Fragment (Rylands Library Papyrus P52).
Scholars differ on the date of the papyrus, but a range of dates determined by scholars extends from before AD 100 to past AD 150. The papyrus is written in Greek on both sides. The side shown here (verso) is from John 18: 37-38. Words visible from the gospel include "the world to bear witness" and "of the truth."

PRACTICAL EXERCISES

1. Discuss the practical consequences for the social and political order that can be drawn from the following texts:

> Christian tradition has never upheld this right [of ownership or property] as absolute and untouchable. On the contrary, it has always understood this right within the broader context of the right common to all to use the goods of the whole of creation: the right to private property is subordinated to the right to common use, to the fact that goods are meant for everyone.[36]

> The ownership of any property makes its holder a steward of Providence, with the task of making it fruitful and communicating its benefits to others, first of all his family (CCC 2404).

2. Evaluate the morality of the individuals in the following cases in light of the Seventh and the Tenth Commandments:

- George's parents went out of town for the weekend and left the car keys home, so that George could use their car for necessary errands. George took the car one evening to go out with his friends, which his parents would almost certainly not have allowed. While they were out, he permitted his friend Katie to drive the car as well. Did he do anything wrong?

- Perry found a credit card and charged some sports equipment before destroying the card. Later, his conscience started to bother him, and he realized that he must make restitution. How do you think he should go about it?

3. Look for and comment on some passages of the New Testament that praise the spirit of poverty and condemn the anxiety for riches (e.g. Lk 16: 19-31). What is the Bible trying to say about the use of riches?

4. Resolve the following case: Margaret, Theresa, and Ann went to California on the train. In the station, Margaret found a wallet with $1,000 in it, but there was no identification in the wallet. They decided to distribute the money among themselves.

They considered this an extraordinary piece of luck, and proceeded to spend the money. Some days later, Ann told her mother about the incident, and her mother said she should not have spent the money. Ann told Theresa and Margaret about what her mother said and they started to worry. Should they have spent the money? If your answer is no, then what do you think they should do now?

5. Based upon your understanding of the principles contained in this chapter, resolve the following questions:

- Terence's friend is dating a girl who had an abortion five years earlier. Terence knows they are talking about getting married. May he tell his friend that the girl had an abortion?

- Maria and her friend Anita had a terrible argument. As a result, Maria told another person at the law firm where she and Anita work that, while they were in college, Anita had cheated on an important final exam, using information she had obtained illicitly. (The story is untrue, because although Anita did have the opportunity to find out what was going to be on the exam before the test, she never followed through. Her conscience would not permit her to do it.) As a result, Anita's reputation at the firm has been severely damaged. One of the senior partners at the firm has even said that she is concerned about Anita having access to confidential documents, because she is afraid that she will misuse the information. What is the specific nature of the sin of which Maria is guilty? What sort of restitution do you think Maria needs to make to Anita for the damage that has been done to her reputation? How do you think she can do this?

PRACTICAL EXERCISES Continued

6. Do you know of any instances in which the media has distorted or misrepresented the truth in their reporting of the news? What obligations does the media have with regard to the truth?

For questions 7 through 12, evaluate the situation and determine whether the person has a moral obligation to tell the truth.

7. A woman in a car stops and asks Monica for directions to a particular street in the neighborhood.

8. Roger is out past curfew, and his mother wants to know where he was and what he was doing.

9. Jake, Patti, Susan, and Rodrigo are in the parking lot after school planning a surprise birthday party for Sarah, a mutual friend. Sarah happens to walk by and asks what they were talking about.

10. Camilla is filling out a job application. She tries to make herself sound more qualified by embellishing certain facts about her previous job experience.

11. Tim, a physician's assistant at the local hospital, is helping to care for little six-year-old Austin after his bicycle accident. Mrs. Kelly, a neighbor who lives three doors down from Austin, phones Tim and asks about Austin's condition.

12. A couple of rough boys from another school show up at the city park and ask Pedro where Pablo is. Pedro knows exactly where Pablo is, but he doesn't want to say it for fear Pablo would get hurt. The rough boys seem very angry and talk about wanting to beat up Pablo for something he did.

Christ Before Pilate by Munkácsy. As Roman governor of Judea, it is possible that Pilate chose to use symbolism that the crowds would recognize as Mosaic Law—the washing of hands to "purge from yourselves the guilt of shedding innocent blood,..." (Dt 21:1-9)

FROM THE CATECHISM

2450 "You shall not steal."[37] "Neither thieves, nor the greedy..., nor robbers will inherit the kingdom of God."[38]

2451 The Seventh Commandment enjoins the practice of justice and charity in the administration of earthly goods and the fruits of men's labor.

2453 The Seventh Commandment forbids theft. Theft is the usurpation of another's goods against the reasonable will of the owner.

2457 Animals are entrusted to man's stewardship; he must show them kindness. They may be used to serve the just satisfaction of man's needs.

2504 "You shall not bear false witness against your neighbor."[39] Christ's disciples have "put on the new man, created after the likeness of God in true righteousness and holiness."[40]

2507 Respect for the reputation and honor of persons forbids all detraction and calumny in word or attitude.

2508 Lying consists in saying what is false with the intention of deceiving one's neighbor.

2509 An offense committed against the truth requires reparation.

2552 The Tenth Commandment forbids avarice arising from a passion for riches and their attendant power.

2556 Detachment from riches is necessary for entering the Kingdom of heaven. "Blessed are the poor in spirit."

2557 "I want to see God" expresses the true desire of man. Thirst for God is quenched by the water of eternal life.[41]

ENDNOTES – CHAPTER NINE

1. Cf. Lk 16:19-31.
2. Lk 12:48.
3. Cf. Lk 21:1-4; 1 Kgs 17:8-16.
4. Cf. CCC 1907.
5. CA 48 § 4; cf. Pius XI, Quadragesimo anno I, 184-186.
6. Cf. CCC 1895.
7. Cf. Gn 2:15.
8. Cf. Gn 1:26.
9. Cf. CCC 2428; CCC 2460.
10. CCC 1947.
11. Cf. Gn 3:14-19.
12. Cf. LE 27.
13. Cf. VS 99-100.
14. John Paul II, Sollicitudo Rei Socialis, 38.
15. CCC 1948.
16. Cf. CCC 2461.
17. CA 57; cf. Lk 6:20-22, Mt 8:20; Mk 12:41-44.
18. Eph 4:28.
19. Cf. CA 57.
20. Cf. SRS 17; 45.
21. CA 28; cf. 35.
22. Cf. SRS 16.
23. Cf. CCC 2455.
24. Cf. Gn 1:28-31.
25. Cf. CA 37-38.
26. Cf. GS 69 § 1.
27. Mt 5:3.
28. Lk 19:8.
29. Nm 23:19.
30. Cf. 1 Jn 4:9.
31. Cf. Jn 14:6.
32. Jn 1:3.
33. Jn 8:31-32.
34. Mt 5:37.
35. Moralia in Job, VII, 21, 24: PL 75, 778: "huius mundi aspera pro æternis præmiis amore."
36. LE 14.
37. Ex 20:15; Dt 5:19.
38. 1 Cor 6:10.
39. Ex 20:16.
40. Eph 4:24.
41. Cf. Jn 4:14.

Epilogue:
Living the Christian Life

CHAPTER 10
Epilogue:
Living the Christian Life

Christ Giving the Keys to St. Peter.
Central panel from a Venetian altarpiece dated 1369 by Lorenzo.

"He encounters us ever anew, in the men and women who reflect his presence, in his word, in the sacraments, and especially in the Eucharist." Pope Benedict XVI, *Deus Caritas Est*, 17.

THE IMITATION OF CHRIST

Christian morality is more than a set of rules. Based on the principles taught by Jesus, it is a morality of love. The Christian life, because it stems from a call from God, is also a vocation. Unless the Christian responds affirmatively to this call from God, however, his or her faith cannot flourish.

The Christian draws closer to God by his or her efforts to imitate the life of Christ. This imitation is not a literal re-enactment of Christ's life but rather a commitment to living according to Jesus' moral perspective. The goal is to act in every human situation with the same moral disposition that Christ exemplified. "For I have given you an example, that you also should do as I have done to you."[1]

The sanctifying grace of Baptism enables a Christian to participate in the life of Jesus in such a way that Christ rightly can be said to dwell within him or her. The person becomes united to Jesus and his transforming grace, which in turn causes the Christian to turn to Christ and to act more like him. It is in this sense that we can say that every Christian is "another Christ."

For Christians, the moral life is, by definition, the imitation of Christ. In this way, the words of the Lord's Prayer, "thy kingdom come, thy will be done," can become a reality. This goal of bringing about God's kingdom and doing his will cannot, however, be reached by human strength alone. Christian life and morality are not merely exercises that reach perfection through practice; instead, the goal can be fully attained only with the assistance of the Holy Spirit. Prayer and the transforming grace of the sacraments (particularly the Eucharist and Penance) are the normal ways through which Jesus and the Holy Spirit act, so it is not possible to live a full moral life in Christ without them.

> Following Christ is not an outward imitation, since it touches man at the very depths of his being. Being a follower of Christ means becoming conformed to him who became a servant even to giving himself on the Cross.[2] Christ dwells by faith in the heart of the believer[3] and thus the disciple is conformed to the Lord. This is the effect of grace, of the active presence of the Holy Spirit in us. (*Veritatis Splendor*, 21)

ENCOUNTER WITH CHRIST

Being Christian is not the result of an ethical choice or a lofty idea, but the encounter with an event, a person, which gives life new horizons and a decisive direction.[4] While each individual begins his or her journey of faith in this way, it is important to remember that this encounter is not the fruit of our own human efforts. It is Christ who comes seeking us. In speaking to his Apostles, Christ tells them, "You did not choose me, but I chose you."[5]

From the moment of the first sin, God has reached out to his people, both as a community and as individuals. This reconciliation offered by God reached its fulfillment in the Incarnation of Jesus Christ, when God became man and entered human history to redeem his people. However, even as God comes to us and offers us the grace to respond to his call, he nevertheless respects the freedom that he bestowed on our first parents even when we misuse our free will by making wrong decisions. This means that each person can freely choose to accept the divine calling or to reject it.

The Christian vocation or call is not simply an invitation to live one's life according to a philosophy; rather, it is an invitation to enter into a personal relationship with Jesus Christ. Referring to the call of the Apostles, Pope Benedict XVI states, "This is how the Apostles' adventure began, as an encounter of people who are open to one another. For the disciples, it was the beginning of a direct acquaintance with the Teacher, seeing where he was staying and starting to get to know him. Indeed, they were not to proclaim an idea, but to witness to a person."[6]

How is it possible for us to encounter Christ two thousand years after the Ascension? This question is no different today than it was for those believers who accepted Christ on that first Pentecost, when the coming of the Holy Spirit upon the Apostles inspired them to preach publicly for the first time since Jesus' Death, a witness that resulted in the baptism of thousands of converts that same day.

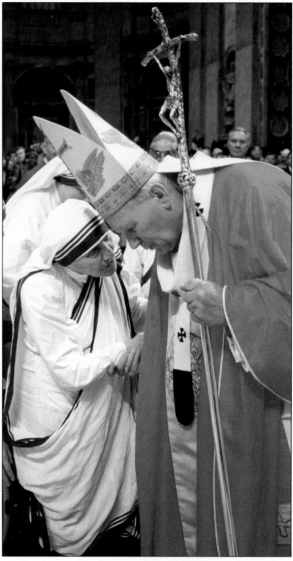

How is it possible for us to encounter Christ two thousand years after the Ascension?
Pope John Paul II and Blessed Teresa of Calcutta in St. Peter's Basilica, 1997.
"Following Christ is not an outward imitation, since it touches man at the very depths of his being."
—Pope John Paul II, *Veritatis Splendor*, 21.

Christ addressed this issue in the Gospel when he spoke to St. Thomas after his Resurrection: "Have you believed because you have seen me? Blessed are those who have not seen and yet believe."[7]

Christ has also provided the means of encountering him in the world today. He established his Church and appointed Apostles who would act with his authority. To ensure that his saving mission would neither end nor become corrupt, he promised that he would be with them always, until the end of time.

Just as he promised, the Church that Christ founded continues today. Through the successors of the Apostles, the bishops, she continues to manifest his presence in the world, teaching the nations the fullness of the apostolic Faith. It is here, in the Church and in her sacraments, that the faithful can encounter the presence of the living and eternal Lord.

Jesus Ordains the Twelve by Tissot. "He went up into the hills, and called to him those whom he desired; and they came to him. And he appointed twelve, to be with him, and to be sent out to preach, and have authority to cast out demons: Simon whom he surnamed Peter; James the son of Zebedee and John the brother of James, whom he surnamed Boanerges, that is, sons of thunder; Andrew, and Philip, and Bartholomew, and Matthew, and Thomas, and James the son of Alphæus, and Thaddæus, and Simon the Cananæan, and Judas Iscariot, who betrayed him." (Mk 3: 13-19)

"He encounters us ever anew, in the men and women who reflect his presence, in his word, in the sacraments, and especially in the Eucharist. In the Church's Liturgy, in her prayer, in the living community of believers, we experience the love of God, we perceive his presence and we thus learn to recognize that presence in our daily lives." (*Deus Caritas Est*, 17.)

THE SPIRITUAL LIFE OF A CHRISTIAN

The spiritual life of a Christian can be summarized as knowing God, loving God, and serving God. This is the journey which is begun in this life and culminates with eternal life with God in Heaven.

KNOWING GOD

The first step in the Christian journey is getting to know God. Even on a purely human level, we must get to know a person before we can love them, and we must love a person before we can truly serve them.

Through the use of reason, mankind is capable of obtaining a certain level of knowledge concerning both the existence of God and the moral and ethical truths. However, the fullness of knowledge is possible only through the Revelation of God.[8] As Scripture tells us, "[God] desires all men to be saved and to come to the knowledge of the truth."[9] It is for this reason that God chose to reveal himself to his people at key moments throughout human history, culminating with the Incarnation of Jesus Christ. Only through the Person of Jesus Christ is it possible for us to gain knowledge of the fullness of Divine Revelation and, therefore, of the meaning of our own lives.

The Gospel of St. Matthew relates how, prior to his Ascension, Jesus granted divine authority to his Apostles and entrusted them with transmitting his salvific message to all nations, promising that he would be with them always.[10] Throughout the ages, the Church has remained faithful to our Lord's command through her mission of bringing this message of salvation to all people.

The Holy Trinity with Saints by Andrea. This altarpiece features (left to right) Sts. Augustine, Sebastian,
Lawrence, Peter Martyr, Francis, and Mary Magdalene.
Only through the Person of Jesus Christ is it possible for us to gain knowledge of the fullness of
Divine Revelation and, therefore, of the meaning of our own lives.

LOVING GOD

> And he said to him, 'You shall love the Lord your God with all your heart, and with all your soul,
> and with all your mind. This is the great and first commandment. And a second is like it, You shall
> love your neighbor as yourself.' (Mt 22:37-39)

Once, while Jesus was teaching, a lawyer came to him, and wishing to test him, asked, "Teacher, what shall
I do to inherit eternal life?" (Lk 10:25). Jesus, who could read all men's hearts, knew that the lawyer was not
concerned with the truth, and so he turned to him and responded: "What is written in the law?" (Lk 10:26).

The lawyer answered: "You shall love the Lord your God with all your heart, and with all your soul, and
with all your strength, and with all your mind; and your neighbor as yourself" (Lk 10:27).

Jesus himself had taught that these two principles—love of God and love of neighbor—summed up the
entire law of the Old Covenant; a law which he had come not to abolish, but to fulfill and perfect. So he told
the lawyer: "You have answered right; do this, and you will live."[11]

However, the lawyer was not satisfied. So he asked Jesus another question. "And who is my neighbor?"
(Lk 10:29). The lawyer was seeking the letter of the law. He wanted to know with certainty who the law
obliged him to love and who he was allowed to hate.

In explaining his new commandment of Love to the lawyer, Jesus told the Parable of the Good Samaritan. For his listeners, this parable would have been shocking: the good neighbor was a Samaritan, someone who was considered an outsider, an enemy. No observant Jew would associate with a Samaritan, much less love him.

As a consequence of Original Sin, the call to love God and neighbor is difficult. We often do what we know is wrong and ignore what we know we should do. These sins cause us to drift away from the Lord. Left to our own devices, we often are too weak to seek God and to follow his teachings.

God, however, never abandons us. He has called us into existence and has given us life. He freely loves us and calls us to love him in return. God makes his grace available to us through our prayer and participation in his sacraments, thus enabling us to return his love and to love our neighbor for his sake. With God's grace, it becomes possible for us to love Christ and to follow his teachings.

SERVING GOD

If our love for God is not to remain at a philosophical level, then it must translate into deeds of love for both God and neighbor. Christ himself said, "If you love me, you will keep my commandments,"[12] and later, "This is my commandment, that you love one another as I have loved you."[13]

Before the Last Supper, Christ gave his disciples an example of how they were to put their love of neighbor into action. The Gospel of St. John relates: "When he had washed their feet, and taken his garments, and

resumed his place, he said to them, 'Do you know what I have done to you?...If I then, your Lord and Teacher, have washed your feet, you also ought to wash one another's feet.'"[14]

Later, Christ gave his ultimate expression of love on the Cross when he died to redeem us from our sins. In doing so, he fulfilled his own teaching: "Greater love has no man than this, that a man lay down his life for his friends."[15]

These deeds of loving service and self-sacrifice spring from an inner conversion in which Christ sanctifies us with his grace. In Baptism, Jesus plants the seed of holiness within us. With this great gift comes the obligation to nurture this seed into a life of holiness in imitation of Christ. We are called to live as holy people, God's chosen ones, with hearts of mercy, humility, kindness, meekness, and patience.[16]

> The followers of Christ are called by God, not because of their works, but according to his own purpose and grace. They are justified in the Lord Jesus, because in the baptism of faith they truly become sons of God and sharers in the divine nature. In this way they are really made holy. Then too, by God's gift, they must hold on to and complete in their lives this holiness they have received. (*Lumen Gentium*, 40)

The Holy Trinity by Coecke van Aelst.
Christ is essentially teaching that only a total union with God can satisfy the longing of the human heart.

THE UNIVERSAL CALL TO HOLINESS

Pentecost by El Greco. "So those who received his word were baptized, and there were added that day about three thousand souls." (Acts 2: 41)

The Church has never tired of spreading the message of Jesus Christ, which is a universal call of every human person to holiness. "You, therefore, must be perfect, as your heavenly Father is perfect."[17] The Second Vatican Council spoke of the Universal Call to Holiness. "All Christians in any state or walk of life are called to the fullness of Christian life and to the perfection of charity."[18] God wants us to be holy. Indeed, it is only in this life of holiness that an individual can be personally united to God and thus achieve true happiness.

It is human nature to ask, "What must I do?" What exactly is this call to holiness? As a first step in living the Christian life, we must turn to God, and in particular to the Holy Spirit. He is the one who calls us to a life of holiness, and it is he who will give us the grace to respond to that call.

The Acts of the Apostles shows us clearly how the early followers of Christ lived this call. Following the outpouring of the Holy Spirit at Pentecost, St. Luke tells us that "they devoted themselves to the apostles' teaching and fellowship, to the breaking of bread and the prayers."[19]

This verse of Scripture is rich in its meaning for us today. The lives of the first Christians were centered on prayer and the Eucharist. They were united as a Christian community with the Apostles and the apostolic teachings. Put in modern language, they prayed together and went to Mass together. They were united to the pope and the bishops (the successors to the Apostles) and adhered to the Magisterium (the teaching authority) of the Church.

The first step in living a life of holiness is to have an interior life. It is only when our lives are centered on Christ in communion with his Church and nourished by the sacraments and a meaningful life of prayer that we will receive the graces needed to put his teachings into practice.

Secondly, a life of holiness involves living our daily lives in accordance with the plan of God. When the events of our lives are seen through God's eyes, they become opportunities of loving him and serving our neighbor in an entirely new way. By dedicating our worship, prayer, work, family life, and friendships to God and living these very human circumstances in the light of Christ and his teachings, we cooperate with him in the building of his kingdom on earth.

Christ in Heaven with Four Saints by Ghirlandaio.
Christ offers eternal life that can only be reached through a total gift of self to God through
one's whole heart, mind, and strength.

CONCLUSION

The encyclical Veritatis Splendor strikes at the heart of moral theology in its analysis of the encounter between Jesus and the rich young man. The youth asks the question: "Teacher what good deed must I do, to have eternal life?"[20] Essentially the young man is asking about the meaning of life and what must be done to achieve happiness. These questions are especially typical of young people who are searching for their vocation in life.

Christ gives a threefold response. First, "No one is good but God alone";[21] secondly, "If you would enter life, keep the commandments";[22] and thirdly, "If you would be perfect, go, sell all what you possess and give to the poor, and you will have treasure in heaven; and come follow me."[23]

The encounter between Christ and the rich young man typifies Christ's dialogue with humankind through his Church. To find the meaning of life one must turn and speak to Christ because he is the Good par excellence. This meeting between Christ and the young man begins with a simple question posed by the youth; Christ responds with a simple but profound statement that only God is good. In saying that "only God is good," Christ is essentially teaching that only a total union with God can satisfy the longing of the human heart. Every other good, as lofty or attractive as it may be, leaves the human heart unsatisfied. "Our hearts are restless until they rest in you."[24]

With the words, "If you love me, you will keep my commandments,"[25] Christ is teaching that a life of happiness is directly connected to the commandments. The Commandments, which include the teachings of Christ in the Sermon on the Mount and in the Beatitudes, are not arbitrary decrees but divinely inspired standards of human behavior that invariably lead to true happiness. They are not ends in themselves but rather means to seriously follow Christ, which lead a person toward the fullness of Christian love. Both the Commandments of the Decalogue and the Beatitudes give the human person the freedom and self-possession for the total gifts of self necessary to follow Christ.

The conversation between Jesus and the rich young man ends with this radical invitation to discipleship: "If you would to be perfect, go, sell all what you possess and give to the poor and you will have treasure in heaven, and come follow me."[26] The Commandments make sense from the perspective of Christ's invitation to holiness. He offers eternal life that can only be reached through a total gift of self to God through one's whole heart, mind, and strength. All of the Commandments and teachings of Divine Revelation are at the service of this total generosity in laying down one's life for Christ and his Gospel, usually in ordinary life, but always with extraordinary love.

The Agony in the Garden by Bloch.
"And he withdrew from them about a stone's throw, and knelt down and prayed, 'Father, if thou art willing, remove this cup from me; nevertheless not my will, but thine, be done.' And there appeared to him an angel from heaven, strengthening him. And being in an agony he prayed more earnestly; and his sweat became like great drops of blood falling down upon the ground." (Lk 22: 41-44)

CHRISTIAN MORALITY: A Program For Life

Now that you have completed your instruction in "Our Moral Life in Christ," here is a handy "decalogue" of questions and answers to help you remember the main themes you have studied throughout this course.

1. What is our purpose in life?

God created us to share in his divine life and, in doing so, to enjoy eternal happiness. The happiness which God envisions for his children, however, is not a momentary or fleeting happiness, but one that is real and lasting—the type of happiness that can only come from a genuine friendship with God.

> He chose us in him before the foundation of the world, that we should be holy and blameless before him. He destined us in love to be his sons through Jesus Christ, according to the purpose of his will, to the praise of his glorious grace which he freely bestowed on us in the Beloved. (Eph 1: 4-6)

Created in the image and likeness of God, Adam and Eve shared in God's friendship and lived in perfect accordance with his will. This was the reality of the human condition in the paradise God created for our first parents. However, as a result of Original Sin, Adam and Eve lost their friendship with God, and the image and likeness of God in which they were created became disfigured as a result. Left to our own devices, we would never be able to regain the true happiness that God intended for us.

> When God created man "in his image," he looked toward the Christ who was to come, and created man according to the image of the "new Adam," the man who is the criterion of the human. (Pope Benedict XVI, *Jesus of Nazareth*, 138)

It was for this reason that God sent his Son, Jesus Christ, to reconcile us to himself. In Baptism, a Christian becomes re-created in the image of Christ. Through Christ, it is possible to have a foretaste of the eternal happiness intended by God, but it is only in Heaven that God will reward us with perfect happiness.

2. How do we achieve true happiness?

In the Old Testament, we see God continually reaching out to his people, revealing himself and showing them the path to correct moral conduct so that they could follow his path and progress toward human perfection. In the fullness of time, God himself entered into human history in the Person of Jesus Christ, fulfilling the promises made to our first parents. At the time of the Fall, God had promised a Messiah who would defeat Satan.

> I will put enmity between you and the woman, and between your seed and her seed; he shall bruise your head, and you shall bruise his heel. (Gn 3: 15)

Through the Incarnation of Jesus Christ, God made himself accessible to mankind. In Christ, we have the fullness of Divine Revelation and are privileged to enter into a personal relationship with God so as to enjoy his divine life. As members of the Church, the Mystical Body of Christ, we share an intimate communion with God and can once again live as his sons and daughters. Living the virtues, as revealed by God in both the Old and New Testaments, having a personal friendship with him, and following his will for our lives lead to happiness and true freedom.

3. How do we know the will of God?

> But what is "God's will"? How do we recognize it? How can we do it? Scripture works on the premise that man has knowledge of God's will in his inmost heart, that anchored deeply within us there is a participation in God's knowing, which we call conscience.[27] (Pope Benedict XVI, *Jesus of Nazareth*, 148)

As we noted earlier, every person is created in the image and likeness of God. Although this likeness is disfigured by Original Sin, God has left his imprint in the depths of the human heart. This means that each individual possesses a hunger for God and a desire to search for truth and everlasting happiness.

> When Gentiles who have not the law do by nature what the law requires, they are a law to themselves, even though they do not have the

CHRISTIAN MORALITY: A Program For Life Continued

law. They show that what the law requires is written on their hearts, while their conscience also bears witness and their conflicting thoughts accuse or perhaps excuse them on that day when, according to my gospel, God judges the secrets of men by Christ Jesus. (Rom 2: 14-16)

Each person, then, has the moral law inscribed on his or her heart—that is, a conscience. When our consciences are properly formed in accordance with the Divine Revelation given by Jesus Christ and transmitted by the Church, and when we sincerely seek the light of Jesus through prayer, we are enabled to know the will of God and to find the truth that we seek.

4. How does God reveal his law?

And we know that the Son of God has come and has given us understanding, to know him who is true; and we are in him who is true, in his Son Jesus Christ. This is the true God and eternal life. (1 Jn 5: 20)

In addition to the natural law that is inscribed on the human heart, God chose to reveal himself through his prophets. Through Abraham, he established a covenant with his people, and, through Moses, he revealed the moral law in the form of the Ten Commandments.

However, wishing to reconcile himself fully with his people, God became man, and it is through the teachings of Jesus Christ that we have the fullness of Divine Revelation.

He who has seen me [Christ] has seen the Father. (Jn 14: 9)

As outlined so beautifully in the first chapter of St. John's Gospel, the Church has always proclaimed the divinity of Jesus Christ. The doctrine of the Blessed Trinity—one God in three Persons, Father, Son, and Holy Spirit—is the central mystery of the Christian Faith. The Son, Jesus Christ, and the Father are one. Through the Person of Jesus Christ, God redeemed his people and revealed the fullness of moral law, which is handed down to us through the Magisterium of the Catholic Church.

The purpose of human existence is to be united to God the Father, through his Son, Jesus Christ, by the power of the Holy Spirit. It is Jesus Christ, God the Son who became man, who teaches us about the Father and shows us the way that will bring us to him. Through his Death and Resurrection, he justifies us. In Baptism, we die to sin and are united to Christ, striving to conform ourselves to his example.

By the grace of the Holy Spirit, we are united to Christ and led to the Father. The Holy Spirit sanctifies us and dwells within us, so that we become Temples of the Holy Spirit. Through the Holy Spirit, we are renewed, enlightened, and strengthened to follow the will of God. In this way, the mystery of the Blessed Trinity is at the very heart of our Christian Faith.

The mystery of the Most Holy Trinity is the central mystery of the Christian faith and of Christian life. God alone can make it known to us by revealing himself as Father, Son, and Holy Spirit. (CCC 261)

5. How did Jesus perfect the moral law given through the prophets?

Think not that I have come to abolish the law and the prophets; I have come not to abolish them but to fulfill them. (Mt 5: 17)

The truths revealed by God to his people in the Old Testament were given in order to set the stage for the truth that would be fully revealed by Christ in the New Testament. Christ did not come to abolish or detract from any of the truths God had revealed, but instead came to perfect these teachings.

Unless your righteousness exceeds that of the scribes and Pharisees, you will never enter the kingdom of heaven. "You have heard that it was said to the men of old, 'You shall not kill; and whoever kills shall be liable to judgment.' But I say to you that every one who is angry with his brother shall be liable to judgment; whoever insults his brother shall be liable to the council, and whoever says, 'You fool!' shall be liable to the hell of fire. (Mt 5: 20-22)

CHRISTIAN MORALITY: A Program For Life Continued

As illustrated in this example, Christ did not change the Fifth Commandment, "Thou shall not kill," but rather elevated it to reflect the plan for human relationships that God had originally intended in creation.

The teachings of Christ are transmitted by the Church in Sacred Tradition and Sacred Scripture and can be found in the *Catechism of the Catholic Church*. The Sermon on the Mount, in which Christ perfected the teachings of the Old Law, relates the primary teachings of Christ on the moral life. The Beatitudes show us the way to perfection.

The teachings of Christ can be summed up as a "law of love"—love of God and love of neighbor. While these teachings were already contained in the Old Law, Christ perfected them, radically redefining the meaning of "neighbor." Christ showed us that our neighbor includes everyone, even those the Old Law allowed us to hate. With the heart of Christ, we are to love everyone as ourselves, for it is only when our hearts are one with Christ that we can conform our will to God's will.

6. Why do we need to educate our conscience?

It is our conscience that allows us to discern good from evil. In creation, Adam and Eve were privileged to know the mind of God. However, in committing Original Sin, they chose to reject God as the fountain of all truth and desired to make themselves the arbiters of good and evil.

Even after Baptism, we still suffer from concupiscence—the effects of Original Sin. We still have a desire to make ourselves the center of truth, to be our own arbiters of good and evil. Taken to its logical extreme, this temptation leads to moral relativism, which denies the existence of moral law and makes the individual the only standard for deciding right and wrong.

The Christian life involves a continual education of the conscience. For this, we can look to the Church. Christ gave us the fullness of Revelation, and in founding his Church, he guaranteed that his truth would be transmitted in its entirety and without error.

In speaking of the moral life, it is also important for us to acknowledge that we are imperfect. In other words, we often fail to live up to the standards taught by Christ. Even when we know the truth, we sometimes fail to follow it in our lives. This is when we need the grace of God, which enables us to exercise our freedom wisely, choosing that which is truly good and which will lead us to eternal life.

7. How do we exercise our freedom wisely?

"If you continue in my word, you are truly my disciples, and you will know the truth, and the truth will make you free." (Jn 8: 31-32)

Among the many gifts that God bestowed on our first parents was the gift of freedom. Before the fall, Adam and Eve exercised their freedom in complete accordance with the capacity given to their intellect and will. However, through their act of disobedience, they lost their friendship with God and introduced sin and suffering into the world.

Considering all the human suffering that is caused by sin, we can sometimes question the value of freedom. However, the exercise of free will is at the very core of human existence. God created us to have a personal relationship with himself, to share in his divine life, to reflect his glory, and to possess the complete happiness that only he can give. For God's friendship to have value, we must be free to accept or reject it.

In giving us freedom, God, as it were, took a chance on us. We are completely free to accept his offer of friendship that will lead to genuine happiness, or to reject it. It is when we reject the will of God that we lose our freedom as children of God and enslave ourselves to sin.

As indicated in St. John's Gospel, it is in following God's will that we are set free. We are thus enabled to fulfill the plan for which we were created. It is when we misuse our freedom that we become slaves to sin. Common sense dictates that when drivers follow the rules of the road, they are free to travel anywhere in relative safety. However, when the rules are disregarded, they lose this freedom.

CHRISTIAN MORALITY: A Program For Life Continued

Wishing what is best for his people, God gave us the norms for correct moral behavior. Through the Ten Commandments and the teachings of Jesus Christ, God revealed the path that we must follow. When we exercise our freedom in accordance with his plan, we become free to enjoy the friendship that God is offering and are enabled to achieve true and lasting happiness.

8. What kind of love is demanded for those who are children of God?

A new commandment I give to you, that you love one another; even as I have loved you, that you also love one another. By this all men will know that you are my disciples, if you have love for one another. (Jn 13:34-35)

As we have seen, the New Law taught by Christ was a "law of love"—love of God and love of neighbor. This attitude of love must permeate the life of a Christian.

As followers of Christ, we should be recognizable by the way we love our neighbors. While the love of God is the Greatest Commandment, it is impossible to separate love of God from love of neighbor; that is, it is impossible to love God but hate one's neighbor.

If any one says, "I love God," and hates his brother, he is a liar; for he who does not love his brother whom he has seen, cannot love God whom he has not seen. And this commandment we have from him, that he who loves God should love his brother also. (1 Jn 4:20-21)

The New Testament makes it abundantly clear that it is not sufficient for a Christian to simply say, "I love my neighbor," and then do nothing further. These words must be translated into deeds of love. In other words, our interior attitude of love of God and neighbor must be reflected in our lives.

If a brother or sister is ill-clad and in lack of daily food, and one of you says to them, "Go in peace, be warmed and filled," without giving them the things needed for the body, what does it profit? (Jas 2:15-16)

In living Christ's commandment of love, it is natural that we first love those closest to us— parents, brothers and sisters, relatives, friends, classmates, and so on. We cannot truly live as a follower of Christ if we do not show love and consideration to those who are intimately connected to our lives.

If you love those who love you, what reward have you? Do not even the tax collectors do the same? (Mt 5:46)

However, as a Christian, it is necessary to go beyond those that the world considers worthy of love. As Christ taught, we must love our enemies, the poor, the sick, the homeless, the imprisoned. It is precisely in our love for those who are difficult to love that we conform our lives and our hearts to Christ, who loved and died for all people.

9. How is this new commandment of love put into practice?

God wants to share his divine life with us. It was for this reason that he sent his Son, Jesus Christ, to be born of the Virgin Mary and to die for our sins. However, like those at Pentecost, we often ask, "What shall we do?"[28] God offers his friendship and gives us every grace that we need in order to respond to that friendship. Endowed with free will, each person must make the choice to accept the gift that God is offering: We must say "Yes" to God.

As outlined in the Acts of the Apostles, it is in Baptism that a person takes the first step in responding to the will of God. However, this is not a once-and-for-all event. We are asked to live out our baptismal promises each and every day. With our consciences properly formed, and making proper use of our free will, God will give us the grace to continually say "Yes" to his will.

The Christian life is one of integrity. A Christian cannot be two-faced, saying one thing and doing another. It would be hypocritical to appear pious on Sunday and then live the rest of the week as if God did not exist. The life of a Christian must be a unified whole, reflecting in deeds the faith that exists in the heart.

CHRISTIAN MORALITY: A Program For Life Continued

> Either make the tree good, and its fruit good; or make the tree bad, and its fruit bad; for the tree is known by its fruit. (Mt 12:33)

Integrity demands that we are honest with ourselves and honest with others. This, in turn, requires God's grace and strength of character. However, as Jesus relates, the Christian has nothing to fear.[29] While the followers of Christ must carry their own crosses and sometimes suffer for the truth, God is with them, and in being faithful to the truth in thought and deed, and through the sacramental life of the Church, they can become more closely united to Christ.

> Clean hands and a pure heart entail man's refusal to deceive or commit perjury; this requires honesty, truthfulness, and justice toward one's fellow men and toward the community—what we might call social ethics, although it actually reaches right down into the depths of the heart. (Pope Benedict XVI, *Jesus of Nazareth*, 94)

10. What do we accomplish by following the law of Christ?

> These things I have spoken to you, that my joy may be in you, and that your joy may be full. (Jn 15:11)

The ultimate goal of life is to enjoy the divine life of God that leads us to eternal happiness. For a Christian, true and lasting happiness can only be accomplished by a friendship with God. While sharing in God's divine life brings us a foretaste of happiness in this life, it is only in Heaven that a person will possess perfect happiness. In this sense, we can say that the goal of the Christian life is complete unity with God in Heaven for all eternity.

> The essence of heaven is oneness with God's will, the oneness of will and truth. Earth becomes "heaven" when and insofar as God's will is done there; and it is merely "earth," the opposite of heaven, when and insofar as it withdraws from the will of God. (Pope Benedict XVI, *Jesus of Nazareth*, 147-148)

With their sights on eternal life in Heaven, Christians strive to do the will of God on earth, thus cooperating with him in establishing the kingdom of Heaven on earth. In communion with God and following his moral law, a Christian shares in the joy of the life to come and eternal life in Heaven.

Raising of the Cross by Rembrandt.
"I am the way, and the truth, and the life; no one comes to the father, but by me." (Jn 14:6)
While the followers of Christ must carry their own crosses and sometimes suffer for the truth, God is with them.

VOCATIONS IN THE CHRISTIAN LIFE

The Second Vatican Council emphasized that every Christian has a vocation, referred to as the "universal call to holiness":

> The followers of Christ are called by God, not because of their works, but according to His own purpose and grace. They are justified in the Lord Jesus, because in the baptism of faith they truly become sons of God and sharers in the divine nature. In this way they are really made holy. Then too, by God's gift, they must hold on to and complete in their lives this holiness they have received. "Be you therefore perfect, even as your heavenly Father is perfect." (*Lumen Gentium*, 40)

For each individual, then, an essential part of the Christian journey involves discerning the plan to which God is calling him or her.

The word *vocation* comes from Latin meaning "to call." Most Christians are called to serve God and others as laypersons. Ordinarily, this call is to remain in their particular state of life, either the married state or the unmarried state, seeking holiness through their ordinary daily work, studies, duties, and relationships. Some may find their search for greater holiness leads them to participate in any of a number of lay apostolates, third orders, associations of the faithful, or personal prelatures. Other laypersons will discern a call to the Consecrated Life.

CONSECRATED LIFE

A vocation to the consecrated life is one way of living out the baptismal commitment and involves following the three evangelical counsels of poverty, chastity, and obedience.

> The life consecrated to God is characterized by the public profession of the evangelical counsels of poverty, chastity, and obedience, in a stable state of life recognized by the Church. (CCC 944)

It can take various forms depending on the particular charism or spirit of each congregation, society, or institute. The consecrated life can also be lived individually or with others in a community. The main types of consecrated life are *religious orders and congregations* and *secular institutes.*

Religious orders (congregations) are communities whose members make vows of poverty, chastity, and obedience and live a life of prayer centered on the Eucharist. Although there are some differences between orders and congregations, the terms are often used interchangeably. These communities are specifically for men or for women. Members in men's communities are referred to as brothers, although some are usually chosen to receive Holy Orders in order to serve the sacramental needs of their community. Members of women's communities are called sisters, nuns, or women religious.

Religious orders or congregations have their origin in the monasticism of the early Church, when certain individuals felt a call to leave society to live a life of solitude and prayer. Eventually organized according to a rule, they strove to live a life of holiness in community. Many of the first monastic orders in the West were organized according to the rule of St. Benedict.

In addition to a special focus on prayer and penance, some orders may be involved in particular works of mercy, such as service to the poor, education, and preaching. Some of these religious orders would include the Benedictines, the Franciscans, and the Dominicans.

Secular institutes first began in the twentieth century. Their membership is comprised of laity, who have been called to live in the midst of the world for the purpose of sanctifying the world. While making private vows of poverty, chastity, and obedience, they retain their ordinary professions and lay status. Normally, members of secular institutes do not live in community, but will meet regularly with the other members of their institute to receive formation and spiritual direction.

VOCATIONS IN THE CHRISTIAN LIFE Continued

SOCIETIES OF APOSTOLIC LIFE

Societies of apostolic life were founded to serve society and the world outside of the traditional cloistered life (the monastery or convent). Like religious orders, societies for apostolic life are specifically for men or women, and as in the case of religious orders, some of the men are ordained to the priesthood. However, unlike those in religious orders or congregations, they do not take public vows of poverty, chastity, and obedience, although they may embrace these vows privately.

The distinguishing characteristic of societies for apostolic life is their involvement in the world. Their members normally perform works of service, such as missionary activities, charity, social work, education, and health care. Examples of societies for apostolic life would include the Missionaries of the Precious Blood, whose principal aim is to give parish missions and retreats, and the Daughters of Charity, who serve the poor.

THIRD ORDERS

Third orders, or tertiaries, are lay members of religious orders, who do not make vows of poverty, chastity, and obedience. These members live in the midst of the world, retaining their ordinary professions and family lives. They receive formation from the religious order to which they are attached, aiding them in living a life of holiness. According to their state in life, each member lives according to the charism of his or her religious order and assists in the fulfillment of its mission. An example of third orders would include the Third Order Carmelites and the Third Order Secular of St. Francis.

LAY ECCLESIAL MOVEMENTS

A lay movement is an organization of laity, normally following the teachings and example of a particular founder. It assists its members in their vocation to holiness through different means of Christian formation, education, spiritual direction, and fraternity. There have been hundreds of new movements founded in the twentieth century, many since Vatican II. Each movement has a unique charism or spirit, such as working with the poor or disabled, education, or the Christian family. Members remain members of their local parishes, while participating in the activities of the movement. Two of the more well-known movements include *Communion and Liberation* and the *L'Arche Community*.

Communion and Liberation was founded in 1954 by Fr. Luigi Giussani. Its particular charism emphasizes three factors. First, it proclaims the event of the Incarnation—that God became man. Secondly, it recognizes that Christ is present in the Church guided by the Bishop of Rome. And thirdly, it witnesses that only in Christ can man find his ultimate fulfillment. Communion and Liberation proposes that the Christian event, lived in communion, is the basis for the authentic liberation of man.

The **L'Arche Community** was founded by Jean Vanier in 1964. Its members strive to recognize the inherent dignity of persons with developmental disabilities and witness to the reality that human suffering can lead to growth and healing. Persons with mental disabilities are invited to share their lives, work, and prayers with those who assist them, creating an authentic Christian home, based on the values of Jesus Christ.

PERSONAL PRELATURES AND MILITARY ORDINARIATES

A personal prelature is a canonical structure comprising a particular group of faithful. It is headed by a prelate and assisted by its clergy. It provides spiritual formation and direction for the faithful of the prelature, who remain active members of their local parishes and dioceses. Its function is to foster Christian life and the Church's evangelizing mission in a way that complements the local Church.

An example of a personal prelature is the Prelature of Opus Dei, founded by St. Josemaria Escriva in 1928. Its mission is to spread the message that work and the ordinary

VOCATIONS IN THE CHRISTIAN LIFE Continued

circumstances of everyday life are the occasions for living the Gospel in its fullness. The faithful of the Prelature of Opus Dei live in the midst of the world and engage in ordinary professions and family life. It is precisely from within the world that they strive to place Christ at the summit of all human activities. While remaining members of the local church, they receive classes, talks, retreats, and pastoral care to help them strive for holiness and evangelize through their daily activities, particularly by promoting the universal call to sanctity in the world.

A military ordinariate is a diocese without geographical boundaries that serves the members of the armed forces. Its goal is to meet the spiritual needs of its members and assures that they have access to the liturgy and sacraments, wherever they may be present in the world.

ASSOCIATION OF THE FAITHFUL

Associations of the Faithful can be comprised of clerics or laity, or clerics and laity. Approved by the Church, members devote themselves to works of apostolate and charity, while striving for holiness in life. Examples of Associations of the Faithful include the Society of Saint Vincent DePaul, the *Militia Immaculata*, Cooperators of Opus Dei, and the Legion of Mary.

Christ Taking Leave of the Apostles by Duccio.
"And he said to them, 'Go into all the world and preach the gospel to the whole creation.
He who believes and is baptized will be saved.'" (Mk 16: 15-16)

ENDNOTES – CHAPTER TEN

1. Jn 13: 15.
2. Cf. Phil 2: 5-8.
3. Cf. Eph 3: 17.
4. Pope Benedict XVI, *Deus Caritas Est*, 1.
5. Jn 15: 16.
6. Pope Benedict XVI, *The Apostles* (Our Sunday Visitor, 2007), p. 15.
7. Jn 20: 29.
8. Cf. CCC 35.
9. 1 Tm 2: 4.
10. Cf. Mt 28: 18-20.
11. Lk 10: 28.
12. Jn 14: 15.
13. Jn 15: 12.
14. Jn 13: 12, 14.
15. Jn 15: 13.
16. Cf. *LG* 40.
17. Mt 5: 48.
18. *LG* 40.
19. Acts 2: 42.
20. Mt 19: 16.
21. Lk 18: 19.
22. Mt 19: 17.
23. Mt 19: 21.
24. St. Augustine, *Confessions*, Bk. 1.
25. Jn 14: 15.
26. Mt 19: 21.
27. Cf. for example, Rom 2: 15.
28. Acts 2: 37.
29. Cf. Mt 10.

ART AND PHOTO CREDITS

Cover

Sermon on the Mount, Carl H. Bloch; Frederiksborg Palace Chapel, Denmark

Front Pages

iii   *See* Cover Credit
iv   *Madonna and Saints Altarpiece*, ca. 1336, Maso di Banco; Brooklyn Museum, New York
vii *The Marriage of the Virgin*, Michelino Molinari Besozzo; The Metropolitan Museum, New York
ix   *Central Dome*, Cathedral Agios Andreas (Saint Andrew), Patras, Achaea, Greece; Eusebius, photographer
x   *Crucifix: Christus Patiens*, ca. 1250; Galleria degli Uffizi, Florence, Italy,

Chapter 1

1   *The Transfiguration*, Raphael; Vatican Art Gallery
2   *Bible of Ripoll*; Vatican Library; Archivo Oronoz
3   *Moses on Mount Sinai*, Nicolas of Verdun; Klosterneuburg Monastery, Austria
4   *The Samaritan Woman at the Well*, Annibale Carracci; Pinacoteca di Brera, Milan, Italy
5   *Temptation on the Mount*, Duccio di Buoninsegna; Frick Collection, New York
6   *Baptism of Christ*, Cima da Conegliano; San Giovanni in Bragora, Venice, Italy
7   *Mother Teresa*; AP/Wide World Photos
8   *The Holy Trinity*, Antonio de Pereda; Museum of Fine Arts, Budapest, Hungary
9   *Expulsion of Adam and Eve*, Aureliano Milani; Private Collection
10 *The Disciples of Jesus Baptizing*, Giulio Procaccini; Palacio Real, Segovia, Spain; Archivo Oronoz
11 *Jesus Preaching on the Mount*, Gustave Doré; Private Collection
12 *St. Augustine Reading the Epistle of St. Paul*, Benozzo Gozzoli; Apsidal Chapel, Sant'Agostino, San Gimignano, Italy
13 *Apostles Peter and Paul*, El Greco; The Hermitage, St. Petersburg, Russia
14 *Transfiguration of Christ* (detail), Giovanni Bellini; Museo Nazionale di Capodimonte, Naples, Italy
15 *Last Judgment and the Wise and Foolish Virgins*, Unknown Flemish Master; State Museum, Berlin, Germany
16 *Parable of the Good Samaritan*, G. Conti; Church of the Miraculous Medal, Messina, Italy
17 *St. Paul Writing His Epistles*, Nicolas Tournier; Blaffer Foundation Collection, Houston, Texas
18 top left: *Moses and the Tablets of Law*, José de Ribera; Chiesa della Certosa di San Martino, Naples, Italy
    top right: *Sermon on the Mount*, Carl H. Bloch; Frederiksborg Palace Chapel, Denmark
19 *Fetus in Bubbly Surroundings*; Blend Images Stock Photos
20 *The Adoration of the Trinity*, Albrecht Dürer; Kunsthistorisches Museum, Vienna, Italy
21 *The Baptism*, Pietro Longhi; Fondazione Querini Stampalia, Venice, Italy
22 *Jesus Blessing the City*, Lombardo Simonet; Malaga Museum of Art, Malaga, Spain; Archivo Oronoz
23 *St. Mary of the Angels Church*, Chicago, Illinois; Julie Koenig, photographer
24 *The Inspiration of St. Matthew*, Caravaggio; Contarelli Chapel, San Luigi dei Francesi, Rome, Italy
25 *Transfiguration*, Andrea Previtali; Pinacoteca di Brera, Milan, Italy
26 *Pope Benedict XVI during visit to São Paulo, Brazil*; Fabio Pozzebom, photographer; Agência Brasil
27 *Triumph of St. Thomas Aquinas* (detail), Benozzo Gozzoli; Musée du Louvre, Paris, France
28 *Crucifixion*, Andrea Mantegna; Musée du Louvre, Paris, France
29 *Cupola of Genesis*, thirteenth century mosaic; Basilica of St. Mark, Venice, Italy
30 *Pope Benedict XVI Celebrates the Eucharist*; Fabio Pozzebom, photographer; Agência Brasil
33 *Communion of the Apostles*, Luca Signorelli; Museo Diocesano, Cortona, Italy
35 *Evangelist Matthew and the Angel*, Rembrandt; Musée du Louvre, Paris, France
37 *Statue of Pope John Paul II*; Cathedral de la Almudena, Madrid, Spain; Juan de Ávalos, sculptor; Greg O'Beirne, photographer
38 *Calling of the Apostles*, Domenico Ghirlandaio; Sistine Chapel, Vatican

Chapter 2

39 *The Agony in the Garden*, El Greco; Toledo Museum of Art, Toledo, Ohio
41 *Denying Satan*, Carl H. Bloch; Frederiksborg Palace Chapel, Denmark
42 *The School of Athens* (detail), Raphael; Stanza della Segnatura, Palazzi Pontifici, Vatican
43 *Christ and the Woman Taken into Adultery*, Alessandro Turchi; Private Collection
44 *Three Temptations of Christ* (detail), Sandro Botticelli; Sistine Chapel, Vatican
45 *The Temptation of Adam* (detail), Tintoretto; Gallerie dell'Accademia, Venice, Italy
46 *Midtown*, Chicago, Illinois; Julie Koenig, photographer
47 *Christ in the Wilderness*, Ivan Kramskoy; Tretyakov Gallery, Moscow, Russia

ART AND PHOTO CREDITS

48 *Fathers of the Church*; Midwest Theological Forum Archives
49 *St. Paul*, Andrea di Bartolo; Private Collection
50 *Statue of the Virgin Mary*; St. Paul of the Cross Church, Park Ridge, Illinois; Julie Koenig, photographer
51 *Homer and His Guide*, William Bouguereau; Milwaukee Art Museum, Milwaukee, Wisconsin
52 *St. Augustine*, Vincenzo Foppa; Castello Sforzesco, Milan, Italy
53 *St. Dominic in Prayer*, El Greco; Private Collection
54 *Willows Academy*, Des Plaines, Illinois; Julie Koenig, photographer
55 *Christ Carrying the Cross*, Titian; Museo del Prado, Madrid, Spain
56 *St. Paul Preaching in Athens*, Raphael; Victoria and Albert Museum, London, England
58 *Second Vatican Council*; St. Peter's Basilica, Vatican; Archivo Oronoz
63 *St. Peter Preaching in the Presence of St. Mark*, Fra Angelico; Museo di San Marco, Florence, Italy

Chapter 3

65 *Christ before Pilate*, Tintoretto; Scuola Grande di San Rocco, Venice, Italy
67 *Lincoln Memorial*; Washington, D.C.; AG Archives
69 *St. Thomas Aquinas in Glory between St. Mark and St. Louis of Toulouse*, Vittore Carpaccio; Staatsgalerie, Stuttgart, Germany
70 *Cleansing the Temple*, Carl H. Bloch; Frederiksborg Palace Chapel, Denmark
71 *Martin Luther King*; AP/Wide World Photos
72 *Sts. Christopher, Jerome and Louis of Toulouse* (detail), Giovanni Bellini; San Giovanni Crisostomo, Venice, Italy
73 *Parable of the Sabbath*, Martin van Valckenborch; Kunsthistorisches Museum, Vienna, Austria
74 *Parable of the Blind Leading the Blind*, Pieter Bruegel the Elder; Museo Nazionale di Capodimonte, Naples, Italy
75 Rubberball Productions, Stock Image
76 *Parable of the Good Samaritan*, Domenico Feti; Museo Thyssen-Bornemisza, Madrid, Spain
77 *Parable of the Workers at the Eleventh Hour*, Domenico Feti; Gemäldegalerie Alte Meister, Dresden, Germany
78 *He Sent Them Out Two By Two*, James Tissot; Brooklyn Museum, New York
79 *Christ with the Virgin Mary and St. John the Evangelist*, Rogier van der Weyden; Musée du Louvre, Paris, France
80 *Pope John Paul II speaks after being honored with the Medal of Freedom*, June 2004; Eric Draper, White House photographer
82 *Mary and Elizabeth*, Carl H. Bloch; Frederiksborg Palace Chapel, Denmark
84 *Moses Receiving the Tables of the Law* (detail), Tintoretto; Madonna dell'Orto, Venice, Italy
85 *Portrait of Dred Scott*, Louis Schultze; Missouri Historical Society, St. Louis, Missouri
86 *Agony in the Garden*, Giovanni Bellini; National Gallery, London, England

Chapter 4

87 *Christ on the Cross* (detail), Velázquez; The Prado Museum, Madrid, Spain
89 *The Creation of Adam*, Michelangelo; Sistine Chapel, Vatican
90 *Cain and Abel*, Titian; Santa Maria della Salute, Venice, Italy
91 *Famine*; AP/Wide World Photos
92 *Jeroboam Offering Sacrifice for the Idol*, Jean-Honoré Fragonard; École des Beaux-Arts, Paris, France
93 *Christ and the Woman Taken in Adultery*, Rembrandt; National Gallery, London, England
94 *Allegory of Freewill and Sin*, François Maître; Illustration for City of God by St. Augustine (ca. 1475-80); Museum Meermanno Westreenianum, The Hague, Netherlands
95 *Las Vegas Strip at Night*; AG Archives
96 *Pope Pius XII*; Midwest Theological Forum Archives
97 *The Capture of Christ*, Dieric Bouts; Alte Pinakothek, Munich, Germany
98 *The Flagellation*, Michael Pacher; Österreichische Galerie Belvedere, Vienna, Austria
101 *Scenes from the Life of Christ: 19. Crucifixion*, Giotto; San Francesco, Assisi, Italy
103 *The Last Judgment*, Altarpiece, Master of the Bambino Vispo; Alte Pinakothek, Munich, Germany
104 *The Last Judgment*, Stefan Lochner; Wallraf-Richartz-Museum, Cologne, Germany
105 *St. Francis Rescuing Souls From Purgatory*; Native American, ca. 1805-1850, New Mexico; Brooklyn Museum, New York
106 *The Rich Man in Hades*, James Tissot; Brooklyn Museum, New York
107 *Christ Pantocrator and the Last Judgment*, Late thirteenth century mosaic; Baptistry of St. John, Florence, Italy
108 *Book of Deuteronomy Frontispiece*, Bible of San Paolo Fuori le Mura, ca. 870; Rome, Italy
109 *Moses Receiving the Law*, Lithograph, ca. 1877; Library of Congress Prints and Photographs Division, Washington, D.C.

ART AND PHOTO CREDITS

110 *Moses on Mount Sinai*, Jean-Léon Gérôme; Private Collection
111 *The Resurrection of Christ*, Paolo Veronese; Gemäldegalerie, Dresden, Germany
112 *The Lord's Prayer*, James Tissot; Brooklyn Museum, New York
113 Luke Mata, photographer; Midwest Theological Forum Archives
114 *Mount of Beatitudes Hillside in Spring*; Pictorial Library of Bible Lands; Todd Bolen, photographer
117 Mosaic, Early tenth century; Monastery of Hosios Loukas, Mount Helicon, Greece
120 *Return of the Prodigal Son*, James Tissot; Brooklyn Museum, New York
124 *Zacchaeus in the Sycamore Awaiting the Passage of Jesus*, James Tissot; Brooklyn Museum, New York
126 *Men's Ward at Kalighat* (Home for the Dying), Calcutta, India; Mark Makowiecki, photographer

Chapter 5

127 *Resurrection of Christ with Sts. Leonardo and Lucy*, Marco d'Oggiono; State Museum, Berlin, Germany
129 *God Resting After Creation*, Byzantine Mosaic; Cathedral of Monreale, Sicily, Italy
130 *Adoration of the Golden Calf*, Nicolas Poussin; National Gallery, London, England
131 *Christ and the Canaanite Woman*, Ludovico Carracci; Pinacoteca di Brera, Milan, Italy
132 *St. Athanasius*, Master of St. Ildefon; Museum of Culture, Valladolid, Spain; Archivo Oronoz
133 *Child Praying*, Puebla, Mexico; Wojciech Dubis, photographer; Midwest Theological Forum Archives
134 *The Charity of St. Elizabeth of Hungary*, Edmund Blair Leighton; Collection of Fred and Sherry Ross
135 *Blessed Virgin Mary*; La Chapelle Notre Dame de la Medaille Miraculeuse; Yvon Meyer, photographer
136 *Satan Carries Jesus to the Pinnacle of the Temple*, James Tissot; Brooklyn Museum, New York
137 *God the Father*, Raphael's Stanza, Vatican
138 top right: *Swearing-in Ceremony*, Secretary of the Interior, June 7, 2006; Eric Draper, White House photographer
    bottom left: *King David and His Harp*, Gerard van Honthorst; Centraal Museum, Utrecht, Netherlands; Archivo Oronoz
139 *The Oath of St. Hedwig* (Jadwiga) the Queen, Józef Simmler; National Museum, Warsaw, Poland
140 *The Sistine Madonna*, Raphael; Gemäldegalerie, Dresden, Germany
142 *The Lord's Prayer*, James Tissot; Brooklyn Museum, New York
143 *St. Christopher with the Infant Christ and St. Peter*, Cima da Conegliano; Private Collection
145 *The Adoration of the Christ Child* (detail), Fra Bartolomeo; Galleria Borghese, Rome, Italy
146 *Jesus Unrolls the Scroll in the Synagogue*, James Tissot; Brooklyn Museum, New York
147 *The Resurrection*, Carl H. Bloch; Frederiksborg Palace Chapel, Denmark
148 *Communion of the Apostles*, Fra Angelico; Museo di San Marco, Florence, Italy
149 *The Immaculate Conception*, Giovanni Battista Tiepolo; Museo del Prado, Madrid, Spain
150 *Assumption of the Virgin*, Juan Martín Cabezalero; Museo del Prado, Madrid, Spain
151 *Holy Mass at the Cathedral*, Easter 2007, Puebla, Mexico; Wojciech Dubis, photographer; Midwest Theological Forum Archives
156 *Adoration of the Shepherds*, Bartolomé Esteban Murillo; Museo del Prado, Madrid, Spain
160 *Christ Falls on the Way to Calvary*, Raphael; Museo del Prado, Madrid, Spain
162 *The Widow's Mite*, James Tissot; Brooklyn Museum, New York

Chapter 6

163 *Holy Family with Palm*, Raphael; Sutherland Collection, Gallery of Scotland, Edinburgh, Scotland
165 *Christ Returning to His Parents*, Martini Simone; Walker Art Gallery, Liverpool, England
166 Digital Vision, Stock Image
167 *St. Joseph and the Christ Child*, El Greco; Museo de Santa Cruz, Toledo, Spain
168 Rubberball Productions, Stock Image
169 left: Digital Vision, Stock Image; right: Design Pics, Stock Image
170 Blend Images, Stock Image
171 Rubberball Productions, Stock Image
172 *The Tribute Money*, James Tissot; Brooklyn Museum, New York
174 Digital Vision, Stock Image
175 *The Holy Family with the Infant St. John*, Niccolò Frangipane; Private Collection
176 Rubberball Productions, Stock Image
177 *The Child Jesus Going Down with His Parents to Nazareth*, William Charles Thomas Dobson; Tate Collections, England
178 *Sts. Anne and Joachim with the Virgin* (detail), Francesco Mancini; Galleria Nazionale dell'Umbria, Perugia, Italy

ART AND PHOTO CREDITS

Chapter 7

179 *The Passion* (detail), Hans Holbein the Younger; Kunstmuseum, Öffentliche Kunstsammlung, Basel, Switzerland
181 *Cain and Abel*, Pietro Novelli; Galleria Nazionale d'Arte Antica, Rome, Italy
182 *Christ and the Child*, Carl H. Bloch; Frederiksborg Palace Chapel, Denmark
183 *The Prodigal Son*, Gerrit van Honthorst; Alte Pinakothek, Munich, Germany
184 *The Good Samaritan*, James Tissot; Brooklyn Museum, New York
185 *The Flagellation of Our Lord Jesus Christ*, William Bouguereau; Musée des Beaux-Arts, La Rochelle, France
186 *Study of an Embryo in the Womb* (detail), Leonardo da Vinci; Royal Library, Windsor, England
187 *Pope John Paul II*; AP/Wide World Photos
189 *Cloning*; AP/Wide World Photos
190 *Cemetery at Hadamar*, April 1945; United States Holocaust Memorial Museum, Washington, D.C.
191 *St. Thomas Aquinas*, Carlo Crivelli; (detail) The Demidoff Altarpiece, The National Gallery, London, England
192 *Hiroshima*, 1945, from top of Red Cross Hospital; buildings in photo erected after bombing; U. S. Government Image
193 *Christ Taken Prisoner*, Giuseppe Cesari; Staatliche Museen, Kassel, Germany
194 *Christ Before Pilate*, Hans Multscher; Staatliche Museen, Berlin, Germany
195 *Human cell-line colony being cloned in vitro through use of cloning rings*; Bob Walker, photographer
197 *Neonatal Intensive Care Unit*, Jacoplane, photographer
199 *Cain Flying Before Jehovah's Curse*, Fernand-Anne Piestre Cormon; Musée d'Orsay, Paris, France
201 *And the Earth Shook*, James Tissot; Brooklyn Museum, New York

Chapter 8

203 *Christ and the Adulteress*, Polidoro da Lanciano; Museum of Fine Arts, Budapest, Hungary
205 *Creation of Eve*, Michelangelo; Sistine Chapel, Vatican
206 Stockbyte, Stock Image
207 Rubberball Productions, Stock Image
208 Rubberball Productions, Stock Image
209 Comstock, Stock Image
210 *The Fall of Man*, Andrea Mantegna; Section of the Madonna della Vittoria, Musée du Louvre, Paris, France
211 *Pope John Paul II*; Midwest Theological Forum Archives
212 Comstock, Stock Image
213 Rubberball Productions, Stock Image
215 Comstock, Stock Image
216 *Pope John Paul II*; © L'Osservatore Romano; from the book *John Paul II: A Light for the World*
217 Rubberball Productions, Stock Image
218 Corbis, Stock Image
219 *Head of Christ*, Titian; surviving fragment from *Noli Me Tangere*, Museo del Prado, Madrid, Spain
221 *The Supper at Emmaus* (detail), Titian; Musée du Louvre, Paris, France
223 Corbis, Stock Image
225 *The Annunciation*, Fra Angelico; Museo Diocesano, Cortona, Italy
231 *Christ Blessing Little Children*, Sir Charles Lock Eastlake; Manchester City Galleries, Manchester, England
233 *The Betrothal of Joseph and Mary*, James Tissot; Brooklyn Museum, New York
234 *Christ with the Woman Taken in Adultery*, Guercino; Dulwich Art Gallery, London, England

ART AND PHOTO CREDITS

Chapter 9

235 *Christ before Caiaphas*, Giotto; Cappella Scrovegni (Arena Chapel), Padua, Italy
237 *Parable of Lazarus and Dives*, Illumination from Codex Aureus of Echternach; German National Museum, Nuremberg, Germany
238 top left: Rubberball Productions, Stock Image; top right: Luke Mata, photographer; Midwest Theological Forum Archives
239 *Homeless in L.A.*; Chris Sansenbach, photographer
240 *Creation of the Animals*, Tintoretto; Gallerie dell'Accademia, Venice, Italy
241 Flat Earth, Stock Image
242 Luke Mata, photographer; Midwest Theological Forum Archives
243 *Pope Leo XIII*, AG Archives
244 Midwest Theological Forum Archives
245 *Gypsy Boy in Serbia*; AG Archives
246 *Shanty Town in Soweto*, South Africa; AG Archives
247 Flat Earth, Stock Image
248 *Slot Machine*; Jeff Kubina, photographer
249 *The Man Who Hoards*, James Tissot; Brooklyn Museum, New York
250 *Old Lady at San Miguel Allende*, Guanajuato, Mexico; Tomas Castelazo, photographer
251 *Christ Before the High Priest*, Gerrit van Honthorst; National Gallery, London, England
252 *Peter Denouncing Christ*, Rembrandt; Rijksmuseum, Amsterdam, Netherlands
253 *Judas Tempted by Thirty Pieces of Silver*, fifteenth century fresco; St. Sebastian Chapel, Lanslevillard, Savoy, France
254 *The Pharisees Question Jesus*, James Tissot; Brooklyn Museum, New York
255 *Judas Returns the Thirty Pieces of Silver*, AG Archives
257 *What is Truth?*, Nikolai Nikolaevich Ge (Gay); Tretyakov Gallery, Moscow, Russia
258 *Ecce Homo*, Antonio Ciseri; Galleria d'Arte Moderna, Florence, Italy
260 *Ascent to Calvary* (detail), Tintoretto; Scuola Grande di San Rocco, Venice, Italy
263 Digital Stock, Stock Image
265 *St. John's Fragment* (verso), Rylands Library Papyrus P52; John Rylands University Library, Manchester, England
267 *Christ before Pilate*, Mihály Munkácsy; Hungarian National Gallery, Budapest, Hungary

Chapter 10

269 *The Ascension of Christ*, Garofalo; Galleria Nazionale d'Arte Antica, Rome, Italy
270 *Christ Giving the Keys to St. Peter*, Lorenzo Veneziano; Central panel of a Venetian altarpiece, 1369; Museo Correr, Venice, Italy
271 *Pope Benedict XVI Celebrates the Eucharist* during visit to São Paulo, Brazil; Fabio Pozzebom, photographer; Agência Brasil
272 *Pope John Paul II greets Mother Teresa*, 1997; © L'Osservatore Romano; from the book *John Paul II: A Light for the World*
273 *Jesus Ordains the Twelve*, James Tissot; Brooklyn Museum, New York
274 *Disputation on the Trinity*, Andrea del Sarto; Galleria Palatina (Palazzo Pitti), Florence, Italy
275 *The Holy Trinity*, Coecke van Aelst; Museo del Prado, Madrid, Spain
276 *The Pentecost*, El Greco; Museo del Prado, Madrid, Spain
277 *Christ in Heaven with Four Saints and a Donor*, Domenico Ghirlandaio; Pinacoteca Comunale, Volterra, Italy
278 *The Agony in the Garden*, Carl H. Bloch; Frederiksborg Palace Chapel, Denmark
283 *Raising of the Cross*, Rembrandt; Alte Pinakothek, Munich, Germany
286 *Christ Taking Leave of the Apostles*, Duccio di Buoninsegna; Museo dell'Opera del Duomo, Siena, Italy

INDEX

INDEX

INDEX